RUFUS THOMAS
AND MEMPHIS SOUL

Matthew Ruddick

FOREWORD BY ROB BOWMAN

UNIVERSITY PRESS OF MISSISSIPPI / JACKSON

The University Press of Mississippi is the scholarly publishing agency of
the Mississippi Institutions of Higher Learning: Alcorn State University,
Delta State University, Jackson State University, Mississippi State University,
Mississippi University for Women, Mississippi Valley State University,
University of Mississippi, and University of Southern Mississippi.

www.upress.state.ms.us

The University Press of Mississippi is a member of
the Association of University Presses.

First printing 2023
∞

Library of Congress Cataloging-in-Publication Data

Names: Ruddick, Matthew, author. | Bowman, Rob (Robert Maxwell James), writer of
foreword. Title: Funkiest man alive : Rufus Thomas and Memphis soul / Matthew Ruddick ;
foreword by Rob Bowman.
Other titles: American made music series.
Description: Jackson : University Press of Mississippi, 2023. |
Series: American made music series | Includes bibliographical references and index.
Identifiers: LCCN 2022051938 (print) | LCCN 2022051939 (ebook) |
ISBN 9781496838407 (hardback) | ISBN 9781496838414 (epub) | ISBN 9781496838421 (epub)
| ISBN 9781496838438 (pdf) | ISBN 9781496838445 (pdf)
Subjects: LCSH: Thomas, Rufus, 1917–2001. | Rhythm and blues musicians—United States—
Biography. | Soul musicians—United States—Biography. | African American musicians—
Biography. | Stax Records—History. | Rhythm and blues music—Tennessee—Memphis—
History and criticism. | Soul music—Tennessee—Memphis—History and criticism.
Classification: LCC ML420.T4607 R83 2023 (print) | LCC ML420.T4607 (ebook) |
DDC 782.42166092/2 [B]—dc23/eng/20221227
LC record available at https://lccn.loc.gov/2022051938
LC ebook record available at https://lccn.loc.gov/2022051939

British Library Cataloging-in-Publication Data available

This book is dedicated to my two amazing daughters, Eden and Jordan.
Love you lots!

Contents

Foreword

ROB BOWMAN

Rufus Thomas was known far and wide as the "World's Oldest Teenager." He was also Memphis's Greatest Ambassador, proclaiming his love of the people, the nightlife, and the music of the city's African American culture every chance he got. Just off Beale Street lies a stretch of roadway named Rufus Thomas Boulevard, evidence of his stature in his hometown. He was also awarded an honorary parking spot just off Beale that was reserved for his use 24/7. It is worth noting that not even the city's mayor was given such an honor. A tap dancer, comedian, blues, soul, and funk singer and songwriter, undoubtedly, Rufus Thomas was the most diversified entertainer in Memphis's incredible lineage of entertainers.

Born in 1917 in Cayce, Mississippi, by the time Rufus was ready to attend school, the Thomas family had relocated to Memphis. It is telling to recognize that Rufus Thomas was born three years before the first vaudeville blues record was released, five years before the first Black jazz record was cut, and six years before the first country blues record was recorded. Rufus came of age in a world where jazz, blues, and gospel were central to Black American life and where Black minstrel and vaudeville shows still barnstormed across the South, playing tent shows in rural areas and Black theaters in more urban confines.

Rufus Thomas literally saw it all. By the time he was ten, he was tap dancing on Beale Street for tips. When he was fifteen, he appeared for the first time on Amateur Night at the city's crown jewel, the Palace Theater. Soon thereafter, he was tap dancing at numerous Memphis nightclubs. By the time he was nineteen, he was on the road with the Rabbit Foot Minstrels, initially, as was the custom, performing with burnt cork on his face. He would later tour with the similarly styled Royal American company.

In 1940, Rufus formed a comedy team with Robert Couch. They performed under the sobriquet Rufus and Bones. Within a year, he added another weapon to his arsenal: writing and singing blues songs. Rufus was now a triple threat—he was a dancer, comedian, and singer. All three skill sets would serve him well for the rest of his life.

There was more. Rufus became a master emcee, using his timing and comedic skills to cohost Amateur Night at the Palace with legendary educator, writer, radio personality, and activist Nat D. Williams. Nat D. would play the role of the straight man while Rufus busted up the audience with the punchlines. When Nat D. stepped down to focus on his newspaper writing, Rufus and Bones cohosted Amateur Night at the Palace for eleven straight years.

In 1950, Rufus added another feather in his cap when Nat D. offered him a job as a disc jockey on WDIA, the first Black appeal radio station in America. Rufus was heard hooting and hollering over the Memphis airwaves through 1974 and then again from 1986 until just before his passing in 2001.

Clearly a Renaissance man, Rufus is best known as a hit-making recording artist starting in 1949 when he cut his first 78s for the Dallas-based label Star Talent. Subsequent recordings followed on Bullet, Chess, Sun, and Meteor before Rufus and his daughter Carla signed with Stax in 1960, then operating under the name Satellite. Incredibly enough, Rufus recorded the very first hit records for both Sun and Stax.

With Stax, Rufus had an incredible run of hits from 1960 through 1975. Eighteen of his Stax recordings made the national charts; several others received significant regional airplay and sales. The majority were dance singles such as "The Dog," "Walking the Dog," "Do the Funky Chicken," "The Breakdown," and "Do the Push and Pull." Rufus wrote them all. Incredibly, he was in his fifties when he embarked on his stunning run of funk anthems, starting with "Do the Funky Chicken" in 1969.

I first met Rufus in September 1983 and subsequently became close to his whole family: wife Lorene, daughters Carla and Vaneese, and son Marvell. I attended family birthday parties and visited him regularly at his home. We went out to lunch together at the Piccadilly Cafeteria and the Four-Way Grill. I interviewed him on numerous occasions and saw him perform more times than I can count. We hung out together in Memphis, Toronto, New York, Washington, DC, and all over Mississippi. When he passed away, I was honored to be asked by the family to speak at his funeral.

What struck me throughout our friendship was that Rufus Thomas the man and Rufus Thomas the stage persona were one and the same. His facial gestures, his hilarious one-liners, the warm, oversized, feel-good-all-over grin, the absolute love of life were always plainly in evidence.

Each time I saw him, on or off stage, he never failed to lift the spirits of all those around him or in the audience.

I often think that life and relationships, at their essence, are about the transformation of energy. If that is true, Rufus was a master of the art. It should be obvious that I loved Rufus. I still do. I miss him and literally think good thoughts for him every night before I go to sleep. I feel blessed and honored that Rufus was such a big part of my life for close to twenty years.

By any measuring stick, Rufus Thomas made a gigantic contribution to American music. He has long deserved a full biography. Thanks to Matthew Ruddick, that biography is now in your hands.

Acknowledgments

The writing of this book would not have been possible without the help and support of the amazing Thomas family. I would particularly like to thank Vaneese Thomas, who was so positive about the project from the very beginning and who gave me her full support every step of the way. Thanks for putting up with my endless questions, not just about your father, but also your mother, you, and your siblings, too. I know that this process can be quite intrusive, but you handled everything with such warmth, patience, and good grace that it made my job easy.

I also want to thank you for putting me in touch with so many family friends who were close to your father; this really helped readers understand that what people heard on the radio and witnessed on stage was just an extension of your father's larger-than-life personality. Finally, thank you for allowing me access to the family archives, which help to bring his amazing story alive. I hope the book is everything you envisioned it to be and look forward to working on new projects together next year.

It would be impossible to tell the incredible story of Stax Records and the key role of the Thomas family in that story without the help and support of Rob Bowman. Rob's book, *Soulsville U.S.A.: The Story of Stax Records*, is the definitive history of the record label, and his Grammy Award-winning liner notes to *The Complete Stax/Volt Soul Singles* were the starting point for my research. Rob was not only incredibly supportive of the project, but he was also kind enough to proof the book for me, making sure I'd gotten my facts straight about all things Stax and beyond. Rob's love of both the music and Rufus Thomas, the man, was integral to the book, not only in terms of the source material but also helping to set the tone of the story. When Rob kindly agreed to write the foreword, I was thrilled, as it felt like a huge endorsement from one of the leading authorities on popular music. I can't thank you enough, Rob.

I'd also like to thank Robert Gordon, whose book, *Respect Yourself: Stax Records and the Soul Explosion*, was also hugely important in terms of background information and anecdotes. Robert was generous with his time and helped me to access some important archival material that he had kept from his own research into the history of Stax Records.

Everyone in the Stax family wanted to see Rufus's story told, but I have to single out the wonderful Deanie Parker for a special mention. Deanie has been a central part of the Stax story for many years as a singer, publicist, and later, as the first president and CEO of Soulsville, which established the Stax Museum of American Soul Music and other important ventures. Every anecdote that Deanie told me was insightful and beautifully phrased, and she was also kind enough to introduce me to other key people in the Stax family, which was helpful beyond belief.

Thanks to Jim Stewart, the man who launched Stax Records. It was an honor to talk with you and hear your memories of working with Rufus, Carla, and Marvell over the years. William Bell was one of the first people I interviewed for this book, and his fond memories of Rufus as a mentor, colleague, and friend, and his friendship with Carla were invaluable.

It was a great pleasure to talk to the legendary Booker T. Jones and Steve Cropper, both of whom took time out of their busy schedules to help with this project. Booker's memories of working with both Rufus and Carla were a vital part of the story, and his insights into life at Stax were fascinating. Steve told me so many amazing stories, and not all of them made it into this book, but his love of Rufus certainly did.

Bobby Manuel knew Rufus well and had some funny and heart-warming stories to tell. He was also helpful with putting me in touch with numerous other people who knew Rufus over the years. Thanks also to David Porter, James Alexander, Willie Hall, and Harold Scott, all of whom shared their memories of Rufus for this book.

Jeff Kollath, executive director of the Stax Museum of American Soul Music, helped me on so many levels, connecting me to people, sourcing photographs owned by the Museum, and offering to host a launch party for the book. I look forward to thanking you in person!

Outside of the Stax family, many other musicians who knew Rufus over the years were happy to share their stories. Don Bryant and the late Howard Grimes talked to me about the importance attached to music education in the city of Memphis in their formative years and the music scene in the 1950s. The late James Nelson shared some musical memories, but more importantly, his love of the Thomas family and the ways in which they had helped and supported him. Jim Spake was very generous with his time, sharing his stories about working with Rufus in his later years and giving me contact details for many other musicians who knew Rufus around that time. Toni Green also spoke to me about the advice and support that Rufus had offered her over the years.

I had the loveliest time talking to Mark Stansbury, who shared his memories of Rufus at WDIA and beyond and his time in the Teen Town Singers with Carla. He was also kind enough to share some memorabilia with me and connect me with James Nelson.

Some of my favorite anecdotes about Rufus's later years came from Graziano Uliani, the mastermind behind the Porretta Soul Festival. He had so many great stories to tell and photos and memorabilia that he made available to me. I'm extremely grateful for your help and look forward to bringing the book to Porretta in 2023!

Other authors were generous, too. It was wonderful to talk to Peter Guralnick, whose *Sweet Soul Music* is probably the most thumbed music book on my shelf, where it has sat since it was first published. He was very happy for me to quote from that book and his definitive bios of both Elvis Presley and Sam Phillips. I also had a fascinating talk with Charles Hughes, the author of the essay "You Pay One Hell of a Price to Be Black," which put Thomas's career into a broader perspective and was not afraid to tackle some difficult topics. He helped me to think about and navigate some of those subjects as well as point me toward some useful sources of information. Thank you both.

Trent Cobb and Ted Spencer, close friends of the Thomas family for many years, gave me considerable insight into the family life of Marvell, Carla, and Vaneese growing up, and Rufus and Lorene as parents, which was fascinating, while the late Bobby O'Jay told me about Rufus's final years at WDIA and the high regard in which he held Rufus as a person.

Bruce Iglauer, the founder of Alligator Records, told me the story behind the making of "That Woman Is Poison!" and gave me his thoughts on why Rufus was such an important artist.

I also need to thank Leslie K. Nelson, who does so much with the Memphis music community and was very kind to me; Mark Caldwell of the Memphis Blues Society, who put me in touch with several musicians that Rufus knew and worked with; and Geddes Bootwright, who connected me with Steve Cropper.

Michelle Duerr, the digitization archival assistant for the Special Collections Department of the University of Memphis, also gets a shout-out. She went out of her way to help me find appropriate images for the book and arrange permissions for me. Your help was much appreciated, and I look forward to finally meeting you and giving you a copy of the book.

Thanks to Craig Gill, Jackson Watson, and the team at the University Press of Mississippi for believing in the project, and Debbie Burke for her kindness and patience in the editing process.

To family and friends, thanks for putting up with my endless music talk and encouraging me to write this second book.

And last but not least, special thanks to Lucy Williams for all of her love and support over the last year. Wading through not one but two of my books requires a special kind of dedication, and I love you for that!

Funkiest Man Alive

Introduction

At the peak of his fame, in August 1972, Rufus Thomas played to a crowd of over 100,000 people at Wattstax, a benefit concert organized by Stax Records at the Los Angeles Coliseum. Resplendent in a pink cape and white boots, he walked onto the stage and asked the crowd, "Can I ask you something?" Opening his cape to reveal a matching pink jacket and Bermuda shorts, he used one of his famous catchphrases, asking the audience, "Ain't I'm clean?"

For many in the audience, Thomas stole the show that day, delivering a fun-filled set of back-to-back hit singles: "The Breakdown," "Do the Funky Chicken," and "Do the Funky Penguin." First, he brought the crowd to its feet, and then over fences onto the stadium pitch itself.

And yet there were some people within the Stax organization, including chief executive Al Bell, a former DJ, who felt that Thomas had misjudged the occasion. Bell felt that Thomas's dance-oriented novelty songs did not fit with the message being delivered by the likes of the Reverend Jesse Jackson and the Staple Singers and that his outfit looked back to the days of minstrelsy rather than looking forward to a new era of Black power.

♦ ♦ ♦

To be fair, it's easy to see how he might be seen as a "novelty" R&B singer. Many of his biggest hit singles were "animal-themed," whether it was his 1953 "answer song" to "Hound Dog" titled "Bear Cat," his dog-themed songs from the mid-1960s ("The Dog," "Walking the Dog," and "Can Your Monkey Do the Dog") or even his biggest hit, "Do the Funky Chicken."

But to see Rufus as specializing in novelty R&B songs is a disservice to his long and varied career, which began with his work on the minstrel circuit in the mid-1930s and extended right up until his death in 2001. Rufus worked as a tap dancer in minstrel shows as an MC, or Master of Ceremonies, hosting an Amateur Night in the theaters of Memphis, as a disc jockey at a local radio station, and as a blues songwriter, then a singer. Later, he became a soul and funk star, recording for Stax Records, even appearing in Hollywood movies toward the end of his life. He was also an important symbol and advocate of the Memphis music scene. And in all of these activities, humor played a pivotal role.

Rob Bowman, the author of *Soulsville U.S.A.: The Story of Stax Records* and a close personal friend of the Thomas family, noted that his humor stemmed from his background in the minstrel shows of the 1930s. It could be heard in his vernacular, through his catchphrases like "I feel so unnecessary!" his radio show introductions, and some of his songs. "He understood the role that humor had played historically, in many ways as a survival mechanism, for African Americans living in a world that was incredibly harsh, incredibly oppressive, and incredibly discriminatory," Bowman explained. "It was the kind of humor that helped a lot of African Americans survive in a world designed to mitigate their ability to survive."[1]

And despite the concerns of Al Bell, who went on to sign comedian Richard Pryor to Stax subsidiary Partee, Thomas's humor was still seen as being relevant to many in the audience at Wattstax, as clearly demonstrated by the audience reaction that day. "Doctors and lawyers may have related to it a little less," Bowman suggested, "but to your average Black citizen, someone like Rufus embodied who and what they were."[2]

A second point to note is that Thomas saw himself as being an all-around entertainer, not just a singer. His early role models included Louis Armstrong and Fats Waller, and in many ways, one could draw a parallel with the likes of Louis Jordan and Cab Calloway, who—while jazz-influenced—still incorporated elements of song, dance, and comedy into their performances. And while Jordan and Calloway were also bandleaders, it's worth noting that Thomas also arranged all of his own songs.

Bowman agrees with this view. "That's why those dance routines were such an important part of his show," he said. "Rufus doing the Funky Chicken, inviting people up onto the stage to do it with him, was a schtick that went on forever. It's kind of like James Brown and the cape, Fats Domino bumping the piano across the stage with his stomach—this was a schtick that audiences adored. It's like Prince waving his purple rain guitar . . . if he doesn't do it, you feel cheated."[3]

Rob Bowman takes the argument a stage further and suggests that you can even extend that line out to Parliament-Funkadelic in the 1970s and early 1980s. "All that stuff with spaceships, Garry Shider wearing a diaper on stage, George Clinton taking a bedsheet, cutting a hole for the head . . . all that was out of the same tradition. It was fantastical, it was humorous, and part of a long tradition of African American expressive culture. P-Funk just took it to outer space!"[4]

And while it's true that many of Thomas's biggest hit singles were based on the latest dance trends, he was somewhat unique in that he was able to stay in touch with the latest developments over a prolonged period of time. Songs like "The Dog" and "Walking the Dog," recorded in the early 1960s, were blues-oriented dance tunes, while "Funky Chicken" and "The Breakdown" were quite different in style and funk-oriented. And as disco came along, Rufus adapted his style once more—albeit with less commercial success—producing more disco-oriented songs like "I Ain't Gettin' Older, I'm Gettin' Better."

The final point to note on this subject is that Thomas also recorded countless great tunes that were neither "novelty" nor "dance"-oriented songs; from his early R&B cuts such as "I'm Steady Holdin' On" and "The Easy Livin' Plan;" early Stax pop-oriented songs like "'Cause I Love You," "Jump Back," and "The World Is Round;" covers such as "Night Time Is the Right Time;" classic late 1960s recordings such as "The Memphis Train" and "Funky Mississippi;" deep funk cuts like "Funkiest Man Alive" and "Funky Hot Grits;" and even later, blues recordings including "All Night Worker."

In short, Rufus Thomas was far more than just a singer of "novelty" R&B songs, as some have suggested; he was an important all-around entertainer whose career spanned from the 1930s right through to the late 1990s when he was still headlining R&B and blues festivals in the United States, Europe, and even Japan.

◆ ◆ ◆

When asked what made Thomas an important figure, fellow Stax historian and author of *Respect Yourself: Stax Records and the Soul Explosion*, Robert Gordon, pointed to the fact that without him, Sun Records and Stax Records may never have gotten off the ground.

"He made the single that gave Sun Records its foundation, its establishing single, and less than ten years later, gave Stax Records [then Satellite] its establishing single," he suggested. "That makes him essential to Memphis music history to me."[5]

Indeed, Rufus's recording of "Bear Cat"—an "answer song" to "Hound Dog" by Big Mama Thornton—was a hit in March 1953. It is entirely possible that were it not for the success of that recording, Elvis Presley would not have thought to walk into the Memphis Recording Service at the Sun Record Company in July 1953, a few months later.

In the same vein, Rufus laid the foundation for Stax Records, one of the most important R&B record labels of all time. Before he walked in the door with his seventeen-year-old daughter, Carla, Stax was still known as Satellite Records and had yet to attract the attention of Atlantic Records, the New York-based major label. The success of "'Cause I Love You" in the summer of 1960 refocused Jim Stewart's attention away from country music to R&B and paved the way for the label's success in the years that followed.

The point about Memphis music history was also made, albeit with a slightly different emphasis, by Rob Bowman. "Besides the things I've said, he was also extremely important as a Memphis icon," he suggested. "Memphis had other icons. Elvis Presley was the obvious one, Isaac Hayes was another. But Elvis and Isaac both left Memphis, although Elvis kept returning. But neither one of those people was as wedded to Memphis, Memphis culture, Beale Street, what Sun had been, what Stax had been. Rufus embodied all of that. And he never stopped talking about the city of Memphis as an important place period and certainly the heart and soul—as far as he was concerned—of southern Black culture."[6]

In his later years, in particular, Rufus became an unofficial ambassador for the city of Memphis. It was a role he took seriously, both on stage and off. He appeared at the very first Porretta International Soul Festival in Porretta, Italy, in 1988, as a special guest of the Memphis Horns World Rhythm and Blues Band, and he was a big supporter of the festival in the years that followed, appearing on numerous occasions and introducing festival organizer Graziano Uliani to numerous other Memphis musicians. In honor of his contribution, the park in which the festival took place was later renamed Rufus Thomas Park.

His enormous contribution to the city of Memphis was recognized in early 1997, on the occasion of Rufus's eightieth birthday, when the city Mayor renamed a section of Hernando Street—where it intersected with Beale Street—as Rufus Thomas Boulevard. In addition, the city gave him an honorary reserved downtown parking space which he used on a regular basis.

◆ ◆ ◆

In addition to his long and varied career as an all-around entertainer and his importance to the cultural history of Memphis, Rufus's role in the history of African American radio is also noteworthy. He was one of the first disc jockeys to join Memphis-based WDIA—in September 1950—which was one of the first radio stations in the South to hire a Black disc jockey and the first to introduce all-Black programming.

By 1954, Rufus hosted two daily shows—*Sepia Swing Club*, which started at 3 p.m. and *Hoot 'n' Holler*, which began at 9:30 p.m., and that was after working an eight-hour shift at a textile plant (the American Finishing Company). He also had a Saturday morning show, *Boogie for Breakfast*, which meant an early start even if he had been playing at a Memphis nightclub into the early hours.

Rufus stayed on at WDIA long after he started having regular hit singles at Stax Records. He did leave, reluctantly, in 1974, when the station went through a management change, but was invited back in 1986 and cohosted the *All Blues* show every Saturday morning until his final days.

♦ ♦ ♦

The role of an all-around entertainer is regarded as something of an old-fashioned concept these days, and artists tend to specialize in one particular skill. "I think that's what young people today are missing. They don't come to the table with much talent, if you want to know the honest truth," explained Rufus's youngest daughter, Vaneese Thomas, an accomplished singer and songwriter in her own regard. "You've got Beyoncé, who's a more rounded entertainer; there are a few of those, like Lady Gaga, but not many. Most of them come with very little singing talent that they can parlay into anything else. The singer/dancer/actor—we don't have much of that anymore."[7]

Aside from humor, the unifying element that made Rufus so successful in all of these diverse roles and brought the longevity to his career was the warmth of his character, which his audience could clearly relate to.

"You might be tempted to describe Rufus Thomas as a larger-than-life personality, but that would be doing him an injustice," suggests author and music historian Peter Guralnick. "[He] was a life force, as anyone who ever encountered him on stage, screen, or simply on the street would attest. His music—blues and Louis Jordan-influenced jump to start off with, then nothing but pure cosmic (and comic) funk—brought a great deal of joy to the world, but his personality brought even more, conveying a message of grit, determination, indomitability, [and] above all, a bottomless appreciation for the human comedy that left little room for the drab or the dreary in his presence."[8]

The grit and determination were evident throughout his career. In the early 1950s, for example, with three children under the age of ten, Rufus worked three jobs: in a textile mill, hosting two radio shows at WDIA, and as a musician, playing gigs in and around Memphis. In the mid-1950s, he overcame the disappointment of being dropped by Sun Records to relaunch himself as Rufus Thomas and the Bear Cats, eventually landing at Satellite Records, later known as Stax Records. And in the late 1960s, he rebounded from the hurt of being left out of Al Bell's Soul Explosion, becoming the label's best-selling singles artist of 1970.

Rufus's life force was nowhere more evident that when he was on stage, dressed in his flamboyant custom-made cape and shorts, an outfit that only he could carry off. He would utilize an amazing array of facial expressions, whether he was imploring the audience to sing with him, encouraging them to dance, or adopting his wide-eyed expression for comic effect.

"[As a live performer,] I didn't want to come on behind him, I tell you!" recalled singer William Bell, laughing. "Rufus was a character—he would set an audience on fire! If you were coming behind Rufus, you really had to step up your game because he was a performer, bar none!"[9]

On stage, Rufus was happy to give the impression of the jovial clown, but he was deadly serious about his art; his band was always well-drilled, and if they missed a beat, he would turn around and quietly remind them what was expected. Likewise, in the studio, he was a notorious perfectionist, never happy until the band was playing precisely what he heard in his head.

His more serious side would also emerge during interviews, when he would opine on the history of the blues and R&B as he saw it or issues such as racism and religion in Memphis, which had played such an important role in his development.

◆ ◆ ◆

To a certain extent, Thomas's numerous achievements were recognized during his lifetime.

He received a Pioneer Award from the Rhythm and Blues Foundation in 1992, the W. C. Handy/Howlin' Wolf Award at the Chicago Blues Festival for Outstanding Blues Performer, and three lifetime achievement awards—from Wings of Change, the Beale Street Merchants Association, and the American Society of Composers, Authors and Publishers (ASCAP) in 1997.

He also received an award in 1998 from the Rock & Roll Hall of Fame for five decades promoting Black music on radio.

It seems strange that the Rock & Roll Hall of Fame singled him out for his contribution to radio rather than as a musician; while he was never a pioneer, he was arguably one of the "founding fathers" of rock and roll with his early R&B cuts. And even more importantly, he provided the first hit singles for two of the most iconic record labels of all time—Sun and Stax. He also championed funk in Memphis, producing a steady stream of hit singles in the late 1960s and early 1970s. And even now, his music is regularly sampled by hip-hop artists who recognize the importance of the rhythms that he laid down.

Funkiest Man Alive tells Thomas's life story from the birth of the blues through the glory days of Stax Records to disco and beyond. But more than this, it tells the story of Memphis soul; the factors that fed into that distinctive southern sound that for several decades—from the early twentieth century through the mid-1970s—made Memphis as important as any other US city from a musical perspective.

Chapter One

Memphis Blues

The Early Years, 1917-1950

Rufus Thomas Jr. was born in Cayce, Mississippi, a small rural town around forty miles southeast of Memphis, Tennessee, on March 26, 1917—although his social security records say March 27. Thomas described Cayce as "a little town about as wide as the back of my hand."

Rufus Jr. was the youngest child of Rufus Sr. and Rachel Thomas, coming up behind his sisters Elizabeth, Willie, Eva, and Dorothy, and his brother, Morris. The family lived on Mt. Carmel Road.

Growing up as the youngest, Rufus Thomas Jr. was always pampered as a child. "Daddy was such a baby—he was the baby of his family, with four older siblings," explained Vaneese Thomas, his younger daughter. "The girls in his family, in particular, used to spoil him rotten—as my mother used to say!"[1]

Rufus Thomas Sr. was born twenty-eight years earlier, on April 13, 1889, and was working as a sharecropper when Rufus was born. In the Reconstruction era, after the Civil War, sharecropping was one of the few ways in which rural freedmen could support themselves and their families, and by 1900, it was estimated that 85 percent of Black farmers in Mississippi were sharecroppers.

There were various types of arrangements: workers could rent a plot of land and keep their own crops, or sometimes no money would change hands, and both the worker and landowner would each keep a share of the crop.[2]

Vaneese Thomas believes her paternal grandfather had four brothers, all of whom eventually moved to Memphis. The information contained in the 1917–18 draft registration forms for Marshall County, Mississippi, provides more detail than the census data and suggests that the two eldest brothers, Arthur and Bud, had already moved by that time. A third brother, Morris Thomas, is listed as having just moved to Collierville, Tennessee, just outside Memphis.

That left the two youngest brothers, Rufus Sr. (1889) and Willie Thomas (1894), still living in Cayce, Mississippi, when the draft registrations were being completed.

We know that Rufus Thomas Sr. made the decision to move to Memphis around 1920 or 1921, when his youngest son was just three or four years old. Relocating a family of that size cannot have been easy, and it seems likely that he made the move on the advice of his older brothers. They had all found work in Memphis in a variety of different jobs.

"One was an ice man, one was a market man—he would grow his own produce and take it around the neighborhood," recalled Vaneese. "He had one who was a metalworker. They were all very talented."[3]

It's also worth noting that all five brothers were musicians, so music clearly ran in the family. "One of my aunts told me they all sat around and played together," said Vaneese. "Rufus Sr. played the [jaw] harp, that you play with your mouth; one played a homemade string instrument, like a cross between a banjo and a guitar; one played the harmonica very well . . .they were all musical."[4]

◆ ◆ ◆

The journey undertaken by Rufus Thomas Sr. and his family was, by the 1920s, a well-trodden path. Since the end of the Civil War, many thousands of African Americans from Mississippi had made the journey to Memphis and beyond to escape the state's poverty and racial politics.

Memphis had seen its population grow from roughly twenty thousand, at the time of the outbreak of the Civil War, to forty thousand by 1870—five years after it had finished; a doubling in just ten years. Sixty percent of this increase was from African Americans, who accounted for close to 40 percent of the city's population as early as 1870.

The city's growth was slowed by the yellow fever epidemics of the 1870s but picked up again in the 1880s, once the city had started to invest in a sewage system. By 1910, the population had exceeded one hundred thirty thousand—a threefold increase in just forty years.

This rapid growth meant that Memphis was a city of opportunity. Robert Church Sr., an African American entrepreneur, took advantage of the lower property prices during the epidemic to build a real estate portfolio and ended up owning several properties along Beale Street, which became the Black entertainment district. He also became a philanthropist, building many facilities for the African American community who were excluded from many of the city's amenities because of segregation.

One such facility was the Church Park and Auditorium on the corner of Beale Street and 4th Street.

But that growth also came at a cost. A study carried out by the Prudential Insurance Company of America found that between 1900 and 1910, Memphis had the highest homicide rates of the thirty-one major cities it surveyed and labeled the city as the "murder town" of the nation. And it wasn't just murder; gambling and prostitution were also rife.

Two key figures came to the city around this time—one Black, one white: a Black blues musician who labeled himself "the Father of the Blues," W. C. Handy, and a white businessman-turned-politician, E. H. Crump, later known as "Boss" Crump.

William Christopher Handy was already a well-established and much-traveled musician by the time he reached Memphis. Born in 1873 in Florence, Alabama—later the hometown of Sam Phillips, founder of Sun Records—Handy was the son of former slaves. His father was a Methodist preacher. An uncle, Whit Walker, was an ex-slave and a fiddler, one of the few jobs offering upward mobility on the plantation. There was lots of other music around Florence, and Handy caught the bug early. He bought a guitar from a local store, but his father was angry when he brought it back to the house. His father was staunchly opposed to his taking up "secular" music and encouraged him to learn the organ instead. Against his father's wishes, he got hold of a cornet and was reportedly taught to play by a circus bandleader who was stranded in Florence for a few days.

Handy went on to study at the Teachers' Agricultural and Mechanical College in Huntsville, Alabama, receiving his degree in 1892. He then found work as a schoolteacher, but in his time off, he continued to pursue his music career.

Handy played cornet at the Chicago World's Fair in 1893, but his big break came in 1896 when he was invited to join W. A. Mahara's Minstrels, initially as a musician. He later became the bandleader and stayed with the group for three years, traveling across the country, and even abroad, to places like Cuba where Handy learned the Latin rhythms used in the tango section of "St. Louis Blues."[5]

Tired of life on the road, Handy and his wife Elizabeth moved to Huntsville, Alabama, in 1900, where Handy worked as a music teacher. The job paid poorly, however, and in 1902 he hit the road again, returning to Mahara's Minstrels.

In 1903, nearing thirty years of age, Handy settled in Clarksdale, Mississippi. At that time, Clarksdale was primarily known as a wealthy cotton town, but now—together with its sister town across the river, Helena,

Early photograph of W. C. Handy. Photographer unknown. Photograph courtesy of the Special Collections Department, University of Memphis Libraries.

Arkansas—it is best known for producing a number of the great blues musicians, including Muddy Waters, John Lee Hooker, Sonny Boy Williamson II (born Alex Miller), Roosevelt Sykes, and Ike Turner.

In Clarksdale, Handy headed up the band organized by the Knights of Pythias. Over the next few years, he gradually immersed himself in the local variation of folk blues that he heard in and around the town. He got his first taste through a slide guitarist in a railroad station in nearby Tutwiler. In his groundbreaking 1941 autobiography *Father of the Blues*, Handy described "a lean, loose-jointed [N]egro . . . plunking a guitar beside me . . . . As he played, he pressed a knife on the strings of the guitar in the manner popularized by Hawaiian guitarists who used steel bars. . . . The singer repeated the line three times, accompanying himself on the guitar with the weirdest music I had ever heard."[6]

It's fair to say that Handy did not invent the blues, but he did effectively merge field or folk blues with European instrumentation, which helped to create a new musical form.

Around 1907, Handy relocated to Memphis. At night, Handy based himself at Pee Wee's saloon, which was then located on the corner of

Hernando and Beale Streets. "Through Pee Wee's doors passed the heroic darktown figures of an age that is now becoming fabulous," he later wrote. "They ranged from cooks and waiters to professional gamblers, jockeys and race track men of the period. Glittering young devils in silk toppers and Prince Alberts drifted in and out with insolent self-assurance. Chocolate dandies with red roses embroidered on cream waistcoats loitered at the door . . . ."[7]

W. C. Handy's arrival in Memphis happened to coincide with a local mayoral election campaign being fought between three men, one of whom was Edward Crump, better known as E. H. Crump, and later, "Boss" Crump.

Crump was born in northern Mississippi but relocated to Memphis in September 1893. In 1902, he married a wealthy local socialite before getting involved in the local political scene. In 1907, he became Commissioner of Fire and Police, which was an influential role, then he stood as the Democratic candidate for mayor in 1909.

Handy wrote an instrumental tune to support Crump's campaign and later added lyrics based on comments he heard from the audience—not all of which were flattering about the potential mayor. The song, "Mr. Crump," became an unofficial campaign anthem and was popular in and around Beale Street.

Crump was elected and served three successive two-year terms. His political "machine" essentially controlled the Memphis political system for the next forty years until his death in 1954. His legacy is deeply divisive; while it is outside of the scope of this book, it should be noted that just as he openly courted the city's Black vote, he also set out to destroy the political and economic power of Robert Church Jr., the son of the local Black entrepreneur, and flattened an area of middle-class African American housing to make way for the city's first housing project which further segregated housing within the city.

W. C. Handy later rewrote his election song as "The Memphis Blues." In 1912, Handy made a deal to get the song published and became a trailblazer in bringing song structures of the blues to a larger audience. Unfortunately for Handy, he was in debt to the printer, so he sold the tune for just $50 and all the unsold sheet music. As a result, he became famous but was not yet wealthy.

Because of this experience, Handy decided to set up a structure to retain ownership of his songs and created his own publishing venture with a songwriter named Harry Pace. Handy released his next hit, "St. Louis Blues," in 1914; the song became a massive success and would be recorded many times over the next several years. Other Handy hits include "Yellow Dog Blues" (1914) and "Beale Street Blues" (1916).

Handy left Memphis for New York in 1918 and based his now successful publishing company in Times Square. In 1926, he published *Blues: An Anthology—Complete Words and Music of 53 Great Songs*, which helped to cement his reputation as the "Father of the Blues."

◆ ◆ ◆

W. C. Handy had left Memphis by the time the Thomas family arrived, but he frequently revisited, often for honorary events. All the while, his rich musical legacy lived on in the bars and clubs of Beale Street and beyond, attracting a new generation of blues musicians to the city.

After moving to Memphis, Rufus Sr. worked several jobs to support his wife and children. According to Thomas Jr., his father "worked at Bluff City Coal and Ice Company and other various jobs and (as a) nightwatchman and that kind of thing." [8]

Rufus Thomas Jr. attended Kortrecht Grammar School as a young child. He made his stage debut in a school production playing a frog. "On Beale Street years ago was a theater by the name of the Grand," Thomas later recalled. "And I was a child of six in elementary school—of course we didn't call it elementary at that time. We called it a grade school, grammar school, and I played the part of a frog on this stage. And that was actually as far back as I can remember, that was my beginning." [9]

Rufus Thomas Sr. instilled in his son a respect for hard work and progress but also a love of music. "His father evidently loved music," explained Carla Thomas, many years later, "because he said they used to stand outside and he'd teach them how to tap (dance) and he played [the jaw] harp." [10]

Before he had even reached his teens, Rufus Thomas Jr. would head down to Beale Street, most likely without his parents' knowledge, to see some of the blues singers who were playing in the city. "There were three, maybe four, that came to Memphis when I was a kid," Rufus explained to author Hugh Merrill. "Let me see here. There was Bessie Smith, there was Mamie Smith, then there was another called Ida Cox. Now she was my blues singer. I liked her better than the rest of them. Bessie got the name, but to me, Ida Cox was the best." [11]

Ida Cox was born in Toccoa, Georgia, in the 1890s; her birthdate was long thought to have been February 25, 1896, although more recently, researchers have suggested she was born earlier—in 1894, or possibly earlier still. She came to fame as a vaudeville singer with the traveling minstrel shows but by 1920, was primarily working as a blues singer. She was extremely popular in Memphis; in March 1922, her concert at the Beale Street Palace was aired on radio station WMC to rave reviews, which resulted in a much wider audience. Rufus Thomas Jr. would have been far too young to see that show, of course, and probably saw her around 1930 when she returned to the city with her popular tent show, *Raisin' Cain.*

Other singers that Rufus Thomas Jr. remembered seeing at that time included local favorite Memphis Minnie. "Then came one called Memphis Minnie and then came Ma Rainey, then another woman who called herself Ma Rainey number two! Now those were the woman blues singers!"[12]

If Thomas did get the chance to see Memphis Minnie, then again, it was most likely around 1930, before she moved to Chicago.

Memphis Minnie was born Lizzie Douglas in Walls, Mississippi, about twenty miles south of Memphis, on June 3, 1897. She had learned to play the banjo by the age of ten, guitar by eleven, and at the age of thirteen, she ran away from home to move to Memphis, only returning home to her family's farm if she ran out of money. Between 1916 and 1920, she toured the South with the Ringling Brothers Circus before returning to Memphis, making her living as a performer but supplementing her income through prostitution.

In 1929, she recorded a song called "When the Levee Breaks" with her second husband, "Kansas" Joe McCoy; the song was later recorded by Led Zeppelin in 1971, albeit with a different melody. She and McCoy were "discovered" by an executive from Columbia Records around this time and moved to Chicago soon after, where they released a series of singles.[13]

It's worth noting that Thomas only mentions female blues singers. Female blues singers were the big stars in the 1920s, especially in the theaters and traveling shows, and they were more welcome in the bars and clubs of Beale Street in Memphis than in many other towns.

Despite his early exposure to the blues, it was tap dancing that initially caught the imagination of the young Rufus Thomas. Around the age of ten, he was evidently impressed by the tap dancing skills of his school friend Edward Martin, and he soon started copying and then surpassing him. He told author Rob Bowman, "I don't know where the drive came from. All I know is that I wanted to be a tap dancer. So I continued to work at it, mixing what I had seen with some steps of my own. During those days, there was no such thing as dancing schools for Blacks."

Soon after this, encouraged by his mother, Rufus started to dance for loose change on Beale Street. "She was pushing me to do it. She knew I loved entertainment," he recalled. "She said, 'Son, if this is what you want, do it. Do it, but always respect the feelings of other people.' And I did."[14]

Rufus was close to his mother and described her as "a great church woman" with "the kind of deep-seated intelligence that you don't get out of books."

He would sometimes return to Cayce, Mississippi, with his mother in the summer holidays and even recalled picking some cotton there when he was a teenager. "But that was not a life I wanted to know," he said forcefully, some seventy years later. "No, I was always a city boy, there was always something going on there for me to take an interest in."[15]

Even at this young age, Thomas knew that the city was deeply divided. "During those days, when I was young and segregation was prevalent, I lived, I just lived," he once explained. "I knew at that time that Blacks didn't attend school with whites. I knew that you did not ride on the front of the bus; you had to go to the back. And I know you didn't eat at the lunch counters . . . in department stores. And I know you didn't live in hotels. I knew all of these things, and I guess maybe it was a matter of survival with me."[16]

Around this time, he became acutely aware of the institutional racism that went hand-in-hand with segregation. "[The] only thing I can remember that really happened real, real bad to me as a child . . . in the neighborhood in which I lived—just a bunch of us kids sitting on the porch one day—we had a hydrant that set right in the middle of the neighborhood we called Gray's Town. It had a spigot that came up and over like this, and then there was a sink there, where water ran out, and this spigot that ran over. I'd go up to the spigot to get some water and one of the fellows playingly threw a glass or something at me and it broke and rolled over where another man lived, so he calls the police. Now I'm only eight or nine years old. The police came; everybody ran but me. Now, I hadn't done anything, so why run? And I always figured if you run and something happens and they catch you, you're a part of it anyway. So I sat there. And he, a policeman, came up, [a] big burly white man—I'm just a kid of eight years old—grabs me on the back of my collar, sort of puts me on exhibition out in front of people on the street. And I got two whacks with a billy club on my arms, of which I will never forget [sic]."[17]

The incident scarred Thomas deeply, and he later admitted it would be many years—until he signed with Satellite Records, more than thirty years later—before he felt that he could like or trust a white man. "People say we should let bygones be bygones," he explained. "But for years, for years and years, I didn't like white folk at all. But I knew that I had to survive; I knew that I had to live, I had to work, and that's how I had to make my living. And I made it."[18]

Religion also played an important role in Thomas's life in his formative years and would continue to do so even in later life. Looking back, he struggled to square the circle between what he was taught at home and in church, and what he witnessed on the streets of Memphis. "What does the Bible teach you? Do you get out of the Bible that you should mistreat anyone, I mean *anybody*, anytime?" he asked when interviewed by the Smithsonian Institution many years later. "I just cannot believe that anything is in the Bible like that. But, yet, you can go to church and come right outta that church and mistreat me *only* because of the color of my skin. And you tell me that you're religious and God-fearing people—it's a bunch of hogwash."[19]

◆ ◆ ◆

Thomas attended Kortrecht Intermediate School until ninth grade, when he moved to Booker T. Washington High School. The school's principal was Blair T. Hunt, who was a pillar of the African American community in Memphis. In addition to his work at the school, he was pastor of the Mississippi Boulevard Christian Church, a position he maintained for some fifty years. He was also a founding member of the Memphis Urban League and the Negro YMCA.

Hunt had served in World War I, and after experiencing first-hand the poor treatment of Black soldiers, he became a champion for the cause of equality. His aim was not only to educate the young Black students at the school but also to give them hope for a brighter future. Hunt was also a champion of the arts and encouraged participation in music and theater.

One of the most popular teachers at the school was Nat D. Williams, who taught social studies, history, sociology, and economics. Williams was academically quite brilliant, having graduated college with two degrees. But he was also a larger-than-life character. "He could be a clown and put on a show," recalled Robert Morris, who taught at the same school, "but then, all of a sudden, he would turn serious. His mind was so good, he could be typing and talking to you at the same time."[20]

Like Hunt, he was a high-profile member of the tight-knit African American community in Memphis. In addition to his job as a teacher, he was a journalist with regular columns in the Memphis World and Tri-State Defender, among others, and he later became one of the first African American disc jockeys in the South, accepting a job with WDIA, a new radio station.

Outside of work, Williams was just as busy. He taught a Sunday school class in church, sang in the church choir, and was one of the key organizers of the Cotton Makers' Jubilee, an annual carnival arranged by the African American community in response to the segregated (and at that time, openly racist) Memphis Cotton Carnival. In addition, he hosted the weekly Amateur Night—a talent show—at the Palace Theater on Beale Street.

A bright and enthusiastic student, Thomas was clearly inspired by Nat D. Williams, who discussed African American history and encouraged his students to recognize their own position in a rich legacy of resistance and reinvention. Years later, Thomas was asked about the impact of his teaching and said, "He had a mind like you just wouldn't believe . . . so much stuff was stored in that man's mind. He was just an awesome man but [also] a very good, articulate person."[21]

As a high school teacher, Williams became involved in producing a high school show known as the BTW (Booker T. Washington) Ballet. The show had started out in the 1920s as a highbrow performance to raise money for the newly formed Black high school and put on ballet performances. Under the influence of Williams, the Ballet broadened its range and became more of a high school talent show, showcasing song, dance, and comedy. Preparing for the annual Ballet was evidently a school-wide affair, with classes devoted to creating costumes.

Williams became aware of Thomas's skill as a tap dancer and invited him to audition for the Ballet when he was in tenth grade. "This was when things really began happening for me," Thomas later revealed. "I had learned the craft, and the first rehearsal at school Nat D. said to me, 'What's your name, you want to be in the Ballet?' and I said, 'Yeah.' He said, 'Let me see your smile,' so I had a funny little grin on my face, and he said, 'You got it!'"[22]

Nat D. Williams recognized Thomas's raw talent and became something of a mentor at this time. He schooled him in the art of comic timing and performing in front of an audience. Over the next couple of years, Thomas progressed from being a tap dancer to a comedian, helping Nat D. with comedy routines at the Ballet. "He chose me out of a bunch of kids to work with him. Nat was the straight man and I was the comic," Thomas remembered. "I used to wear the big pants and the big shoes and the big tie that would hang almost to the floor. I was hot stuff—I was so sharp I could stick up in concrete."[23]

The shows themselves were compiled by Williams in conjunction with his collaborator, Maurice Hulbert Jr., a popular local dancer and entertainer. Thomas remained immensely proud of these shows in his later years. He once joked that "the old Ballet was sophisticated and pretty. We had no sophistication and we were ugly, but we had some kinda show!"[24]

Another time he added, "Under Nat D. Williams . . . we performed on stage there. I mean real, live, good performances, so good that the youngsters, the children, not even twenty years old, had a show—we had a show so good out of that school that we played the Palace Theater on Beale Street for a week. That's the way shows used to come in because the Palace was the showplace for the South."

While he was still in high school, Thomas made his first appearances in the clubs of Memphis, working as a tap dancer. "At seventeen, I think, I started to tap dance in a nightclub," he later recalled. "The Morocco, [the] Cotton Club, Brown Derby, Elks Club—all of these clubs I worked in as a tap dancer."[25]

Williams also encouraged Thomas to try his luck as a dancer at the Amateur Night he hosted at the Palace Theater. Thomas is thought to have first appeared in 1934 with a fellow Booker T. Washington high school student by the name of Johnny Dowdy. "We were dancing up and down steps, doing wings and all that fancy stuff, but it was mostly flash," Thomas told Louis Cantor.[26]

By all accounts, he was considered one of the finest tap dancers in town. "I heard from people in Memphis who knew him when he was a teenager, that he was a better tap dancer than Bill Robinson," his youngest daughter, Vaneese Thomas, revealed. In later years, Thomas laughed about his former dancing prowess. "If I try it today, I can't last no more than eight bars!"[27]

Thomas graduated from Booker T. Washington High School in the summer of 1934 and faced something of a dilemma. He was inclined to try his luck as a professional tap dancer until a trip to Chicago made him realize that he still had a lot to learn. "I went to Chicago, right out of high school. And I watched the tap dancers in Chicago; I would go to the various clubs. Fellows that I knew that was formerly of Memphis, had gone to Chicago to live. And I had met these people and they took me around to the various clubs, and then I watched these tap dancers. I said, "Woo! Haven't quite learned enough yet."[28]

Thomas returned to Memphis, where Nat D. Williams again acted as a mentor—as he would continue to do so over the next several years. That summer, he took Thomas under his wing and tried to persuade him that he would progress further in life if he had a college education. "He had a mind like nobody I ever met," Thomas explained to author John

Floyd. "He used to take me round to adult functions. I'd be the only kid in there. I guess he just wanted to show me how the other side worked."[29]

Thomas took Nat D.'s advice and enrolled at Tennessee Agricultural and Industrial State College in Nashville, a university that was originally established as the Tennessee Agricultural and Industrial State Normal School for Negroes back in 1912. In the end, Thomas dropped out of college after just one semester, in part because of economic constraints but also because he was homesick. "I didn't stay there because from the start I was troubled," he later revealed. "I'd never been that far away from Memphis, and I went back home in 1935. Then I started working all around the city as a tap dancer and I would do some scat singing and comic songs like Louis Armstrong or Fats Waller. I would do everything there was to do really, whatever came under the name of entertainment."

In early 1936, Thomas and his friend Johnny Dowdy joined a touring group known as the Rabbit Foot Minstrels. The Rabbit's Foot Company was a long-running minstrel and variety troupe that toured as a tent show between the 1900s and the late 1950s.

It was originally established and managed by Pat Chappelle, an African American guitarist and entrepreneur who also had experience as a theatre operator. The business grew rapidly, and by 1904, it featured more than sixty performers, including blues singers, dancers, acrobats, comedians, actors and even opera singers. When Chappelle died in October 1911, at the age of just forty-two, his widow sold the business as a going concern to Fred Swift Wolcott, better known as F. S. Wolcott—a white farmer from Michigan who also owned a small carnival company that put on a touring show as F. S. Wolcott's Fun Factory.

Wolcott maintained the company as a touring show, initially as both owner and manager. He was always looking to attract new talent; Thomas's favorite blues singer, Ida Cox, joined the company in 1913, while Ma Rainey encouraged a young Bessie Smith to join in 1914, working with her until Smith left the troupe in 1915. Louis Jordan also performed with the troupe in 1923, sometimes with his father, who was a bandleader.

In his book *The Story of the Blues*, Paul Oliver wrote, "The Foots traveled in two cars and had an 80' x 110' tent which was raised by the roustabouts and canvass men, while a brass band would parade in town to advertise the coming of the show. The stage would be of boards on a folding frame and Coleman lanterns—gasoline mantle lamps—acted as footlights. There were no microphones; the weaker voiced singers used a megaphone, but most of the featured women blues singers scorned such aids to volume."[30]

Advertisement for the Rabbit Foot Minstrels Show. Date and photographer unknown.

Of note, it was Wolcott who referred to the show as a "minstrel show," a term that Chappelle had always avoided. The company, by this time known as F. S. Wolcott's Original Rabbit's Foot Company or F. S. Wolcott's Original Rabbit Foot Minstrels, continued to perform annual tours through to the late 1950s, playing small towns during the week and bigger cities on weekends.

"Vaudeville at Rabbit's Foot, boy that was something," Thomas later recalled. "We had the chorus girls, we had the dancers, we had the singers, we had the whole works, we had everything that big-time shows had on this Rabbit's Foot Minstrels . . . . And as a tap dancer I went with a fellow by the name of Johnny Dowdy and the both of us as a team were one of the finest dance teams that Rabbit Foot had ever seen. We were good!"[31]

Thomas and Dowdy did two tours with the Foots, May through October in 1936 and then again in 1937. Back in Pat Chappelle's day, the company would perform as far north as Baltimore and Washington, but under Wolcott, they primarily played in Mississippi, Arkansas, and parts of Louisiana. "We played Hernando, Mississippi, which is close to

Memphis, but we never played Memphis itself," Thomas explained to author Hugh Merrill.[32]

The performers would travel by bus, and because hotels were segregated across the South, they would generally have to rent a private room when they arrived in each town. "We'd get a room for fifty cents a night," Thomas recalled. "I think tops was seventy-five cents when you'd get into a plush house. That's how we survived out there, by living in people's houses."

One interviewer once asked Thomas if the room they rented had a color television. "Color television?" he said, laughing. "There wasn't even radio in those days!"[33]

On the day the show came to town, a number of the performers would assemble in the town square to promote that evening's performance. "Up around noon, we would parade around the square—you know, to show some of the stuff we had so people would come out. It was sort of a visual advertising. And you'd see a few people on the square, not many. Then you'd wonder where in the world those people came from that night. Man, they came out of the cotton patches. All out from the thickets and the woods! And they would pack that old tent—a big old tent, like a circus tent; and sometimes they'd be so full they had to let up the sides of the tent. But we had great shows and a great audience."[34]

The Rabbit's Foot shows were segregated but did play to both a Black and white audience. "On one side, it was white, on the other side it was Black, and they had an aisle right down the middle that separated the audience," Thomas recalled. "But there was never a problem."[35]

Thomas had fond memories of the shows themselves, which were pure vaudeville—offering a mix of song, dance, comedy, and acrobatics. "You had one blues singer in the show—I can't remember her name right now," Thomas told Hugh Merrill. "But I can remember this. There was a pretty girl sittin' right down front one night. The chorus girls came out and did all them high kicks and all that. And when they finished, this pretty girl in the audience did just a little applause. Then came a singer, a pretty singer. Man, it was the whole nine yards! When she finished, just a little applause. Then the dancer came out. Still not much. But there was a blues singer on that show, and the minute the blues singer started singing them blues, that chick jumped out of her seat, started to poppin' her fingers, had her dress above her knees. Boy, and she went! She turned herself a-loose! And that was in 1937."[36]

The one element of the Rabbit's Foot show that Thomas could never get comfortable with was the use of blackface, which was still being used by African American entertainers for "comic" effect at that time.

Thomas later talked to the GRAMMY Foundation about the issue of discrimination within entertainment. "Minstrel comes in two phases," he explained. "If you saw Al Jolson and a couple of others, they were doing what they call blackface—[as] comedians. Wanting to be Black, they had white lips because they put that black stuff all over their face. Burnt cork they called it. To be Black. They weren't Black, but they wanted to be Black . . . to make money off of it. See, they could make money off of trying to be Black, but we couldn't make the money trying to be white. Because it weren't [sic] there. I don't care what you put on me, I ain't white. And you're not gonna get it. But you put that Black on them now, he's playing the part of being Black. And they earned and got big time. Al Jolson and Eddie Cantor, they were two of the best—playing the part of somebody Black."[37]

The second element of the minstrel show, according to Thomas, was the use of burnt cork to exaggerate the dark features of an African American performer to try and "entertain" their mixed or sometimes all-white audience. "And I used to put that burnt cork on my face, you know," he explained. "I'm a Black comedian and I want to put that blackface on that they were doing so I could be a comedian too. And then I woke up one morning and I asked myself, 'why in the hell am I putting this black stuff on my face? I'm already Black! And I got a pretty black skin. Ain't nobody finer than me!'"[38]

Elsewhere, however, Thomas suggested he gave it up for medical reasons. "My doctor told me I had what they called hypersensitive skin. It would break me out in big splotches and I had to stop."[39]

Despite these reservations, Thomas had few regrets about his time with the Rabbit Foot Minstrels. By all accounts, Wolcott treated all of the performers with respect. Thomas always claimed he had a lot of fun, even if the money wasn't great. Most important, he further developed his skills as an entertainer. He learned how to project his voice as the tents had no microphones, and he got the chance to work on his comedic chops too, exaggerating his facial features to make the audience laugh and improving the timing of his delivery.

The tours finished in October, after which Thomas and Dowdy would return to Memphis to look for work. After the second tour with the Rabbit Foot Minstrels, they landed a job in Nashville, working as a dance duo at Kyle's nightclub. Thomas also earned money by waiting tables for white diners. "I was what you'd call a singing waiter," he said. "During that time the white fellow was quite boastful, if he was out with his woman—but he'd pay well. At the end of the night, I had the money, and that's what I was working for—so you ask yourself, 'who's the fool?'"

Photograph of the *Harlem in Havana* show, date and photographer unknown. Photograph courtesy of Leslie Cunningham, the *Harlem in Havana Project*, www.harleminhavana.com.

In the summer of 1938, Thomas was lured back to the tent shows—without Johnny Dowdy, it seems—joining a company called Royal American Shows that advertised itself as the "Most Beautiful Show on Earth."

The company was established by Carl Sedlmayr in 1923, and he ran the business in conjunction with two brothers, Curtis and Elmer Velare, who specialized in fairground rides. Royal American Shows always claimed to have the world's largest "midway" or carnival area; Tom Parker—later known as "Colonel" Tom Parker, the manager of Elvis Presley—started out as a "carnie" with the Royal American Shows, working there from 1931 until 1938. The shows also featured a vaudeville tent, typically featuring African American performers. The show used to tour state fairs and festivals across Minnesota, Oklahoma, Kansas, Arkansas, Mississippi, Louisiana, Tennessee, and western Canada.

In 1936, Leon Claxton, an African American vaudeville performer-turned- producer, took over the vaudeville section of the show. His first themed show, produced that year, was an all-female show called *Hep Cats*. Soon after, he started to produce a more broad-based show featuring a variety of different performers known as *Harlem in Havana*, which went on to run for many years.

Unlike the Rabbit Foot Minstrels, the show was completely segregated. "Later on, I was with the Royal American Shows, which was (another) tent-show carnival, and it played Memphis every year during the month of May," Thomas recalled. "Of course, it was strange at that time. We had Black entertainers and all, but it was a segregated show with Royal American. And Black people didn't come. It was Black people performing for white people, but the Black patronage was not welcome."

Occasionally, when one of the other performers did not show up, Thomas got the chance to try his hand at comedy and singing blues tunes. "I was just doing tap dancing around the time with maybe a bit of singing on the side," he explained. "It was hard. I was working on stage before there were microphones. You really had to have some kind of voice."[40]

Despite the segregation that existed with the *Harlem in Havana* shows, Rufus had no regrets looking back. "I wouldn't have traded the world for that foundation," he told author Peter Guralnick. "Even with all the racism, all the hold backs [*sic*], all those things, it was still quite likeable [*sic*], people were having fun. We didn't make a lot of money but we had a damn good time!"[41]

After four consecutive summers on the road with vaudeville shows, Thomas returned to Memphis in late 1939, in part to be able to spend more time with his girlfriend, Cornelia Lorene Wilson, known as Lorene. "They knew each other back in junior high," explained Vaneese Thomas, their younger daughter. "According to my mother, they were introduced by her brother; her brother was Henry Young. He was slightly older than Daddy, but Daddy and Uncle were friends. My mother had long, beautiful hair down to her waist and she wore it in a long braid, and he would pull her braids. He used to pull her pigtails, even though she was only two years younger!"[42]

Around this time, Rufus Thomas Jr.'s mother, Rachel Thomas, passed away quite suddenly. "My parents were not married yet when Daddy's mother died," Vaneese explained. "Because they grew up in the same neighborhood, on Lucy (Avenue), my mother was familiar with his parents. Apparently, Daddy was at work—he was not yet at the American Finishing Company. They called him to tell him that his mother had died. My mother said she would never forget—he came by her house first to tell her. She remembered the look of total horror and dismay on his face when they told him. She said that it was one of those tender moments that let her know what a nice guy he was, that he thought so much of his mother, and probably helped her decide to marry him."[43]

In 1940, Thomas formed a new duo, performing both comedy and dance with a gentleman by the name of Robert Couch, who was nicknamed "Bones." "And when Bones came aboard with me, I was the straight man, and he was the comic," Thomas explained.[44]

Harlem in Havana chorus line, 1940. Photographer unknown. Photograph courtesy of Leslie Cunningham, the *Harlem in Havana Project*, www.harleminhavana.com.

"Bones" had enjoyed a previous brush with fame, appearing in the groundbreaking 1928 movie *Hallelujah*, which was shot in Memphis. This was one of the early "talkie" movies, recorded with sound. The first of those, *The Jazz Singer*, featured the Jewish entertainer Al Jolson, who famously appeared in blackface in a few scenes. *Hallelujah*, by contrast, featured an all-African American cast—which was a first—despite being directed by a white Hollywood director, King Vidor. Vidor was nominated for an Academy Award for the movie, but given the nature of the film and widespread segregation at that time, it was not shown in many parts of the country.

Most of the main cast of *Hallelujah* was drawn from the African American communities of Chicago and New York, but some were hired locally, including Robert Couch—who played a character known as Half Pint. Robert Golden, the assistant director, later recalled discovering Couch while he was "dancing in the Hotel Peabody lobby for pennies." Many of the extras from the movie were hired in the local churches of Memphis.[45]

Thomas later recalled that he also took up singing and songwriting around this time. "I was working in a comedy team at the Elks Club on

Beale," he explained to John Floyd. "There was a blues singer there by the name of Georgia Dickerson and I used to write blues for her every week, and she'd sing them. But she left town and that left space in the show, so I thought *I'm going to try to take up that space.* That's all there was to it. I sang a song by Lonnie Johnson called 'Jelly Roll Baker.'"[46]

The song went:

She said, Mr. Jelly Roll Baker let me be your slave.
When Gabriel blows his trumpet, then I'll rise from my grave.
For some of your good jelly roll, crazy 'bout that good jelly roll.
You know it's good for the sick, and it's good for the young and old.

The reaction from the crowd surprised Thomas as they applauded wildly and threw coins. One female patron reportedly came on to the stage and gave him a kiss, coupled with a five-dollar tip.

"And from that night on, blues has become a part of me," Thomas later explained. "It was my roots . . . I never really sang gospel, just a tiny bit in church. But there's all the good voices, usually, especially down south here, comes out of the church. But I had a [*sic*] old, ragged voice that wasn't considered good, but I got lucky and fortunate—blessed, I suppose—and a good ragged blues voice came out of it."[47]

"Then I learned other songs and I did a few love songs like 'For Sentimental Reasons' and I even did 'Stardust,'" Thomas recalled. "But my voice then was beginning to turn and I couldn't sing anything sweet with all that gravel in it!"[48]

◆ ◆ ◆

Thomas proposed to Lorene Wilson around this time, dedicating a song to her one evening while he was performing at the Harlem Theater on Florida Street.

In November 1940, the two of them married in the New Salem Baptist Church in Memphis. "The Reverend C. L. Franklin (the father of Aretha Franklin) was the pastor at the church at that time," said Vaneese Thomas, their youngest child. "She was in the choir, and they were friends, so she asked him to marry them and he did!"[49]

Incidentally, the Reverend Franklin married his second wife, Barbara Siggers, in June 1936, and their third child, Aretha, was born in 1942. Many years later, Vaneese Thomas ended up working with Aretha Franklin, performing as a backing vocalist. "I've had many discussions with Aretha about that very thing," Vaneese explained. "We felt a kinship—same earth, same ground, same air!"[50]

Soon after, the newlyweds moved into Foote Homes, a newly built housing complex. The development had proved controversial as "Boss" Crump had effectively demolished a prospering middle-class African American neighborhood to make way for the project, prompting concern that he was promoting a segregated housing policy within the city.

Those concerns were probably well-founded, but the development proved popular with young families, with the Memphis Housing Authority receiving over 5,200 applications to fill the development's 900 residences, which set a national record.

Among the early residents of Foote Homes was author Gloria Wade-Gayles, whose 1993 memoir, *Pushed Back to Strength: A Black Woman's Journey Home*, includes a passage about her childhood there. "My housing project—called the Foote Homes—was a thirty-minute walk from Main Street and only fifteen minutes from Beale Street," she wrote. "It was a colorful city within a city composed of attached red-brick apartment buildings: cheap versions of Philadelphia row houses. In the back, units faced one another across a wide driveway that snaked through the entire community."[51]

The young couple was hoping to start a family, so Thomas accepted a day job at the American Finishing Company, a textile bleaching plant, a job he maintained for the next twenty-three years. "He worked in the boiler room. They prepared cloth, so he was also working with chemicals. He was fortunate, in that the American Finishing Company was an important wartime supplier (for uniforms), and he didn't have to go join the army, because they needed him as a worker in the textile mill. So that's the reason he was not drafted in the war," explained his younger daughter, Vaneese Thomas.

Not only was it grueling work, but the working conditions were miserable. The job was scheduled to start at 7 a.m. and finish at 3 p.m., but this was moved to a 6:30 a.m. start to avoid a confrontation between white and Black workers on the streetcar. "White folks had the same shift, and during those days, whites not only got the front of the streetcar, they got the front of the line waiting for it," Thomas explained many years later.[52]

The factory itself was also segregated. "I never sat down and talked to my boss the entire time I was at the American Finishing Company," Rufus later revealed. Still, his coworkers remembered him as something of a comedian, making everyone laugh with his one-liners and making the day brighter for everyone.[53]

Workers in the boiler room were required to wear a standard-issue denim boiler suit. "He wore jeans every day, and it got to the point that as soon as he was able to quit, he'd never wear jeans again in his life, because he hated it," Vaneese laughed. "He changed later, because he could wear his own jeans, but he hated having to wear them every day!"[54]

The fact that his shift finished at 2:30 p.m. made it easier for Rufus and Bones to perform in nightclubs by night. "I took my wife to one of my shows one night and, as fate would have it, she sat very close to the stage," Thomas later recalled. "And the women would come up and put money in my hand, and fold it up in my hand like that, and they'd stop and kiss me, and I could see *daggers* coming out of my wife's eyes. So she didn't blow off any steam, but I knew she did not like it and I did not take her anymore. Because these things do happen to entertainers, and especially if they're fairly good entertainers. And I thought I was pretty good at that time!"[55]

Rufus's mentor from high school days, Nat D. Williams, continued to look out for his former pupil, too, and occasionally suggested that the two of them perform at the Amateur Night he hosted at the Palace Theater. "Daddy danced so well that he eventually got barred from competition," recalled Carla Thomas, laughing. "That's how he got to be emcee."

It seems that Williams tried to help Thomas's career as an entertainer by hiring Rufus and Bones to work with him, initially as a comic foil and later to host the show itself.

♦ ♦ ♦

Rufus and Lorene Thomas had their first two children in quick succession. On August 22, 1941, they had a son, Ronald Marvell Thomas—who was always known as Marvell. "The name Marvell came from my mother," he later recalled, "but I don't have any idea where she got it."

"I used to tease my parents all the time," Marvell later revealed. "I think I was born nine months and 21 days after they were married. So, they weren't wasting any time!"[56]

Less than eighteen months later, Carla Venita Thomas was born on December 21, 1942.

Both children had fond memories of growing up in that neighborhood, which was very family oriented. "We lived in a public housing complex," Marvell recalled. "They wound up being called 'the projects' later, but it was fun growing up there. Nice people and a lot of kids to play with."[57]

Carla remembers being introduced to music by her father, even before she started school. "Even at a young age, Daddy was teaching us rhythmic patterns," she says. "We learned them streetwise from my dad. My dad was a tap dancer in his early days, so he was really into rhythmic patterns. He would teach us things that Bo Diddley ended up doing on record. We would sing those kinds of songs, and then he'd teach us how

Robert "Bones" Couch and Rufus Thomas, circa 1950. Photograph courtesy of the Vaneese Thomas family collection.

to do our hands in different rhythmic patterns. So even at three and four years old, we were doing drum licks, I guess you would call it, and bass rhythms and humming things that were rhythmic."[58]

Beale Street was only a few blocks away and quickly became a second home—even if their parents were not always aware. "You could call it a second home," Marvell Thomas said in 2011. "It was just three blocks from our house. I was a little kid, five years old, running up and down Beale Street all the time, much to my parents' chagrin when they found out. Of course, I was there a lot legitimately too, when my father was hosting the talent show every Thursday night at the Palace Theatre."[59]

Around this time, Nat D. Williams decided to focus more of his time on his teaching and effectively promoted Rufus and Bones to cohost the show in his place. "We were together for eleven consecutive years at the Palace Theater, every Wednesday night," Thomas later explained to Peter Guralnick. "We were making five dollars a night and you had the Al Jackson band and they were only making 25 dollars and they had a big band too! The show was only a nickel (entry) then, but the place was packed."

With a more prominent role in Amateur Night, Rufus made sure he looked and sounded the part, as Williams had always taught him. He was always sharply dressed, and as he walked on, made sure the audience was aware of how good he looked with the catchphrase, "Ain't I'm clean?" Another catchphrase that he devised at this time that always brought a laugh was, "Oh I feel so unnecessary!"

Rufus liked to include new jokes in his routine, and Carla remembers that he used to rehearse his jokes at home first before trying them out on stage. "Our upbringing was so heavily musical and performance-oriented. That's kind of how our house was. We heard jokes—Daddy would try them out on us."

As the children got a little older, Rufus would bring them down to the Palace Theater as a special treat. The show would start with a movie, then go on to the talent show section, after which there would be another movie. "Occasionally, he would take Carla and me with him to the Palace Theatre, and a fellow worker would keep an eye on us while Rufus emceed the weekly Amateur Hour," Marvell recalled many years later. "They sometimes played movies before the show. I saw the first *Mummy's Curse* with Boris Karloff—scared the hell out of me! I love scary movies to this very day."[60]

Carla's favorite part was the talent show itself. "Beale Street was right there—it was like a way of life for us," she recalled. "I was around music all the time and around Dad all the time. And he would take a lot of the kids to (the Palace Theater). We'd all be holding hands—Mom and all of us—and we'd go watch the show. It was interesting because people would just allow their feelings (to come out). "Man, get off the stage! It was just fun."[61]

As a result of her early exposure to the entertainment district, Carla came to regard the area as the city's beating heart. "It seemed to me then that to be associated with Beale Street was to be associated with creativity, strength and pride," she explained. "That's why many Blacks, especially on the weekends, would congregate up and down Beale Street to feel the pulse of life it had to offer."

This was a view that her father clearly shared. "Beale Street was the Black man's haven," he once told an interviewer. "They'd come into town and forget all their worries and woes!"[62]

But childhood wasn't just about Beale Street. Marvell remembers that while his father worked very hard to provide for the family, he was always there for outdoor activities, too. "As father and son, Rufus and I made homemade kites," he remembered. "From the textile mill, he would bring home heavy brown paper and string. We'd go out in the woods, and he'd cut twigs to use as the framework; we'd use some of his old ties for the kite's tail. We'd do that all the time."[63]

As Marvell grew older, Rufus taught him how to play corkball, a child's version of baseball using a cork, weighted with a coin and then wrapped in white tape. "Rufus also played semi-pro baseball, and for a couple of summers, I was the batboy," Marvell recalled.[64]

Rufus also encouraged his children's musical education, not only teaching them rhythmic patterns but also how to sing and even yodel! Carla later recalled that she and her brother could yodel in harmony, while Marvell also showed off his yodeling skills at local talent shows. "It was so odd to see a Black kid yodeling that I always won," he later recalled.[65]

The influence of Lorene Thomas, their mother, was no less important. She kept the children grounded and instilled in them both the importance of a good education and good manners. "From my mother, I got an inner strength, a tenaciousness that is hard to describe," Marvell later recalled. "She was extraordinarily giving and helpful to people. She was always there for them, selfless—and she expected her children to be, too."[66]

Like Rufus, she also had a strong work ethic. Once the children were old enough, she started studying to become a nurse. "My mother, Lorene, was a stay-at-home mom until I was about six years old, and she decided to go to nursing school," said Marvell. "I admired her sitting up burning the midnight oil studying medical textbooks. It was a lot of very heavy stuff. She (later) became a nurse at John Gaston Hospital."[67]

She was also busy every Sunday and continued to take an active role in the New Salem Baptist Church in Memphis, which played an important role in her life. In addition to singing in the choir, she would also help out with community projects. It was important to her that her children had a spiritual upbringing, too, and she made sure they attended every Sunday. "Mother and Dad worked a lot of times on Sunday, so this teacher would take us to this church," Carla recalled. "But then my mother's church, her pastor was C. L. Franklin, Aretha's dad—so we got all the good heavy gospel, and then we had the conservative hymns. Our upbringing was so heavily musical and performance-oriented."[68]

Despite raising two young children, studying to be a nurse, and working with the church every Sunday, Lorene Thomas still found time to play a vibrant role in the local community. She looked out for other children in the neighborhood and always had fresh-baked cookies or cake for other children who came to visit. "My mother and I liked to cook," Marvell recalled. "She and her sister and first cousin would all cook together, and I'd watch them. How did they put all these separate things into one place and out came such a wonderful result? How do they do that? The first thing I cooked was a coconut cake from scratch—my mother's favorite, but not nearly as good as hers."[69]

◆ ◆ ◆

Back on Beale Street, Thomas noticed that Amateur Night was starting to heat up. The first generation of blues musicians, starting with W. C. Handy, and continuing with the likes of Ida Cox, Ma Rainey and Memphis Minnie, had inspired a new generation of younger blues musicians to come to Memphis and try their luck. Typically, these musicians would compete at the various talent shows around town but also try to find work in the various nightclubs around town.

In the summer of 1946, a twenty-one-year-old singer and guitarist named Riley King hitchhiked to Memphis, staying with his mother's first cousin, Booker T. Washington White. White had made some recordings for Victor Records in 1930 and later became known as Bukka White, with "Bukka" being a phonetic spelling of his first name. His 1937 song, "Shake 'Em on Down," was later referenced by Led Zeppelin on "Hats off to (Roy) Harper," which featured on the band's third album. White went on to record "Parchman Farm Blues" in 1940, which would later be recorded by Jeff Buckley, and "Fixin' to Die Blues," which was adapted by Bob Dylan on his debut album.

Riley King, later known as B.B. King, stayed with White in Memphis for ten months. "At that time we had contestants come up to perform, and then after everybody performed they'd all come back on stage and the audience would applaud for first prize. They used to have $5, $3 and $2 but they cut that out and later everybody who came up on stage would get a dollar," Thomas explained to Beale Street historians Margaret McKee and Fred Chisenhall. "B.B. King used to come with holes in his shoes, his guitar all patched up, just to get that dollar."[70]

King missed his wife and returned to Indianola in 1947 before returning to Memphis in 1948, arriving with his guitar and $2.50. The second time around, he teamed up with Bobby Bland, Johnny Ace and Earl Forrest in a coalition of musicians known as the Beale Streeters. As a result, he acquired the nickname "Beale Street Blues Boy," which in time was shortened to "Blues Boy" and then to just "B.B." "Beale Street was where it all started for me," King said. "That's where it all came from."

Another famous name to make his way through Amateur Night at the Palace Theater was Johnny Ace himself, then known as John Marshall Alexander Jr. Ike Turner, who worked as a talent scout, later arranged for Alexander and the Beale Streeters to record for Modern Records in 1951, and it was shortly after this that he changed his name to Johnny Ace.

Sadly, his fame was short-lived, and he died of an accidental, self-inflicted gunshot wound backstage in Houston, Texas, on Christmas Day, 1954.

But there were signs of another new phenomenon, too. The influence of W. C. Handy had started to be felt in the high schools which served the African American community in Memphis; schools like Booker T. Washington that Thomas had attended, but also Manassas High in North Memphis. Both schools took the performing arts very seriously, knowing that this was one avenue for the students to make a living in the segregated city of Memphis. With that in mind, both schools had hired gifted musicians as teachers and encouraged the formation of school bands and vocal choruses, too. The fruits of that investment were now starting to come through, as a new generation of young Memphis-born musicians was starting to emerge.

Jazz saxophonist Charles Lloyd was one of the new generation of musicians emerging and appeared at the Palace around 1948. "When I was about nine or ten, I played alto sax on the amateur show at the Palace Theater on Beale Street in my hometown (of) Memphis," he later remembered. "Rufus Thomas was the MC and Al Jackson Sr. was the bandleader, the great Hank O'Day played lead alto in the big band. I recall I played a mixture of 'Ornithology' and the 'Huckelbuck.' I won first prize of $5 and had a standing ovation. When I walked offstage, a young man of sixteen or seventeen said to me, 'You need lessons bad!' He promptly walked me around the corner to Mitchell's Hotel on Hernando and Beale and knocked on a door. It was Irving Reason, the great alto player. The young man left me saying, 'He needs lessons.'"[71]

Another Memphis jazz musician emerging at this time was guitarist Calvin Newborn, who recalled being presented with five dollars by Thomas at the Palace Theater for playing a duet with his brother, pianist Phineas, on "Hey! Ba-Ba-Re-Bop;" most likely this would have been in 1946, when the two boys were thirteen and fifteen, respectively.

Saxophonist Herman Green was another. He didn't perform at the talent show but ended up in Al Jackson's band at the Palace in 1945, at the age of just fifteen. He later claimed that Thomas got him his first start in showbusiness, recommending him to B.B. King, who was in the process of putting a band together. He played with King when he was still in high school, graduated in 1948, and later played on some of Thomas's early singles in the 1950s. Soon after that, he moved to New York, where he tried to break into the burgeoning jazz scene.

Thomas stayed at the Palace Theater with his sidekick, Bones, until 1950, when he had a falling out with the Palace Theater's management over money. As a performer, comedian and MC, he felt that they deserved a pay rise after ten years of service. "I wanted more, but I couldn't get Bones to go ask for it with me," he explained to Peter Guralnick. "So the man got with Bones and asked him if he would work with someone else, and I got fired."

Rufus was not out of work as an MC for long and was quickly offered a job hosting the competing talent show at the nearby Handy Theatre, named after W. C. Handy itself—a role he kept until 1954.

Looking back in later years, Rufus was very proud of his role in the Memphis talent shows over the years. "They called it amateur, but Memphis amateurs are the world's professionals," he said. "Everybody that came on the show was given a dollar and out of those shows, which lasted over many years, have come so many talented people, such as B.B. King, Bobby Bland, and later on Isaac Hayes and Junior Parker. They all came by me first, so you know I gotta feel proud when I see them making it today."[72]

♦ ♦ ♦

While Thomas spent Wednesday nights hosting the Palace Theatre Amateur Night in the 1940s, his weekends were typically spent trying to make a name for himself as an all-around entertainer.

Despite having young children, Rufus continued to ply his trade in the numerous bars and clubs around town. "The Elks Club, that was the foundation; Maurice Hulbert ran the place," he explained to the Smithsonian Institution. "Then I started to work with the various bands in the city. I'd learned enough songs where I could sing with bands. I sang with, first, Bill Fort, saxophone player, tenor saxophone player; very good. Then I worked with Al Jackson, Sr., which [sic] was the father of Al Jackson, who was the drummer for Booker T. & the M.G.'s. This was early; he was nothing but a kid then; he wasn't even playing. I wasn't a drummer, but I used to show Al Junior little licks in drumming. I could never actually play them, but I could show you what I wanted, and you could go from there."[73]

Despite Thomas's dislike of performing in segregated spaces, his growing popularity meant that he spent a great deal of his time entertaining white audiences at venues such as the Cottage Inn. "That was during the time we had to come in through the back," he later recalled. "We didn't come in through the front. There was no such thing as fraternizing, and if you had to go to the bathroom, you went out in the back, because there were no facilities for you." [74]

By the late 1940s, Thomas had spent several years singing in Memphis nightclubs with a number of good local bands, including the aforementioned Al Jackson, Bill Harvey and Tuff Green. He had not originally seen singing as his main forte but as part of his game plan to be an all-around entertainer. He said, "My models were Fats Waller and Louis Armstrong, and a fellow named 'Gatemouth' Moore, Dwight Moore out of Memphis. They were all good entertainers, very, very versatile."[75]

And as one of the city's leading African American entertainers, both as an MC and a singer, it wasn't long before Thomas attracted the attention of local Memphis radio station WDIA, which was looking to expand its ground-breaking lineup of Black radio announcers.

This would raise his profile significantly in the years ahead, turning him from a local star, in the city of Memphis, into a regional star.

Chapter Two

WDIA

Rufus on the Radio, 1950-1960

Rufus Thomas felt that the founders of WDIA Radio in Memphis helped to break down the color barriers in the city in the late 1940s. "Bert Ferguson and John Pepper, they were sort of a Branch Rickey of radio—like Branch Rickey was with Jackie Robinson, the first to enter professional baseball," Thomas recalled. "He said, we are going to do this because this is the way it is, it's the way it's supposed to be."[1]

In some respects, Rufus was right; WDIA was one of the first radio stations in the South to hire a Black disc jockey and the first to introduce all-Black programming, and their actions paved the way for other important changes in the years that followed. But the changes introduced by Ferguson and Pepper were less altruistic than Thomas suggests and were taken out of financial necessity rather than because that was the way it was supposed to be.[2]

Jackie Robinson was originally signed by Rickey to a minor league contract in 1945 and started for the Brooklyn Dodgers two years later, in 1947. One year later, there was no sign of similar progress being made in Memphis. The Memphis Chicks, the white baseball team, played in the Southern Association, while the Black team, the Memphis Blues, played in the Negro Southern League at that time.

The situation in baseball simply mirrored day-to-day living. Housing was largely segregated, as dictated by the policies of Boss Crump, the former mayor turned political leader, who had supervised the dismantling of a middle-class Black neighborhood west of Lauderdale in the mid-1930s to make way for a major public housing complex built by the Memphis Housing Authority. Schools were still segregated, of course, and would remain so well beyond the landmark Brown vs. Board of Education decision in 1954.

African Americans were also excluded from most public facilities within Memphis at that time, including Memphis Zoo, the Memphis Fairgrounds and city museums. When the Zoo did finally open its doors to Blacks several years later, it famously erected a sign stating 'No white people allowed in the zoo today', indicating that this was the one day of the week that African Americans were permitted to visit.

In terms of nightlife, the African American community had long developed its own forms of entertainment, as highlighted in the preceding chapter. Theaters were effectively segregated, with most white theaters offering segregated seating areas for Blacks and Black theaters offering special white-only shows, known as "midnight rambles." In the same vein, Thomas regularly played in 'white only' nightclubs around this time, in addition to the clubs around Beale Street.

The media were no different. The African American community had its own newspaper, the *Memphis World*, but the main white newspapers, the *Commercial Appeal* and the *Memphis Press-Scimitar*, refused to use titles such as Mr. or Mrs. when referring to Black citizens. Radio was even more one-sided; Memphis had five radio stations in 1947, not one of which was aimed at the Black community; and when WDIA opened its doors that same year, that became six.[3]

All of this was reflected in employment opportunities, which were just as segregated at this time. In 1953, the Memphis Urban League reported that the median income for Black households was $1,348 annually, less than half the white median of $3,085. Roughly 23,000 Black families lived in extreme poverty, making less than $1,000 annually, and more Black families were grouped in the sub-$500 category than in any other bracket.

But as the 1950s approached, there were the first signs of change in the air. In July 1948, President Harry Truman mandated the integration of the US armed forces. In the same year, Memphis appointed its first Black postal clerks, which was front page news in the *Memphis World*. Even more significant was the hiring of thirteen Black trainee police officers to Memphis Police Academy in October 1948. Of note, they received the same salary as their white counterparts, even if they were not yet able to arrest white citizens; they could, however, hold them until their white counterparts came on to the scene.

It was amid these changes that WDIA considered a change in its approach. The radio station was launched in 1947 by Bert Ferguson and John R. Pepper, two white men and veterans of the radio business. When the new station started broadcasting on June 7, 1947, it was intended to be a country and western station. When that approach failed to find much of an audience, Ferguson and Pepper switched to what they described as "good music." In practice, this meant a mix of country and western music and light pop, homemaker shows, and "block programming," which included soap operas and classical music.

A year down the line, WDIA was floundering, with low listening figures and mired in red ink. When the station's two biggest advertisers both canceled, the two owners briefly considered selling out. Ferguson, it seems, was particularly keen to make it work and started toying with the idea of moving to Black programming. "When I was with WHBQ—years before we put 'DIA on the air—we aimed several individual shows at the Negro audience," he later recalled. "Even though the on-air personality was no Negro, the music was performed by Negroes. The shows were very successful, so that idea of programming stuck in my mind."

He mentioned this idea to John Pepper and Chris Spindel, WDIA's first female program director, and both agreed that it might be an option. According to Spindel, the turning point came when she and Ferguson attended a convention held by the Tennessee Association of Broadcasters, at which one speaker emphasized that the secret of success was finding the right audience. On the journey back to Memphis, Ferguson leaned over to her and whispered, "What do you think of programming for Negro people?" As the possibilities raced through her mind, Ferguson elaborated further. "We could play records by Negro musicians and singers and then branch out, experimenting with other programs," he whispered. "We would start by hiring a Negro disc jockey."[4]

In the weeks that followed, Ferguson researched the business opportunity and discovered that half of the listeners who could hear WDIA's signal—which was originally 730khz—were African Americans. He convinced his business partner, John Pepper, that they needed to make the change. They decided to introduce a half-hour show aimed at "a big segment of the population that had musical tastes and community needs that were not being answered," recalled Ferguson, some twenty years later. The reason for starting with a half-hour show was simple; they could not afford to alienate their few existing advertisers, given the fragile state of the company.[5]

Ferguson knew immediately whom he wanted to hire as the station's first Black disc jockey: Nat D. Williams, who was already a pillar of the African American community. He was a charismatic and much-loved history teacher at Booker T. Washington High School but also a highly respected journalist.

An announcer also needed to be an entertainer, of course, and Williams had all the experience required. He had been MC of the weekly Amateur Night at the Palace Theater, a show which was also broadcast on WNBR radio and later on television. He was also MC of the Grand Jubilee Parade, the highlight of the annual Cotton Makers' Jubilee. "I think he was one of the most popular Black people in the entire city," his daughter Naomi Williams Moody noted with justifiable pride.[6]

Choosing a name for the new show also proved to be a delicate matter. "We needed to send a message to our future listeners, preferably without alerting white listeners, but there was no time to poll people and find out what they wanted to be called," Chris Spindel remembered. "At that time, you never called anyone 'Black.' Black was an insult. Ebony? We decided it was too obscure. Negro was the polite term but we couldn't say 'Negro' in the newspaper's weekly radio guide. Overruling my list, Bert chose 'jamboree' for the last part of the name. He also liked 'tan' and 'town.'" Eventually, Ferguson settled on *Tan-Town Jamboree*, and the matter was settled.[7]

The first *Tan-Town Jamboree* took place at 4 p.m. on October 25, 1948. Williams had come straight from high school, where he taught until 3:15 p.m., and arrived clutching a selection of his own records. Everyone was nervous ahead of the new show, and when the staff announcer opened Williams's microphone, he let out a huge belly laugh to relieve the tension. "A laugh is a pretty good foil for fending off a lot of unpleasantness," he noted later, "if it's used at the right time with the right sound effects."[8]

His laugh quickly became one of his trademarks, and he would follow that up with his regular introduction: "Well, yes-siree, it's Nat D. on the Jamboree, coming at thee on seventy-three (on the dial), WDIA. Now, whatchubet." The first tune that day was "Stompin' at the Savoy"—presumably the Chick Webb version rather than Benny Goodman's recording.

Predictably, Williams's opening appearance provoked a handful of irate phone calls, but these soon died down. The radio station did continue to receive letters of complaint—some of them threatening—but Ferguson did his best to protect his new hire from any such threats. In any case, the feedback was overwhelmingly positive, and his main concern was how to expand Black programming.

One of the first things WDIA looked to do was to expand the hours that Nat D. Williams was on the air. After just ten days, the *Tan Town Jamboree* moved from a 4:45 p.m. finish to 5:30 p.m.; this was the latest it could finish in the winter, as WDIA was a "dawn-to-dusk" station at that time.

Another early change was the adoption of gospel programming, with regular fifteen-minute live slots being given to popular groups such as the Spirit of Memphis, the Southern Wonders and the Sons of Jehovah, and from early 1949, a female group, the Songbirds of the South. This additional programming proved very popular with the African American community and had the added advantage that it was a cheap way of filling airtime.

In early 1949, as the days began to lengthen once more, Nat D. Williams was offered longer hours once again. The *Jamboree* was extended until 7 p.m., with the last hour becoming known as *Nat D.'s Supper Club*. He was also given a breakfast show, the *Tan Town Coffee Club*, from 7:15 a.m. until 8 a.m., after which he'd have to rush off to school. The morning show was later brought forward to a 6:30 a.m. start, making the hard-working Nat D.'s day even longer.

As WDIA looked to expand its Black programming, Williams played an essential role in recommending potential candidates. One of the first that he looked to hire was Maurice Hulbert, whose father, Maurice "Fess" Hulbert Sr., had established the first Black dancing school in Memphis in the 1920s. His son had worked variously as a dancer, comedian, bandleader, and nightclub MC; at the time he was hired, he was working as the band conductor for Tuff Green's orchestra.

Hulbert was known to Williams because he was the producer of the Booker T. Washington's annual Ballet. Williams encouraged him to audition for WDIA, and Hulbert was initially reluctant, concerned that he would tread on his friend's toes. But WDIA needed more "name" disc jockeys, and Hulbert's colorful personality was perfect for the role.

Hulbert became adept at changing his on-air persona to suit each show. His biggest show, the *Sepia Swing Club*, was broadcast every afternoon from 3 p.m. until the news at 3:55 p.m. The program was designed to showcase hot new music, and it was here that Hulbert developed his nickname, "Hot Rod," describing a spaceship that listeners would be transported on through a solar system of hot music.

Hulbert quickly took on other shows, too, and changed his style accordingly. At 8 a.m. every weekday—right after *Tan Town Coffee Club*—he would host *Delta Melodies*, a program of spiritual music which required a more reverential persona. And then, in the late morning, from 11 a.m. until 11:55 a.m., he hosted *Moods by Maurice*. This late-morning program catered primarily to housewives, and Hulbert became the "Sweet Talking Man," playing more romantic tunes for his audience.

Another Nat D. recommendation was the Reverend Dwight "Gatemouth" Moore, a blues singer-turned-preacher. He was one of Nat D.'s former high school students and, as a budding blues singer, had regularly entered—and won—Amateur Night at the Palace Theater. His "conversion" had taken place at the Club DeLisa in Chicago in early 1949. He had stepped on stage to sing, and nothing had come out. When he tried again, he said, "I started singing 'Shine on Me,' a religious number, and most of the audience thought I'd lost my mind."[9]

Moore was a natural showman and brought a mix of spiritual fervor and outspoken opinion to the airwaves in his early afternoon gospel show. "My program was called *Prayer Time*," Moore later recollected, "and my phone would ring and I've had white people to say, 'What is happening on that radio station? My maid is tearing up the house!'"[10]

Moore was not averse to the odd and outrageous publicity stunt, which would occasionally cause conflict with WDIA's management. On one occasion, he announced that he would walk on water and asked listeners to meet later that day where Beale Street meets the Mississippi River. A sizeable crowd gathered, awaiting his appearance, and for a while, there was no sign of him. As the crowd started to disperse, Moore finally appeared, wearing a white suit, white shoes, and a white, wide-brimmed hat. He walked to the banks of the river and crouched down to touch the water before turning back to face the crowd. "Children, the water is troubled today," he announced. "Reverend Moore cannot walk on troubled waters."[11]

Not all of WDIA's initial hires were Nat D's recommendations. In the spring of 1949, a young musician walked twenty blocks in the rain, from the bus station to the radio station, to audition for work. "One rainy spring morning I was working at my desk upstairs when Bert called me to come down," recalled Chris Spindel. "He wanted me to hear a musician who had arrived unannounced at the station. He introduced a thin young man who stood waiting with his guitar, nervous and shy. He was neatly dressed in a black suit with a tie. Bert told him to go back into our unused front studio, stand at the microphone, and play two of his songs again so I could hear them."[12]

The self-effacing young man turned out to be a blues singer called Riley King, who later became known as B.B. King. He was looking for a radio station where he could play his songs and maybe cut a record. Ferguson informed him the station didn't make records but asked if he could write a jingle for a new "blood-building" tonic distributed by Ber-jon, a company in which he was a partner. The tonic was called Peptikon. King started singing:

Pep-Ti-Kon sure is good, Pep-Ti-Kon sure is good,
Pep-Ti-Kon sure is good, you can get it in your neighborhood.

Ferguson hired him on the spot, and King was originally given a fifteen-minute slot within Nat's Tan Town Jamboree starting at 5:30

p.m. He was not paid for his appearance but got the chance to plug some of his original songs while opening and closing with the Peptikon jingle.

Much later, King finally discovered why Peptikon had been so popular back in the day. "It was supposed to be good for anything that ails you," he revealed. "I'm 83 now, and people my age then—especially church people—boy, they bought it like there'd never be anymore . . . I picked up a bottle of it, and it was 12 percent alcohol, so now I know why a lot of those old people bought it!"[13]

Riley King's slot became very popular, and he was given a standalone slot of his own, adopting the on-air persona of the "Beale Street Blues Boy." His show was later sponsored by Lucky Strike cigarettes. This was one of the first national brands to advertise on WDIA, and it helped to attract other major advertisers in the months that followed.

By the summer of 1949, Bert Ferguson and John Pepper had been made aware that their initial foray into Black programming was successful and that WDIA was moving up in the ratings. At this time, they printed 40,000 copies of a four-page promotional leaflet that featured photographs of Nat D. Williams, "Hot Rod" Hulbert, and B.B. King, as well as some of the gospel groups that appeared on Sundays. The brochure also showed the times each show took place, but there were still large gaps in the schedule, which were still filled with block programming.

Around this time, Ferguson later recalled, he and Pepper made the decision to move to all-Black programming. "It took a year to get complete all-Black programming, and even then, there were skeptics," he remembered. "But the ever-soaring ratings confirmed the soundness of our original idea. By the early 1950s, we unquestionably had the largest radio audience in the Memphis market, and this was done with a dawn-to-dusk license, which was no small handicap in those days."

One of the next hires in August 1949 was the station's first female DJ, Willa Monroe. Her *Tan Town Homemakers* show ran from 9 a.m. until 9:55 a.m. It was not the first traditional women's show aimed at housewives, but it was probably the first to be specifically directed at women in the Black community. Monroe featured music by Black pop singers, along with recipes, society news, and homemaking tips, as well as interviews with Black female newsmakers. She paved the way for other Black women to host similar shows and to eventually branch out into programs about current affairs.

A second female disc jockey was hired in 1950; a former Cotton Makers' Jubilee Queen by the name of Star McKinney, who features in several early WDIA publicity shots. Her role was more peripheral, however, and in the early years, she simply read "society news" in a fifteen-minute slot on Saturday mornings.

More important was the arrival of A. C. Williams, who, like Nat D. Williams, was an important figure within the African American community. Like Nat D., he was also a teacher, teaching biology at Manassas High School. He was also an MC at the Cotton Makers' Jubilee, meaning that he had the personality required for radio.

It was one of his other projects that first brought him to WDIA, however. He was the founder and organizer of the Teen Town Singers, a vocal group that featured singing talent from the various high schools across the city. While the young singers used to rehearse after school, membership was as much about camaraderie, discipline, and leadership as it was about singing. The Teen Town Singers first appeared on WDIA one Saturday morning in June 1949, and Williams himself seems to have been hired a few months later.

Like "Hot Rod" Hulbert, Williams ended up hosting a number of different shows, filling in the various gaps in WDIA's schedule. The Teen Town Singers got their own show, appearing every Saturday morning at 10:30 a.m. when they would typically sing everything from classical to gospel and standards to the latest pop hits.

A tall man, Williams acquired the nickname "Moohah" at college, which apparently referenced an old Native American word for "mighty." Pretty soon, he was hosting *Moohah's Matinee* on Sundays and, later, more R&B-related shows, including *Saturday Night Fish Fry*. Moohah played a vital role at the station for many years and eventually became WDIA's first full-time African American employee when he was appointed as a promotions consultant.

Ferguson and Pepper's bold gamble paid off and, within a year, WDIA had entirely converted to African American programming and quickly became the number one station in Memphis. By the time the Hooper Survey was published for September-October 1949, WDIA had 28.1 percent of the morning market, compared with WREC, their nearest rival, with just 21.6 percent.

WDIA's rapid rise meant that the station was always going to be vulnerable to the risk of larger stations poaching their biggest stars. The first to leave was "Hot Rod" Hulbert, who left in April 1951 to work at WITH in Baltimore, Maryland, making him the first Black DJ at what had hitherto been an all-white station. The move was seen as a step up, and Hulbert left on good terms. B.B. King initially took over his flagship show, *Sepia Swing Club*, an arrangement that lasted until 1951, by which time his performing and recording career had started to take off.

The second departure was the Reverend Dwight "Gatemouth" Moore, who left to join another new all-Black station, WEDR in Birmingham. His early afternoon gospel show was also filled by B.B. King, who launched a

Rufus Thomas (left) and Stokes Trent at the textile mill, circa 1950. Photograph courtesy of the Thomas family.

new program called *Bee Bee's Jeebies*, in which he predominantly played blues music rather than gospel.

Reverend Moore was effectively replaced by a musician named Ford Nelson, who had started working as B.B. King's pianist earlier that year. Although he was still playing regular gigs with King in Memphis nightclubs and on the chitlin circuit, he was given an audition as a disc jockey and initially landed a fifteen-minute lunchtime R&B show called *Let's Have Some Fun* in 1950. WDIA later decided that his personality was well-suited to hosting a gospel show, which also plugged an important gap in their programming. Amazingly, Nelson went on to become WDIA's longest-serving DJ and only retired in 2014 after an amazing sixty-four-year career at the radio station.

The other new major arrival, joining in September 1950, was Nat D. Williams's protégé, Rufus Thomas. Given that he had worked closely with Williams for a number of years, first on the Booker T. Washington Ballets and then as cohost of Amateur Night at the Palace Theater, it might seem surprising that he had not been approached earlier. The most likely explanation was that Thomas already had a day job at the American Finishing Company, which started at 6:30 a.m. and did not finish until 2:30 p.m. and was occasionally working at night too, either hosting Amateur Night or working in one of the nightclubs. As a result, Williams may have thought it was difficult to get a firm commitment.

When Williams did propose Thomas, David James Mattis, who had taken over as program director, agreed that he would be a good fit. If

"Make my lips go oooo-bedoo!" Rufus at WDIA, circa 1951. Photograph courtesy of the Vaneese Thomas family collection.

you gave Thomas a good line, "you could guarantee he'd tear the house to pieces," he told WDIA historian Louis Cantor. "Give the line to four or five other guys, and nothing." Years of working in vaudeville and then at the Palace Theater had honed Thomas's delivery and comic timing to near perfection.[14]

Thomas was initially hired to host two hour-long shows on a Saturday: *House of Happiness* and *Special Delivery*. Rufus had no experience on the radio and initially tried to imitate the style of the more stoic white announcers, failing to project his own personality. "When I first got into radio, we used to listen to WREC," he told author Peter Guralnick. "They would have this big booming voice, you know—'This is WREC broadcasting from the South's finest hotel, the Hotel Peabody'—and thought you had to be like that, too."[15]

In particular, Thomas had problems selling product on-air, which was a key part of the role because his voice sounded so contrived. Mattis recalled working with him for many hours. Thomas was a proud man and would get upset by this. He would be "stubborn, hang the lip out, pout, and he couldn't sell," Mattis recalled. "He did the lousiest commercials in the world and he thought he did the best."[16]

At one point, Thomas thought he would be terminated from his new job, but Mattis persevered, encouraging him to relax and have fun and showcase his natural entertainment skills. In later years, Thomas credited Mattis with helping him to overcome his anger over segregation issues and enjoy the working environment at WDIA. "After that," he recalled, "I was off like a freight train." The respect was evidently mutual, with Mattis describing Thomas as "the best Black entertainer I ever saw in my life"—which, given the competition at WDIA, was high praise indeed.[17]

With his radio career now up and running, WDIA made a couple of important changes to Thomas's schedule, which helped to raise his profile.

First of all, he was offered the Saturday morning breakfast show, *Boogie for Breakfast*. The only problem was that this started at 7 a.m. and, given that many of his nightclub gigs were on a Friday night, it was not unusual for Thomas to come directly to the radio station from the club!

Then, in late 1951, Rufus inherited the *Sepia Swing Club* from B.B. King, who, by this stage, was too busy touring to appear on a regular basis. *Sepia Swing Club* was on at 3 p.m., and Rufus's shift at the factory did not finish until 2:30 p.m. In the early years, he used to jump on the streetcar to the radio station, often leaping into his chair at or just beyond the opening of the show, ready to take off "like a late freight!" After a while, he would hitch a lift in his friend's car, and it was not until 1954 that he finally bought a car of his own.

By this stage, Thomas had developed his own radio talk, and he soon began to stamp his own authority on the afternoon show, always opening with:

Come in the club, we're ready and right,
Got records and jive, no fuss—no fight,
This is Rufus Thomas of *Sepia Swing*,
Gonna try to make you laugh and sing.

♦ ♦ ♦

The WDIA success story resulted in other radio stations, both in Memphis and elsewhere, trying to replicate what they had achieved. Thomas noted that this also began to impact the local music scene, too, with a number of blues artists trying to follow B.B. King's lead and make an impression on the radio and in the nightclubs.

One such artist was the Mississippi-born singer and guitarist Chester Arthur Burnett—better known by his stage name, Howlin' Wolf. "Now in West Memphis, across the bridge, you're talking the blues language," Thomas explained to author Hugh Merrill. "Howlin' Wolf was on the radio over there. Howlin' Wolf had a fifteen-minute show on KWEM [later KWAM] radio. [But] there ain't nothing in West Memphis now."[18]

The popularity of Wolf's radio show soon spilled out in the nightclub scene not just in West Memphis but in Memphis too. "Howlin' Wolf drew more people in a club than anybody that's ever been in town," Thomas continued. "There was a club there called the Paradise and they'd have a thousand, maybe two thousand people. But Howlin' Wolf had 'em hanging off the rafters. He had maybe five thousand people in a two-thousand-seat house. Everywhere you could see was people. Howlin' Wolf drew more people than Ray Charles."[19]

In 1951, Ike Turner, who was a freelance talent scout, heard Howlin' Wolf playing in West Memphis and brought some of his songs over to Sam Phillips at the Memphis Recording Studio (later renamed the Sun Studio). Phillips praised his singing, saying, "God, what it would be worth on film to see the fervor in that man's face when he sang. His eyes would light up, you'd see the veins come out on his neck and, buddy, there was nothing on his mind but that song. He sang with his damn soul." Sun Records had not yet been formed, so Phillips licensed his recording to Chess Records in Chicago and Modern Records in Los Angeles. In December 1951, Leonard Chess was able to secure Howlin' Wolf's contract, and at Chess's urging, he relocated from Memphis to Chicago in late 1952.[20]

The success of Howlin' Wolf was not lost on Thomas, who soon reached out to Sam Phillips himself, as discussed in the next chapter. His initial singles recorded at the Memphis Recording Studio were sent to Chess Records, but once Phillips had established his own label, Sun Records, Thomas landed his first hit single.

♦ ♦ ♦

The additional money that Thomas was starting to earn from his new afternoon show at WDIA proved to be timely as, in the spring of 1952, Thomas and Lorene discovered they were expecting their third child. They made the decision to move from their apartment at 440 Vance Avenue, which was located within the Foote Homes housing complex, to a bigger stand-alone house located at 1376 Kerr Street.

Kerr Street was a more family-oriented neighborhood, which was perfect for the Thomases' larger family. The street itself was full of similar young families, which in part reflected its proximity to Hamilton Elementary School, which backed onto Kerr. In addition, Kerr was effectively a dead-end at one end of the street at that time, which limited the amount of traffic, making it a safe place for children to play.

Lorene Thomas gave birth to a second baby daughter on August 24, 1952, and named her Vaneese Yseult Thomas. The name "Vaneese" was a derivation of Vanessa, which Lorene thought was too common. "Yseult" is the French version of "Isolde" and appears to have been taken from Wagner's opera *Tristan and Isolde*. "My mother had no idea that I would grow up to speak French!" Vaneese laughed. "I'm sure it was taken from the opera, because she was a well-read, well-spoken person, and always read to us from a very young age."[21]

The Thomases' new house was a good size, with space at the back of the house to expand and a yard in the front where the children could play. When "Bear Cat" became a hit single in the summer of 1953, Rufus used part of the royalties to build a large den at the back of the house, which expanded the footprint of the house substantially. "That's where they had all the musical instruments, the TV, a record player, microphones, the whole works," recalled Vaneese's childhood friend Trent Cobb, who grew up three doors down on the same street.[22]

Once the extension had been built, Lorene and Rufus arranged for a piano to be delivered to the house. "My first piano came from a friend of my mother's, whose daughter took piano lessons under duress," Marvell later recalled. "As soon as the daughter went off to college, the mother offered the piano to my mother. I remember six guys pulling up in the driveway in a truck and unloading a huge player piano. I saw them and went outside. I was playing on that piano before they could get it into the house!"[23]

Marvell was clearly excited about piano, and it was Lorene who first suggested he take lessons. "After about three weeks of just banging on this thing and making no intelligible sounds, my mother decided maybe I should get piano lessons," he said. "So, I was ten, eleven, when I took my first piano lesson." He started to take lessons from the daughter of the jazz bass player and local high school bandleader, Tuff Green.[24]

In the years that followed, Rufus and Lorene Thomas both became immersed in the neighborhood. When the children were younger, Rufus would make up little stories to tell the younger children. "He was a great storyteller, in fact," said Trent Cobb, laughing at the memory. "He'd be so dramatic! As little kids, our eyes would grow so big!"[25]

And in the summer months, the Thomases would fill an inflatable pool in their front yard for the younger children to play in. "Mr. and Mrs. Thomas would pull out a little portable pool, fill it with water, and pull out the water hose and spray us," Cobb recalled. "We thought we could swim! It was a wonderful time."

Rufus playing baseball at the Foote Homes, 1945. Photograph courtesy of the Vaneese Thomas family collection.

Rufus was a decent baseball player in his younger days, and as Marvell grew older, Rufus would teach the boys in the neighborhood how to play a version of corkball. "When Rufus got home from work, he would start playing corkball with those guys," said Cobb. "It's kind of like baseball, but you'd take a piece of cork, put a penny on the large part of the cork to give it some weight, wrap it in white tape. You would pitch it underhand, and the bat was a broomstick!"[26]

By the time the younger generation of children was coming through, Thomas was an established star with a well-established radio show and numerous hit singles to his name. But as Cobb recalled, he still found time to play with the kids. "As we started getting older, he started teaching us how to play corkball, too—he taught us how to pitch it, how to catch it, how to throw it. Our school was directly across the street from us, and he would come and play with us directly after work."

Trent Cobb remembered Lorene Thomas as a sweet mother and a loving, caring individual. "That house was always joyful," he remembered. "If she didn't bake cookies for us, she always had treats for us."

Lorene always took a keen interest in the children's education, not just of her own children but others living on the street. "She was a great teacher, extremely patient," Cobb explained. "She would make sure we could read, knew how to pronounce words, understood our times tables. We didn't realize that she was trying to reinforce what we were learning in school."[27]

She also taught the young boys in the neighborhood how to behave like gentlemen. "You had to let the girls go first, guys had to walk on the outside of the sidewalk to protect the girls, and every time we came into the house, we had to remove our cap," Cobb recalled. "Little things like that, she taught us as boys. And she would compliment us when we did those things, not knowing we were being taught to be a gentleman."

Above all, Kerr Street was a safe neighborhood in Memphis to bring up young children. Cobb remembered how parents always felt safe knowing the whole neighborhood would look out and keep an eye on the children. "We were either on Kerr Street or the next street along, which was Gill Street. The third street over to the north, in fact, was Quinn. There was a store at the corner of Quinn and Wilson—and as children, we thought that was a long way! If we went to the store, we'd have to let our parents know. When walking across to the first main thoroughfare, there would be people sitting out on the porch. We had to speak to each one of them, going up and coming back—every last one of them. The people in the store knew us, too. A dime and a quarter went a long way back then. Sodas were like six cents, and you could put a penny in the peanut machine and get a handful of peanuts. Then coming back, we'd have to speak to the same people we'd just spoken to!"[28]

And when it was time for the children to head back home, Thomas devised a special method of calling each of his three children individually. "When we would be outside playing, we had to come in before the street lights came on," said Cobb. "But Mr. Thomas would whistle for his children! He had one whistle for Marvell to come home, another for Carla to come home, and a third whistle for Vaneese to come home! We used to ask them, 'how do you know which one is which?' But they'd go home, one at a time. I said to myself, 'this is amazing!'"

"To this day, we call the people who lived on that block the Kerr Street Gang," recalled Marvell Thomas in his later years. "We grew up with three partial generations. The oldest kids were mentors to the younger ones. They kept us out of trouble, and they never allowed any older bully types to give us any grief at all. In retrospect, it was a great neighborhood to grow up in."[29]

◆ ◆ ◆

Back at WDIA in 1954, important changes were taking place. The most significant occurred in June, when WDIA increased its signal power massively from 250 watts to 50,000 watts, allowing the station to broadcast not only to the Memphis area but the entire South. The station estimated that this brought them an audience of 1.5 million African American listeners, a move which proved immensely popular with its sponsors, who had a much bigger target audience.

There were other important changes associated with this move. First of all, WDIA now had permission to broadcast from 4 a.m. until midnight, a big leap in airtime from its previous dusk until dawn license and one that required more people and programming. In addition, WDIA moved from 730 on the dial to 1070, a move that understandably confused listeners. Even six months later, the radio station was receiving calls from listeners wondering what had happened.

WDIA had to make a number of staff and programming changes to fill the additional airtime. One of the new hires was Theo "Bless My Bones" Wade, who first joined the station in 1953. Wade had been a member of the gospel group the Mount Olive Wonders in the late 1920s and in the 1940s joined the popular local gospel group Spirit of Memphis, originally as a manager and later as a singer. Wade was hired to provide additional gospel programming. He started with just a thirty-minute show as he had a full-time position with the Federal Compress Company, a cotton warehouse business in West Memphis. When the station extended its hours, however, he was given the early morning slot, from 4 a.m. until 6:30 a.m., when he ran the *Hallelujah Jubilee*. Despite the early hour, the show became popular with advertisers, in part because Wade was one of the best salespeople. Later, he also ran the *Jubilee Roll Call* on Saturday mornings, on which he would play his top ten gospel songs of the week.

And that nickname? Wade's early start required a morning coffee, and on one occasion, he spilled the drink in his lap on-air. He knew not to curse on-air and said, "Doggone, bless my bones, I knocked over my coffee!" The name stuck, and he was known as "Bless My Bones" by everyone in Memphis and well beyond.

Brother Wade was responsible for arranging the gospel portion of the radio station's annual fundraising event, the Goodwill Revue, and he also played a major role in the station's day-to-day charity work, fulfilling a vital role that helped the radio station bond with the local community.

Another important new hire was Martha Jean Steinberg, who joined in 1954. Program director David James Mattis had arranged a contest to attract another full-time female announcer. Steinberg actually came second in the contest and started with some weekend work at the station. But when the winner—Gerry Brown, a local schoolteacher—quit to get married, Steinberg took over her evening show, *Nite Spot*, and quickly made it her own. While James had set out to provide more programs aimed at its female listeners, Steinberg's sultry voice seemed to be aimed squarely at the male audience, earning her the nickname "Martha Jean the Queen."

Steinberg became one of the station's biggest stars. She was given another show at noon on Saturday called *Premium Stuff*, in which she would play a number of new releases, and when Willa Monroe's health started to fail, Steinberg later took over the morning *Homemaker* slot—a position she held until 1963 when she left for WCHB in Michigan.

Other new hires around this time were Robert "Honeyboy" Thomas, who joined in March 1954 after winning WDIA's Disc Jockey Derby, a contest to find a new announcer, and Robert "Honeymoon" Garner, a former student of A. C. Williams's and one of the original Teen Town singers.

With the longer air-time now available to WDIA, Thomas—more prominent now after his hit single "Bear Cat"—was rewarded with a prime-time evening slot. As a result of this scheduling change, he was forced to give up his role as MC of Amateur Hour at the W. C. Handy Theatre.

The daily two-hour gospel show *Hallelujah Jubilee* used to end at 9 p.m., and the rest of the evening was devoted to pure R&B.

Martha Jean Steinberg kicked off with her thirty-minute show *Nite Spot*, which tended to feature "crossover" R&B groups such as the Platters and the Drifters.

At 9:30 p.m., Thomas would take over with a brand-new show, *Hoot 'n' Holler*. He insisted on a low-key introduction before bursting onto the airwaves with his famous introduction:

I'm young, I'm loose, I'm full of juice,
I got the goose so what's the use,
We're feeling gay, though we ain't got a dollar,
Rufus is here, so Hoot 'n' Holler!

"The name of my show—you know everybody had a theme song back in those days—you'd always identify the disc jockey by his theme song—and mine was *Hoot and Holler*, a song done by Sonny Terry and Brownie McGhee," Thomas explained. And without fail, that song would open the show.[30]

With two radio shows a day, Thomas's working day now started at 6:30 a.m., when his shift at the American Finishing Company would begin, and ended at 11 p.m. when the *Hoot 'n' Holler* show finished; and that was assuming he wasn't playing in a nightclub. To make life easier, he finally bought his first car. "When we were little boys, our families didn't really own cars," recalled Trent Cobb, who lived a few doors down. "Mr. Thomas came down the street in this beautiful car—it was a 1954

Chevy. It was orange and white, with some beautiful white tires—man, that thing was so pretty! He kept it so clean and shiny!"[31]

Buying a car meant that Thomas just about had time to go home and freshen up after his shift finished at 2:30 p.m. "He'd have to come home, take a bath, change clothes and get to the station by 3 p.m.," recalled his daughter Vaneese. "We'd all have his bathwater ready. Mummy would have his clothes laid out on the bed so he could do all this stuff, hop in the car, and get to WDIA. The radio station would usually play a record right at the top of the hour, just in case he was late!"[32]

Knowing that Thomas was sometimes a few minutes late for *Sepia Swing*, the radio station eventually recorded his introduction, which by 1955 went like this:

> Come in the club, we're ready and right,
> Got records and jive, no fuss—no fight,
> This is Rufus Thomas of Sepia Swing,
> Gonna try to make you laugh and sing.
> Right here in the club, we're willing and able,
> So Mable, Mable, sweet and able,
> Get your elbows off the table, and let's rock!

The first record would then come on, courtesy of the control board operator, giving Thomas another two to three minutes to make it to the studio. "I'd start hollering, 'I'm there, I'm there,'" he told Louis Cantor, author of *Wheelin' on Beale*. "And when that record would end, I'd be sitting there on air."

Carla Thomas remembers listening to her father's radio show every afternoon when she got home from school. "And that's when I started listening to the Teen Towners," she recalled. "I must have been nine or ten. And I'd be, 'Am I gonna be in there?' Daddy would reply, 'You're too young. You can't be in there.'"[33]

Still, Carla persisted, and one Saturday morning, Rufus brought her to the radio station and let her enter the *Big Star Talent Show*. "One day he said, 'I tell you what. You're about to get on my nerves. Okay, I gotta go put on my show. Now, you sit there with Martha Jean [Steinberg], and you just sit there 'til I finish.' He goes in the back and he sits me with Martha Jean. And she was so gorgeous. She was just so beautiful. And she said, 'Hey, you're Rufus's little girl.'"[34]

The Teen Towners had just finished their Saturday morning broadcast when Rufus went over to speak to "Moohah" Williams and arranged for Carla to perform. "Someone said, 'Can you sing, little girl?'" Carla remembered. "And I said, 'No, ma'am, I can't sing,' because my Daddy had already told me I couldn't sing. And then I thought, 'Oh my God, the Teen Towners are still in there!' And I said, 'Mm-hmm, I sing!' I didn't know I could sing a note. I just knew I wanted to tell Daddy I could actually sing with the Teen Towners. Anyway, I went in, and they had a little riser she found and stood me on it. And they had the little mic come down right in front of me."[35]

Carla sang "Here Comes Peter Cottontail" that morning, live on air, and after she had performed, the phones lit up, and listeners cast their votes for her. "So I got my little Brownie camera—they used to give you a little Brownie camera when you won. They had those things there for kids, but [today] it's not that simple. It has to be a big production."[36]

Around the same time she started singing with the Teen Towners, Carla also started taking music lessons with Memphis-based opera singer Florence Cole Talbert-McCleave, who was known to Carla as Madam Florence McCleave. "She was a philanthropist," Carla later recalled. "She loved young people. And just one little street on this side of the projects separated her big house."[37]

Carla initially took piano lessons there, but when she heard singing coming from the next room informed the teacher that she wanted to sing. Even then, Carla's singing voice took on elements of music she'd heard through her father. "You may end up singing pop music," Madam McCleave explained to her. "You know, it's good to have good training for your voice, but we're not going to make an opera singer out of you."[38]

From that time, both Carla Thomas and her older brother, Marvell Thomas, formally joined the Teen Town Singers, which helped to further their musical development in their teenage years. "That was the beginning of a real serious music education for me, because I learned things that I probably would have never been exposed to otherwise, musically," Marvell revealed. "We had just been like most kids who grew up listening to radio. We learned big bands. We did Count Basie. We did a lot of jazz things. And we actually sang big band arrangements, as though we were the instruments and not singers. So, we learned a lot of things. And what I have learned and I've been complimented for this on numerous occasions as a pianist, is that I make a great accompanist for singers. And the reason why is I knew all the songs. I knew all the lyrics, because I learned them all in this group in high school."[39]

◆ ◆ ◆

WDIA's strong signal and all-day broadcasting helped to make its disc jockeys major stars, not just in Memphis but across the whole of the

South. Dora Todd, a teacher at Washington High, said, "Most folks in the 1950s may not have been able to tell you who the mayor or governor was, but they sure knew the names of Nat Williams and Rufus Thomas."[40]

To truly understand the significance of WDIA in the 1950s, it is important to appreciate the degree to which the radio station was embedded in the local community. Toni Bell, who grew up listening to WDIA and worked at the station in the 1980s, said that hearing Nat D. Williams, Thomas, and other African American personalities on the radio meant so much because no one on the air before spoke directly to their community or addressed the issues that concerned them. "WDIA was the only place we could get someone Black talking to us," she said.[41]

Fairly early in the station's history, a woman came running into the offices saying she'd lost her child. She asked the station to announce a description; the child was found, and soon after, WDIA was making all sorts of community announcements: missing persons, church events, even lost false teeth. These became known as "goodwill announcements."

Station owner Bert Ferguson initially thought these announcements were a waste of time and would only be of interest to the person who had lost the item concerned. At one point, he chastised one of the members of staff broadcasting about "all the umbrellas that were lost in Memphis." "She reminded me that a five-dollar umbrella is a pretty important item to someone with a low income," Ferguson recalled.[42]

In addition, WDIA would get involved in a number of community projects within Memphis. They sponsored a local talent show, put on a spelling bee at the Tri-State Fair (where they also bought the championship hog), and on summer nights, they set up a movie projector in different low-income housing projects, providing free entertainment to the children.

In late 1949, shortly after it had made the switch to all-Black programming, Bert Ferguson thought it would be good to host a Christmas fundraising event harnessing the newly hired talent from the radio station. "They had stage experience," Ferguson said. "Nat emceeing Amateur Hour, and so on. So we decided to put on a regular show."[43]

The shows became known as the Goodwill Revue. The early Revues were divided into two parts: the gospel show, which would include a "song battle" between two vocal groups, and the R&B portion, which would typically be hosted by Nat D. Williams, Thomas, and "Moohah" Williams. The early shows were modest in scale, and the money raised was typically donated to local Black charities such as the Beale Street Elks.

By the mid-1950s, the Goodwill Revue had expanded massively and was held in the North Hall of Ellis Auditorium, which could seat 6,000 people. WDIA would contact the major R&B labels and request they send their biggest stars to perform free of charge. In 1955, former WDIA disc jockey B.B. King flew in from California, Chess Records sent pianist Willie Mabon, while the gospel portion of the show featured the Soul Stirrers, which included a young Sam Cooke, and the Skylarks.

As a consequence, the money being raised was much higher than expected, and Ferguson decided to establish the Goodwill Fund so that the radio station could administer its own charity rather than contribute to others. The first beneficiary of the Goodwill Fund was a newly estab-lished school for physically handicapped Black children. In 1955, WDIA provided two white and yellow buses for the school with drivers and also with disc jockey Theo "Bless My Bones" Wade driving the southern route himself, without pay.

The success of the Goodwill Revue eventually prompted the radio station to organize a second annual event, the Starlight Revue. This event was held outdoors every summer, and with the additional capacity, it dramatically increased the funds available to the Goodwill Fund.

The next big charitable project that WDIA became involved in was the establishment of the WDIA Little League for Black schoolchildren. In 1955, there were over 200 white teams in the city of Memphis and not a single Black team. The radio station ultimately established more than 150 baseball teams in the years that followed, providing both uniforms and equipment. WDIA also helped to establish the Goodwill Home for Black Children, working with churches and other organizations to establish a home for Black children from broken families.

As a result of work like this, WDIA was effectively an extension of the community. "WDIA entertained, educated, enlightened, and expanded our music," explained Deanie Parker, who was later a Stax recording artist and executive and went on to become the first president and CEO of Soulsville, which built and managed the Stax Museum of American Soul Music. "It was a supplement for people without opportunity for quality education, the people working in the kitchens and laundries and what have you, who needed encouragement to keep going, people who needed to be informed about social changes and challenges of the time, people who needed a helping hand. It touched the churches; it touched every aspect of life in the African American community. It was a galvanizer. It was a part of our families."[44]

In many respects, WDIA also established a template for improved racial integration within Memphis, a model that was later replicated by Stax Records. Although the radio station would remain white-owned for a number of years, the back-office staff was mixed-race, which was rare in the 1950s. "WDIA was like a family," recalled Mark Stansbury, who started out as a control board operator in 1958 at the age of sixteen and went on to become a gospel disc jockey in his own right, still working at WDIA sixty years later. "You know we had Blacks and whites working together and you didn't call Larry 'Mister' and didn't call such and such 'Missus.' You called her Barbara or Larry or Joe, just like you would A. C. or Nat."[45]

Rufus didn't remain with WDIA for quite as long as Ford Nelson, who finally retired in 2014 after sixty-four years with the station, or Mark Stansbury, who was still hosting Sunday's Best Gospel in 2020, sixty-two years after joining. But he remained at WDIA long after he signed to Stax Records, still hosting both Sepia Swing and Hoot 'n' Holler, except when he was away on tour.

He did leave in 1973 when WDIA underwent a management change but was invited back in 1986 by WDIA's new program director, Bobby O'Jay. At that time, he cohosted the All Blues show every Saturday morning with Jaye Michael Davis, a show he continued to host until his final illness.

Upon rejoining in 1986, Thomas made it clear that he was delighted to be back on-air. "WDIA is more than a radio station," he said. "It is an institution!"

The key role that Thomas played in the history of African American radio was recognized in 1998 when the Rock & Roll Hall of Fame gave him an award for five decades promoting Black music on the radio. Hopefully, they will eventually recognize his own contribution to making music, which surely deserves greater recognition, as the chapters that follow make abundantly clear.

Chapter Three

Bear Cat

Rufus and Elvis, 1950-1956

By late 1949, Rufus Thomas was something of a veteran on the Memphis nightclub scene. He had spent the best part of ten years honing his skills with a number of highly regarded local bands, including Bill Harvey, Tuff Green and his Rocketeers, Al Jackson Sr., and Bill Fort.

Around this time, Thomas put together a band of his own featuring Evelyn Young on tenor saxophone, Robert Carter on guitar, Evans Bradshaw on piano, and Red Davis on drums. This was a highly accomplished combo; Evelyn Young had been playing on Beale Street since the age of fourteen and, in 1952, went on to join B.B. King's band. Pianist Evans Bradshaw later moved to New York, where he recorded two jazz LPs for Riverside Records.

The band attracted the attention of Jesse Erickson, the owner of the small, Dallas-based record labels Talent and Star Talent. The business seems to have been established around his daughter's record store, Louise's Record Shop, which was situated at 3313 Oakland Avenue in South Dallas. "Jesse and Louise did a lot of advertising on the radio, and he wholesaled and retailed records," said country guitarist Boots Bourquin. "That was a pretty big thing because all them stars had records in there and they would come by and meet him. It was a gathering place for musicians, all those guys that was trying to get a start in country music."[1]

Around Christmas 1949, Thomas and his band were performing at Currie's Club Tropicana, a nightclub on the north side of Memphis. The imposing Erickson—who was six feet, four inches tall—had made arrangements to record the band at the club. Thomas had not previously heard of the record company but was excited to finally be a recording artist. "It was a chance," he told a newspaper reporter in the mid-1990s. "I just wanted to make a record. I never thought of getting rich. I just wanted to be known, be a recording artist. At that time, we really didn't have a lot of big names with Black artists anyway—not a lot. I just wanted to be on that record."[2]

Many of the songs that Thomas was writing around that time seem to have been fairly formulaic blues-oriented songs, frequently about trouble with women but injected with a dash of his trademark humor. The song chosen as a single, "I'll Be a Good Boy," was very much in that vein. The lyrics mention that he and his baby had a few words last night and how good he'll be if she comes back. Thomas sings it well, his voice far less gravelly than in later years, and there are two fine saxophone solos from Evelyn Young.

The B-side was a slow blues titled "I'm So Worried." There's a lovely late-night sax intro from Young before Thomas warns of the perils of having an affair with a married woman. "It's an awful shame," he warns, "to be in love with a married woman when she's in love with another married man."

The Star Talent label was primarily known for its country recordings, but the single was released on its Folk Series. While that sounds misplaced, the label says in smaller letters that this was part of the "blues and rhythm series," which sounds more appropriate. The single was issued in February 1950 and got a cursory mention in *Billboard* magazine under the "New Rhythm & Blues Releases" for the week of February 25. The magazine picks out the B-side, "I'm So Worried," and says, "Thomas shows first-class style on a slow blues, but the combo work is amateurish behind him." That seems a little harsh given the quality of the band, and hindsight suggests it's probably the quality of the recording that's at fault rather than the band.

The single sank without a trace, and in later years, Thomas laughed it off. "The record sold five copies," Thomas said, "and I bought four of them."[3]

At the time, Thomas was probably more optimistic that the label was going to release one of the other songs recorded that day as a second single. After all, in a March edition of *Billboard*, the label took out an advertisement highlighting its "Star-Studded Star Talent," listing fourteen country artists and six blues and gospel acts, including Thomas.

No second single was ever released, however. Many years later, two more recordings were uncovered: "Double Trouble" and "Who's That Chick?" The former is in the "women trouble" category, with Thomas falling for two women at the same time and having to sign up for the army so he can leave town. "Who's That Chick?" is perhaps the more likely second single. It's a Louis Jordan-style jump blues featuring some swinging piano, a delicious sax riff, courtesy of Evelyn Young, and some

Jordan-like call-and-response vocals. The "chick" concerned has "long dark hair, she wears some beautiful clothes," with Thomas presumably basing the song on someone he'd seen around town.

Two other songs were apparently recorded by Erickson that day; the splendidly named "Take Me Home, I'm Tired, He Lied" and "Paper Doll." The additional songs were apparently located at a studio in Dallas, Texas, but were not released, perhaps because the quality of the acetate disc had degraded over time.

If Thomas was disappointed that a second single was never released by Star Talent, it would have been short-lived because by June 1950—just six months after recording his first single—he was recording once more. By this stage, he had left his role as MC at the Palace Theater and started running a Saturday midnight amateur show at the W. C. Handy Theatre on Park Avenue in the city's Orange Mound district. The theater was built for Black audiences at the time of segregation, but Thomas used to lead the so-called "midnight ramble" whereby a white audience would be admitted to see a top-name band around midnight on a Sunday night. "I remember very well seeing the Count Basie Band, the Lionel Hampton Band, and Lucky Millinder Band," one reader later recalled on the Historic Memphis website. "Those musicians would play their hearts out to a packed house. I remember how entertaining Lionel Hampton was."[4]

Indeed, the recording session took place after one such appearance by Lionel Hampton and his Orchestra in mid-June. On this occasion, Thomas sang two more self-composed tunes—"Beer Bottle Boogie" and "Gonna Bring My Baby Back"—backed by Bobby Plater's Orchestra. Bobby Plater was an alto saxophonist in Hampton's orchestra and an accomplished songwriter and arranger himself, best known for cocomposing "Jersey Bounce," which was recorded by the likes of Glenn Miller and Ella Fitzgerald. Bobby Plater's Orchestra was a miniature big band that included an unknown trumpet player, three saxophonists, Milt Buckner on piano, Rudy Mason on guitar, and a rhythm section comprised of Roy Johnson on bass and Ellis Bartee on drums.

"Beer Bottle Boogie" is a fantastic tune, and under different circumstances, could easily have been a hit single. The lyrics focus on various problems driving him to drink, including getting burned at poker. Unsurprisingly, things don't end well, with "the bartender kicking him in the pants." For someone who was a teetotaler, Thomas certainly tells a good story about a big night out. His voice also sounds more polished here. The band is also first-class, with a rolling piano intro, courtesy of Milt Buckner, and the bigger horn sound, which works well. The B-side,

"Gonna Bring My Baby Back," is almost as good and only let down by the somewhat cliché lyrics.

A record deal was hastily arranged with Nashville's Bullet label. The deal was drawn up by Overton Ganong, the head of Bullet Records, Robert Henry, the manager of the W. C. Handy Theatre, and Bert Ferguson of WDIA, who had been instrumental in sending B.B. King's first recordings to Bullet—and would go on to hire Thomas as a disc jockey just four months later.

The single was released in late July but credited to "Mr. Swing" rather than Rufus Thomas. This presumably reflected the fact that Thomas was unsure whether he was still contractually signed to Star Talent in Dallas. The two songs were not credited to Thomas until 1996, when he played them in a blind test. "Hey, that's me," he said. He remembered little about the recording session almost five decades later but was quick to note the quality of the musicians. "I do remember that 'Beer Bottle' song," he said, "and that is a good band, a quality band on there. I think so." [5]

Once again, the single failed to get much airplay. The main reason is probably that Bullet Records was facing financial difficulties by this time. The label was predominantly known for its country recordings, but in 1947, they enjoyed a pop hit with "Near You," recorded by orchestra leader Francis Craig. The label then spent considerable sums trying to replicate this success over the next two years, and by the time Mr. Swing's single was released, the game was almost up. The label eventually folded in 1952.

Rufus was hired by WDIA in October 1950, and before the end of the year, he was hosting two one-hour shows, *House of Happiness* and *Special Delivery*. Given that he had been working on the Memphis nightclub scene for ten years, Thomas would probably have been aware that a new recording studio, originally called the Memphis Recording Service, had been opened at 706 Union Avenue by a radio engineer by the name of Sam Phillips. He tried to launch his own record label, The Phillips Records, in the summer of 1950, and when that failed, he started to record "Negro artists of the South" with a view to leasing or selling those recordings to more prominent labels.

As a radio announcer, Thomas would have known that by late 1950, Phillips had recorded the likes of B.B. King and Rosco Gordon. But the big breakthrough came in the spring of 1951 when Phillips recorded "Rocket 88," which was credited to Jackie Brenston & his Delta Cats but was written and conceived by Ike Turner and performed by his band, the Kings of Rhythm. The song was leased by Phillips to Chess Records in Chicago and released as a single in April 1951. [6]

It became a massive success, reaching No. 1 on the *Billboard* R&B charts, and is considered by many to be one of the first rock and roll recordings. "Everyone was just going up there, and I found out about it, so I went, too," Thomas told author Peter Guralnick. "You could come right off the street and go in there."[7] This quote referenced the fact that Sam Phillips operated an open-door policy. His original slogan for the Memphis Recording Service was "We Record Anything, Anywhere, Anytime." In fact, for a modest fee, you could walk in and make your own recording, as Elvis Presley later discovered.

Thomas is thought to have made his way to the recording studio in May 1951. Sam Phillips was out, an event that was not uncommon; in the early days, he used to drive tens of thousands of miles every year, plugging his artists to radio stations and distributors across the country. Thomas introduced himself to Phillips's assistant, Marion Keisker, who was also a radio show host over at WREC. In all likelihood, she recognized Thomas and suggested he return to the studio a few days later, when Sam Phillips was back in town.

Sam Phillips was excited at the prospect of recording Thomas, an established nightclub singer and rising star at WDIA. He arranged a recording session in late May or early June of 1951, and Thomas started the process of putting together a new band. The saxophonist he had used on his first recordings, Evelyn Young, was unavailable, but Thomas was able to recruit Herman Green, who had played behind him at the Palace Theater on tenor saxophone. Richard Sanders joined on baritone, Billy "Red" Love—an accomplished musician who had worked with Rosco Gordon—played piano, while Houston Stokes played drums. Sun's records do not identify who played trumpet, trombone, guitar, or bass players on these sessions.

The first song the band recorded appears to have been "Night Workin' Blues," which opens with a neat horn riff from Green and Sanders. Although the tune is credited to one Marty Witzel, it sounds like a Rufus Thomas tune. The lyrics highlight the perils of working the night shift: "Well I'm a hard night worker and I work hard every night, and I can't understand, why my woman won't treat me right." By all accounts, it was a song that had been in Thomas's live repertoire for some time, and the reason why it was credited to Marty Witzel has been long forgotten.

There are some other interesting things to note about this recording. First, Thomas's voice has more of its trademark gravelly tone here, something he later admitted came quite naturally early in his singing career. Secondly, the song also shows Thomas moving away from his blues roots toward a more R&B-oriented sound, presumably influenced by what he was hearing on the radio at WDIA. While Thomas never pretended to be a rock and roll pioneer, there is a strong case to be made that he was at least one of the founding fathers, given that these recordings were made in the summer of 1951.

The second song recorded and chosen as the B-side to "Night Workin' Blues" was a more straight-ahead blues tune titled "Why Did You Dee Gee?" which sees Thomas lamenting the departure of his "girl," the strangely named Dee Gee. Thomas's vocals crack in apparent pain on this one, which was probably a touch of theater from his live performances. He once claimed that the song was about an old acquaintance name Doris Genius, but this sounds like another Thomas joke made at the expense of the interviewer![8]

A third song was recorded at that first session—the splendid "Crazy About You Baby." This song further underlines Thomas's role in the early development of rock and roll. The song is clearly influenced by Ike Turner's "Rocket 88," but as you would expect from Rufus, the song is about a girl, rather than a car, the Oldsmobile Rocket 88. Lyrically, the song echoes the themes of "Crazy About You Baby," with Rufus complaining: "You take advantage of me baby, 'cos I work all night." It's entirely possible that the "complaints" were partly autobiographical, given that he was effectively working three jobs to support his family—at the factory, the radio station, and playing regular nightclub gigs too. Whatever the truth of the matter, the band kicked up a storm here, creating a real party vibe complete with call-and-response vocals from the band. There's also a fantastic tenor sax solo from Herman Green to enjoy.

The single "Night Workin' Blues" was licensed to Chess Records in Chicago and released as a single in the summer of 1951. The record failed to chart but would appear to have sold in respectable numbers as Chess agreed to release a second single.

The records kept by Marion Keisker at Sun suggest that at some stage—the date is not clear—the band may have recorded a fourth song titled "Xmas Song." Most likely, the song's title had not yet been finalized, but the recording had been sent to Chess together with "Crazy About You Baby" by the autumn of 1951. While most of Thomas's Sun recordings have been reissued over the years, "Xmas Song" has never been found. One possible explanation is that Chess thought September was too early to release a Christmas song, even as a B-side, and the song was pushed to the side.

Thomas was invited back to the studio to record a follow-up in October 1951. He returned with the same band to record "No More Doggin' Around (Ain't Gonna Be Your Dog)." Rufus clearly had a penchant for dog-related tunes. This particular song was not dance-related but about a man being mistreated by his woman. The tune is built on a simple horn riff, probably arranged by Thomas himself. Put simply, it's another example of a good early rock and roll number; there some's fine rolling piano, courtesy of Billy "Red" Love, and another strong solo from Herman Green, who impresses on all of these early Sun recordings.

The master was sent to Chess Records in early October, and they made the decision to release "No More Doggin' Around" as the A-side, with the superior "Crazy About You Baby" mysteriously relegated to the B-side, with the record given the catalog number of Chess 1492. The single would appear to have achieved steady sales in the months that followed without building sufficient momentum to trouble the charts.

By early 1952, Sam Phillips was beginning to experience some teething problems with his business model; he did not have his own publishing company at this time and did not benefit from the ownership of the songs themselves. Moreover, the artists were only tied to Sam Phillips by loosely phrased "personal service" contracts. In addition, following the success of "Rocket 88," both Chess Records in Chicago and Modern/RPM in Los Angeles claimed that they had the right of first refusal on Sam's recordings.

One of the artists whose deal was under discussion was Rosco Gordon, the blues singer and pianist, whose singles had been recorded at Sam's studio but licensed at various times to three different labels. Modern/RPM eventually signed Gordon on an exclusive basis in mid-February 1952, and as part of this deal, most of the songs recorded at his final session with Sam Phillips went with him to California. There was one exception, a Gordon song called "Decorate the Counter." Chess Records in Chicago had already expressed an interest in this song, and as a result, this song was excluded from Gordon's new contract with Modern/RPM.

Thomas became the beneficiary of this contract anomaly. Phillips also thought the song had potential and invited Thomas back to the studio for a recording session on April 21, 1952. The band on this occasion was Rosco Gordon's old band, which included Willie Wilkes on tenor saxophone, Richard Sanders on baritone saxophone, and John Murray Daley on drums. Billy "Red" Love sits in for Rosco Gordon at the piano.

The song itself was apparently a reference to Robert Henry, one of the great characters of Beale Street at that time. He was the manager of the W. C. Handy Theatre and also the first manager of B.B. King. He also ran a pool hall, and if people wanted to be served, he told them to "decorate the counter," meaning put some cash at the bar. Thomas's take on the song is near identical to that of Rosco Gordon, which is presumably what

Chess Records was looking for. It's good, raucous fun, particularly the honking baritone sax sound produced by Richard Sanders, but arguably it was not as strong as Thomas's previous Chess singles "Night Workin' Blues" and "No More Doggin' Around."

The song recorded as a B-side, "Juanita," was again part of Thomas's live repertoire at that time. It's a slow, piano-driven comedy-blues song featuring mock sobbing and a quavering lead vocal. The song is very much of its time and has not dated well. One can imagine how it must have worked better on stage, given Rufus's comic timing and mannerisms, but it's not an easy listen without the visual effects.

The single was sent to Chess that same week but not released as a single until July. Although Chess had apparently been keen to release that song as a single, it failed to catch fire, and there are no records of any royalty payments being made to Thomas.

The same band recorded three additional songs that day. The first of those was "Married Woman," a straight-ahead piano-driven blues, with Thomas turning to the bottle in an attempt to shake off his troubles. "I'm just sitting here drinking, trying to drink my blues away." The song's highlight is probably the fiery tenor solo by Willie Wilkes, who steals the show. The band also recorded a second take, which includes a deliberately slurred intro by Thomas; again, the comedy element was probably more effective on stage than on record. The second song, "I'm Off That Stuff," is a mid-paced R&B number, this time featuring Richard Sanders on baritone. The song was probably intended as a possible B-side but features some good one-liners from Thomas, including "no more pistols, no more knives, no more messin' around with wives." The final song recorded that day was apparently "Beale Street Bound," but sadly, the tape of this song has not been found.

In all likelihood, Sam Phillips had intended to send two of these songs to Chess as a potential single in the autumn of 1952, but there is no evidence that this ever happened. In his defense, Phillips was in the process of setting up his own label, Sun Records, and was probably in the midst of trying to secure distribution at that time, which would have meant a lot of traveling across the country. Thomas would have been well aware of these developments, and Phillips would no doubt have made clear that Thomas was part of his plans.

On March 14, 1953, *Billboard* announced the birth of Sun Records. "Sun Record Label launched In Memphis—a new indie rhythm and blues label headed by Jim Bulleit and Sam Phillips. The Sun label plans to give every opportunity to untried artists to prove their talents, whether they play a broomstick or the finest jazz sax in the world." In actual fact, the label had been established back in February 1952, the label's name a sign of Phillips's optimism: a new day and a new beginning.

Despite Sam's optimism, Sun Records was slow to take off. The first single, an R&B instrumental by Johnny London, sank without a trace, and Phillips spent most of the remainder of the year trying to license out his recordings, as he had done previously. It was only once he had partnered with Jim Bulleit—the former owner of Bullet Records in Nashville—that the new label began to take shape.

Around the same time that Sun Records "relaunched," Thomas was invited back into the studio, this time to record a song called "Bear Cat." The song was intended to be an "answer song" to a recently released single titled "Hound Dog" by blues singer Willie Mae "Big Mama" Thornton. This was quite a widespread practice within R&B at that time; in fact, Jackie Brenston had provided his own answer song to "Rocket 88" called "My Real Gone Rocket." More often, a different artist would seek to provide an answer song.

"Hound Dog," of course, was later recorded by Elvis Presley. But the song itself had been written by the young songwriting duo of Jerry Leiber and Mike Stoller, then just nineteen years of age, in the summer of 1952. They had been invited to write a song for "Big Mama" Thornton. She was nicknamed "Big Mama" for a reason, and confronted with her appearance, they composed a song in which the woman berates her selfish, no-good man. When she came to record the song in August 1952, she initially crooned the song Sinatra-style, and Jerry Leiber faced the unenviable task of suggesting that she sing the song with a bit more aggression and humor. "Big Mama" Thornton nailed it, of course, injecting howling dog sounds and her own vocal mannerisms, and they had a take. The song was eventually released as a single in late February 1953.

According to Phillips's biographer, Peter Guralnick, he was blown away by "Big Mama" Thornton's "Hound Dog" the very first time he heard it. "Performed with ripsaw gusto by the singer . . . the record struck a communal chord somewhere between low comedy and bedrock truth. It totally tickled Sam on both levels. 'I said, my God, it's so true. You ain't nothing but a hound dog. You ain't met your responsibilities. You didn't go to work like you [should].' And it gave him an immediate idea for a follow-up—from the *man's* point of view . . . 'Bear Cat.'"[9]

Phillips knew that Thomas would be perfect for the song that he had written and invited him to the studio on March 8, 1953—less than two weeks after the original had been released.

According to Guralnick, in his book *Sam Phillips: The Man Who Invented Rock 'n' Roll*, Thomas initially rejected the idea, unsure what

Phillips meant by the term "bear cat." "I said, 'Rufus, hell, you don't know what a damn bear cat is? That's the meanest goddamn woman in the world,'" Phillips explained.[10]

The problem was that "Bear Cat" was not so much an answer song as a near-copy, borrowing heavily from the original; "Copy Cat" would probably have been a more appropriate title. "Bear Cat" employed the same sparse instrumentation—in this case, Joe Hill Louis on electric guitar, Tuff Green on bass, and Houston Stokes on drums. Although he's no match for "Big Mama" Thornton, Thomas sings his heart out, employing cat noises and catcalls. Strangely, his vocals are more nasal on this than his previous recordings, but it's still a great listen.

Thomas, however, was reportedly disappointed by the recording, which he felt was hurried. In particular, he felt that the guitarist, Joe Hill Louis, had played a few wrong notes, and he would rather have recorded another take.

The same lineup also recorded a B-side, "Walkin' in The Rain," that day. Listening to the two back-to-back, it's hard to tell they are by the same singer, illustrating that Thomas was a more flexible singer than many gave him credit for. It's a fantastic slow blues, showing Thomas maturing as both a songwriter and singer and probably deserved a better fate than being a forgotten flip side.

The record was rushed to market with the catalog number Sun 181, with the singer credited as Rufus Hound Dog Thomas Jr. on the label. Two weeks later, with "Hound Dog" gaining nationwide radio airplay, *Billboard* itself commented on the speed at which the "answer song" had been released.

> "The so-called answer record craze is still going strong in the rhythm and blues field. This week a new diskery [sic] came out with an answer to Peacock's smash waxing of 'Hound Dog with thrush Willie Mae Thornton. 'Hound Dog' was released only about three weeks ago and has turned out to be one of the fastest-breaking hits in recent years. It has already popped into the best-selling r&b [sic] charts. The answer to 'Hound Dog' comes from Sun Records, Memphis, Tenn., diskery, a wild thing called 'Bear Cat sung by Rufus Thomas Jr. It used to be that the answers to hits usually waited until the hit had started on the downward trail, but today the answers are ready a few days after records start moving upwards [sic]. This has led some to remark that the diskeries soon may be bringing out the answers before the originals are released."

Promotional photograph of Rufus Thomas, circa 1955. Photograph courtesy of the Special Collections Department, University of Memphis Libraries.

Billboard raised a valid point. "Bear Cat" may have been the fastest "answer song," but there were others hot on its tail—pun intended. On March 18, blues singer Roy Brown recorded "Mr. Hound Dog's in Town" for King Records, which also boasted the same melody, while on March 22, singer Charlie Gore and guitarist Louis Innis recorded "(You Ain't Nothin' but a Female) Hound Dog," also for King Records. Numerous other versions were recorded in the months that followed.

Two weeks later, on March 28, 1953, *Billboard* suggested that song publishers might look to seek legal action. "In an effort to combat what has become a rampant practice by small labels—the rushing out of answers which are similar in melody and/or theme to ditties which have become smash hits—many pubbers [sic] are now retaining attorneys."

Don Robey of Lion Publishing Company acted swiftly to defend his copyright, responding to the "answer song" with an "answer letter." In late March, around the same time as the second *Billboard* article appeared, he instructed the Harry Fox Agency to write to Sun Records asking it to seek a formal license that would allow them to formally "copy" "Hound Dog" following the correct legal protocol. When no response was received within one week, he followed up with a formal letter dated April 4, 1953.

It said,

> Please be advised that first, you should have contacted the owner prior to the release of the record, as release of the composition leaves you liable for 5 cents to 8 cents per record royalty for the intrusion upon the rights of others.
>
> I advised Mr. Harry Fox to license you for the statutory 2 cents per record royalty, allowing you to continue with pressing the record, the same as all of the Companies who were properly licensed prior to the release of their own versions of our composition.
>
> This is to also inform that unless contracts are signed and in the office of Mr. Harry Fox by Wednesday, April 8th, 1953, I will be forced to take immediate steps with Court Actions, plus apply charges for full 5 cents to 8 cents per record royalty.[11]

Phillips took his time to respond, presumably waiting to see how "Bear Cat" would fare from a sales perspective. "Hound Dog" itself entered the charts on March 28, 1953, and ended up spending seven weeks at the top of the R&B charts. "Bear Cat" entered the charts just two weeks later, and while it didn't sell anywhere near as many copies, it still made No. 3 on the R&B charts, providing the newly formed Sun Records with its first hit.

For Phillips, this proved to be something of a double-edged sword. On the one hand, he was delighted to achieve the first hit single on his own label; but the more successful it became, the more likely it was that he would have to face Lion Publishing in court. Lion eventually filed for royalties and "triple damages" in the Memphis courts, claiming that "Bear Cat" was a "dead steal." In May, Phillips sent a formal response. "There's a lot of difference in the words," he claimed. "As for the tune, there's practically no melody, but a rhythm pattern," adding that it is hard to differentiate between any two 12-bar blues songs.

The courts ruled against Phillips and upheld the charges of plagiarism, finding the tune and some of the lyrics of "Bear Cat" to be identical to those of "Hound Dog." On June 4, *Jet* magazine reported: "The Sun Record Company of Memphis agreed to pay $2,080 to a Texas recording firm because its blues tune, 'Bear Cat,' is too similar to 'Hound Dog.' Sam C. Phillips of Sun Record agreed to pay 'Hound Dog' owners two cents per record for 79,000 waxings of 'Bear Cat' already sold and two cents a record for future sales."

Years later, Phillips admitted that he should have known better. "The melody was exactly the same as theirs," he confessed to author Robert Palmer.

It has been suggested that the lawsuit almost drove Sun Records into bankruptcy, but that was not the case. The label made less money from "Bear Cat" than it might have, but the song was still a sizeable hit, and in the months that followed, Thomas received his first big royalty checks.

That being said, the record label's financial position was still precarious and would remain so until it started to record regular hits once the likes of Johnny Cash and Carl Perkins had signed to the label in 1956.

The guitarist on "Bear Cat," Joe Hill Louis, wrote a new song of his own in May 1953 titled "Tiger Man." He wrote it as a straight-ahead blues, but the lyrics cheekily reference both "Hound Dog" and "Bear Cat."

> Yeah, I get up on a mountain, and I call my bear cat back
> Yeah, I get up on a mountain, and I call my bear cat back
> My bear cat comes runnin', and the hound dogs get way back

Louis seems to have recorded two versions for Sun Records: an initial demo and a band version that features Walter Horton on harmonica. Sam Phillips clearly heard the song's potential and invited his biggest star, Rufus Thomas, to record his own version of the song on June 30. The recording session featured Floyd Murphy on guitar rather than Joe Hill Louis and Houston Stokes on drums. They were joined by three regular Sun Records session musicians—James Wheeler on tenor sax, Bill Johnson on piano, and Kenneth Banks on bass.

The arrangement of the song is totally different from the original and was probably dreamed up by Thomas himself. The rolling drums are more prominent, lending the song a more dramatic, almost tribal feel, while Floyd Murphy contributes some wiry fills and a fine solo. But Thomas steals the show with his Tarzan-style opening and a powerhouse vocal, which make it one of his early standout recordings.

The B-side, recorded with the same band, was a Rufus Thomas original, a slow blues called "Save That Money." The lyrics seem to reference the Great Depression: "You'd better save that money, things are gonna get tough again." James Wheeler's tenor saxophone plays a more prominent role here, and Thomas demonstrates once again that he is a fine blues singer.

The single was not released until late September, presumably when sales of "Bear Cat" had started to diminish. It is interesting to note that "Tiger Man" is cocredited to Sam Phillips's wife, Rebecca Burns. It's not clear why this arrangement was made; Phillips may have come to some financial arrangement with the song's actual composer, Joe Hill Louis.

The single received mixed reviews. *Billboard* referred to it as a novelty blues whose "lyric does not make sense, but will get some attention because of its weird quality." They did not much care for the B-side, "Save That Money," either, describing it as "good advice, but not a noteworthy record." The record sold relatively well but failed to chart. It did seem to make an impression on a young man by the name of Elvis Presley, however. He went on to record the song—using Thomas's arrangement— as part of his *'68 Comeback Special*. By then, sadly, Louis had passed away, dying of tetanus as a result of a cut to his thumb at the age of just thirty-five.

Later that year, by virtue of his hit single, Thomas made his first appearance at WDIA's annual Goodwill Revue as a performer rather than just a radio personality. On November 7, *Billboard* announced plans for the station's "Fifth Annual Goodwill Revue for Handicapped Negro Children [which] will present one of the strongest spiritual and rhythm and blues talent lineups ever. A crowd of up to 60,000 [sic; probably 6,000] is expected to fill the Ellis Auditorium on December 4 to see B.B. King, Lloyd Price, Muddy Waters, Eddie Boyd, Little Walter, Helen Thompson, the Soul Stirrers, and WDIA personalities Alex Bradford, the Caravans, Rufus Thomas, Moohah Williams, the Spirit of Memphis Quartet, the Southern Wonders, and Al Jackson's band. All the artists are giving their time in order to raise money for the charity. And their diskeries— Specialty, Chess, United and Starmaker—are defraying their expenses."[12]

Little did he know at the time that "Tiger Man" was to be Thomas's final single for Sun Records—and the last time he would enter a recording studio for four years.

Sam Phillips does not appear to have made a conscious decision to drop Thomas from the label. Rather, a strange chain of events seems to have led Sam Phillips toward a radically different business model, a model that apparently had no room for Rufus Thomas or any of the other blues artists he had been recording up to that point.

Unfortunately for Thomas, "Tiger Man" was overshadowed by a recording made just three weeks earlier. The second hit record recorded by Sam Philips was as controversial as the first, but for quite different reasons. The Prisonaires—as the name suggests—started up within the confines of the Tennessee State Penitentiary in Nashville. The group was led by Johnny Bragg, who had been a penitentiary inmate since 1943 when, at the age of 17, he was convicted of six charges of rape and sentenced to 594 years in prison. The band was formed when Bragg joined up with two prison gospel singers, Ed Thurman and William Stewart (each of whom was serving ninety-nine years for murder), and two new penitentiary arrivals, John Drue Jr. and Marcell Sanders, who were serving shorter sentences for larceny and involuntary manslaughter, respectively.

The group's doo-wop style singing was heard by the local radio producer, Joe Calloway, who apparently heard them while he was preparing a news broadcast from the prison. He arranged for them to perform on the radio, a performance that attracted the attention of Red Wortham, a Nashville song publisher.

Wortham then contacted his friend Jim Bulleit, who had teamed up with Sam Phillips at Sun Records. Bulleit then called Sam Phillips and told him he had "something sensational." Phillips was initially skeptical until Bulleit played him a tape of the radio recording.

The two business partners got in touch with the local prison warden, James Edwards, who was in favor of prisoner rehabilitation and quite receptive to the idea of recording them. On June 1, 1953, Bulleit arranged to collect the five members of the group from prison and take them to Sun Records in Memphis accompanied by an armed guard and trustee from the prison—with all expenses paid by Sun Records.

The band recorded a single for Sun Records called "Just Walkin' in the Rain." The song itself had an interesting history. The idea for the song came about in 1952 when Johnny Bragg was walking across the prison courtyard in the rain with his fellow inmate, Robert Riley. Bragg allegedly said, "Here we are just walking in the rain, and wondering what the girls are doing." Riley suggested that this would make a good basis for a song, and within a few minutes, Bragg had composed two verses. However, because Bragg was unable to read and write, he asked Riley to write the lyrics down in exchange for being credited as one of the song's writers. While Riley was fortunate to be credited as the cowriter, he was no singer, and was left behind when the group was allowed out for the day to make their debut recording.

A few weeks later, "Just Walkin' in the Rain" was released as a single and eventually sold 250,000 copies and became a hit on the US *Billboard* R&B chart, the second hit single for the Sun Records label. The song became an even bigger hit three years later when it was recorded by Johnnie Ray; his version reached No. 2 on the Billboard Hot 100 and also topped the charts in the UK.

The Prisonaires' version of the song is thought to have been heard by the eighteen-year-old Elvis Presley, who had graduated high school earlier that summer and just landed a job at M. B. Parker Machinists. Legend has it that Presley dropped into the studio without an appointment to make a record to surprise his mother. But as Peter Guralnick pointed out in his acclaimed Presley biography *Last Train to Memphis*, he could have done this for just twenty-five cents at the local W. T. Grant store on Main Street.

Instead, Presley walked into a professional recording studio, where he would have to pay $4 to make a recording of his own voice. It was clear that Presley hoped to attract the attention of the label's proprietor, Sam Phillips, who now had a couple of recent hit singles under his belt: "Bear Cat" and "Just Walkin' in the Rain."

He was greeted by Sam's receptionist and office manager, Marion Keisker. The young man was clearly nervous, and she tried to make him feel more relaxed by making small talk while Phillips set up the recording equipment. "What kind of singer are you?" she asked. "I sing all kinds," he replied. "Who do you sound like?" "I don't sound like nobody," the young man replied. And of course, he did not.[13]

The two songs he recorded that day, "My Happiness" and "That's When Your Heartaches Begin," were never intended for commercial release, and amazingly, the original acetates were found in the possession of one of Presley's high school friends many years later in 1988. Presley's voice is uneven on these early recordings, but there is an earnest, yearning quality to his voice that is quite unique. Presley explained to Keisker that he was interested in joining a band and asked her to let him know if she heard of any opportunities.

After the relative failure of "Tiger Man" as a single, Sam Phillips seems to have started questioning his own business model, wondering whether there was enough of a market to sell blues as well as rhythm and blues records to a crossover audience. As Keisker later recalled, "Over and over I remember Sam saying, 'If I could find a white man who had the Negro sound and the Negro feel, I could make a billion dollars.'"[14]

By early 1954, Phillips had taken to recording the likes of Earl Peterson, Michigan's singing cowboy, and the hillbilly music of Hardrock Gunter.

There was still room for blues artist Little Milton, who recorded another single in the spring of 1954, but it was clear that Sun Records was no longer a pure blues label.

Buoyed by the success of "Just Walkin' in the Rain," Phillips stayed in touch with the prison warden at the Tennessee State Penitentiary, and several months later, he received a second demo from another inmate. While this demo did not leave the same strong impression, there was something in the singer's voice that reminded him of the young high school graduate he had recorded the previous summer. He mentioned this to Marion Keisker, who arranged to invite Presley back to the studio to record a formal demo.

In the intervening months, Presley had auditioned with a local vocal quartet, the Songfellows, but been rejected because he couldn't sing harmony. He had also tried to join rockabilly guitarist Eddie Bond, who informed Presley that "he was never going to make it as a singer," a rejection that left him heartbroken.

Elvis returned to the Sun studio on Saturday, June 26, 1954. The ballad Phillips had chosen, "Without You," did not seem like a good fit, and after the recording had been completed, Elvis sang him excerpts of various songs in his repertoire ranging from Bing Crosby's "Harbor Lights" to "If I Didn't Care" by the Ink Spots. "I guess I must have sat there at least three hours," Elvis later told the *Memphis Press-Scimitar* reporter Bob Johnson in 1956. "I sang everything I knew—pop stuff, spirituals, just a few words of [anything] I remembered."[15]

While they had yet to find the right material to suit his distinctive voice, both Phillips and Keisker had a special feeling about what they'd heard. A few days later, a guitarist by the name of Scotty Moore was in the studio. He had just made a record with Phillips with his band, the Starlite Wranglers, when Keisker mentioned Presley's name and suggested they could get together.

Moore took her up on the suggestion and invited the young singer to his house to jam with the band's bass player, Bill Black. The very next day—Monday, July 5, 1954—the three of them went into Sun Records to record their first session. The first few songs didn't seem to gel, and the musicians took a break, enjoying a cold drink to escape the summer heat. "All of a sudden," Scotty later recalled, "Elvis just started singing this song and acting the fool, and then Bill picked up his bass and he started acting the fool, too, and I started playing with them. Sam . . . had the control booth open, and he stuck his head out and said, 'What are you doing?' And we said, 'We don't know.' 'Well, back up,' he said, 'try to find a place to start, and do it again.'"[16]

The song, it turned out, was an up-tempo version of "That's All Right," an old blues song by Arthur "Big Boy" Crudup. The band was aware that they'd finally captured something special, and at the end of the recording session, Bill Black turned to Scotty Moore and said, "Damn. Get that on the radio and they'll run us out of town," which seems to have been a reference to white musicians performing in a Black style.

But that's exactly what Phillips looked to do. He gave copies of the acetate to local disc jockeys Dewey Phillips (no relation) of WHBQ, Uncle Richard of WMPS, and Sleepy-Eyed John Lepley of WHHM. The song received its first airplay on July 7, 1954; Dewey Phillips played the tune on his popular radio show *Red, Hot & Blue*. Dewey later recalled that the song caused quite a stir; he received over forty telephone calls that day alone and even persuaded Presley to go into the radio station later that night to record his first interview. One of the questions he asked was what high school Presley had attended, which was intended to indirectly inform listeners of Presley's race without broaching the subject directly.

The single, "That's All Right," was officially released two weeks later, on July 19, 1954, and eventually sold around 20,000 copies. This number was not enough to chart nationally, but the single reached number four on the local Memphis charts.

At the end of July 1954, the newly formed trio appeared at the Overton Park Shell in Memphis, where they were supporting country star Slim Whitman. Presley was understandably nervous playing in front of such a big audience, and the combination of this and the band's strong rhythm caused him to shake his legs, which caused an immediate reaction from the girls in the audience. "During the instrumental parts, he would back off from the mike and be playing and shaking," recalled guitarist Scotty Moore, "and the crowd would just go wild."[17]

The same trio recorded a follow-up single, "Good Rockin' Tonight," in September 1954. The live shows had given the band a growing confidence in their new sound, and Presley's vocal sounded far more assured, too. The single failed to chart, despite the best efforts of Phillips, who drove extensively across the country to plug the new singer. Many of his traditional R&B contacts thought the new singer was "too country," while one pop-oriented disc jockey told him, "Your music is just so ragged—I just can't handle it right now." Nevertheless, Phillips remained confident that this was precisely the sound he had been looking for. "I needed the attention that I got from the people that hated what I was doing, that acted like: 'Here is somebody trying to thrust junk on us and classify it as our music,'" he later recalled.[18]

While still not known outside the South, Presley's early singles and regional success became a drawing card for Sun Records, as singing hopefuls soon arrived from all over the region. One such singer was Johnny Cash, who had just left the US Air Force, got married, and moved to Memphis. He had met guitarist Scotty Moore in Memphis and asked his advice on how to get an audition at Sun Records. Moore suggested that he simply try his luck at the reception desk as Elvis Presley had done, but every time he tried, Phillips was away from the studio. "Finally, one day I was sitting on the stoop just as he came to work and I stood up and said, 'I'm John Cash and I want you to hear me play,'" he later told Peter Guralnick. "He said, 'Well, come on in.' I sang two or three hours for him. Everything I knew—Hank Snow, Ernest Tubb, Flatt and Scruggs . . . I even sang I'll Take You Home Again Kathleen."[19]

The young singer was offered a contract and recorded his first single, "Hey, Porter," in September 1954.

Another musician who fell in love with the new sounds coming out of Sun Records was a singer from rural Tennessee by the name of Carl Perkins. By mid-1954, he had made crude tape recordings of him playing with his brother, Jay, and sent them to RCA and Columbia but heard no response. In July 1954, he and his wife heard a song called "Blue Moon of Kentucky" on the radio and were blown away by what they heard. As the song faded out, Perkins reportedly told his wife, "There's a man in Memphis who understands what we're doing. I need to go see him." He successfully auditioned for the label in October and released his first single in early 1956.

These developments obviously came to the attention of Thomas, who had not been invited back to record a follow-up single to "Tiger Man." "Me and Sam Phillips, we were tighter than the nuts on the Brooklyn Bridge," he later recalled. "But when Elvis and Carl Perkins and Johnny Cash come along, no more Blacks did he pick up at all."[20]

In fact, not only did Sam Phillips not sign any new Black artists—with the exception of the occasional single by Little Milton, Billy "The Kid" Emerson, and Rosco Gordon—Sam Phillips stopped recording most of the African American artists that had been signed to his label. "We called Elvis and the rest the Four Horsemen," Thomas told a reporter from the *Telegraph* newspaper in the UK. "When they came along, all the people in the studio that was Black—we all got discarded."[21]

The "four horsemen" Thomas referred to were Johnny Cash, Carl Perkins, Jerry Lee Lewis, and Roy Orbison.

Many years later, Thomas was asked whether Sam Phillips loved R&B music or was simply trying to make a buck. Thomas conceded that it was probably a bit of both. "I'm looking at Sam in those days as trying to make a buck and I guess he would have to have some kind of a liking to this kind of music because I think even B.B. King came through there, Howlin' Wolf came through—so he had to have some kind of a feeling. But he was still capitalizing and trying to get something going where Black music was concerned."

The same interviewer pushed Thomas on whether he felt Phillips's love of R&B was ever really genuine. "I just don't think that was genuine," Thomas admitted. "He was spreading it around alright . . . but if you ever listen to him and try to . . . visualize in your head . . . why should he kick us all out because a white boy came along? He was doing something . . . (but) the whole time he was doing this, he was looking for a white boy who could sing Black, who could sing like a Black boy which means his head . . .was not really there." Thomas exaggerated slightly here, as Sam Phillips only hit upon this idea in 1954.[22]

The stark contrast with Satellite Records—later known as Stax Records—that Thomas eventually signed with in 1960 couldn't be clearer. "A few years later in came Stax—which proved that maybe, just maybe, Sam was thinking that Blacks and whites couldn't make it together—Stax proved it wrong, so wrong."[23]

♦ ♦ ♦

It's worth noting that Sam Phillips had a different view of the events which saw Thomas leave Sun Records. He explained to Peter Guralnick in *Sam Phillips: The Man Who Invented Rock 'n' Roll* that Thomas's contract had expired and that he had announced his intention to sign with Starmaker, a short-lived label run by WDIA. In the meantime, Starmaker soon collapsed, and as he recalled, Thomas never returned to Sun. This story seems far-fetched; Thomas was a proud man, but he was also ambitious, and it seems unlikely that he would have turned down the chance to record another single with Sun Records.

Phillips also points to the economic necessity of his decision-making; the label was losing money, and the business model needed to change if the label was going to survive. That much is certainly true, but as Thomas himself asked, why not record both Black and white artists?

♦ ♦ ♦

In later years, Thomas would regularly encounter Sam Phillips at industry events around Memphis such as the W. C. Handy Awards, now known as the Blues Music Awards, and would always talk politely with him. The experience had clearly burned him deeply, however, and it does seem to have been one of the few episodes over which Thomas continued to hold a grudge, even as he got older. "Daddy always harbored bitterness with Sam," recalled his daughter Vaneese Thomas. "How could he not?"[24]

Thomas may have held a grudge against Sam Phillips, but he never held a grudge against Elvis Presley himself.

On November 21, 1955, RCA Victor struck a deal with Sam Phillips and Presley's "special advisor" at the time, "Colonel" Tom Parker, to acquire Presley's contract with Sun Records for the unprecedented sum of $35,000—equivalent to almost ten times that in 2020. In the months that followed, Elvis hit the No. 1 spot on the *Billboard* Hot 100 with "Heartbreak Hotel," "I Want You, I Need You," "I Love You," "Don't Be Cruel," and "Hound Dog." In addition, his debut album became the first rock 'n' roll album to top the charts, spending ten weeks at No. 1, catapulting the singer to national and international stardom.

As the days shortened, the staff at WDIA—still Memphis's top radio station—turned their attention to which music stars they could attract to their annual charity fundraising event, the Goodwill Revue. Normally, the radio station approached R&B labels, such as Chess, Sun, and Vee-Jay, so to approach RCA Victor, one of the majors, was always going to be a long shot. Still, Elvis Presley was a local boy, and Louis Cantor, one of the control board operators at WDIA, was in the year above Presley at Humes High School. More importantly, Cantor was a close associate of George Klein, one of Presley's best friends. Cantor and Klein had studied Hebrew together as children, and both attended Memphis State University. In Cantor's view, it was still a long shot—but worth a try.

In November 1956, with the Revue less than one month away, Cantor asked Klein if he would be willing to help. He was glad to help out but was informed that Presley's new contract would not allow him to perform for benefits of any kind. However, the young singer was happy to help out his old school friends and agreed to make a personal appearance at the Revue.

By 1956, the Goodwill Revue had become a sizeable event and featured some big names. While the appearance by Elvis was not publicized before the show, it featured Ray Charles, a former WDIA disc jockey; B.B. King; an R&B group, The Moonglows; a doo-wop group, the Magnificents; and a gospel group, the Five Blind Boys of Alabama. According to Cantor, both halls of the Ellis Auditorium were used, meaning there was an audience of 9,000 Black fans in attendance.

George Klein was able to bring Elvis Presley to the stage entrance. At this stage of his career, there were no bodyguards in attendance, although he was accompanied by a group of Memphis policemen who were presumably concerned about how the crowd might react. Looking back, Thomas was surprised that the young singer agreed to even attend. "For a young white boy to show up at an all-[B]lack function took guts," he recalled.[25]

Elvis was introduced to the members of the WDIA staff, most of whom were dressed in Native American costumes for the evening. The event had been "themed" for a few years, and in 1956, the R&B segment saw the "Indians" taking over the auditorium. The "tribe" featured "Moo-hah" Williams as Big Chief, Willa Monroe as Sweet Mama, his squaw, Rufus Thomas as Rocking Horse, and Martha Jean Steinberg as Princess Premium Stuff. The evening's MC, of course, was Nat D. Williams, who was the medicine man, Great Googa-Mooga.

The plot—such as it was—saw the "square" leader, Big Chief, upset that his tribe had been infiltrated by a new brand of music, rock 'n' roll, which had been brought in by Thomas as the "hep" Rocking Horse. This was 1956, after all! To make matters worse, Rocking Horse had eloped with Big Chief's daughter, Princess Premium Stuff.

What the young Elvis Presley made of the plot has not been documented, but he was apparently taken by Thomas's costume, and photographer Ernest Withers captured an amazing photograph of the two men backstage.

Elvis Presley's music was already popular in the Thomas household at that time, according to Vaneese Thomas. "We were a multi-genre family—we played everything—we played country, we played jazz, we played the beginnings of rock'n'roll," she remembered. "Because Daddy was a DJ, we had all those records. And I used to tell my family that Elvis was my boyfriend! So when I met him that night, I pulled on his coattail and said, 'Did you know you were my boyfriend?' He thought that was so cute and stooped down and sat me on his lap. And that was when Mr. Withers—Ernest Withers—always in the right place at the right time—took the photograph of us."[26]

Elvis Presley also got the chance to talk to B.B. King backstage at the Ellis Auditorium, an encounter that was later described as the meeting of the two "Kings." When they met, Presley turned to King and said, "Thanks, man, for all the early lessons you gave me," according to the *Tri-State Defender*.

Don Kern, who worked as the production manager at WDIA, planned to introduce Elvis at the beginning of the R&B portion of the show, given that he was not going to be performing. He—and others at the station—underestimated the popularity of Elvis Presley among the African

"Did you know you were my boyfriend?" Vaneese Thomas meets Elvis Presley backstage at the WDIA Goodwill Revue at Ellis Auditorium, Memphis, December 7, 1956. © Dr. Ernest C. Withers Sr., courtesy of the Withers Family Trust.

American community. Luckily, Thomas, who, as a disc jockey, was more in touch with popular culture, was able to set him straight. "I told Don, 'Don't do that!'" Thomas later recalled. "You do, the show is over."

As a result, Elvis Presley watched from the wings, joining the audience as they laughed at Nat D. Williams as Great Googa-Mooga, holding a tomahawk and telling the crowd he had killed many buffalo.

Toward the end of the evening, Nat D. returned to the stage and said, "Folks we have a special treat for you tonight—here is Elvis Presley." He was led on stage by the hand by Thomas, still dressed as Rocking Horse, and met by mass hysteria. "He did that [thing] with his leg two or three times and it was over—the show was really over—and the people, these were Black people, his first all-Black show, they stormed that place trying to get to Elvis."[27]

George Klein later told his friend Louis Cantor that they struggled to get out of the auditorium that evening. "We barely got out of there, you know. Everybody started charging toward the stage, and so Elvis ran and he grabbed me!" Luckily, the police were present, and he was able to make a well-choreographed getaway before the girls reached him.[28]

Rufus Thomas later claimed that up until that moment, WDIA's program director had been reluctant to let him play Elvis Presley. "Our program director, he was a Southern white man, he was from St. Louis and I guess he thought—being white—that [B]lack folk just didn't like Elvis which means that he was so wrong."[29]

The very next day, Thomas played Elvis on his show, later claiming to be the first Black disc jockey to have played Elvis on the radio. "See, there's no one individual who can think for a group of people," he argued. "People like music and if it's good it makes no difference who's doing it— Black, blue, green, even plaid if it's like that! I love good music and Elvis was doing good music for me at that time. He was doing blues, rhythm and blues because that was his beginning."[30]

However, it seems that Rufus was developing his own myth with that particular story. "Elvis got so big and so hot that we naturally had to play a few of his records sometimes," recalled "Honeymoon" Garner. He also recalled "Moohah" Williams playing some of Elvis's early singles.[31]

Even if there is an element of urban myth in that particular story, the fact remains that Thomas was one of the first Black disc jockeys to appreciate that Presley's appeal transcended color boundaries.

But did Elvis Presley mark the beginning of rock 'n' roll? "They say that once he [Sam Phillips] got white people, it was the beginning of rock and roll," Thomas explained to author Hugh Merrill. "But we were already doing it! It was already there. Joe Turner had rock and roll long before these white people came. Chuck Berry, Little Richard . . . a direct copy of Little Richard was Jerry Lee Lewis. Listen to the piano that Jerry Lee Lewis played back in the 1950s. Identical. Jerry Lee is a copy. So was Elvis in the beginning. So were all of them." Thomas makes some good points. Certainly, the term "rock 'n' roll" was in use before Elvis Presley and was predominantly used to refer to R&B music that also appealed to a white audience, but it became more mainstream when white musicians started to perform it themselves.[32]

Chapter Four

Steady Holdin' On

Memphis Talent, 1956-1960

Memphis in 1956 was a melting pot for music; the main ingredients were blues, the mainstay of the city for so many years; gospel, which obviously stemmed from the church; jazz and R&B, both of which were extensions of blues; doo-wop, a form of R&B featuring harmony singing that was becoming increasingly popular at that time; and rockabilly—also an extension of the blues—courtesy of Elvis Presley and Sun Records.

And if a nightclub found itself short of one particular ingredient, it was always possible to find a substitution. Many of the city's emerging jazz musicians found themselves playing in R&B bands, for example, while doo-wop singers might find themselves singing jazz standards with a big band on the weekend.

Adding spice to the pot was an amazing array of young African American talent that was emerging from the Memphis school system at that time. Singers like William Bell, Don Bryant, Maurice White, David Porter, Deanie Parker; musicians like Charles Lloyd, Booker Little, George Coleman, Booker T. Jones, Isaac Hayes, Howard Grimes—to name but a few. And then there were Rufus Thomas's two eldest children, Marvell and Carla, who showed immense promise as a pianist and singer, respectively.

To put this into context, remember that Memphis was a city of less than half a million people, and with a segregated school system, these singers and musicians were all emerging from just two high schools—Booker T. Washington in the central city and Manassas High School in North Memphis. There was something in the water flowing through the Mississippi River.

♦ ♦ ♦

As noted in the previous chapter, the early singles of Elvis Presley attracted young, country-oriented musicians to Sun Studios in Memphis, which signed Johnny Cash in 1954 and Carl Perkins in 1955. Other key musicians drawn to Sam Phillips's studio were Texas-born Roy Orbison and Louisiana-born Jerry Lee Lewis, both of whom signed to the label in 1956.

In truth, the rockabilly boom was explosive but short-lived. Presley's original backing musicians, Scotty Moore and Bill Black, walked out in 1957 in a dispute over money, noting that Elvis had been turned into a "corporation," a remark that was pretty close to the truth as "Colonel" Tom Parker started to manage every aspect of his career.

Roy Orbison's career failed to ignite at Sun Records. He briefly quit the music industry altogether in 1958, and it wasn't until he signed to Monument Records in 1960 that his career really began to take off. Johnny Cash also had a falling out with Sam Phillips and quit the label in 1958 to sign with Columbia. "I think Johnny left because he got his feelings hurt," recalled guitarist Jack Clement. "One day Johnny dropped by and wanted to talk to Sam or have lunch or something and Sam was too busy. He was doing something with Jerry Lee . . . I think that's what started it."[1]

Carl Perkins followed Cash to Columbia Records in 1958, where he recorded a string of singles, but by 1959 his career had also started to peter out, and he had returned to the southern honky-tonks. In the meantime, Jerry Lee Lewis was the architect of his own downfall. He had enjoyed massive hits in 1957 with singles like "Whole Lotta Shakin' Goin' On" and "Great Balls of Fire," but in 1958, against the recommendation of Sam Phillips and others, he married his thirteen-year-old cousin. When the British press found out ahead of a UK tour in the spring of 1958, all hell broke loose, and most of the concerts were canceled.

In 1959, Sam Phillips opened a larger recording studio, the Sam C. Phillips Recording Studio, better known as Phillips Recording. When a reporter asked him that year if rock 'n' roll was dead, he replied that it was not—the music was simply "modifying the beat." In a sense, he was right, but the glory days for Sun Records were effectively over.

♦ ♦ ♦

It might easily be argued that the glory days were also over for Memphis blues. B.B. King might have made his name in Memphis as the Beale Street Blues Boy, but by the early 1950s, he was signed to Modern Records in Los Angeles, and by 1956, he was a nationwide star, playing an incredible 342 one-night concerts in the US in a single year.

Howlin' Wolf had also left Memphis by this time. His early recordings had been made by Sam Phillips at the Memphis Recording Studio,
then licensed to either Chess Records in Chicago or RPM Records, a
subsidiary of Modern Records in Los Angeles. In December 1951, however, Leonard Chess was able to secure his contract from Phillips and
suggested Wolf relocate to Chicago in order to advance his career. Wolf
also persuaded Memphis-born guitarist Hubert Sumlin to join him a
year later.

Wolf was not alone in relocating to Chicago. Another Memphis-born
blues pianist and singer, Memphis Slim—born John Chatman—signed
to United Records in Chicago around this time and later teamed up
with Willie Dixon, appearing on his debut album, *Willie's Blues*, in 1959.

Despite these big-name departures, blues music was still a big draw
in the clubs of Memphis. One of the singers keeping the flame burning
was Rufus Thomas. Undeterred by the fallout at Sun Records following
the signing of Elvis Presley, Thomas initially found work singing with
other bands, including the big band run by Al Jackson Sr.

Around 1955, he decided to put together his own, more blues-oriented
band. "Since I had recorded 'Bear Cat' [in 1953], I got me a little group
together and called it Rufus Thomas and the Bear Cats. And we played
all down in Mississippi, over in Arkansas, and in parts of Tennessee,
within the tri-state area. And in the meantime, I was [still] holding down
a job in a textile mill."[2]

The lineup varied over time, but according to Thomas, the band was
originally comprised of himself and four other musicians. "The piano
player was Benny Murrell. We had a trumpet player and piano player,
uh, golly Moses, his name is Willie D. Northington. Willie Clark was on
bass. Harvey Simmons was on saxophone. Jeff Grayer was on drums. Let
me see, I think that's about all . . . in the early stages of the Bear Cats, we
didn't have a guitar. But the trumpet player played piano *and* trumpet if
Benny Murrell wasn't there."[3]

The whole band used to travel to gigs in a single car, a two-door '54
Chevrolet. "Five of us got in there, plus an upright bass," Thomas said,
laughing. "Now you wonder how all that happened, but we made it. As I
say—here we go again—[it was] a matter of survival. You would take the
bottom of the bass, put it in the, like, in the window, and put the neck
of it across the seat. And that's the way we rode, just like that. And had
a good time in there. We didn't make a lot of money, but we sure had a
good time then."[4]

Sometimes the Bear Cats would be joined by another Memphis singer
known as Big Ella. "She was always talkin' about her size in a song,"

Thomas recalled. "But, boy, the girl was a riot. She couldn't come off very well on a record but, boy, she could tear a house apart. And she had some moves with her big self that you would not believe! She was a good singer—and, well, recently she passed—but she was a good performer, and she was a great asset to the Bear Cats."[5]

By 1956, the lineup seemed to have changed and included Evelyn Young and Harvey Simmons on saxophone, trumpeter Willie Dee, future Booker T. & the M.G.'s bass player Lewie Steinberg and drummer Jeff Grayer. While the band never achieved any commercial success, they had a considerable reputation in and around Memphis at that time. "Everybody wanted to be a Bear Cat," recalled Isaac Hayes at Thomas's funeral many years later.

Rufus Thomas later remembered the band playing over at a club over in West Memphis. "Eighth Street used to be the place in West Memphis— The Little Brown Jug," he told Hugh Merrill, author of *The Blues Route*. "I used to go over there—boy, it was a joint. They did a lot of gamblin' and stuff over there. But it was the place. I used to work over there in a club with my little band called the Bear Cats. Then this sheriff came along and broke that shit up. Broke it up, man. A sheriff named Culp. He was awful. But he didn't pick 'em. If you were white and screwed up, he kicked your butt. If you were [B]lack and screwed up, he kicked your butt. Didn't make no difference to Culp! He cleaned it up and wasn't no more fun, man."[6]

Another important band at this time was Willie Mitchell and his Jumpin' Band, who were the house band at the Plantation Inn in Memphis.

Mitchell was born in Ashland, Mississippi, in 1928 but moved to Memphis when he was still a toddler. He started playing trumpet at the age of eight and played in the big bands fronted by Tuff Green and Al Jackson Sr. when he was still a teenager.

The army disrupted his musical development somewhat when he was drafted in 1950, but in 1954, when he returned to Memphis, he formed his own band, which took up residency first at Danny's Club in West Memphis, then at the Manhattan Club, eventually settling at the Plantation Inn.

The musicians that had passed through his band over that period include some of the finest local jazz musicians, including saxophonist Charles Lloyd, fellow trumpet player Booker Little, and saxophonist George Coleman, who went on to join the Miles Davis Quintet, and Frank Strozier, to name but a few.

The Plantation Inn had a long and varied history. It was once a cotton plantation house in West Memphis and later a gambling hall before being launched as a music venue and supper club in 1942. Author Robert

Gordon, who devoted a chapter to the Plantation Inn in his 1995 book *It Came from Memphis*, notes that the club provided a whole generation of white musicians—often underage—with their first serious dose of Black music. "Kids could get into clubs more easily across the river, and the exposure to bands like Willie Mitchell's or Phineas Newborn's group or the many others who came and went was crucial," says Gordon. "It provided those kids with a kind of primer for R&B—for the rhythms and the repertoires and the unusual horn arrangements."[7]

Saxophonist Charles "Packy" Axton, the son of Stax cofounder Estelle Axton, was a regular attendee, as were his bandmates in the Mar-Keys, guitarist Steve Cropper and Donald "Duck" Dunn.

Another highly influential band at this time was a more jazz-oriented band led by drummer Phineas Newborn Sr.—father of pianist Phineas Newborn Jr. and guitarist Calvin Newborn—and affectionately known as "Old Man Phineas" by most members of his band. The band had started out at the Plantation Inn and, around 1956, moved across to the Flamingo Club, which was located in downtown Memphis on Hernando Street, just a block or two down from Beale Street.

Like Willie Mitchell's band, it attracted some of the city's finest musicians, including jazz saxophonists Charles Lloyd and Hank Crawford, the latter of whom went on to play with Ray Charles. It was also something of a family affair with sons Phineas and Calvin on piano and guitar, respectively, and Calvin's wife, Wanda Jones, on trombone.

There were numerous other bands playing regularly across Memphis at this time. Trumpet player Gene "Bowlegs" Miller was also a regular at the Flamingo Club with his band, Bowlegs and His Band, while tenor saxophonist Ben Branch played with his band, the Largos, at Curry's Club Tropicana in North Memphis.

"There was another group from Beale Street, which was over at Club Handy, which was Sam Jones and the Vel-Tones," recalled drummer Howard Grimes. "Some of the blues acts that were passing through were friends of W. C. Handy, and were close friends with Sunbeam Mitchell at Club Handy."[8]

♦ ♦ ♦

One of the many hot new talents emerging into the burgeoning Memphis music scene was a young singer by the name of William Bell. "I started in church, of course," Bell later recalled. "From around seven years old, I was singing in the choir. And by nine, I was singing solo with the choir behind me. I was kind of like a prodigy."[9]

In his early teens, he joined WDIA's Teen Town singers, which was where he first encountered Rufus Thomas and his daughter Carla. "I was roughly fourteen years old, around 1954 or 1955," he later recalled. "I was in the group at the same time as Carla, and that's how I got to know the family. We went along to the WDIA studio. They had a DJ by the name of 'Moohah' Williams, and I ran into Rufus at the radio station. I used to listen to him on the radio all the time."[10]

In 1955, at the age of sixteen, Bell entered a local talent contest. "That was my first contest," he remembered. "It was a Mid-South Talent Contest that they held in a Tri-state area for talent from Tennessee, Mississippi and Arkansas. I got the first prize, which was a trip to Chicago to work with the Red Saunders band it was just for the weekend at Club DeLisa. That was my first trip to Chicago."[11]

On the back of his talent show success, Bell landed a job singing jazz standards with the band led by "Old Man Phineas." "Phineas and Red Saunders were friends," said Bell. "Red had called and told him of the good job I had done and he, of course, contacted me. He had to get permission from my mom, which was not an easy task, but he got the okay from her for me to work at the Flamingo [Club] on weekends."[12]

Singing with a fourteen-piece band, including some of the finest jazz musicians in the city, gave the young singer a strong musical grounding. "We did all the standards," he recalled. "'Moonlight in Vermont,' 'A Pretty Girl is Like a Melody'—oh, and 'Unforgettable' by Nat King Cole! He and Arthur Prysock and a lot of singers were on the scene, and those were the kinds of tunes we did."[13]

Rufus Thomas heard about Bell's work at the Flamingo Club and took the young singer under his wing, becoming something of a father figure in the process. "He would host the Wednesday night talent show at the Handy Theatre," Bell remembered. "I was just watching the show at the time—I wasn't supposed to be in there! But they all knew me from working at the Flamingo [Club], so they'd let me in, and I'd stand in the wings and watch him perform, dance, and tell jokes.[14]

Outside of the Flamingo Club, Bell also tried his hand at doo-wop. The origins of doo-wop go back to the late 1930s, with early proponents being groups like the Ink Spots and the Mills Brothers. By 1956, doo-wop recordings were topping the R&B charts with hits like "I'll Be Home" (The Flamingos) and "Why Do Fools Fall in Love" (Frankie Lymon and the Teenagers), which effectively fused doo-wop with rock 'n' roll.

Incidentally, the term "doo-wop" was not coined until much later. Doo-wop included many "nonsense" phrases, but music historians have traced the phrase "doo-wop" back to a song called "Just A-Sittin' and A-Rockin'" which was recorded by The Delta Rhythm Boys back in 1945.

"David Porter, Maurice White (later of Earth, Wind & Fire) and I all lived within a couple of blocks of each other—we all came out of LeMoyne Gardens, which was a housing project there," Bell recalled. "And in the night time, we'd sing under the streetlights. I'm telling you, we would have sessions out there until the neighbors would run us in! Yeah, Maurice, David and I, we would do all those doo-wop songs by the Flamingos and Billy Ward and the Dominos and all those old '50s songs."[15]

Doo-wop was also becoming more popular with the patrons of the Flamingo Club. "On Sunday afternoons they had a fashion show and what they called 'a tea dance,' and we would do jazz stuff. Then they wanted more of the current stuff, and most of it was like the doo-wop groups, so I formed a group of guys."

The new vocal group was called the Del-Rios, which was originally comprised of five singers—Bell, Harrison Austin, Louis Williams, David Brown, and Roy Webb. The group rehearsed at Bell's mother's house during the week, and on Sunday evenings, they sang the latest R&B tunes with Phineas Newborn Sr. Besides Phineas, the group also worked with the combos of Gene "Bowlegs" Miller, Ben Branch, and Willie Mitchell.

The new group quickly gained a good reputation in and around the Memphis area and on the college circuit. "We did some backup work with Rufus and performed a couple of gigs with him at the Plantation Inn, an all-white club at the time, but it was very popular with the college kids and the people from Memphis and West Memphis."[16]

It was this gig at the Plantation Inn that is thought to have attracted the attention of Lester Bihari, the founder of a small Memphis-based record label, Meteor Records, which was located at 1794 Chelsea Avenue.

In fact, Lester Bihari was the older brother of Julius (Jools), Saul, and Joseph, who had established Modern Records in Los Angeles in 1945. In the early 1950s, the brothers launched a number of subsidiaries, including RPM Records and Flair Records. At this time, Ike Turner worked as a talent spotter for the label in Memphis and introduced B.B. King to the Biharis, who signed him to the RPM label. Other Memphis-based artists introduced by Ike Turner included Rosco Gordon and Howlin' Wolf. Modern Records went on to become one of the leading R&B labels of the 1950s, signing artists such as Etta James, Little Richard, John Lee Hooker, and Ike and Tina Turner.

Lester Bihari only had a peripheral involvement in Modern Records, it seems, but was placed in charge of Meteor Records—another subsidiary of

Modern Records—in Memphis, Tennessee, with the new label launching in November 1952.

The label met with some initial success. Lester Bihari's first release was a single called "I Believe" by blues singer and guitarist Elmore James. The single sold well, but Lester Bihari struggled to replicate this success, and subsequent singles flopped badly.

Two years later, Meteor enjoyed a second regional hit, this time with hillbilly singer Bud Deckelman's single "Daydreamin." The same song was then recorded by Jimmy Newman, who scored a bigger hit, and Deckelman was promptly lured to one of the major labels, MGM.

Meteor underwent another stylistic shift in the mid-1950s, signing a number of rockabilly artists that were not able to sign with Sam Phillips at Sun Records. So almost by default, Lester Bihari made some fine rockabilly recordings by the likes of Charlie Feathers and Jess Hooper. Unfortunately, his distribution network relied on that of the parent company, Modern Records, which was more accustomed to R&B-type songs, so most of these fine recordings failed to sell.

By 1956, it was apparent that Meteor Records was struggling financially. Lester Bihari seems to have made a conscious decision to go back to his R&B roots and may well have been encouraged to do so by Rufus Thomas himself, who would have pointed out that there was an obvious gap in the market with Sam Phillips having dropped most of his African American artists.

Lester Bihari was clearly impressed by both William Bell's band, the Del-Rios, and Rufus Thomas and the Bear Cats, and decided to record them both, probably at the same recording session.

Like the original Sun Studio, Meteor Records was another self-contained recording studio and office, all under one roof. "I made my first recording for (the) Meteor label, when I was still in high school," William Bell remembered. "I recorded a song I had written called 'Alone on a Rainy Nite.' Rufus Thomas's band, the Bear Cats, was the rhythm section on the recording. 'Alone on a Rainy Nite' is one of those—before it was fashionable—Southern soul ballads [laughs] and "Lizzie" on the B-side is an uptempo [sic] song, almost like 'There Is Love' [a later release on Stax Records]." [17]

The single was credited to "The Del Rios with The Bear Cats," and it was released on Meteor 5038 in late 1956 and it made some noise, but only locally.

Rufus Thomas and the Bear Cats seem to have been joined in the studio by a pianist, who is thought to have been Billy Morrow, and a guitarist, who remains unknown. The A-side they recorded was "The Easy Livin' Plan," which was a storming R&B number. The Bear Cats deliver a formidable shuffle led by that fine horn section. Thomas is also in fine form, both vocally and lyrically; the chorus invokes a list of characters, all living life to the fullest:

> That preacher, that teacher, that gamblin' man,
> They're all trying to make it on the easy plan,
> The lawyer, the doctor, even down to the baker,
> They're all trying to keep up with the undertaker . . .

The song clearly demonstrates how far Thomas had advanced as a songwriter since his early recordings just five years earlier.

The B-side, "I'm Steady Holding On," was a slow blues, but again, far superior lyrically to his earlier efforts. "I wrote one of the first songs that Bobby Bland ever sung," Thomas later told Peter Guralnick.

> I got a new kind of loving that other men can't catch on,
> While they losing out, I'm steady holding on.

"It was a good tune. Bobby sang it on the Amateur Show and won first prize," he recalled. Thomas later rerecorded the song as a B-side to his 1968 Stax single, "Down Ta My House."

Sadly, the recording studio on Chelsea Avenue was fairly rudimentary, and the sound quality of the recording was poor compared with his earlier recordings at Sun Studios.

The A-side received a favorable review in *Billboard*, reproduced below, but failed to make the charts.

Sadly for both William Bell and Rufus Thomas, Meteor Records continued to struggle financially. Neither artist recorded a follow-up single for the label, and it eventually folded in May 1957, according to *Cashbox* magazine. After the label folded, Lester Bihari worked for his brothers' Crown budget label as a sales representative, first in Memphis, then later in Texas. He eventually returned to Los Angeles, where he remained on the payroll for a number of years.

◆ ◆ ◆

William Bell was one of many new artists emerging from the Memphis high school system at this time. Another was William Bell's one-time doo-wop partner, a budding singer and songwriter by the name of David Porter.

David Porter was born in November 1941, the ninth of twelve children. Like Bell, he was something of a child prodigy, forming a gospel quartet with Maurice White while he was still in junior high. By 1956, at the age of just fifteen, he was in a band called the Marquettes, which would occasionally sing at venues such as the Flamingo Club where he appeared with Barbara Griffin.

Porter remembered appearing on Rufus Thomas's talent show at the Handy Theatre in the early 1950s. "At different times they would host that evening for high school kids, and I was one of the kids that would come in and try to win $3 on stage," he recalled. "I started out singing; I was [already] writing, but had no hit records, and nowhere to go with it. The talents would vary from week to week, depending on how popular the doo-wop group was and the song that you were singing—that's what mattered, rather than how great you were! If you got the right song on that Wednesday night, that was popular, you could win!"[18]

Porter would go on to record his first single at the age of nineteen for the local label, Golden Eagle Records, and was one of the first musicians to start working at Satellite Records after it moved to McLemore Avenue, singing background on some of the earliest sessions there.

One of the people Porter competed with at the local talent shows was a singer and musician by the name of Isaac Hayes. Hayes was nine months younger than Porter, born in August 1942. Similarly, while still in high school, he formed a vocal group called the Teen Tones. It has often been suggested that, like Carla Thomas, Isaac Hayes was a member of WDIA's Teen Town singers, but that was never the case. The confusion seems to have arisen from the similarity of the band's names and also the fact that Isaac Hayes and the Teen Tones did appear on WDIA's Saturday morning *Big Star Talent Show*, a program that appeared directly after the Teen Towners had performed.

Years later, Hayes had fond memories of the Memphis talent shows. "I was a raggedy kid with holes in his shoes up on stage singing the Nat King Cole song 'Looking Back,'" he recalled. "All of a sudden, I win this contest and I'm signing autographs and the pretty girls are noticing me."[19]

Hayes ended up having to retake one year of high school and did not graduate until 1962. He made three attempts to audition for Stax Records at that time—one with the Teen Tones, one with an R&B group, Sir Isaac and the Do-Dads, and finally with a more blues-oriented band, Sir Calvin Valentine and His Swinging Cats. When all three failed, he ended up playing piano with saxophonist Floyd Newman over at the Plantation Inn.

Hayes was eventually signed by Jim Stewart as a substitute piano player rather than as a singer when Booker T. Jones started college. His first session was playing organ with Floyd Newman on "Frog Stomp," and Hayes went on to form a highly successful songwriting partnership with David Porter before becoming a massive solo star in his own right.

Another singer emerging at that time, the same age as Hayes, was Don Bryant. Born in Memphis in April 1942, he began singing in church at the age of five. He soon joined his father's gospel group, but in high school, he was also bitten by the doo-wop bug. "Just about every neighborhood had a group; three or four guys that would get together," he remembered. "They came from all over Memphis—you would hear good voices everywhere. We would have rehearsals in the park, people would gather 'round and listen to the songs. Music just became a part of us."[20]

Bryant's vocal quartet was noticed by a local disc jockey, "Cane" Cole, and the group became known as the Four Canes. "He became our manager," said Bryant. "He had a radio show. Before we went to school in the morning, he'd have us on the show, and we'd be singing a couple of songs. Things like that kept me interested in the music industry."[21]

The vocal quartet, later renamed the Four Kings, ended up fronting Willie Mitchell's band for a considerable period of time. "We played at the Manhattan Club, which was a private club; at the Flamingo [Club]; we played at Danny's Club in West Memphis; we played all over, really—we played weekly at Danny's for a while on the weekends," noted Bryant. "There was so much good talent, the clubs were full all the time. Many of them would have a house band and bring on another band. I guess you could say it was like a talent show, in some ways, because you wanted to do better than the group before you!"[22]

It was while he was fronting Willie Mitchell's band that Bryant first encountered Rufus Thomas, who was clearly from a different generation, who acted like a father figure in some respects. "There were a lot of artists around—people like Rufus Thomas—who were so knowledgeable about what they were doing. You had the opportunity to listen to them and then see what you had to do," he said. "Just to be with them, it inspired me, to tell you the truth. It got a hold of me, and I got a hold of it!"[23]

When Willie Mitchell accepted a job over at Hi Records, Bryant also became a songwriter for the record label while continuing to record with the Four Kings. He recorded a solo album of his own for Hi, *Precious Soul*, in 1969, before starting to write songs for a singer by the name of Ann Peebles, who later became his wife.

Another Hi Records alumnus who started around the same time was a young drummer by the name of Howard Grimes. Grimes was no prodigy but was effectively self-taught. "The music came from my mother," he revealed. "She was the one. Her name was Mary Grimes. I used to hear all of her music, the blues and jazz and the country and western music from my granddaddy—Hank Williams, Hank Snow, all of those people were on the Grand Old Opry, and my granddaddy would listen in. So, I had all this music between them. That's how it all got started. It was a gift that God gave me—I was self-taught."[24]

Most of his learning was informal and took place in the clubs of Memphis when he was still in his mid-teens and attending Manassas High School. "I was playing in the clubs, but I was too young to be in them," he recalled. "Back in the day they had vice squads. I was covered by the club, but the vice squad used to come in to check up on me. As long as I wasn't sitting out in the audience with people with alcohol, because I was too young. I had to be in the dressing room or the kitchen on the break. All the music I was learning was from greats like Floyd Newman, Fred Ford—all these musicians that people don't know anything about. It was one of the greatest times of my life, being the kid I was. That's how it all began . . . ."[25]

By 1960, still eighteen, Grimes landed a gig with a pianist and bandleader by the name of Bob Talley, and it was through Talley that Grimes landed his first recording session at Satellite Records with Rufus and Carla Thomas. At Satellite, he was given further guidance by Al Jackson Jr., the drummer for Booker T. & the M.G.'s, and in later years, both drummers ended up working with Willie Mitchell over at Hi Records.

◆ ◆ ◆

All of this begs the question as to why so much young talent was suddenly emerging from the African American community in a city the size of Memphis—rather than New York, Chicago, Los Angeles, or San Francisco. It's a question that music historians have been struggling to answer for many years, largely because there is no simple answer.

Or is there? For drummer Howard Grimes, it all goes back to the Father of the Memphis blues. "That's where it started," he explained. "I was at Manassas (High School). The band teacher was Mr. Emerson Able—he was the one that put the history up on me [sic]. The music that I was playing under his instruction basically started with W. C. Handy, who wrote the blues. He came later on to Cannonball Adderley, Ray Charles, jazz . . . it all connected the same."[26]

Keyboard player Booker T. Jones agreed that it started with W. C. Handy but had a more academic, metaphysical explanation as to how it evolved from there to the generation coming through in the late 1950s. "I feel that in time there are centers of energy on the earth," he explained. "They coagulate, they gather, like cells. There is energy for literature, for painting, for music, and I think that's what I was caught up in, a certain, special energy that was in Memphis during that period. People were drawn to it from Mississippi, from Arkansas, from other places. That's what I really believe. If you were there, you were lucky, and things fell into place for you. There was Charles Lloyd, there was Elvis Presley, there was my first mentor, Willie Mitchell, Lucie Campbell and her gospel songs. In the human body, when microbes gather in one place, they do good or bad; I think it happens with the arts." [27]

Jones's explanation makes a great deal of sense. Memphis was well-positioned geographically, with no major cities within a few hundred miles, so the potential catchment area was huge. It also boasted a well-established entertainment district that had been in place for many years courtesy of Memphis's position as a cotton-trading hub. Beale Street, for example, had become a Black entertainment district by the turn of the century, and by the time W. C. Handy got to Memphis in 1909, it was already well established.

Guitarist Steve Cropper, Jones's bandmate for many years in Booker T. & the M.G.'s, essentially shared this view. "Memphis was a melting pot," he explained. "You had artists coming in from Arkansas, Mississippi, Missouri, Kentucky, of course Tennessee, Alabama, Georgia. People came here because it was an old gambling town—a riverboat gambling town. This was way back in the 1920s, and even before that. It was a gambling town, and a music town. It always had clubs."[28]

So, by the time you added Black radio to the mix in the late 1940s, it's easy to see why the city was attracting a new generation of musicians such as B.B. King, originally from near Indianola, Mississippi, and Howlin' Wolf, from West Point, Mississippi, to play at the clubs and on the radio stations.

But there's an important missing link touched on by Grimes, which allowed this musical knowledge to be passed on to the next generation—young musicians like Grimes, Booker T. Jones, William Bell, David Porter, Isaac Hayes, Carla Thomas and the like—and that was the education system that existed in Memphis at that time.

As stated earlier, the African American community in Memphis was quite tight-knit, and most of these musicians attended either Booker T. Washington High School in downtown Memphis or Manassas High School to the north.

Of note, both schools were blessed with inspirational music teachers. At Booker T. Washington High School, the attitude toward the performing arts came from the very top, according to Rufus Thomas's youngest daughter, Vaneese Thomas. "The principal was a really brilliant professor,

Blair T. Hunt," she recalled. "He loved the arts, and every year they would have these things called 'ballets'—but basically, they were variety shows, and they would have all the kids come up and perform."[29]

Booker T. Jones attended Booker T. Washington High School and singled out one teacher as exerting a huge influence on the young musicians coming through. "There was one particular figure that was responsible for so many successful jazz musicians, and that was the band professor, W. T. McDaniel," he explained. "He was the band instructor . . . one of those exacting people who directed the band for many years and it was a famous band. I was in the band, Maurice White was in the band, so many people before us. He was in the same age group as Rufus Thomas."[30]

The pioneering gospel singer Lucie E. Campbell also taught at Booker T. Washington High School and organized choral groups there.

In the same vein, Emerson Able served as band director at Manassas High for around thirty years, with students including jazz musicians Booker Little, Frank Strozier, and George Coleman, and R&B musicians such as Isaac Hayes and Howard Grimes.

Deanie Parker, the Stax singer and executive, confirmed that the Memphis school system played a vital role but also questioned whether that is still the case now. "Memphis had better sense then than it does now," she argued. "It cared for and did more to nurture the musical talent that either migrated to this area or were born and bred in this area. For a half-century, Memphis has benefited from those achievements and that unique culture that existed then, and it has not re-invested, which is a tragedy. Because Memphis is a musically, culturally, unique city."[31]

With the education system playing its part, at least at that time, all that was needed was an outlet for the emerging talent, and that's where the talent shows, hosted by the likes of Nat D. Williams at the Palace Theater, Rufus Thomas at the Handy Theatre, and WDIA on Saturday mornings came in. As did the nightclubs, where older musicians would nurture the budding musicians, and one new band could compete against another.

The last word on this subject goes to David Porter. "What made Memphis so impactful is the Black talents that were able to get the opportunity to show their wares," he explained. "And giving them that opportunity, it was the understanding of the people who opened the door for them, because they were equally amazed. And when they were able to get comfortable and do what they do, the individuality . . . came out . . . and the rest is history."[32]

◆ ◆ ◆

In the meantime, Rufus Thomas's two eldest children, Marvell and Carla, who in 1956 turned fifteen and fourteen, respectively, were also taking their first steps toward a career in music.

Marvell had taken full advantage of the piano that had been delivered to the house at Kerr Street three years previously. "Playing the piano came quite naturally to me, and it was something I had an intense interest in," he later revealed. "I took lessons from the daughter of a famous high school bandleader at that time, Tuff Green. We ran out of things she could teach me pretty quickly."[33]

Marvell, like Carla, was also a member of WDIA's Teen Town singers, and they also helped to further his musical education at this time, giving him his first experience writing and arranging for a small group. "Inside this choral group that I was in, the Teen Town Singers, there were many groups," he explained. "I mean, the kids were encouraged to do other things inside the group. Like, there were two or three, like smaller, like quartets or quintets that were formed inside the group. . . . And we were given the opportunity to perform those songs. So, it wasn't just, have rehearsals and just learn. We had some outlet for it."[34]

Marvell landed his first paid gig at the age of sixteen, playing for Ben Branch's group, the Largos, at Curry's Club Tropicana at the corner of Thomas and Huron in North Memphis. "I was legally too young to be in there, but one of the guys in the band, Floyd Newman, convinced my reluctant mother that he would make sure nothing happened to me," he later revealed. "My first night, I got paid by Ben Branch, who wound up being an extraordinary bandleader. But Ben had this habit of folding everyone's money 300 times, down to the size of a postage stamp. By the time the musicians unfolded their money, Ben was long gone home. I was supposed to get paid $15, but when I unfolded the money, there was only $7 there. Fortunately, Ben's girlfriend had stopped him at the exit because she was mad at him. I told Floyd about my short payment, and he got the rest of my money for me. So, I got paid short on my very first gig—and it's been the same way ever since!"[35]

Marvell remembered the gig as a steep learning curve. "The first set, the first hour, would be a jazz set, and the guys got a chance to really stretch out and play and show what they could do with their instruments," he later explained. "The jazz stuff was musically over my head at the time . . . it was [like] going to school for me. Just sitting there listening to these guys play, because I was, by far and away, a baby by comparison in age and in musical experience."[36]

The gig with the Largos ended up lasting for several months and caused a significant amount of friction within the Thomas family. "I

Lorene Thomas, Kerr Street, Memphis, circa 1956. Photograph courtesy of the Vaneese Thomas family collection.

started playing weekends and nights in clubs when I was 16 or 17 and going to school during the day," said Marvell. "I wouldn't get home until 3 a.m., and my mother was not at all fond of that. Rufus just stayed out of the way and let my mother argue the point!"[37]

At this stage, Marvell was not considering a career in music. At the age of nine, he suffered from severe pneumonia and almost died. "I was in the hospital's children's ward for about a month. I started getting better, and I began running errands and doing chores for the interns, such as getting blood samples and doing blood count studies. I was fascinated with it! I also got to watch operations with the surgical students. I thought, 'I want to do this!'" As a result, Marvell's high school studies were focused on science and math-oriented subjects with a view to eventually attending medical school.

After graduating high school, Marvell studied at LeMoyne College for one year. His music professor was known as "Doc Whitaker"—it wasn't until later that the Thomas children learned of his importance to American music history. Whitaker had served as part of James Reese Europe's military band during World War I, widely recognized for having pioneered orchestral jazz both at home and abroad. But by that stage, Marvell Thomas was finding regular paid work as a musician and thoughts of going to medical school began to fade.

While Marvell was playing his first gigs, Carla found the Teen Town singers took up most of her spare time, with two nights of rehearsal every week and weekend events to attend. By this stage, she had become one of the group's featured soloists. "Lord, I was sometimes late for this and late for that. I was a kid—how'd I do that? But I did it," she remembered. "It was get off school every Wednesday and go straight to class. Get off school every Friday and go straight to rehearsal. [I] had to catch the bus and go, 'cause we had moved by that time. And Saturday we had to go down to the [radio] station and sing. It was just a whole bunch of us. It was a lot of fun, it really was!"[38]

The Teen Town radio show went out live every Saturday morning, between 10 and 10:30 a.m. and drew a broad audience, attracting both young and old. In addition, the Teen Towners sometimes provided background vocals for artists appearing at WDIA fundraising events. "They were called the Goodwill Revue—that was in the winter—and the Starlight Revue in the summer. So we got a chance to really meet a lot of artists—blues artists, gospel artists," Carla recalled.[39]

The Teen Towners would also go out on the road and tour the local area, which helped the teenage Carla Thomas develop her stagecraft. "We would go to a lot of schools and sing for their programs," she remembered. "And, a lot of my shyness, getting in front of people, began to kind of go away. I was taught how to use a mic."[40]

Carla's childhood friend and fellow Teen Town singer, Mark Stansbury, remembers that the Teen Town singers didn't just teach you about music but gave you valuable life lessons too. "Mr. ['Moohah'] Williams was such a great inspiration to young people," he noted. "Even if you weren't a great singer, he would teach you good things. Taught you to be on time, if you tell someone you're going to do something, do it. As a result of the training from Mr. Williams, I have never been late. I always set my watch fifteen minutes ahead of time!"[41]

In her early teens, Carla would often listen to country music at home—especially Brenda Lee—and this influence could be heard in her earliest recordings for Stax Records, too. "We grew up on all kinds of music. There was a lady that lived next door that taught ballet, so we heard classical music all the time. And my mother loved country music. She was kind of raised on country music, so we listened to that every morning going to school. She had *Bob Neal's Breakfast Club* on, and Red Foley. So, we grew up with the real country people. I'm talking about Hank Williams and Hank Snow and Ferlin Husky, long before Elvis."[42]

Carla's love of Brenda Lee fed into her work with the Teen Town singers, and she used to sing songs like "I'm Sorry" on the Saturday morning broadcast. "I even used to do some audition tapes for her to listen to," she recalled. "I remember for some reason they (the WDIA staff) knew

Carla and Vaneese, Kerr Street, Memphis, circa 1955. Photograph courtesy of the
Vaneese Thomas family collection.

I liked country, so they'd come get me when I was at school and I'd go
down there and sing some audition tapes. A lot of times I know they sent
them to Brenda, 'cause that's all that I cared about. As a young girl my
age, she was kind of like a role model."[43]

Carla doesn't remember exactly what happened to the tapes but sus-
pects that they may have been sent to the Tree Publishing Company,
a country music publishing house owned by Dial Records' founder,
Buddy Killen.

Once she had reached fifteen years of age, Carla got her first visual
exposure to R&B, watching television with her mother. "We were sitting
watching Jackie Wilson on Bandstand. We were sitting there watching
him sing, and I said, 'Ooh, I'm so glad to get a chance to see Jackie
Wilson.' You know, back in those days there was that pride of seeing an
African American on TV. My mother told me, 'You know what? You're
gonna be on there.' That was prophetic, because I didn't get on [American
Bandstand] until I was a freshman in college"[44]

Carla Thomas started composing her own songs around this time, while she was still in high school, blending sounds she heard on the radio and on records her father brought back from WDIA. "I used to sit around just like Daddy and write songs," she said. One of these songs turned out to be "Gee Whiz," which was her first solo recording.

Thomas could see that his eldest daughter had a talent for singing and one day brought a reel-to-reel tape recorder back from the radio station so that they could cut a demo together. "He put it down there on the floor one day, right near the piano. He had a song called 'Deep Down Inside,'" she recalled. "So I started singing it with him, and he taped it. By this time, I guess I was getting ready to graduate [from high school], and I had not really focused on a singing career. I just loved being around the business, and him and my mother too because she just loved just about everything that had to do with music."[45]

Carla graduated from Hamilton High School that summer and didn't give the demo another thought until one Saturday morning when her father suggested they take a ride and check out a new recording studio that was being built over on McLemore Avenue.

Chapter Five

Gee Whiz

The Birth of Stax, 1957-1962

In July 1960, the postman delivered good news to the Thomas household. The postman in question was Robert Talley, who by night was a blues pianist and occasional bandleader. "Robert Talley came by my house and told us that there's a new recording studio down on McLemore and College," Rufus explained.[1]

Talley had heard from his friend, a fellow songwriter who doubled as the local mortician, that the studio had installed brand-new recording equipment, and local musicians could record demos there. "They had this Ampex 350 recorder," Talley later recalled. "So, I told Rufus Thomas, 'Hey, man, let's go over there and do some demos on McLemore.' And that's how we got hooked up."[2]

The recording studio belonged to Satellite, a fledgling record label established by a gentleman by the name of Jim Stewart. Stewart worked in the bond department at the First National Bank in Memphis. He also played the fiddle and, on the weekends, occasionally played with a country swing band called the Canyon Cowboys.[3]

In late 1957, encouraged by the success of Sun Records, which had been established by Sam Phillips in 1952, and the more recent establishment of Hi Records in South Memphis by two former producers at Sun Records, Stewart decided to set up his own recording studio. The original studio was located in a garage belonging to his wife's uncle, decked out with a monoaural recording deck borrowed from his barber and a new set of curtains.

The first song recorded in the new studio was "Blue Roses," a country song composed by Jim himself. It featured a local country singer and disc jockey, Fred Byler, on vocals.

The record sank without a trace despite Byler's radio connections. Nevertheless, the new record label had been launched; it was christened Satellite, after the October 1957 Sputnik launch, which had dominated the news.

The second single cut at the new studio was a rockabilly tune titled "Boppin' High School Baby," sung and composed by a guitarist named Don Willis. The song was more in tune with the music being recorded by Sun Records post-Elvis, but at this stage in his nascent music career, Jim Stewart had yet to learn the basics of music distribution, which required a relationship with both distributors and local disc jockeys.

Around this time, Stewart started working with a young guitarist and sound engineer by the name of Lincoln Wayne Moman, nicknamed "Chips" because of his prowess at the poker table. Moman was born in LaGrange, Georgia, and had hitchhiked his way to Memphis in 1950, when he was fourteen years old. Having taught himself to play guitar, he moved to Los Angeles in 1957, where he played with rockabilly singer Johnny Burnette. He later toured with Gene Vincent before a car crash brought him back to Memphis to recuperate.[4]

Later that year, however, the new label ran into problems. Jim's wife's uncle wanted the garage back, so they would need to find new premises. More importantly, Jim's barber left town, taking his monoaural tape recorder with him.

At this point, two people came to Jim's rescue: his new barber and his older sister, Estelle Stewart Axton, who worked as a bank teller at the Union Planters Bank in Memphis.

His new barber, Mr. Mitchell, learned of Jim's dilemma and offered the use of an old storage facility in Brunswick, around twenty miles east of Memphis. The location was an issue not just because of the distance from the city center but because it was right next to a railroad track. "It seemed like every time we tried to do a professional session, these trains would come by and jar the building," Estelle later recalled.[5]

Stewart and Axton cleaned out the old storage facility and put up new tiles to improve the acoustics. Axton then persuaded her husband Everett that it made good financial sense to invest in a recording studio and remortgaged her family home to invest $2,500 (around $22,000 in 2020) in the company. And it was this investment that enabled Satellite to purchase an Ampex 350 mono console tape recorder and Estelle to become joint owner of the new record label.

In the summer of 1959, "Chips" Moman is thought to have introduced Jim and Estelle Stewart to a Black R&B group from West Memphis called the Veltones. They recorded a song called "Fool in Love," cowritten by

Moman and drummer Jerry Arnold. It featured doo-wop style harmony vocals and some vibrato-heavy twangy guitar, presumably courtesy of Moman himself. It's a far cry from Satellite's early recordings, both in style and the more professional sound of the recording. It also marked Satellite's first exposure to R&B.

Jim Stewart may have been a country boy at heart, but he knew enough about R&B to realize that he needed to approach the city's main African American radio station, WDIA, to get any chance of airplay. And it was there that he first encountered the local disc jockey, Rufus Thomas, who had recorded some earlier R&B singles of his own on local labels like Sun and Meteor. Thomas offered to play the new single, but despite his help and a national distribution deal for the single with Mercury Records, the song failed to make a mark on the R&B charts.

In the months that followed, Satellite recorded just one additional single, by Charles Heinz; again, without success. The Brunswick studio also served as a rehearsal space for a white high school rock group that dabbled in R&B and called themselves—without a hint of irony—the Royal Spades. The band was led by a young guitarist by the name of Steve Cropper.[6]

"A guy comes up to me in the hallway at Messick High School and he says, 'I hear you've got a great band!'" recalled Cropper. "I said, 'Well, thanks,' thinking I'm talking to a guy in another band. He says, 'I wanna be in your band.' I said, 'Well, we're not looking for anybody. What do you play?' He said, 'Saxophone.' I said, 'Really? We don't have any horns, but you never know. How long have you been playing?' He said, 'I've been taking lessons for three months!'"[7]

That guy was Charles "Packy" Axton, the eighteen-year-old son of Estelle Axton.

"Somewhere in that conversation he said that his uncle owned a recording studio," Cropper continued. "Later I found out that Jim Stewart had some recording equipment in a garage in North Memphis! That passed for a studio back then."[8]

In early 1960, Jim Stewart started the process of looking for an alternative location for Satellite's studio, closer to the city and away from the noise of the railroad tracks. It was "Chips" Moman who found the perfect new location, a disused movie house, the Capitol Theater, located on the corner of College and McLemore in South Memphis.

The building had been constructed in 1931, but with the onset of television in the late 1950s had closed down. By 1959, the building was vacant and available to hire for just $150 per month. Jim Stewart was excited by the new location because it had space for a record store where the concession stand used to be located; he thought this would be good for business and bring in regular cash flow. "Chips" Moman had other ideas. He noted the theater was located in a bustling commercial African American neighborhood and thought it was an ideal location to attract some of the emerging new R&B bands from downtown Memphis.[9]

The first task facing Stewart and Axton was to covert the old movie theater into a recording studio. "The studio wasn't designed like studios are today," Cropper remembered. "I mean, we took this old theatre [sic] and pulled the seats out of it. We had to go and hammer all of the screws down into the concrete before we could put carpet down. And we were all there helping to do that, making burlap baffles and so on, without any knowledge at all of what we were doing."[10]

Jim Stewart also enlisted the help of other members of the Royal Spades in the renovation work, including Axton's son Packy and a saxophonist by the name of Don Nix. Stewart opted to save money by keeping the theater's sloped floor and then constructed a wall to divide the old theater, building a control booth on what was the old stage. In hindsight, the unusual shape of the studio, with its sloping floor and ceiling, created a unique sound that musicians claimed produced a "live" feel, with sound reverberating around the walls.

And so it was that one Saturday morning, Thomas invited his eldest daughter, Carla, to join him as he checked out the new studio. "So, he asked me one day, 'These people called me to come down and look at this theater that was being renovated into a new recording studio down near Lemoyne.' And I said, 'Okay!' He never really asked me to go places," she explained. "As I was in school and doing so much and in this singing group, he just probably figured I was too busy. But one day he said, 'I'm going down there. Do you want a ride?' And I was going, 'Ooh, Daddy's asking me to go somewhere!'"[11]

While Rufus Thomas had met with Jim Stewart previously, he still felt reservations as he made his way through the theater's main entrance and introduced himself to Estelle Axton. "At that time, really, I thought nothing about white folk," he later admitted. "I'm thinking that all white folk are the same. I'm trying to get my talent out there and they were the ones who could give me that chance to expose my talent." [12]

Stewart gave them a guided tour of the building and showed them the work that was being carried out. At this stage, Carla recalled, they had not yet put in any sound isolation. "So when we were getting ready to leave, Jim said, 'Well, ask Daddy if he has ever thought about recording again!' Dad said, 'Yeah.' Jim said, 'Well, you got anything? I could hear it right now before you leave.' Now that was weird. In his glove compartment, Daddy had 'Deep Down Inside' that we had taped on that reel-to-reel. And he went there and put it on the board. They had just put this little board in. It wasn't but about four tracks. And Jim said, 'Why don't we cut that?' So Daddy was like, 'Fine!' It wasn't like [it was] planned."[13]

Thomas needed no further invitation, and a few days later—the renovation work presumably completed—he returned to the studio with his eighteen-year-old son, Marvell, who played piano, and Bob Talley's band, which featured an eighteen-year-old drummer by the name of Howard Grimes, who would later go on to play with the likes of Al Green and Ann Peebles as a member of the fabled Hi Records' rhythm section.

The recording process went smoothly until Stewart reminded Thomas that he needed to think about a B-side. "Jim said, 'Well, we need one more song,' Carla said. 'A 45's got to have two sides!' So Dad stood right there by the piano and [wrote] "Cause I Love You' . . . in the studio, right there!"[14]

Jim liked the new song and suggested they record it as a duet, featuring Carla Thomas. "Dad looked at me. I'm going, 'Huh? I'm getting ready to go to college. I don't know about this!' Of course, I started getting a little anxious," she recalled.

Talley assisted Rufus Thomas with the arrangement of the new song, "borrowing" the rhythm from a regional hit—Jesse Hill's "Ooh Poo Pah Doo." With Marvell Thomas playing piano, Robert Talley played trumpet on the session. The young high school guitarist, Steve Cropper, was recruited to play guitar, and Thomas brought in bass player Wilbur Steinberg, who at the age of twenty-six, was a "veteran" on the Memphis music scene, although previously unknown to Jim Stewart.

Once the rhythm section found the groove, Talley suggested it might sound better if they added some baritone saxophone. Talley's regular singer, David Porter, recommended a young multi-instrumentalist he knew by the name of Booker T. Jones; the only snag—he was fifteen years old and still in high school.

Porter borrowed a car, swung by Jones's high school, and asked the high school band teacher if he could use Jones's help for a recording session.

As it happens, Jones was familiar with the new recording studio. He lived in the neighborhood and was a regular customer of the record store that was located to the right of the lobby, where the snack bar had been located. "I had heard the music coming from behind the curtain while I listened to hundreds of records in the store," he later recalled. But he had never summoned up the courage to venture behind the curtain.

Once he finally did enter the studio, he recognized the young guitarist as being the clerk from the record store. They had little chance to interact that afternoon, with the pianist playing behind a sound divider, but would spend plenty of time together in the years ahead as founder members of Booker T. & the M.G.'s.

Jim Stewart was thrilled with both the new song and the arrangement and suggested making "'Cause I Love You" the A-side of the single, which was credited to Carla and Rufus. It features a delightful call-and-response between Rufus and Carla, with Rufus playing the clown trying to win his woman back and Carla sounding mature beyond her years. The arrangement, which was probably down to both Thomas and Talley, allowed plenty of space for Booker T.'s memorable baritone sax line and Marvell's fine piano.

The single was released in August 1960. Part of the publishing for the song was credited to John R. (Richbourg), a disc jockey based at radio station WLAC in Nashville. The station boasted a strong radio signal that could be heard throughout the South, and with a vested interest in the single, he was bound to give it plenty of air time. With little previous experience in promoting R&B, this idea must have come from Thomas, a disc jockey himself and a man never short of marketing ideas.

There were no program directors in those days, so Thomas and his colleagues at WDIA made sure the song was played on a regular basis. Thomas also called in a favor from his friend Dick "Cane" Cole at WLOK, Memphis's only other R&B radio station, who also helped out. Thomas even managed to get some air time in San Francisco through the Sonderling Broadcasting chain, which owned WDIA.

Pretty soon, calls started coming in to the record label from radio stations and record stores across the South. Jim Stewart even recalled getting into his car with Thomas himself and delivering copies of the record by hand. Satellite had its very first local hit record!

But things were about to get a whole lot bigger. Once the single had sold fifteen or twenty thousand copies, Plastic Products—which pressed Satellite's records—mentioned the song to Atlantic's promotional man the next time he came through Memphis, and a few days later, Atlantic producer and partner Jerry Wexler picked up the phone and called Jim Stewart directly.[15]

Wexler introduced himself as the producer of "What'd I Say" by Ray Charles. Even with his country background, Stewart knew what that meant, with the song having hit No. 1 on the R&B chart the previous year and crossed over to the mainstream pop charts, reaching as high as No. 6. He offered Stewart a deal to lease and distribute "'Cause I Love You" nationwide, and a five-year option on what Stewart and Axton took to be all future duets by Carla and Rufus. But with no written contract in place, that deal was soon called into question.

The amount paid by Atlantic for that initial master has been the subject of much debate. In *Sweet Soul Music* by Peter Guralnick, Jim Stewart remembered receiving $2,000. Axton was convinced the figure was just $1,000. But in a 1986 interview with Rob Bowman, Jim Stewart recalled the figure as $5,000.[16]

Now that so many years have passed and with no written contract in place, the truth will never be known. "'Cause I Love You" was eventually released on the Atco label, a subsidiary of Atlantic Records, and went on to sell an estimated thirty to forty thousand records nationwide. "We got a percentage rate so small it was unreal," Jim Stewart told Guralnick. "But it was a start. I was really bitten, and this was the big time for me."[17]

Over the next few months, Satellite Records released a mix of country, pop, and R&B singles, but for Jim Stewart, life had changed, and he felt increasingly drawn toward R&B. "It was like a blind man who suddenly gained his sight," he later claimed.[18]

The transition to a fully-fledged R&B label was made easier by a number of local factors. The new studio was located, as "Chips" Moman had noted, in a thriving African American community. The local Big Star grocery store, where the local community would do its weekly shopping, was located opposite the recording studio.[19]

In addition, a local soul food restaurant, Slim Jenkins' Joint—latter immortalized as "Slim Jenkins' Place" on the Booker T. & the M.G.'s album *Hip Hug-Her* in 1967—was located next door. And on the other side of the old theater was the neighborhood television repair shop.

The newly established Satellite Record Shop, which was run by Estelle Axton herself, also helped to breathe life into the neighborhood. Booker T. Jones was an early customer and later told author Robert Gordon that before it opened, he used to have to drive for twenty minutes to Sears to check out the latest releases.

Estelle Axton was also shrewd at marketing and soon hung speakers outside the entrance to the record store in order to attract younger clientele into the new store. "We would dance outside on the sidewalks," singer William Bell later recalled. "I'm sure it was good for business because the kids dancing would attract potential buyers."[20]

The sheer array of predominantly African American talent emerging from Memphis at this time was another factor, as discussed in depth in the preceding chapter. The budding singer and songwriter, David Porter—still only eighteen years old—got a job at the Big Star grocery and would spend most of his spare time in the record shop.

Another former student of Booker T. Washington High School, William C. Brown, started hanging around outside the record store and used to sing doo-wop with his old school friend, John Gary Williams. Jim Stewart eventually gave him a part-time job helping out in the studio, and he eventually went on to form the vocal group the Mad Lads, who started to record for the label in 1964.

Meanwhile, Booker T. Jones used to come in after school, still wearing his Reserve Officer Training Corps ("ROTC") uniform, according to "Chips" Moman. Jones took this opportunity to remind Moman that he played piano as well as baritone saxophone and trombone and soon made the transition from record shop to studio.

And pretty soon, the word started to spread, and the record store became a neighborhood hangout. "[Drummer] Al Jackson I knew from high school," recalled singer William Bell. "And I knew Booker for a long time—his family and mine went to the same church."[21]

But the glue that held all these parts together was the attitude of Jim Stewart and his sister, Estelle Axton. "Jim and Estelle both were like surrogate parents to all of us," explained William Bell. "This was during segregation back then, and it was wonderful that this white brother and sister would take in all kinds . . . we were all mixed in the confines of Stax!"[22]

Marvell Thomas thought that Estelle Axton was particularly important in this regard. "Estelle was the nucleus," he told Stax biographer Robert Gordon. "Her attitudes about people and her love for people was the reason why the racial harmony existed in that place. Everybody loved her. Black, white, green, purple, we all liked Estelle."[23]

David Porter shared the same view. "She was a person who motivated you to listen to music and to study it and develop an understanding of it. She gave me free access to getting that information," Porter recalled. "I never took a song to her and said 'Estelle, what do you think of this song?' But she was an unbelievable motivator and supporter of me getting into that studio. She was the one who encouraged her brother to take a listen to me. At that time, Jim was still listening to country music."[24]

♦ ♦ ♦

One of the next singles recorded by Satellite was a song called "Gee Whiz" written by Carla Thomas in thirty minutes when she was just fifteen years old. "I had written a lot of songs like that because of Brenda Lee," she later explained. "I used to try to sing all her stuff growing up, and Teresa Brewer and stuff like "A Sweet Old-Fashioned Girl." That was one of my solos in one of the groups I sang in. And Frankie Lymon's 'Why Do Fools Fall in Love.' I sang songs like that, so I was used to writing. Because that was my era, I wrote like that."[25]

Her father Rufus had seen the song's potential at that time and cut a demo for Carla, taking it to Vee-Jay Records in Chicago. "I think at that time, we were so in love with Jerry Butler and The Impressions and Curtis Mayfield . . . so he thought that would be a good label," Carla later recalled.[26]

"I took it to Vee Jay on my vacation and let them listen," Thomas later explained to author Peter Guralnick. "They said, 'Well, you know, this is all right,' but it stayed up there a whole year, and so when I went back on vacation the following year I picked it up and brought it back."[27]

But when Thomas played the same demo to Satellite boss Jim Stewart in the summer of 1960, he immediately heard the hit potential. "I knew 'Gee Whiz' was a great song when I first heard Carla do it," said Jim. "A hit record. You just get this feeling."

Jim wanted to record the song properly and provide Carla with a lush arrangement that would bring out the song's full potential. He booked the Veltones, who had previously recorded a single for Satellite, to do the background vocals. He also arranged for a three-piece string section led by his former violin teacher Noel Gilbert.

However, with Atlantic's money in the bank, he liked the idea of making even higher-quality recordings—even though the record company was not yet generating a steady cash flow. In addition, he was not convinced that his Satellite's Ampex tape machine and four-channel mixer were really up to the task of recording more complex arrangements.

Stewart arranged to record Carla and the musicians at the Hi Records studio in a different neighborhood. It was a decision he came to regret. "It was too fast," he later recalled. "I couldn't hear the magic."

Despite the expense of paying union rates all over again for a string section, Stewart arranged to rerecord the song. The second session took place on a hot August afternoon at the Satellite studio on McLemore Avenue, which lacked air conditioning. As with "'Cause I Love You," piano player Bob Talley had been hired to work on the arrangements. He had played a gig the night before, however, and failed to show up. As a result, Stewart himself took over, working out the arrangement on the fly with Gilbert.

When they were finally ready to go, it was 5 p.m., and the musicians were making overtime. They rolled the tape, and the seventeen-year-old Carla Thomas managed to get it right on the first take, nailing her vocal at the first attempt.

Carla wrote the flip side to "Gee Whiz," "For You," with "Chips" Moman, and the single was released with the catalog number Satellite 104 in November 1960, just after Carla had started her studies at Tennessee

Agricultural and Industrial College, the largest and only state-funded Black university in Tennessee.

Looking back, "Gee Whiz" is still a delightful song, but even in late 1960, it sounded like a throwback to the sounds of the mid-to-late 1950s. The main thing that distinguished it from many other teen ballads was the innocent quality of Carla's vocal, which holds the listener from the very start. It was a far cry from the funkier Stax sound that was later associated with the label. In many respects, it was this more pop-oriented material that Carla felt most comfortable with—which would cause problems for her in the years to come.

The new single initially made little impact on the charts. "They released it in November, but nothing was happening because they were still promoting "Cause I Love You," Carla remembered. "Plus, you know in the record business how the Christmas records all start coming out, so 'Gee Whiz' got kind of lost in there."[28]

Another problem was that, quite coincidentally, a band called The Innocents had also released a single titled "Gee Whiz" around the same time. It was a different song, originally written by R&B duo Bob & Earl in 1957. Bob & Earl would later go on to have a hit single with "Harlem Shuffle," later recorded by the Rolling Stones. "I wasn't on a show with them, so I never got a chance to meet these guys," Carla later recalled. "I only heard their record. But we were saying, 'Oh my goodness, which one is going to do it?'"

In any event, it was Carla's song that started to make an impression, initially in Memphis and the surrounding area and later in cities like St. Louis.

As with "'Cause I Love You," the record soon came to the attention of Jerry Wexler at Atlantic Records in New York. Hymie Weiss, a music executive, heard the single on numerous occasions while traveling through Memphis and put the call in to Wexler.

Once again, Wexler called Jim Stewart, but this time his tone was more bullying, accusing Stewart of reneging on their agreement. "I started promoting the record on Stax, and then I got a call from Jerry Wexler saying it was his record because Carla was on "Cause I Love You," Stewart revealed. He further explained that from his perspective, the original agreement only applied to duets by Carla and Rufus, not solo recordings by either singer.[29]

Stewart explained to Wexler that he was thinking of remaining independent and that he could make more money by cutting out Atlantic. Wexler countered that Stewart was making a big mistake and that Satellite lacked a nationwide salesforce that could guarantee national airplay and distribution. In the end, Stewart agreed that Carla Thomas would remain signed to Satellite, but that all of her future releases would be released on the Atlantic label.

More importantly, Jim Stewart and Estelle Axton agreed to a new distribution deal with Atlantic Records. Satellite would continue to own the masters but deliver them to Atlantic, who would manufacture and distribute on the Satellite (and later Stax) label. In return, Satellite would be paid a royalty fee of fifteen cents per single that was sold. It was a five-year deal, and although it was more comprehensive than their previous agreement, nothing was put in writing. "In those days, no one hired an attorney to do these things," Jim explained. "It was a one-on-one deal, and my deal was with Jerry Wexler."

The new deal with Atlantic paid immediate dividends for both Carla Thomas and Satellite Records. The single was renamed "Gee Whiz (Look at His Eyes)," partly to avoid confusion with the single by The Innocents and issued by Atlantic with the catalog number Atlantic 2086. With Atlantic's backing, the single started to receive national airplay and climb the charts.

The success of "Gee Whiz" resulted in Carla's first public appearance at WDIA's December Goodwill Revue. The event was held at the Ellis Auditorium in Memphis. After a lengthy campaign by the NAACP over the summer, the WDIA station manager announced that for the first time in its history, the event would be held with "mixed seating." He also announced an impressive lineup including Little Junior Parker, Bobby "Blue" Bland, Bo Diddley, the Five Royales, and Carla Thomas, who was billed as "Memphis's newest teenage star."

As Christmas approached, Carla remembers hearing her song more on the radio. "So, December went by, and all of a sudden I start hearing it more. I start hearing a little more around the middle of January. Then eventually by February, I hear it more and more and more. And in the spring [of 1961] I was invited to do Bandstand in Philly. That was actually the first TV show as far as exposure, which was some heck of exposure!"[30]

With the passing of time, Carla got her dates slightly wrong. Her appearance on Bandstand was actually January 27, 1961. "I was singing, and I saw this little bench over there and I thought it was something I could sit on. It was a prop," she laughed. "It was kind of like cardboard or something, but they had it fixed up so beautiful with flowers all over it, and I said, 'I think I'll just go and sit on there.' It looked so sturdy, the way they had it. They said [from the side of the stage], 'Oh no! No, no, no, please!' And then afterwards we talked about it on the interview. [Dick Clark] said, 'I am so glad you did not sit on that. That would have been over!' I'll never forget that!"[31]

Carla Thomas, early promotional photograph, circa 1961. Photographer unknown.

Three days after Carla's appearance on Bandstand, on January 30, "Gee Whiz (Look at His Eyes)" entered *Billboard*'s Hot Top 100 chart; on March 27, it peaked at No. 10, spending a total of fourteen weeks on the Top 100. It also reached No. 5 on *Billboard*'s R&B Singles chart. With the help of Atlantic's distribution, Satellite had achieved their first crossover hit.

The success of both "'Cause I Love You" and "Gee Whiz" had a big impact on the Thomas household. Lorene quit her job as a nurse, although she continued to do voluntary work with the NAACP. "She stopped nursing when Carla got her big hit, because Carla was a minor, and Mother would travel with her," explained Vaneese Thomas. "So she couldn't work anymore. She traveled with her from the time she was eighteen until she graduated from college. My mother was the chaperone!"[32]

As "Gee Whiz" continued its rise up the charts, Atlantic was keen to bring Carla to New York for a promotional show as part of an R&B revue. Jerry Wexler decided to fly from New York to Memphis to discuss the arrangements with Stewart directly. This was in part because he wanted to smooth things over with him after the recent renegotiation of their distribution deal. But in addition, he was keen to meet Carla Thomas, the rising star of both Satellite Records and Atlantic.

After a guided tour of the Satellite studio and record store, Wexler offered to take Jim Stewart out for dinner, inviting Rufus and Lorene Thomas and their daughter Carla to join them. "Of course, during that time, you couldn't go to a restaurant with African American people because segregation was going on in this city," Stewart remembered. "Wexler suggested we meet him at his hotel for dinner. We couldn't meet downstairs for dinner, so we ordered dinner up in his room. We could not go up in the elevator from the lobby. We had to go to the rear of the building and go up in the freight elevator. I still remember this like it was yesterday. I felt hugely embarrassed and angry. Here was a young lady who had a Top Ten record in the country but could not walk through the lobby of the Claridge Hotel in Memphis, Tennessee."[33]

Rufus Thomas was understandably incensed. "I refused to go and ride an elevator," he later revealed. "Now I'm clean, I'm sharp, I got on my good clothes and I'm looking as good or better than Jerry Wexler or any of the rest of the group that was with us including all those white folks. I'm cleaner than, than . . . nineteen yards of chitlins and you clean them up good to eat them. And I rebelled, I decided I'm not going and I turned around to go back."[34]

Lorene Thomas, always a strong advocate for civil rights, persuaded her husband to back down for the sake of Carla's career. But she confronted both Jim Stewart and Jerry Wexler about what had transpired. "Never again will you ask my husband to go in the back door of any establishment and especially on a freight elevator."

Dinner went well, with food served on carts by the hotel staff. "We had dinner in there and we talked," Thomas remembered. "They talked real good about what Satellite and Atlantic were going to do, how they were gonna market the records, about New York and Tennessee, the North and the South coming together for a common cause, and that was the records."[35]

The dinner party broke up amicably at around 10 p.m., and the Thomas family headed home. "Soon after, Jerry Wexler was almost arrested," revealed Jim Stewart. "The police came up, knocked on his door and tried to arrest him for having an African-American in his hotel room. I'll never forget that."[36]

When the police found Wexler's room to be empty, they eventually let him off with a warning. Wexler called the police chief the next morning. "This is the Stone Age," he told him. "And that's what you are, and your cops are—Stone Age!"[37]

Mission finally accomplished, Carla did eventually make it to the Brooklyn Paramount in New York to take her place in a lineup that included the likes of Jackie Wilson and Little Anthony. She was accompanied by her mother, Lorene, who protected her from the numerous backstage visitors to her dressing room. "Mummy became the backstage mother because people like Jackie Wilson and Sam Cooke would drop by the room to say hi, or 'I have a button come off, would you sew that on for me, Ms. Thomas?'"[38]

Carla only performed two songs that evening—"Gee Whiz" and "For You"—but described the experience of being on the same stage as her idols as "one of the highlights of my life."

♦ ♦ ♦

Back in Memphis, Satellite Records had yet to develop its own house band, but with both Jim Stewart and Estelle Axton still engaged in their day jobs during the week, "Chips" Moman was effectively the gatekeeper to the studio.

The combination of the new recording studio, which had just produced a nationwide hit, and the record store produced a steady stream of visitors; they were a mix of old and young, club musicians and high school students, Black and white.

One day there might be experienced horn players dropping by, like baritone saxophonist Floyd Newman, who had just returned to Memphis after going to college in Detroit, or fellow saxophonist Fred "Sweet Daddy Goodlow" Ford, a regular at the Flamingo Club and Club Paradise.

Estelle's son, Packy Axton, used to arrive at 926 East McLemore in the early afternoon, and at various times, depending on their jobs, he would be joined by other members of the band he belonged to, the Royal Spades, such as guitarist Steve Cropper or saxophonist Don Nix. "Chips" Moman would encourage them to play the latest R&B hits or arrange jam sessions with the more experienced club musicians.

And at 4:30 p.m., Estelle Axton would show up, having finished work at the bank, and would be playing the latest hits in the record shop, with graduates (and undergraduates) of Booker T. Washington High School popping in to listen. Booker T. Jones recalls Estelle introducing him to the sounds of John Coltrane at this time while she would also discuss the song structure of the latest hits to David Porter, who was already writing songs of his own.

It was this fertile, creative atmosphere that produced Satellite's next big hit. Since forming in high school days, the Royal Spades had gradually evolved from being an enthusiastic blues-oriented band, playing covers

Rufus Thomas at the Satellite Records shop. Photograph by Don Nix courtesy of the Oklahoma Museum of Popular Culture, Steve Todoroff Collection.

of Jimmy Reed, to a full-fledged R&B band, influenced by the likes of The Fives Royales, Hank Ballard and the Midnighters, and Bill Doggett. "Everybody in that band loved the same music," explained bass player Donald "Duck" Dunn. "Everybody in that band loved Black guys' music. Here was a bunch of white guys trying to do Black guys' music—but we started to get some attention, and we started getting some notoriety."[39]

By this stage, the band included guitarist Steve Cropper, bassist Donald "Duck" Dunn, trumpeter Wayne Jackson, tenor saxophonist Charles "Packy" Axton, baritone saxophonist William Donald "Don" Nix, keyboard player Lee "Smoochy" Smith, and drummer Terry Johnson.

The origins of the band's debut single, "Last Night," are mired in controversy. The simple horn patterns were apparently developed by Floyd Newman, who was messing around in the studio with fellow saxophonist Gilbert Caple, a regular at the Plantation Inn. Newman also claims to have come up with the spoken line "Ooh, last night," which gives the tune a more suggestive feel.

"Chips" Moman heard the potential and brought in some of the Royal Spades, who were in the studio at that time. "Smoochy" Smith came up with the distinctive organ riff, which dovetailed perfectly with the horns. "Packy" Axton and Wayne Jackson joined the horn section. Moman felt there was no need for guitar, so Steve Cropper played piano on the session. "Duck" Dunn was working on the day of the recording, so the experienced Lewie Steinberg—younger brother of Wilbur Steinberg, who played on "'Cause I Love You"—played bass while Curtis Green, another regular at the Plantation Inn, played drums.

Jim Stewart didn't think much of the tune. He and Packy tended to clash at the best of times, and in any case, he was busy working with Carla Thomas on a number of potential new songs. Estelle Axton saw the potential, however, and made a test pressing which she brought to the two Black radio stations, WDIA and WLOK. The response was overwhelming, and Estelle Axton eventually got her way, and the single was released in June 1961.

But that wasn't the end of the story. First of all, she had to convince the band to change its name. While the band claimed the Royal Spades was a poker reference, Estelle was smart enough to realize it had broader connotations and was inappropriate for a white band playing "Black" music. She suggested the Marquees, after the canopy hanging outside the theater, but the guys in the band had issues with the "q" in the name, so it was simplified to the Mar-Keys.

The controversy didn't end there. When the single came out, it was credited to Newman and Caple, who originally developed the horn pattern, but also "Smoochy" Smith, "Chips" Moman, and Packy Axton. Newman and Caple were furious, and felt that the song was their own. To be fair, the organ riff adds a great deal to the tune, and Moman was undoubtedly behind the arrangement as a whole. Packy Axton had little to do with the song, however, and his mother was clearly behind the decision to credit him.

"Last Night" was distributed nationwide by Atlantic on the Satellite label and steadily climbed the charts, peaking at No. 3 on the US pop charts, No. 2 on the R&B charts, and selling over one million copies, earning a gold disc along the way. Guitarist Steve Cropper believes it became a big hit because it was the first instrumental you could do the Twist to. "It had that Hank Ballard twist beat," Cropper noted. "That's exactly why it was popular. It was absolute perfect timing. Everybody was twisting to that song."[40]

It also demonstrated to Jim Stewart and Estelle Axton that instrumentals could be just as successful as vocal recordings.

In September 1961, the record came to the attention of another record label by the name of Satellite in California, which offered to sell the rights to the name to Jim and Estelle Stewart for $1,000. Jim refused to pay, later claiming he never liked the name, anyway. As a result, the label changed its name to Stax Records, the name a portmanteau of the names of the coowners, Jim Stewart and Estelle Axton.

As for the Mar-Keys, the original lineup disintegrated before the year came to an end. They did a few dates with Carla Thomas when she was back for the Christmas holidays. "Miss Axton traveled with us," Carla later recalled. "She was our mother. We went everywhere—all around. I was the Black girl with the white band . . . we would play to a lot of rhythm and blues audiences, mostly Black."[41]

Lorene Thomas, Carla's mother, eventually decided that was a bad idea. The eight guys—Newman and Caple had not been invited to join—continued on their own in a van. Tensions were running high between Cropper, who regarded himself as the founder and organizer, and "Packy" Axton, who saw himself as the "spiritual" leader. Axton's heavy drinking was another factor as the party spirit got out of hand.

"They were horrible to be on the road with," said Cropper, laughing. "They had no manners! I just couldn't take it anymore. So, at Shreveport, Louisiana, at the end of the tour, we got this gig to play at the Show Bar in Bossier City. We were there for about three weeks. In the middle of the second week, we were taking a break and [had] gone to the restroom. We were standing in the stalls, and I looked at Packy and said, 'Packy, you've always wanted to be the leader of this band. You've got it! I'm catching a bus to Memphis tomorrow morning.'"[42]

Cropper quit the band, caught a bus back to Memphis, and reenrolled in Memphis State College. Within a few days, he was back at the record store, working part-time and helping out in the studio.

While Estelle was focused on promoting the Mar-Keys, Jim Stewart was more focused on Carla Thomas, whom he regarded as the label's biggest star. With Carla enrolled at college at Tennessee A & I in Nashville, Jim arranged to record her next two singles in a Nashville studio. The first of these, "A Love of My Own," was written by Carla while she was at the university. The song is lovely but somewhat overpowered by the syrupy Nashville string arrangement and the sterile backing vocals of the Anita Kerr singers. Despite this, the single was a modest success, peaking at No. 20 on the R&B charts in the spring of 1961 and No. 56 on the pop charts.

The follow-up, "(Mama, Mama) Wish Me Good Luck," was another self-penned tune, again recorded in Nashville. The results were less memorable, sadly, and the song failed to make an impression on the charts.

Atlantic Records seemed eager to cash in on their investment in Carla Thomas, and released her debut album, named after her smash hit single, in the autumn of 1961. The remainder of the album was recorded in

Nashville in two separate recording sessions in March and May of 1961. As one would probably expect, the album is a mix of songs composed by Carla Thomas herself, other members of the Stax team, including Rufus Thomas and "Chips" Moman, and covers of recent R&B and doo-wop hits by the likes of The Drifters, the Five Satins, and The Harptones.

"Dance With Me," a No. 2 hit on the R&B charts for The Drifters in 1959, works well, but the other Drifters' cover, "Fools Fall in Love," is marred by another Nashville production-line string arrangement. "I thought I'd get a better string sound," Jim Stewart later admitted. "I was misleading myself, actually. I didn't know what I had in that [McLemore] studio."[43]

Some of the other covers, such as "To the Aisle" (Five Satins) and "The Masquerade Is Over" (The Harptones), again feature the Anita Kerr singers on backing vocals, giving the doo-wop-oriented tunes a country feel. Granted, Carla Thomas had grown up listening to Brenda Lee's more country-oriented songs, but in hindsight, one wonders why they didn't use William Bell's vocal group, the Del-Rios.

Carla Thomas again proved that she was a very promising songwriter with "It Ain't Me" in particular, demonstrating a maturity beyond her years. Rufus Thomas's own contribution, "Your Love," also seemed well-suited to Carla's style and is one of the album's other highlights.

Overall, it's a more pop-oriented album than her later recordings, but it is the arrangements—both string and vocal—that lend the album a somewhat dated feel rather than the material.

The album failed to chart despite being issued by Atlantic Records rather than Stax Records. One would assume that Atlantic's marketing team would have given priority to their own artists rather than those effectively on loan from another label. The fact that Carla was at college when the album was released and had limited time for promotional work may also have been a factor.

◆ ◆ ◆

Singer William Bell, a vocalist in the Del Rios, had been talking to "Chips" Moman about a possible recording session. "'Chips' started asking me, 'Why don't you do a single recording?'" Bell later recalled. "I always resisted it, because I did that Meteor recording and it was popular with the college crowd and in the Tri-state area but not a national hit or anything. I was just kinda disillusioned with the recording industry."[44]

In the meantime, he had landed a six-week gig in New York with the Phineas Newborn Orchestra. When the gig was extended, the homesick young singer wrote a handful of new songs, including the plaintive ballad

"You Don't Miss Your Water." "We had a couple of days off and I was in the hotel one weekend, one Sunday night," Bell recalled. "And it was raining and storming and I was missing home and missing my girlfriend at home. I was just missing stuff, and of course one of those old sayings came up: "You don't miss your water until your well runs dry.""[45]

When he finally returned to Memphis, Moman persuaded him to record a few sides at the Stax studio. "You Don't Miss Your Water" was originally recorded with a three-piece rhythm section that included Marvell Thomas on piano and horns courtesy of some of the members of the Mar-Keys. An organ overdub was added later, courtesy of "Spooky" Butler, which added to the song's gospel feel.

Jim Stewart thought the song was too "churchy" to be a major hit but agreed it should be released as a single in November 1961. The song could easily have gotten lost in the Christmas market, but there was a subtle elegance to Bell's writing and singing that struck a chord with radio listeners. By the time the New Year broke, it was picking up airplay in cities like Baton Rouge, New Orleans, and in Florida. Strangely, it didn't reach the nationwide R&B charts, but It was a big enough regional hit that it made William Bell—not Rufus Thomas—the label's first male solo star.

"You Don't Miss Your Water" is now regarded as one of the cornerstones of Southern Soul, combining elements of country, blues, and gospel. It became a key element of the Memphis sound, feeding into numerous key recordings at Stax Records, Hi Records, and FAME studios at Muscle Shoals. The song itself was later covered by Otis Redding, the Byrds, and Taj Mahal.

Sadly, it was one of the last recording sessions engineered at the Stax studios by "Chips" Moman. He left after a bitter argument with Jim Stewart, claiming that Stewart had reneged on a deal that would allow him to become part-owner of the label. Two years later, in 1964, he established the American Sound Studio in Memphis, where he would go on to record numerous hits for the likes of Bobby Womack, Aretha Franklin, Dusty Springfield, Neil Diamond, and even Elvis Presley himself. "I wish we could have kept 'Chips,'" said Carla, who had worked closely with him on her early recordings. "I really liked him very much. We just seemed to click, you know?"[46]

In the first half of 1962, Jim Stewart—for now the sole producer/engineer—recorded a number of vocal groups, including a female group, the Tonettes, and the Canes. He also released a single by William Bell's group, the Del-Rios, presumably in an attempt to cash in on the success of "You Don't Miss Your Water." Two singles were also released by a new-look Mar-Keys, but the band struggled to replicate their earlier success.

By this stage, a house band had emerged, composed of Booker T. Jones on keyboards, Lewie Steinberg on bass, Steve Cropper on guitar, and drummer Al Jackson Jr., a friend of Booker T.'s who had been playing in Willie Mitchell's band. Depending on the recording session, Stewart would occasionally add the horn section of the Mar-Keys, which later became known as the Memphis Horns.

Quite by accident, the house band recorded a hit single—the label's first in six months. The precise details have been lost in the mists of time, but the four musicians were messing around in the studio, either waiting for the rockabilly singer Billy Lee Riley to show up or winding down after the session was over. They had already recorded a blues tune called "Behave Yourself," which Jim Stewart considered to be good enough to release as a single.

When he suggested they record a B-side, the band started working on a riff that Jones had developed in conjunction with Steve Cropper. The tune is set to the most basic of blues beats, but when Cropper's guitar started to cut across Booker T.'s funky organ, sparks started to fly. "We were all real excited about this thing," Steve Cropper recalled. "I thought it was so good, I needed a dub of it. Scotty Moore was a good friend of mine, and he ran the lathe over at Sun—a Neumann lathe. I said, 'Can you cut me a dub on something we cut yesterday?' He said, 'Absolutely!'"[47]

When Cropper arranged for the new song to be played on WLOK the next morning, the phones lit up. "They were asking who was playing, where they could buy it," Cropper recalled.[48]

Estelle Axton called Jim Stewart at the bank and requested an emergency meeting for that evening. "We had no name for the group, we had no name for the record, and we had to get the damn thing out," said Cropper, laughing. The band all agreed that the tune was funky, and it was bass player Lewie Steinberg who suggested the name "Onions," arguing that they were the funkiest—meaning smelliest—thing he could think of. Estelle Axton added "Green" to the title, and "Green Onions" was born.

The house band also needed a name. Drummer Al Jackson looked outside of the front of the recording studio, saw a British-made M.G. sports car parked there, and suggested Booker T. & the M.G.'s. "The reason we called it that, there were a lot of 'car groups' in them days," explained Steve Cropper. "Later, we got a letter from MG's lawyers saying that we don't endorse anything to do with music. But we thought, 'We ain't changing the name.'" And so "M.G.'s" came to refer to "Memphis Group."[49]

Years later, there was still confusion as to where the name was derived from. "In 1977, we had an album out called *Universal Language*," said Cropper. "The person interviewing us said, 'I know it's been a long time, guys, but what does M.G.'s really stand for?' And Donald 'Duck' Dunn says, 'Musical Geniuses!'"[50]

"Green Onions" was a milestone recording for Stax Records. It entered the *Billboard* pop charts in August 1962, and peaked at No. 3 in late September. The single also made it to No. 1 on the R&B singles chart for four non-consecutive weeks—an unusual feat, in that it fell in and out of top spot three times.

The song also had a considerable impact on the emerging "mod" scene (derived from "modern" or "modernist") in the UK, with pianist Georgie Fame—leader of Georgie Fame and the Blue Flames—claiming it was this song that prompted him to switch from piano to Hammond organ during his three-year residency at The Flamingo Club in London. It put Stax on the map, if not the charts, and eventually paved the way for a highly successful UK tour in 1966.

By the end of 1962, Stax Records was back in ascendancy with a number of crossover hits under its belt, including "Gee Whiz," "Last Night," and "Green Onions," which hit both the Pop and R&B charts. They also had a new house band, which, going forward, helped to provide the label with a "trademark" gritty soul sound, less polished and more funky than Detroit's Motown label—and a sound that, at least for now, was pure Memphis.

Just as important, they had a deal with one of the major labels—Atlantic Records—that gave them nationwide distribution rather than just regional distribution. And if the royalty rate seemed low, that felt like a small price to pay after the success of "Green Onions."

When Rufus Thomas walked into the newly established label just two years earlier, Jim Stewart had suggested he record the duet "'Cause I Love You" with Carla, which was credited to Carla and Rufus, and then he would alternate between solo recordings by both Rufus Thomas and Carla Thomas, interspersed with the occasional duet.

But things hadn't quite worked out as planned. Carla's debut solo recording, "Gee Whiz," had been a smash hit. Jim Stewart then focused his attention on his new solo star, even supervising her debut album.

Rufus Thomas had recorded a couple of solo singles, "I Didn't Believe"—which also featured Carla—and "Can't Ever Let You Go," but neither had made any impression on the charts.

But Rufus remained positive and upbeat, confident that things were about to change.

Chapter Six

Walking the Dog

Rufus and the British "Mod" Scene, 1963-1964

The newly formed Booker T. & the M.G.'s was now the biggest and brightest act on the label, having effectively topped both the R&B and pop charts in the fall of 1962. The only drawback? The young keyboard player and multi-instrumentalist who provided the band with its name, Booker T. Jones, was still in high school when the song was recorded. And while the song started to climb the charts as he was on his summer vacation, he had his heart set on going to college that September. "I didn't want anything to interfere with my obtaining a music education and a college degree like my parents and grandfather wanted," he wrote in his recent autobiography, *Time is Tight: My Life, Note by Note*.[1]

Looking back, Booker T. still feels he made the right decision for himself, even if it was difficult for the other members of the band to accept. "For me, it was essential," he explained. "I was hearing music in my head for years as a boy. My Mum played piano, and I had a good piano teacher, but no one told me how to write it down and tell me exactly what it was. I had to know. That's what I found out in Indiana; how to navigate it and how to write. If I hadn't gone, it would have driven me crazy!"[2]

The band's guitarist, Steve Cropper, remembers being disappointed by his decision at the time. "I was a little bit upset with Booker because we had a number one record on *Billboard* and around the world with 'Green Onions,' and he goes off to college," he recalled. "I thought, 'wait a minute, you can always go back to college.' Years later I thought if he hadn't have done that, there would never have been an Isaac Hayes—because Isaac was a replacement for when Booker was not around."[3]

With Booker about to leave Memphis for Indiana University, Jim Stewart persuaded the band to quickly record a debut album. The resulting album, also called *Green Onions*, was recorded between June and

August 1962. Given the time constraint, the album primarily consisted of well-chosen covers, including "I Got a Woman" by Ray Charles, "Twist and Shout," and Doc Pomus's timeless "Lonely Avenue." Listening now, it's remarkable how quickly the band gelled and established their trademark sound. The album was released in September 1962, by which time Booker T. Jones had already started college.

Amazingly, Booker drove back to Memphis most weekends to help out as part of the house band and to get together with the rest of the M.G.'s, who found the time to record the occasional single. "It was hectic. Every weekend I drove 400 miles back to Memphis," he recalled. "And of course, every summer I spent there. But I was determined to get the degree, and Monday to Friday I was in Indiana. But Stax paid for my education up there; the session money paid for the trips."[4]

The band recorded three brand-new singles in 1963—"Jelly Bread" (released in January), "Home Grown" (February), and "Chinese Checkers" (June). "Jelly Bread" was arguably a little too similar to "Green Onions," and "Home Grown" was perhaps too laid-back for the charts. "Chinese Checkers" is one of the band's finest recordings; however, it features Booker on electric piano rather than organ, and a fantastic horn line, with Booker even doubling on trombone. Amazingly, the song failed to chart, and the band's only success that year was with a song called "Mo' Onions," an original that had appeared on the debut album the previous year.

The first chart success for Stax Records in 1963 came from the man who had recorded their very first hit—Rufus Thomas. In the preceding months, he had struck up a friendship with the young guitarist, Steve Cropper, who used to spend his spare time in Estelle Axton's record store between recording sessions. "Rufus used to come into the record shop; a lot of those DJs did, because the Stax record shop was the place to go, to hear new music and all that," Cropper remembered. "And Mrs. Axton stayed up on all that. She had a great knowledge of music, pop and R&B—but she loved R&B."[5]

One day, Rufus came in with a new song idea that he had developed the previous weekend. "Rufus found out I played guitar," he remembered. "He said, "Well let's go out back and set it up." He knew the studio and knew where to go. I set up my little amp and guitar, and he would kind of hum what he wanted, and I would put some other stuff with it."[6]

A few weeks previously, Rufus's eldest daughter, Carla Thomas, had demonstrated a new dance craze called the Dog to her father. "Carla showed me a new dance," Rufus recalled twenty years later. "But she didn't do it the way it ended up when it was called the Dirty Dog," he added quickly.[7]

Shortly after that, Thomas was performing live in a bar in Tennessee when a girl in the audience started dancing the Dog. Rufus, as ever, was not lost for words and started to improvise. "There was a tall beautiful Black girl, had a long waist line, and she was wearing a black leather skirt; very alluring, slick and sleek. We were playing a rhythm at the time. There is nothing in my head about this song. I was just telling her to do the dog. I changed the rhythm pattern. I was putting it together as we went along. I couldn't think of but three dogs—bulldog, bird dog, hound dog. Then I got to the part where (you) just do any kind of dog, just do the dog."[8]

Rufus brought the idea to Steve Cropper, who brought in other members of the house band, with Marvell Thomas filling in for Booker T. Jones on piano. The house horn section, which would later become known as the Memphis Horns, varied in the early years and would depend on who was available that day. According to Rob Bowman, the Stax historian, it might include Floyd Newman on baritone saxophone, who can be heard on "The Dog," tenor saxophonists that might include Gilbert Caple, Gene Parker, "Packy" Axton, or Andrew Love, and Wayne Jackson or "Bowlegs" Miller on trumpet.

On the final studio recording, the band recorded three choruses, then just played the rhythm while Steve Cropper took a solo. Rufus told everyone in the studio to start barking like a dog over the solo. "I was the lead dog with the bark way up there!" he laughed.[9]

Thomas also remembered stealing the bass line from Willie Mitchell's Hi Records recording of a tune called "The Crawl." Even on these early recordings, Thomas tended to know exactly what he was looking for and arranged most of the songs himself, including the horn section.

"The Dog" was released as a single and hit the charts in February, reaching No. 22 on the R&B chart and No. 87 on the pop chart—his first major solo hit since "Bear Cat." On some dance floors around the country, "Dog" became "Dirty Dog," upsetting some people in the clubs. "In some areas, people were getting arrested for doing it so vulgar," Thomas laughed. "They got all down on the floor . . . had I been the judge, I would have put them in jail, too!"[10]

The church also worried that "The Dog" might be sinful, perhaps concerned that it somehow encouraged people to dance the "Dirty Dog." "My wife went to church a couple of miles from where we lived," said Jim Stewart. "The preacher started his sermon and talked about this awful record, this sinful record, called 'The Dog'! My wife wanted to crawl under the seat. She came home and said people were asking where I was. I told her I was probably in the studio cutting another dog! She was worried they were going to kick her out of the church. The little things like that I remember well."[11]

◆ ◆ ◆

The influence of the song is much bigger than these chart positions suggest, however. Early Stax singles—and the Rufus Thomas singles of 1963 and 1964—had a profound impact on British "mod" culture. They marked the beginning of a British love affair with American "soul" music that arguably culminated in the Stax/Volt Revue UK tour in 1967 but still exists to this day.

To understand the changes taking place in the London music scene at that time, it is helpful to know a little bit about the history of the Flamingo Club in Soho, where Georgie Fame and the Blue Notes were the house band for three years starting in 1962.

The club was originally established in August 1952 by British businessman Jeffrey Kruger, who was a jazz fan. The club was originally situated beneath the Mapleton Restaurant, at the junction of Coventry Street and Whitcomb Street, just off Leicester Square. The club competed with Ronnie Scott's and was promoted as "Britain's most comfortable club," and male visitors were expected to wear ties. The Tony Crombie Quintet, featuring Ronnie Scott and Joe Harriott, became the resident group, and in the years that followed, Sarah Vaughan and Billie Holiday both made appearances at the club.

The club relocated to 33 Wardour Street—still in Soho—in April 1957. The club was run on a day-to-day basis by two brothers, Rik and Johnny Gunnell. The club still focused primarily on jazz, but over the next few years, Kruger's priorities started to change. One problem was that the club had started to arrange "all-nighters" on a Friday and Saturday night, and Kruger felt the jazz musicians took themselves too seriously and didn't provide enough entertainment for the audience. The second issue was the Flamingo's audience had also begun to change. The all-nighters had started to attract a new audience which included West Indians and African American soldiers still based in England.

"[It was] the GIs [from American military bases set up in England during WWII] who influenced the decision I made to introduce the all-nighters," Kruger explained. "They brought records from the States, and from these sounds, new thoughts were conveyed to our jazz musicians and people like Georgie Fame."[12]

To reflect this change, Kruger introduced a Jamaican DJ into the club to host the all-nighters. "First we used Jamaica's Count Suckle and his then-monumental sound system," said Kruger. "He featured Jamaican

Georgie Fame at the Flamingo Club, 1963. Photographer unknown.

music sounds not previously heard in the confines of a jazz venue, and he introduced ska and reggae." At this point, it's fair to say male visitors were no longer expected to wear ties.[13]

The all-nighters were predominantly frequented by the local West Indian population and American GIs in the early days. "There were only a handful of hip young white people that used to go to the Flamingo," Georgie Fame recalled many years later. "When I first went there as a punter, I was scared. Once I started to play there, it was no problem."

Georgie Fame and his band, the Blue Flames, were originally the backup band for the English rock 'n' roll singer Billy Fury. Indeed, it was Fury's manager, Larry Parnes, who convinced the young keyboard player to change his name from Clive Powell to the "cooler" Georgie Fame. In 1962, Fury decided that the band were too "jazzy" for him, and the band went out on their own, with Fame taking over on lead vocals.

Fame had a prodigious knowledge of jazz and blues, including the likes of Mose Allison, who was a key influence. But he was also open to "new" sounds that he heard at the Flamingo, including new releases that he picked up from Count Suckle and other visiting GIs. When Fame heard Suckle play "Green Onions" by Booker T. & the M.G.'s for the first time, he made the decision to switch from piano to organ.

Around this time, in late 1962, Georgie Fame and the Blue Flames started playing at the Flamingo on a regular basis, and before long, they became the house band. Playing the all-nighters was always a challenge, as the band had a limited repertoire in the beginning. "We were always seeking out new material," remembered the band's saxophonist, Mike Eve. "Everyone was eager each week to contribute. Red [Reece], the drummer or me [sic] might turn up with a single we'd acquired and play it to Georgie. We'd always have one or two new tunes each week, otherwise we'd get bored. Once we'd got the organ, 'Night Train' (Jimmy Forrest) and 'Green Onions' were a must. All the Rufus Thomas stuff, plus 'Let the Sun Shine In' [Teddy Randazzo]."[14]

By the time it got to around 4 a.m., the band would be starting to fade, and one of the band members would suggest a ballad to slow the tempo. "So we'd get away with a nice slow tune . . . it would change the mood," Eve continued. "Then John Gunnel [the club manager] would come out and ask us to liven it up so we'd have to do something like 'Do the Dog.'"[15]

The mention of Rufus Thomas's song, "The Dog," is interesting because while it was a single in the US, Stax Records was a relatively unknown label in the UK at that time, and that particular song was never released as a single. In all likelihood, it was one of the singles brought in by one of the American GIs that caught the attention of the band. They started to include it in their repertoire, and it soon became a crowd favorite.

Georgie Fame and the Blue Flames eventually recorded a live version of "The Dog"—as "Do the Dog" in late 1963. It was included on the band's now-legendary debut album, *Rhythm and Blues at the Flamingo*, and released as a single in early 1964. While both the single and album failed to chart, the band and the sound captured the imagination of the growing mod movement in the UK. The mods were shaped by their approach to fashion, shopping in the nearby boutiques of Carnaby Street, and to music, and the Flamingo Club soon became one of the *de rigueur* hangouts in London. As a result, it wasn't long before the West Indian and African American clientele began to be displaced, and the mod audience began to take over the club.

◆ ◆ ◆

Back in Memphis and buoyed by the success of "The Dog," Rufus Thomas started to spend more of his spare time hanging around Stax Records, where he could interact with other local musicians. "Rufus would appear in the lobby of Stax Records, which was adjacent to Satellite Record Shop," recalled Deanie Parker, who had recently won a local talent contest and been offered a recording contract with Stax. "And the lobby became the place for networking for musicians. On any given day, Rufus might be in the lobby with an audience of fellow professionals and novice entertainers who wanted to know where the gigs were, where the sessions were. That area was informally formatted for that purpose. Rufus was not only sharing information about where job opportunities were, but also what artists were coming to town, what emerging artists he'd heard, by virtue of his work as a disc jockey."[16]

In addition to networking with the other musicians, Thomas—who was a generation older—was also happy to offer advice to the younger artists on the label. "He would also share life lessons, because he had his own philosophy, his own sayings about almost everything," said Parker. "And most of what he'd relay to you had a touch of humor, because he was a part-time comedian. I don't know what else he was talking about, because sometimes the guys would lower their voice to a whisper when they were talking about things they didn't want us to hear, you know! Although none of us are perfect, Rufus was a Stax-father in a lot of ways because he was an older person and because by our standards he was doing things the right way. He was an entertainer who had a daytime job, sought to pick up any additional job he could find to support his family of three, bought a home for them, and educated his children. He was an example to other musicians who chose to have other careers, and a life and a family, and do it the right way."[17]

Thomas struck up a close friendship with the young guitarist, Steve Cropper, who, by this time, was always to be found in either the studio or, between recording sessions, the record store. "What Rufus saw in this snot-nosed white kid I have no idea," said Cropper, laughing. "But Rufus was friends with everybody, and to me he was more like a father figure. He taught me a lot. He took me aside and taught me all that stuff he'd learned in the vaudeville days. He was so streetwise, it was amazing."[18]

One Sunday in the early fall of 1963 after attending church, Thomas swung by the studio with another idea for a song, again based on the "Dog" dance, but this time based on an old nursery rhyme. "He walked in and said, 'Steve, I've got a great idea for a song!'" the guitarist recalled. "It was more of a dance than anything else, but that was his idea to put down the wedding march [as the intro]—he'd hum it, and I'd play it on the guitar. When we got into the basics of the music, I sort of took something from Junior Walker's stuff. I think one of the main things was 'Cleo's Mood' or something, and it worked. It was just an R&B riff, and it was easy enough for me to play! I helped him, but I didn't write the song. That's about all I did."[19]

The resulting song, "Walking the Dog," borrows liberally from the words of a children's nursery rhyme and clapping game, "Mary Mack" (also known as "Miss Mary Mack").[20]

The original begins:

Miss Mary Mack, Mack, Mack
All dressed in black, black, black
With silver buttons, buttons, buttons
All down her back, back, back.
She asked her mother, mother, mother
For 50 cents, cents, cents
To see the elephants, elephants, elephants
Jumped over the fence, fence, fence . . . .

Thomas changes this to:

Mary Mack, dressed in black,
Silver buttons all down her back
High, low, tipsy toe,
She broke a needle and she can't sew
Walkin' the dog,
Just walkin' the dog
If you don't know how to do it,
I'll show you how to walk the dog
Asked a fellow for fifteen cents,
See the fellow he jumped the fence
Jumped so high he touched the sky,
Never got back till the Fourth of July
Walkin' the dog,
Just walkin' the dog
If you don't know how to do it,
I'll show you how to walk the dog

As with much of Rufus Thomas's best work in the years that followed, it effectively combines his skills as a singer, dancer, and comedian, developed from his years in vaudeville and in the nightclubs of Memphis.

There are numerous comedy elements to Thomas's delivery ranging from the whistling between verses, calling the "dog," and the additional inclusion of lyrics from another old English nursery rhyme, "Mary, Mary, Quite Contrary," later in the song. Not to mention the song's intro, which quotes the first fourteen notes of Mendelssohn's "Wedding March" from *A Midsummer's Night's Dream*!

The recording process was witnessed by Tom Dowd, the engineer from Atlantic Records, who had flown into Memphis the previous Friday.

Atlantic had been expecting to receive a new single from Carla Thomas, but every time Jerry Wexler called to inquire about it, Jim Stewart told him that the recording equipment was broken. Wexler sent Dowd down to Memphis to fix the problem, which required some spare parts to be flown in from New York. "Next morning, I asked Jim to take me to the airport to pick up the parts," Dowd explained. "I think he was a little taken aback. But we returned to the studio, plugged in a soldering iron, had the machine running in about thirty-five or forty minutes."[21]

Dowd was not flying back to New York until late afternoon on that Sunday and was surprised as various members of the house band came into the studio one by one after attending church. Then Rufus Thomas came in, asked if the machine was now working, and said, "I got a song."

At Atlantic, back in New York, the studio would be booked in advance, session musicians would be hired in accordance with union rules, and the arrangements would be written out in advance. By contrast, Stax Records had a loose, improvisational feel; Thomas sang through the new number for the band once or twice, humming suggestions for their parts and sounding the rhythm by clacking his teeth close to their ears. Once the arrangement was established, Dowd started recording, and Thomas and the band nailed the song in just two takes.

When Dowd returned to New York the next day, he had the tape of Thomas's breakthrough hit, "Walking the Dog," which Jim Stewart lauded as the best-sounding record Stax had yet produced. "Memphis was a real departure," Wexler explained to Peter Guralnick, "because Memphis was a return to head arrangements, to the set rhythm section away from the arranger. It was a return to the symbiosis between the producer and the rhythm section. It was really something new."[22]

The single was released in September 1963. Jim Stewart paid a visit to Atlantic Records shortly after the single had come out. "Right after we released the record I was in New York, in Jerry Wexler's office," he recalled. "We got a call from our Chicago distributor and he said he wanted to place a big order for the record. "I said, "You mean 5,000?" He said, "Hell, no, I mean 20,000!" So that was really the record that broke Rufus nationally."[23]

"Walking the Dog" was a massive success, peaking at No. 5 on the R&B charts and No. 10 on the *Billboard* Hot 100, remaining on the chart for over three months. The single's success meant that Rufus Thomas was finally able to quit his job at the American Finishing Company, a job he had for twenty-two years.

"I made more money in one night than I made at that textile mill in one month," Thomas later revealed. "I only made fifty-seven and a half cents an hour, top salary, 1963. And that's when I left American Finishing Company. The supervisor told me, 'Don't leave. Just stay off a little while, then come back, and your job will be right here waiting on you.' I mean, like, what more could you ask for, you know, with the service of twenty-two years. And I told him, 'No. Uh-uh. I won't be back!'"[24]

When the song became a hit, there was some speculation about what the song was really about. "'Walking the Dog' got banned in I don't know how many countries!" said Steve Cropper, laughing. "They thought it had something to do with sex, but it had zero to do with sex! That bit, 'just walking the dog,' was about a dance!"[25]

Others speculated that "walking the dog" might be some kind of slang for smoking marijuana—after all, this was the 1960s. "Drugs? Well, Rufus didn't do them!" said the guitarist, laughing again. "He didn't drink, he didn't smoke, didn't do drugs. But he did teach me a lot about how to deal with the street as a young kid. Of course, when you're young, you think you know everything, but you don't."[26]

◆ ◆ ◆

As with "The Dog," "Walking the Dog" had a big impact over in the UK. It had been released as a single there by London Records, which had the right to distribute Stax in the UK. Again, the song proved to be popular at Soho's Flamingo Club. Georgie Fame and the Blue Flames recorded a version for BBC Radio in 1964, and it became a regular part of their live shows. Fame eventually recorded the song on his fourth album, *Sound Venture*, which was made with the Harry South Big Band.

The song also came to the attention of an up-and-coming British blues band by the name of the Rolling Stones, which liked the song so much that they included it on their debut album, released in May 1964. In fact, it had been in their repertoire for some time, as the group had performed it on the BBC on February 8, 1964, three months before the album was released. The Stones' version is less of a "novelty" song than the original. The cheesy opening fanfare is replaced by a bluesy guitar intro, and Jagger's vocals are less jokey than Thomas's. The only time he comes slightly unstuck is on the spoken part, where he sounds less convincing. Brian Jones features on backing vocals and also replicates Thomas's whistle, and there's a fine guitar solo by Keith Richards, too.

The Rolling Stones were much admired by another young London-based band, the High Numbers—which later became The Who. "Walking the Dog" also became part of their live set, as did "Chinese Checkers" by Booker T. & the M.G.'s. Although the Who never recorded the song, it was an occasional part of their live set, too; a rehearsal version of the song can be heard on a bootleg of the band's Young Vic concert from 1971.

The Who's singer, Roger Daltrey, also recorded a version of "Walking the Dog" on his 1975 solo album, *Ride a Rock Horse*. It was also released as a single but only reached No. 52 on the UK charts.

In November 1975, Daltrey passed through Memphis as part of the *Who by Numbers* tour. On November 22, the night before the band's gig at the Mid-South Coliseum, Daltrey made the effort to look up Rufus Thomas's address and swung by the house, hoping to talk to him. "I'll always remember when Roger Daltrey came by the house one night," recalled his son Marvell Thomas. "Nine o'clock. It was me and Daddy. Daddy looked out on the porch and saw a skinny white dude standing there. Daddy didn't know who the Who was. He opened the door [and said], 'May I help you?' Roger Daltrey, in his nasal Cockney accent, told Rufus who he was and said that he wanted to meet Rufus Thomas because the band had just finished recording 'Walking the Dog.' We all sat there and talked for a long time."[27]

To further emphasize the song's impact on the British R&B scene, it's worth noting that the song was also included on *Stupidity*, the barnstorming live album by the Canvey Island blues-rock band Dr. Feelgood, which topped the UK album charts in 1976.

Of course, the song's influence was not only felt in the UK. In the US, the song was also covered by Johnny Rivers (1964), the Kingsmen (1964), Aerosmith (1973), and even punk rockers Green Day, who recorded a demo of the song for *Dookie*, their major label debut (1993).

♦ ♦ ♦

With "Walking the Dog" climbing the charts, Jim Stewart was keen to cash in on Thomas's newfound success and suggested they record his debut album—which was named after the single.

The album included a cover of Jesse Hill's "Ooh Poo Pah Doo"—the song whose rhythm Thomas had borrowed for "'Cause I Love You"—and it's no exaggeration to say that Thomas's version outshines the original. It also includes a stellar cover of Lee Dorsey's "Ya Ya," on which the horn section really shines.

Thomas also sings "Land of a Thousand Dances," the song that was later immortalized by Wilson Pickett. Thomas's version is slower, more mid-tempo, and closer to the Chris Kenner original, which had charted earlier that year. In many respects, it was an obvious song for Thomas to record, as the lyric mentions sixteen different dances—but not The

Dog. Given that Thomas would become associated with "dance"-oriented songs, it feels like a good fit.

There's also a nod to Thomas's blues roots with a cover of John Lee Hooker's tune "Boom Boom," which had been released as a single in May 1962. Thomas's version is more horn-driven, inevitably, and while it might lack the impact of the original, it still works well.

Finally, after hits with "The Dog" and "Walking the Dog," it was perhaps inevitable that Thomas would look to record one more "dog"-themed song. He wrote another novelty dance song for the album, this time titled "Can Your Monkey Do the Dog?"

"The 'Monkey Time' was a big dance (written by Curtis Mayfield, performed by Major Lance)," explained Steve Cropper. "'The Monkey Time'—it was an easy enough dance . . . but can it 'Do the Dog?'" The new song was credited to both Rufus Thomas and Steve Cropper, a sign of their emerging partnership and friendship.[28]

Of note, the album didn't include any ballads—the album was clearly pitching Rufus Thomas as the new "king" of the dance floor, and the album cover reflected that, featuring multicolored silhouettes of two couples dancing.

"Can Your Monkey Do the Dog?" was selected as the next single, and charted in January 1964, reaching No. 48 on the pop charts but failing to replicate the success of his previous single.

Incidentally, Thomas had one last try with the "dog" theme, recording a single called "Somebody Stole My Dog," which was released in March 1964. It scraped into the *Billboard* Hot 100 but probably didn't do Thomas any favors; it suggested he was more of a "novelty" song man, and by the spring of 1964, that particular novelty was starting to wear off.

The album itself was released in November 1963, and while it failed to achieve the chart success of the singles, still sold well, peaking at No. 138 on the *Billboard* 200 albums chart, which was no mean feat for a debut R&B album. The album was also released in the UK, where it achieved a cult following.

The recording of the album cemented the friendship of Rufus Thomas and the guitarist, Steve Cropper, with Thomas even inviting him over to the family home for dinner. "That was an honor to be invited over to Rufus's house for dinner," he recalled. "Carla I already knew, and Marvell I knew too—Vaneese was pretty young in those days. I just became part of the family, I guess. We sat around talking music, talking Stax. I read these days that Memphis was the most segregated city in the United States. I didn't know that. I grew up there, and nobody ever talked about it. We just got along as friends at Stax. Stax was a real family. I think it was—everybody respected each other."[29]

Thomas's newfound solo success landed an invitation to record a live album at the Apollo Theater in New York. The album was being compiled by Atlantic Records, which distributed for Stax, and featured a mix of Atlantic recording stars such as Ben E. King, the Coasters and the Falcons, and two artists from Stax/Volt—Rufus Thomas and a new signing to the Volt label, a young singer by the name of Otis Redding.

Otis Redding came to the attention of Jim Stewart at Stax purely by accident. Born in Dawson, Georgia, in September 1941, Redding was the fourth of six children. As a child, he sang in the Vineville Baptist Church, but by his mid-teens, he was leaning toward secular music, citing Little Richard as his main inspiration. He recorded a handful of singles for minor labels in the early 1960s, but his guitarist at this time, Johnny Jenkins, left to front a band called the Pinetoppers, who later employed Redding as a singer.

The manager of the Pinetoppers, Phil Walden, was looking for a record label to sign the band when an Atlantic representative suggested they try Stax in Memphis. The band was scheduled to record an instrumental, but Otis Redding joined the band that day as the chauffeur since Jenkins was unable to drive. The recording session that day—which featured Jenkins backed by Booker T. & the M.G.'s—was not productive and finished early. As a result, Redding was invited to perform two songs. The first of these, a ballad called "These Arms of Mine," impressed everyone. "There was something different about [the ballad]," Stewart remembered. "He really poured his soul into it."[30]

Redding's success was far from instant. "These Arms of Mine" took several months before it eventually charted in March 1963, and the follow-up, "That's What My Heart Needs," was also something of a slow-burn, just scraping into the Top 30 of the *Billboard* R&B charts. Stewart was convinced that Redding had something special, however, and suggested that he join Rufus Thomas in New York.

Otis Redding was driven up there, together with his brother Rodgers, in a '63 Ford XL Convertible. While that sounds glamorous, they were driven by Sylvester Huckaby, an ex-boxer who didn't even possess a driving license.

The musicians stayed at the Hotel Theresa, which was located between West 124th and 125th in Harlem, just around the corner from the Apollo Theater. Huckaby later recalled the hotel as "raggedy," but at that time, it was known as the Waldorf of Harlem. The boxer Cassius Clay—later known as Muhammed Ali—had apparently taken over the whole of the seventh floor. He was not yet the heavyweight champion of the world but regarded as the main contender, and Rufus Thomas and Otis Redding got the opportunity to hang around with him before the show.

The two Stax/Volt stars were paid $400 a week, which they figured was a lot of money, particularly as they had the use of the Atlantic house band led by King Curtis and didn't have to pay for their own backing band. What they hadn't bargained on was that King Curtis was not familiar with the tunes they wanted to play and requested they get sheet music. That ended up costing the musicians over $450, and they had to call Jim Stewart at Stax and request that he wire more money to New York.

When Otis Redding met the star of the show, Ben E. King, King took pity on the younger man and gave him one hundred dollars out of his own pocket to make up part of the shortfall. It may not have been the payday that Redding had been expecting, but it gave him invaluable experience, and his appearance at the Apollo proved to be a watershed moment in his career.

Redding performed two songs, "Pain in My Heart," his new single, and "These Arms of Mine." The effect of his pleading, soulful voice can clearly be heard in the female members of the audience, who clearly loved every second of his performance. The one thing lacking at this time, according to Atlantic's Jerry Wexler, was his stagecraft. "He didn't know how to move in those days," Wexler recalled. "He just stood still, and he'd bend from the waist."[31]

The more experienced and better-known Thomas came on later in the show. He was well-versed in stagecraft, of course, after years of plying his trade in the clubs around Memphis. He was introduced as "the man who invented the thing called 'walking the dog'" and was met with a rousing reception. He played a rocking R&B tune called "Rockin' Chair," which was obviously part of his live set at the time and featured some great call-and-response with the band. The crowd-pleasing "Walking the Dog" inevitably follows and benefits from the much larger horn section, which helps to elevate the song.

Atlantic later released an album of the concert titled *Apollo Saturday Night*, and it's a great way to appreciate how Otis Redding sounded early in his career and what a fine showman Thomas was in his prime.

♦ ♦ ♦

After a busy couple of years, Carla Thomas had kept a lower profile in 1963 and was primarily focused on her studies at Tennessee A&I in Nashville.

She had recorded one single earlier in the year called "What a Fool I've Been," which was cowritten by guitarist Steve Cropper and singer/

songwriter William Bell. It featured a string arrangement that was credited to Steve Cropper and the occasional in-house trumpet player Vinnie
Trauth and was clearly aimed at the pop audience that loved "Gee Whiz"
rather than R&B lovers. The single met with modest success on the R&B
chart, reaching No. 28, but it barely troubled the pop charts.

With Christmas fast approaching, Carla Thomas was back in Memphis
and looking forward to some time away from her studies. Christmas
songs could be big sellers, and somebody at Stax suggested she record a
song of her own. "I said, 'Yeah, I know one—"Gee Whiz, It's Christmas,"'"
she said, laughing. "It was done as a joke. But we sat down and wrote
it." Her collaborators were Cropper and arranger Vincent Trauth. "Gee
Whiz, It's Christmas" might have been intended as a throwaway, but
it's a delight, elevated by Carla's superb vocals and the relatively simple
arrangement.[32]

The B-side was even better. "All I Want for Christmas Is You" is not
the song made famous by Mariah Carey but an original composed by
Carla's Teen Town mentor (and WDIA disc jockey), A. C. "Moohah"
Williams. It's that rare breed, an elegant Christmas song, and deserves to
be better known than it is. Sadly, even with two good Christmas tunes,
the single failed to chart.

After Rufus Thomas's final "dog" singles "Can Your Monkey Do the
Dog?" and "Somebody Stole My Dog" in the spring of 1964, he and Carla
returned with a duet—a fine double-header which consisted of "That's
Really Some Good" and a remake of the Ray Charles hit "Night Time Is
the Right Time." The former was a Rufus Thomas original which opens
with a quote from "Yankee Doodle." It's a great song, but "Night Time"
was even better, with Thomas singing the Ray Charles part and Carla the
part originally sung by Margie Hendricks. The song features a powerhouse performance from Carla, who belts out the word "baby" in her
inimitable style. Fellow Stax artist Deanie Parker told Carla that no one
sang the word "baby" like her, and she had a good point. Both songs made
it to the lower reaches of the *Billboard* Top 100 pop charts but probably
deserved a better fate.

Back in Memphis for the summer holidays, Carla cut another solo
record, "I've Got No Time to Lose." Atlantic still controlled the rights to
solo recordings by Carla and released the song as a single. "There was a
young lady that had come from my high school named Deanie Parker,
who had written it," Carla later explained. "She had cut it too, but it was
cut different with a different melody. I was coming in to talk with Jim
about something, and he had just left from the studio so I didn't get a
chance to. Steve [Cropper] was up there, putting some of the master

tapes away. I said, 'What was that I heard when I was coming here? That was a great song!' He said, 'Jim doesn't like it, and he ain't gonna put it out.' I said, 'Are you sure?' He said, 'He already told us.' I said, 'Play it again!' So, he took it down and he played it over and over, and I said, 'That's a hit record!'"[33]

Deanie Parker was happy for Carla to cover the song and also joined on backing vocals. The song demonstrates Carla's growing maturity as a performer, and with Cropper's lean guitar licks, it has a more soulful feel than Carla's more pop-oriented early recordings. The song reached No. 67 on the *Billboard* Top 100 pop charts. It's worth noting that *Billboard* stopped producing R&B charts for a couple of years, taking the narrow-minded view that many records were now "crossing over." Had they produced R&B charts at that time, the song would probably have been much closer to the Top 20. "That actually is one of my favorite songs," Carla confirmed, smiling at the memory.

◆ ◆ ◆

Now that Thomas was no longer working at the factory, he had more time to perform live; previously, with both factory and radio commitments, he was effectively tied to the Memphis area. WDIA welcomed his chart success and allowed him plenty of flexibility with regards to time off, which allowed him to play extensively now, particularly across the South.

Despite the segregation that still existed, college fraternities were an important ingredient in the development of "southern" soul music, as Peter Guralnick explained in his definitive work on the subject, *Sweet Soul Music*. "College audiences are the greatest audiences in the world," Thomas informed him. "There is no greater audience. I must have played every fraternity house there was in the South. When we played Ole Miss, they'd send the girls home at midnight and then we'd tell nasty jokes and all that stuff. Oh man, we used to have some *good* times down there in Oxford."[34] It turns out that *National Lampoon's Animal House* wasn't so far from the truth, in that respect, at least!

It wasn't just that the colleges made a good audience; it was also a good payday. Thomas didn't have his own full-time band and regularly used pick-up bands from the local colleges. "I started with Rufus in 1963—I was only seventeen years old," explained guitarist Bobby Manuel, who joined Stax himself five years later. "Rufus used to play all these fraternity and sorority colleges and stuff, and most of the time he wouldn't bring his own band. I think he made more money getting those high school bands and he would use them. I played with a high school band called the Blazers—we had a horn section, and just played rhythm and blues.

Rufus live on stage, circa 1964. Photographer unknown.

We were real excited to play his songs. We never rehearsed with him—he just expected you to know "Walking the Dog," "The Dog," "Ooh Poo Pah Doo"—the songs you were playing that day! It was showtime for me!"[35]

By contrast, Carla Thomas was only playing concerts on an irregular basis at this time, given her college commitments. Most of the gigs that she played in the early 1960s were as part of a "package" tour, featuring several artists on the same bill. "You had to bring your charts, you had to bring all your things, and it was very professional," she recalled. "Your rehearsal time was set at this particular time, and you did your rehearsal spot. You maybe had twenty minutes or so to practice it. But that taught me professionalism. You got to be there. You've got to bring your little satchel and your dress."[36]

Indeed, a concert poster from August 1, 1964—during her summer holiday—shows Carla on the same bill as the Isley Brothers, who were headlining Joe Tex, Esther Phillips, and the Drifters, now without Ben E. King as their lead singer.

Over time, however, her promotional commitments increased, which started to eat into her college time. "It eventually got to be harder than I thought," she told author David Freeland. "In the beginning it wasn't—because it was still a lot of fun. Then it got to be I was getting more job offers, and that's when it got to be harder. It was harder because I would have to leave (school), but in a way it was good for a young lady because it wasn't like a club gig, getting off at two or three in the morning."[37]

Independently, Rufus and Carla returned to the studio one more time that year to record a single; on both occasions, they worked with guitarist Steve Cropper, who had built up a close relationship with the Thomas family. "When I'd walk into the room, he'd be like 'Hey! Cropper!'" the guitarist laughed. "We'd have a special handshake, all that kind of stuff."[38]

Thomas's next single, recorded in September 1964, was another self-composed dance-oriented number called "Jump Back," which featured a Stax female vocal quartet, the Drapels, some neat guitar work from Steve Cropper and great work from the Memphis Horns. It was a winning combination that continued Thomas's winning streak, taking him to No. 49 on the pop charts—and what would have been a much bigger R&B hit.

"I played on almost all of his records [in the 1960s] and most of them were famous," recalled Cropper. "'Jump Back' was another one. We had so much fun. He was something else. He was very serious about what he did, and when he got upset, he'd say 'that ain't the way I want it!'—very abrupt. But it didn't take anybody back. That was just his nature, the way he was."[39]

Rufus Thomas was known as a perfectionist in the recording studio. He was particularly fussy about the rhythm, which had to be exactly as he heard it in his head, and he would work closely with the horn section, too, humming the arrangements until the band got them just right. When the hits were flowing and his mood was good and he was working with the house band who knew his methods—this rarely created a problem. But when the hits dried up or he was working with a less experienced band, this would occasionally create some friction in the recording studio.

Booker T. Jones confirmed this view. "He had a very strong personality, very much in charge," he recalled. "To be honest with you, [he was] not always easy. But now that I'm older, I know you have to have a passion in life, you have to have an aim. You had to have that—something you care about."[40]

Steve Cropper was also involved in Carla Thomas's final single that year, cowriting "A Woman's Love" and the B-side, "Don't Let the Love Light Leave." The single confirmed that Carla Thomas was maturing as a lyricist but also that Steve Cropper was becoming a significant songwriter in his own right. "We got along so well," the singer recalled. "I really wish I had sat down and written with him more, but by me being in college, we didn't do as much as I probably could have done with him. I think we would have written well."[41]

By this stage, Carla had completed her degree at Tennessee A&I, but she was about to embark on a master's at Howard University in

Washington, so the songwriting partnership with Cropper failed to develop. As a result, the guitarist went on to form songwriting partnerships with the likes of Wilson Pickett, Eddie Floyd, and Otis Redding, cowriting songs such as "In the Midnight Hour," "Knock on Wood," and "(Sittin' On) The Dock of the Bay."

"A Woman's Love" sold relatively well, reaching No. 71 on the *Billboard* Top 100, again with no R&B chart available at that time. Incidentally, the song was later rewritten as an "answer record" called "That's a Man's Way" by Wilson Pickett in 1965, when Atlantic brought him down to Memphis to record. At that point, the writing credit was changed to Cropper-Pickett, which infuriated Carla, who briefly considered suing Stax Records.

◆ ◆ ◆

In late October 1964, the British music press announced that Rik Gunnell, the manager of the Flamingo Club in London's Soho, was promoting a ten-day UK tour by Rufus Thomas, opening on December 9 at the Flamingo Club itself and later including an all-nighter at the same club where Thomas was the guest of the house band, Georgie Fame and the Blue Flames.

Thomas's backing band for the tour, which also played support most nights, was a British band that had formed in Wolverhampton, near Birmingham, England, earlier that year—Tony Knight's Chessmen. The band featured Tony Knight on drums and vocals, Lol Coxhill on tenor and soprano saxophone, John Gummer on baritone saxophone and trumpet, Terry Martin on bass, and Jeff Reed on organ.

Rufus was the first Stax artist to be invited to tour overseas, and both the record label and his radio station, WDIA, were delighted by the news. "WDIA went crazy, man!" remembered James Nelson, a family friend and member of the Teen Town singers. "A. C. Williams, who was the promotions director, as well as a disc jockey, started calling Rufus 'Milord the Dog.' They made a big deal out of it!"

The following weekend, "Moohah" William built the Teen Town program around Thomas going to London, and he chose Nelson to sing Thomas's songs. "Rufus was at the radio station that Saturday and he said, 'Which one of you boys sang my music? Boy, you did a wonderful job! When I come back, we're gonna hook up.' And he did exactly what he said," said Nelson. "When he came back, he had Mother [Lorene Thomas] call me and I went out to the house. He said, 'We're gonna do some stuff together.' It marked the beginning of a lifelong friendship with

Review of Rufus Thomas's performance at Aylesbury Bluesville club on December 15, 1964, from the Bucks Advertiser.

the Thomas family, and Nelson went on to play piano and organ for both Rufus and Carla Thomas in the years ahead, once he had finished college.

Thomas's debut international tour was well-received. Singer David Essex, who later became successful with hits such as "Gonna Make You a Star" and "Hold Me Close," remembers seeing his opening gig at the Flamingo Club in Soho. "My friend and I joined the queue and, when we got in, the place was packed solid and the atmosphere was electric. The resident band was Georgie Fame and the Blue Flames, and the guest on stage that night was Rufus Thomas. After watching these great performers, I had no doubt in my mind that I wanted to be a musician. It was like a star over Bethlehem!"[42]

Later that month, Thomas played at the Bluesville club in Aylesbury, Buckinghamshire, about forty miles outside London. "His voice is not unlike a young Louis Armstrong," the local newspaper suggested the next day, "and his performance has a similar sort of exuberance and enthusiasm. He gagged about; he told funny stories; his demonstrations of the various 'dog' dances were hilarious."

Rufus Thomas did not get the chance to meet the Rolling Stones, the young British band that had recorded "Walking the Dog," while he was in England. He did finally get the chance to meet with them on November 17, 1965, when the band embarked on their second tour of the United States that year. "They were at the mid-South Coliseum, and Daddy could get in anywhere—of course, he was Rufus Thomas!" explained his younger daughter, Vaneese Thomas. "The Stones were thrilled to death after the show to finally meet Daddy. I was in their dressing room and he introduced me to them. Afterward he asked me about what I thought of them. I was a huge Beatles fan at the time—my brother used to call me 'little white girl,' as I love the British invasion—but after meeting them I realized that they look like reprobates, and I still preferred The Beatles!"[43]

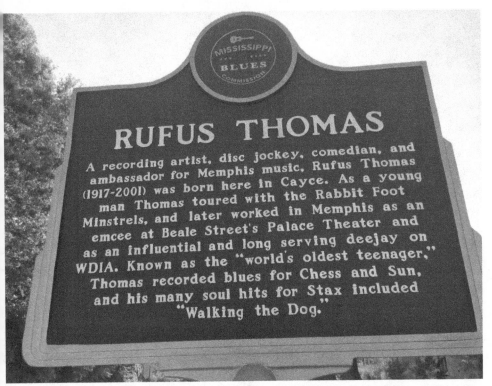

RUFUS THOMAS

A recording artist, disc jockey, comedian, and ambassador for Memphis music, Rufus Thomas (1917-2001) was born here in Cayce. As a young man Thomas toured with the Rabbit Foot Minstrels, and later worked in Memphis as an emcee at Beale Street's Palace Theater and as an influential and long serving deejay on WDIA. Known as the "world's oldest teenager," Thomas recorded blues for Chess and Sun, and his many soul hits for Stax included "Walking the Dog."

Rufus Thomas's plaque in Cayce Mississippi, on the Mississippi Blues Trail. Photograph courtesy of Mark S. Hilton, the Historical Marker Database (HMdb.org).v

Photograph of Rufus Thomas Sr., circa 1925. Photograph courtesy of the Vaneese Thomas family collection.

Photograph of Rachel Thomas Sr., circa 1920. Photograph courtesy of the Vaneese Thomas family collection.

Lorene Thomas with Carla and Marvell, circa 1946. Photograph courtesy of the Vaneese Thomas family collection.

Marvell and Carla, Foote Homes, circa 1947. Photograph courtesy of the Vaneese Thomas family collection.

Rufus Thomas, circa 1947. Photograph courtesy of the Vaneese Thomas family collection.

Rufus Thomas at the Foote Homes Auditorium, 1951. Photograph courtesy of the Vaneese Thomas family collection.

Rufus Thomas WDIA publicity shot. Photographer unknown. Photograph courtesy of the Vaneese Thomas family collection.

Lorene Thomas picketing on Main Street, Memphis. 1963. © Dr. Ernest C. Withers Sr., courtesy of the Withers Family Trust.

A signed promotional photograph of the album artwork used for Rufus Thomas's debut album, *Walking the Dog*. Photographer unknown.

Carla Thomas with Bill Cosby, January 1971. Photograph courtesy of the *Memphis Press-Scimitar*, Special Collections Department, University of Memphis Libraries.

Rufus Thomas and Elvis Presley, backstage at the WDIA Goodwill Revue at Ellis Auditorium, Memphis, December 7, 1956. © Dr. Ernest C. Withers Sr., courtesy of the Withers Family Trust.

Carla Thomas performing on stage at Wattstax at the LA Coliseum, August 20, 1972. Photograph courtesy of the Stax Museum of American Soul Music.

Rufus returns from Liberia, May 1971. Photograph courtesy of the Stax Museum of American Soul Music.

Rufus Thomas performs at the Starlite Review, November 26, 1973. Photograph courtesy of the *Memphis Press-Scimitar*, Special Collections Department, University of Memphis Libraries.

Al Green, Jesse Jackson, Rufus Thomas, and Soul Train host Don Cornelius, circa 1974. Photograph courtesy of the Stax Museum of American Soul Music.

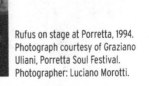

Rufus on stage at Porretta, 1994. Photograph courtesy of Graziano Uliani, Porretta Soul Festival. Photographer: Luciano Morotti.

Rufus Thomas and Mavis Staples on stage at Porretta, 1994. Photograph courtesy of Graziano Uliani, Porretta Soul Festival. Photographer: G. Pradelli.

Rufus Thomas and William Bell, Porretta 1994. Photograph courtesy of Graziano Uliani, Porretta Soul Festival. Photographer: G. Pradelli.

Vaneese, Carla, and Marvell at Rufus Thomas Park, Porretta. Photograph courtesy of Graziano Uliani, Porretta Soul Festival. Photographer: Luciano Marchi.

Chapter Seven

B-A-B-Y

Stax in Ascendance, 1965-1966

In the words of Stax historian Robert Gordon, "Around this time, though nothing changed at Stax, everything changed."[1]

By early 1965, Stax had developed a distinctive sound courtesy of its house band, which was effectively Booker T. & the M.G.'s coupled with the Memphis Horns, whose personnel varied but coalesced around Wayne Jackson on trumpet, Andrew Love on tenor saxophone, and Floyd Newman on baritone saxophone. And they had an established roster of artists scoring regular hits, including Rufus and Carla Thomas. But early 1965 saw the emergence of two brand-new stars—Otis Redding, who was effectively homegrown, and a singing duo called Sam and Dave, who were on loan from Atlantic Records.

Another change, again seemingly minor, was the emergence of a new songwriting duo, David Porter and Isaac Hayes. Porter had been working with the label from the very early days. By 1965, he was twenty-four years old and married with two children. Like Rufus Thomas, he was working hard to make things happen; he still worked at the grocery store opposite the recording studio and sold insurance to earn extra money. He continued to sing; Stax released a solo single in January 1965, and he occasionally sang with the M.G.'s, too. He also wrote his own songs but felt he needed a songwriting partner who could develop musical arrangements.

Isaac Hayes had come on board to fill in for Booker T. Jones, who was at college in Indiana midweek but had started to work as an arranger, too. While they had met as teenagers, they reunited at Stax when Porter tried to sell Hayes an insurance policy. "During our conversation, we discovered that we had similar interests," said Hayes. "He said, 'Ike, I'm a lyric man, and you're a music man, let's do like Holland-Dozier [Motown] and Bacharach and David!'"[2]

The spring of 1965 also saw Stax cement its relationship with Atlantic with a formal written contract rather than relying on the "gentlemen's agreement" that had been in place for the last few years. As part of this arrangement, Stax also agreed to record another Atlantic artist, Wilson Pickett, at their studio in Memphis.

Finally, in the fall of 1965, Jim Stewart hired a disc jockey named Al Bell as director of promotions, which provided the company with a fresh impetus for growth and a more business-like organization.

As Gordon suggests, no one of these changes in and of themselves appeared to be that significant. Taken together, however, they combined to produce a golden era for Stax Records. The hits started to flow, with singles topping the charts on a regular basis, and the label started to gain wider recognition on the West Coast, but more importantly, in Europe too. In the words of the new marketing man, Al Bell, the "temperature of the thermometer was starting to rise!"

But the changes weren't all positive. Jim Stewart had not paid enough attention to the finer points of the contract he had signed with Atlantic Records, which would have far-reaching consequences over the longer term. In addition, more hit records meant more competition for the label's limited resources—studio time, air time, and access to the label's in-house songwriters, and that would lead to the first signs of friction within the Stax "family."

◆ ◆ ◆

In January 1965, Rufus Thomas's son, Marvell, was drafted into the army. He was not engaged in active service but helped to arrange a military band that toured military installations all around the world. "I returned to my duties at Stax in '67," he later revealed. "While I was gone, though, I missed Otis Redding's coming through Stax and his formative years. That's one thing I regret."[3]

In fact, early 1965 saw Otis Redding riding high on the charts with his biggest hit to date, "Mr. Pitiful." The idea for the song came from WDIA disc jockey "Moohah" Williams, who had started referring to the singer as Mr. Pitiful because he sounded so mournful singing ballads. "I got the idea for writing about it in the shower," Steve Cropper remembered. "I was on my way down to pick up Otis. I got down there and I was humming it in the car. I said, 'Hey, what do you think about this?' We just wrote the song on the way to the studio, just slapping our legs. We wrote it in about ten minutes, went in, showed it to the guys, he hummed a horn line, boom we had it!"[4]

"Mr. Pitiful" was Otis Redding's seventh single for the label and reached No. 10 on the newly reinstated *Billboard* R&B charts and No. 41 on the pop charts. His follow-up single, "I've Been Loving You Too Long," was released in April 1965 and was an even bigger hit, reaching No. 2 and No. 21 on the R&B and pop charts, respectively. A new star had emerged.

Singing duo Sam Moore and Dave Prater had emerged from the Miami gospel scene and recorded a handful of singles for Roulette Records in New York before signing with Atlantic Records in the summer of 1964. Jerry Wexler didn't feel that he could capture the raw, gospel feel of the duo and proposed a loan deal whereby they remained signed to Atlantic but recorded with Stax, which would receive most of the royalties.

After a couple of false starts, Sam and Dave struck gold with their third release, the gospel-tinged "You Don't Know Like I Know," in late 1965. The song had been cowritten by David Porter and Isaac Hayes. Porter later admitted that his songwriting craft had improved over time, in part by studying Motown's impressive catalog. The pairing with Hayes was also vital in terms of the arrangements. "When we first started, it was just a verse, chorus, then harmonize it out," Moore later revealed. "Isaac Hayes, bless his heart, gave me and Dave the style, all the call-and-response, the horns became the background singers, the rhythm keeping the beat—it's Isaac Hayes."[5]

The song reached No. 7 on the R&B charts and scraped into the Top 100 on the pop charts, but it marked the beginning of a golden era for both Sam and Dave and the songwriting duo of Porter and Hayes, who were on a hot streak. The follow-up, "Hold On! I'm Comin'," followed in the spring of 1966 and topped the R&B charts while reaching No. 21 on the pop charts, too. After that, there was no looking back, and Sam and Dave, together with Otis Redding, spearheaded the label's golden era.

While Atlantic's lawyers were drafting the terms of the "loan" agreement for Sam and Dave, they noticed that no formal agreement was in place between Atlantic Records and Stax Records. The relationship had effectively worked as a "gentlemen's agreement" between Jerry Wexler and Jim Stewart since 1960, with any disagreements ironed out by telephone or a face-to-face meeting. A formal contract was drafted by Atlantic's lawyers, presumably in conjunction with Wexler himself. Under the terms of the new contract, Stax would continue to receive fifteen cents for every single sold and ten percent of the retail price of each album, and Stax would be responsible for paying each artist. Jim Stewart was happy to formalize this arrangement but did insist on a "key man" clause, meaning that the contract was only valid while Wexler remained at Atlantic Records. He felt they had built up a good relationship over the years and didn't want to find himself dealing with people he didn't know.

Unfortunately for Jim Stewart, he never bothered to read the terms of the contract or hire a lawyer to do so on his behalf—a decision that would later cost him dearly.

With a new contract in the pipeline, Wexler asked Stewart if he would consider recording two other Atlantic artists that he thought might benefit from Stax's informal studio arrangements: Wilson Pickett and Don Covay. Jim Stewart agreed to this, primarily to help out, and arranged for Wilson Pickett to work on some song ideas with guitarist Steve Cropper. "Wilson and I wrote three songs together in one night," Cropper later recalled. "They picked us up at the airport and we checked into the Holiday Inn, which is not there anymore. We wrote 'In the Midnight Hour,' 'I'm Not Tired,' and 'Don't Fight It' all in one night!"

"In the Midnight Hour" was chosen as Pickett's next single but was released on Atlantic, not Stax. It was released in May 1965 and quickly climbed to No. 1 on the R&B charts. The song was also a massive crossover success, reaching No. 21 on the pop charts and selling well in the UK, too, garnering Pickett's first Grammy nomination along the way.

Atlantic was keen to replicate Pickett's success and sent singer Don Covay to Memphis the following month. Again, he teamed up with Steve Cropper, and together they wrote "See-Saw" and "Sookie Sookie," both R&B classics, which confirmed Cropper's growing strength as both a songwriter and arranger.

Covay clashed with both Jim Stewart and the house band, which didn't appreciate the singer's brash attitude or having to effectively work for free for Atlantic. That clash carried over into Wilson Pickett's subsequent studio sessions. By that stage, he was a big star, and he treated the studio musicians badly. They eventually walked out of the third recording session, only for Pickett to offer them one hundred dollars each to return to the studio. The musicians refused, telling Jim Stewart "not to bring that asshole down here again."

As spring turned into summer, the hits continued. Carla Thomas returned to the charts with a song called "Stop! Look What You're Doin,'" which was her biggest hit since "What a Fool I've Been" in 1963. The song had been cowritten by Washington-based disc jockey, Al Bell, and a songwriter by the name of Eddie Floyd. "Carla Thomas was going to Howard University there at that time," explained Floyd. "But I knew Carla. I'd met her when I was with the Falcons. We had 'I Found a Love' and 'You're So Fine' out. She was going to university back there in Tennessee, and we were there playing, so I did know her already."[6]

The song was recorded in Memphis rather than Washington. "Eddie brought a guitarist," explained Carla. "This guy's name was Al McCloud. You know how Curtis Mayfield played? He had that little twirl when he played. Al played a lot like that. That's why 'Stop! Look What You're Doin'' sounds like that, because he's on it, not Steve [Cropper]. You hear the difference in the guitar."[7]

Before the end of the year, both Al Bell and Eddie Floyd would join Stax on a formal basis, with Bell in charge of promotion and Floyd initially working as a songwriter.

Stax was back on the charts again in the early summer. The vocal group, the Mad Lads, scored their biggest chart hit with the delightful but old-fashioned doo-wop song, "Don't Have to Shop Around," which reached No. 11 on the R&B charts.

After producing a steady stream of hit singles, Jim Stewart and Estelle Axton were both aware that the record label needed to devote more time to promotion. Detroit's Motown Records used to host regular Motortown Revues across the country, showcasing their biggest stars but also giving emerging artists like Stevie Wonder and Marvin Gaye the chance to make a name for themselves.

Estelle Axton had long handled most of the record label's promotional activities and had good relationships with many of the country's disc jockeys through her work in the record shop. At that point, Stax Records still had a relatively weak presence on the West Coast, so Estelle Axton started to plan a Stax Revue in conjunction with an LA-based DJ by the name of Magnificent Montague, who worked at the city's leading R&B station, KGFJ.

Montague was known as a "character" DJ, yelling his popular catchphrase "burn, baby, burn" between songs. But he also had a reputation as a shady character, having ripped off various Stax artists in one of his previous jobs in New York. "We had done another gig with Montague [when] I was in college," Carla explained. "He was supposed to pay Booker and left owing everybody. He ran out of the door with the money."[8]

Despite his reputation, Estelle Axton needed Montague's help to get airplay on the West Coast and to secure promotional appearances for the Stax musicians.

The highlight of the trip was a two-night Stax Revue on August 7 and 8 at the 54 Ballroom (pronounced "5–4"), an older club situated on the intersection of 54th Street and Broadway in the South Central district of Los Angeles known as Watts. The Revue featured Booker T. & the M.G.'s, vocal groups the Astors and the Mad Lads, a resurrected version of the Mar-Keys featuring Estelle's son, Packy Axton, William Bell, who had just returned from two years of military service, and Carla Thomas and her father, Rufus, who headlined the show.

Joining the Stax stars on the trip was Atlantic's Wilson Pickett, which probably reflected Stax returning a favor to Atlantic, who had featured Stax performers at their own revues in New York.

"I flew out from Indianapolis for that show," recalled Booker T., who was still at college in Indiana. "That was a prestigious gig for Stax—that was Hollywood. It was one of our first shows outside [as the M.G.'s]—we didn't play live that much."[9]

Montague and Axton had arranged a number of high-profile TV appearances before the weekend shows. Carla Thomas's single "Stop! Look What You're Doin'" was on the charts, and she appeared on Dick Clark's *Where the Action Is*, joined by the Astors, who sang "Candy." Rufus Thomas appeared on *Shindig!* To perform "Walking the Dog" while Booker T. & the M.G.'s played "Boot-Leg," a Top 10 R&B hit, on a program called *Hollywood a Go-Go*. The TV appearances were also the subject of a *Billboard* article on August 7 titled "Stax and Volt Artists on TV." Whatever his shortfalls as an individual, it is clear that Magnificent Montague knew a thing or two about promotion.

The main concerts were a resounding success. Booker T. & the M.G.'s were arguably the stars of the show. As Jones explained, they did not play live that regularly in the early days, but there was a real intensity to their playing. "Green Onions" was effectively refried and served burning hot, while "Boot-Leg," featuring the Mar-Keys horn section, received a rousing reception from the capacity crowd of seven hundred. William Bell's "Any Other Way" contained echoes of Sam Cooke, but his soulful version of "You Don't Miss Your Water" was even better, supported by Booker T.'s gospel-infused organ.

The Magnificent Montague gave the headliner, Rufus Thomas, a James Brown-style introduction: "He needs no introduction, he needs no publicity, he needs no promotion, he only needs you to give a big round of applause . . . " culminating in a "one, two, three—BURN!" Rufus Thomas duly delivered with crowd-pleasing versions of his two biggest hits, "The Dog" and "Walking the Dog."

Years later, a recording of the concert was later released on Ace Records titled *Stax Revue Live at the 5/4 Ballroom*. Given how few live recordings were made of the likes of Booker T. & the M.G.'s, William Bell, Carla Thomas and Rufus Thomas at their prime, it is an invaluable recording.

What the Stax musicians did not realize at the time was that the local African American community was already fired up by a combination of discriminatory local housing laws and police behavior, and the combination of hot R&B and an incendiary DJ yelling "burn, baby, burn!" was simply adding fuel to the fire.

Most of the musicians, including Rufus and Carla Thomas, returned to Memphis on Monday morning, but the Astors flew back on Wednesday, and as their plane took off, they noticed thick coils of black smoke billowing above the urban sprawl. The band was witnessing the outbreak of what became known as the Watts Rebellion, the biggest race riots seen in the United States in the 1960s.

The riots were significant for a number of reasons. The insurrection symbolized a dramatic sea change in the civil rights movement. It was the harbinger of the Black Power era, an age of increased Black militancy. The Black Panthers were formed in Oakland, California, in late 1966, and six months later, the Student Nonviolent Coordinating Committee, or SNCC (known as "Snick")—fronted by Stokely Carmichael—kicked out its white members. This would have far-reaching implications, calling into question Martin Luther King's approach to peaceful protest and also feeding into the music being created by Black musicians, many of whom felt obliged to reflect this change in mentality.

The fact that the riots started in the Watts district, days after a Stax Revue in which the audience was shouting "burn, baby, burn!," meant that the Memphis-based record label felt a lasting bond with the neighborhood. As the music being created by Stax also started to turn more political in the late 1960s and early 1970s, the label arranged a commemorative concert, Wattstax, in the summer of 1972—the seventh anniversary of the riots. According to the Reverend Jesse Jackson, who was the event's MC, it was intended as "a day of Black awareness."

Back in Memphis, Jim Stewart was trying to negotiate a deal to land Al Bell to join Stax as promotions director. He had a strong background in music, having worked as a disc jockey in Arkansas (where he was born), Memphis, and more recently, Washington. He also understood how record companies worked, having established a small label of his own, Safice Records, while in Washington. He was well-known by many of the Stax artists, most of whom felt sure he would be a good fit.

But there were other aspects of Bell's background that arguably made him the perfect counterbalance to Jim Stewart and Estelle Axton. He had a head for business, having studied at Philander Smith College in Arkansas. He also felt a close affinity for the civil rights movement, having worked closely with Dr. King in Georgia before moving to Memphis, which gave him respect among the predominantly African American artists on the label. He was also an imposing man, standing six feet, four inches tall, with a personality to match.

"Jim [Stewart] was an astute business person, but he was not the wheeler-dealer that we needed to work with the disc jockeys, the radio station owners, and the distributors and all that—Al was that kind of person," explained William Bell. "But he was a good person, and he was good for Stax because he knew the industry and knew the disc jockeys, because he worked in radio."[10]

The only issue was compensation. Jim Stewart was relatively tight with money and reluctant to pay much of an advance to sign a recording artist, let alone a promotions man. He initially offered Bell a salary of one hundred dollars per week and persuaded Wexler to match that sum. Bell laughed and explained that he was making far more than that working as a disc jockey and promoter. The only way to tempt him to join was to make him a partner, offering him a percentage of the company. And with that, Al Bell came on board in the early autumn of 1965.

One of the first changes Bell introduced was the concept of the "sales thermometer." He drew a thermometer on a flip chart with a small amount of red ink on the bottom, which was the mercury. As sales and revenue would increase, he would recalibrate the temperature to show the heat rising. "Al told us that when we reached the top, he was gonna give everyone a bonus," explained Steve Cropper. "So we couldn't wait to come in on Monday morning and see!"[11]

The first project to get the temperature rising was the recording of Otis Redding's new album. By the summer of 1965, Otis Redding was one of Stax Records' biggest stars. While he had only been with the label for three years and had been slow to take off, his last five singles had all made the Top 20 on the *Billboard* R&B charts; in fact, the last two singles, "I've Been Loving You Too Long" and "Respect," had both made the Top 5.

Redding's growing success was based on hard work. He toured incessantly, but his approach was radically different from his labelmate, Rufus Thomas. While Thomas tended to play at small venues using a pickup band, Redding was more ambitious. He rented a bus and crisscrossed America with eight to ten acts on the bus, plus an eight-piece band. This meant more up-front costs, but it also meant that they could play in bigger theaters which brought in more money; more money, it turned out, than hit singles. He was not only a successful singer but an astute businessman, too.

The initial contract that Jim Stewart had signed with Otis Redding was for a period of three years. The singer was ambitious and was encouraged by Stax Records to renew its distribution deal with Atlantic. That summer, he agreed to a new five-year deal which saw his royalty rate increase from 3 percent to 5 percent.

With an extensive touring schedule, it was a monumental task to get Redding into the studio to record his new album. He had two free days in his schedule on July 9 and 10, which happened to fall on a weekend, before another gig on that Monday. There were two problems, though: first, he hadn't finalized all of his new material, which meant that he would need some time to polish the songs with guitarist Steve Cropper before they were recorded. The second problem was that some members of the house band had gigs booked that weekend, which meant taking a lengthy break in the limited recording time available that Saturday night from 8 p.m. until 2 a.m. Sunday morning.

Jim Stewart enlisted the help of Atlantic's engineer, Tom Dowd, who flew down from New York to assist in the recording process. The house band featured Booker T. & the M.G.'s, Isaac Hayes, who helped out on piano, and the Memphis Horns.

One of the many highlights recorded during the marathon session was a song Redding had written called "Respect." According to the drummer, Al Jackson Jr., Redding wrote the song after a conversation they had during a break in the recording session in which he told Redding, "You're on the road all the time. All you can look for is a little respect when you come home." "Respect" was the first single to be released from the new album, reaching No. 4 on the R&B charts. It would be an even bigger hit for Aretha Franklin two years later, who added the distinctive "sock it to me" refrain sung by the backing singers.[12]

The album also included a cover of "Satisfaction" by the Rolling Stones, which had been suggested by Steve Cropper. "I went up to the front of the record shop, got a copy of the record, played it for the band, and wrote down the lyrics," he later recalled. Redding had never heard the song but delivered a storming version, famously pronouncing it "satis-fashion." Again, this was later released as a single, peaking at No. 4 on the R&B charts, helping to cement Redding's reputation as the biggest new star in R&B.[13]

The album relied heavily on cover versions, most likely reflecting the time constraints faced by the musicians who may not have had time to complete some of the other songs Redding was working on. There were three songs by Sam Cooke, the gospel and R&B singer who had been shot dead seven months earlier. They included a stirring version of his civil rights song, "A Change Is Gonna Come"—shortened to "Change Gonna Come"—and a swinging version of "Shake."

The resulting album was called *Otis Blue/Otis Redding Sings Soul*, but it is usually referred to as *Otis Blue*. Despite the time constraints in the recording process and the preponderance of covers, it is widely regarded

as Otis Redding's finest album, up there among the best R&B albums
of all time. It was released on September 15, 1965, and topped the R&B
album charts in the US. Notably, it also reached No. 6 on the UK album
charts, prompting his first European tour the following year.

As the year came to a close, Carla Thomas was back home in Memphis
for the holidays, and Jim Stewart set about completing her second full-
length album—which was only the sixth album to appear on the label.

The album included two singles she had recorded back in late 1964:
"I've Got No Time to Lose" and "A Woman's Love," both of which charted.
Both songs were arranged by Steve Cropper, whom Carla clearly enjoyed
working with. Strangely, the album did not include two singles from 1965,
"How Do You Quit (Someone You Love)," which had been composed by
David Porter, Isaac Hayes, and Raymond Moore, and "Stop! Look What
You're Doin'," even though both songs had charted.

The most likely explanation is that Jim Stewart, perhaps in conjunction with Al Bell, wanted to present more new material in the hope of
landing Carla a big hit single. In any event, only one more single was
released from the album.

The single chosen was the album's opening song, which was also the
title track. "Comfort Me" had been composed by the songwriting duo
of Al Bell and Eddie Floyd working in conjunction with Steve Cropper.
The more mature lyrical theme, with Carla asking her lover to provide
comfort in her hour of need, seemed appropriate for her as she was now
older and wiser. Better still, the recording features stunning gospel-like
backing vocals courtesy of Gladys Knight and the Pips. "They might have
been in town for a show, but I had no idea they were going to come on
my [record]. They just came in to say 'Hi.' They heard the tape and they
said, 'Wow, can we do that?' And I was like [gasps in disbelief]. Because
when we were in school, all the young ladies would just croon—Gladys
was singing 'With every beat of my heart,' you know, 'there's a beat for
you.'" It's one of the great Carla Thomas songs, and it remains a mystery
as to why it didn't chart when it was released in December 1965; perhaps
it got lost among the Christmas releases.[14]

Incidentally, Jim Stewart tried to sign Gladys Knight to Stax Records
after the recording session but to no avail. "They said, 'Jim, we're already
signed with Motown!'" revealed Steve Cropper. "They always tried to
sign anyone they thought was real good so they could have hit songs."[15]

Carla's take on Barbara Mason's "Yes, I'm Ready" is perfect; the vocals
are sweet but not too sweet, and a delicate horn arrangement replaces
the strings of the original. "Lover's Concerto" is pure pop, a far cry from

the sophisticated opening track, but good fun nonetheless. Next up is a Hayes and Porter composition, "I'm for You," which is one of the best songs they wrote for Carla. The Stax artists were primarily male, and their songs often seemed better-suited to male singers. But this song was tailor-made, and the horn arrangement elegantly frames her vocals.

Side two wasn't quite as strong but was still impressive. Carla's version of Bacharach and David's "What the World Needs Now" was bold and original, with the strings replaced by an innovative horn arrangement, Stax-style. In many ways, this provided a template for the "adult contemporary" sound that she tried to move toward in 1967 when she started to work with pianist and arranger Donny Hathaway.

The arrangement of Goffin and King's "Will You Love Me Tomorrow" was less successful and didn't really add much to the original, which was perfect in every way. "Move On Drifter," a Baby Washington B-side, was a better choice of a cover, and Carla makes the song her own here. The album's closing track, "Another Night Without My Man," is another highlight; it was another Bell/Floyd/Cropper composition ballad, Carla mourning the fact that her lover failed to come home.

By the time "Comfort Me" was recorded, Carla Thomas was almost twenty-three years of age and a graduate, not a schoolgirl. Stax looked to project a more mature image in terms of both the choice of songs and, indeed, the album cover, which showed her reclining on a sofa in a slightly provocative manner. As an artistic statement, it was pretty much perfect—the sound of an artist finding her own voice, treading a fine line between pop and R&B. The one thing it lacked was a smash hit single; in an ideal world, the title track would have provided just that. The album sold quite well, peaking at No. 11 on the R&B charts but failing to achieve crossover success and only reaching No. 134 on the pop charts.

♦ ♦ ♦

The year 1965 was the most successful one for Stax Records so far, with eight Top 20 R&B hits recorded by a number of different artists—including Booker T. & the M.G.'s, the Astors, Sam and Dave, and their biggest star, Otis Redding. Carla Thomas failed to crack the Top 20 but came close on a few occasions. Perhaps the biggest surprise was that their biggest star of 1963 and 1964, Rufus Thomas, failed to chart that year.

It wasn't through lack of trying. In March 1965, he released a self-composed single, "Little Sally Walker." Similar to "Walking the Dog," the lyrics were inspired by a children's nursery rhyme of the same name. The words of the original vary but are usually given as:

Little Sally Walker, sitting in a saucer,
Rise, Sally, rise!
Wipe your weeping eyes!
Turn to the east,
Turn to the west,
Turn to the one that you love the best.

As one would expect, Thomas tried to turn the song into a novelty dance number, changing it to the following:

Little Sally Walker, sittin' in a saucer,
Rise, Sally, rise!
Wipe your weepin' eyes!
Put your hands on your hips,
And let your backbone slip.
I want you to shake it to the east,
Awww, I moved that-a baby!
Shake it to the west,
I moved I moved that baby!
Shake it to the very one,
That you love the best.

The resulting song didn't work so well as a dance number and failed to catch on with the public. "He cut a difficult path for himself, Rufus," explained Booker T. Jones. "He started with a unique novelty song, "The Dog." How are you going to top that? I mean, that's his first big hit. I think 'Walking the Dog' was even bigger than 'The Dog.' But that's the problem for all these entertainers. How do you top that? He fell right into that trap. That was a big conundrum for us [Booker T. & the M.G.'s] and for Rufus."[16]

In June 1965, Rufus Thomas tried his hand at a novelty song that in-house songwriter David Porter had written for him called "Willy Nilly." The title was inspired by a newspaper headline about Lyndon B. Johnson, according to Porter. "It was on the front page of the paper," he explained. "'Johnson says that the Communist situation is willy nilly.'"[17]

Thomas was less than enthusiastic about the new song. "'Willy Nilly' is the worst song title I heard in my life. I hated it," he said. Coming from the man who wrote "Funky Penguin," that seemed a little unfair to Porter. That being said, Thomas had a point—it wasn't one of Porter's finest lyrics. The public seemed to agree, and the record again failed to chart.[18]

In response to Rufus's criticism, the Hayes-Porter team wrote "When You Move You Lose" for Rufus and Carla to sing as a duet. It was a much stronger song, helped by a powerful performance from Carla Thomas and a Motown-style backing vocal. Perhaps the military-style drumbeat made the arrangement sound too stilted and in need of further development, but the single did not sell particularly well.

Thomas tried his luck again in August 1965, with his third single in three months, which suggested he was starting to feel frustrated. This time he reworked his 1956 single, "The Easy Livin' Plan," into more of a dance tune, renaming it "The World Is Round." It was by far his strongest song of the year, with a swinging arrangement that he worked up in the studio featuring a great drum break, presumably courtesy of Al Jackson Jr.

Once again, chart success eluded him. His version of the song was covered one year later by the British singer Georgie Fame, who had long been a fan of Rufus Thomas's songs. He included it on his third album, *Sweet Things*, which was released in 1966.

Thomas returned to the studio on two additional occasions that year. One session was to record another duet with Carla, a cover of Jewel Akens's hit single "The Birds and the Bees," which had been a big hit on both the pop and R&B charts in the spring of 1965. The song was given the full Stax treatment, including a rousing horn section, but failed to capture the imagination of the public, perhaps because it was so soon after the original.

The final recording session that year took place with the rejuvenated Mar-Keys, with Thomas bringing a new groove to the studio and trying to work up some lyrics for the song. "Rufus's words were not gelling," recalled baritone saxophonist Floyd Newman. "He was a disc jockey at that particular time and he had to go to work. It just wasn't coming off. We had been there so long and his time was running out. So, he left and went to work. Jim [Stewart] said, 'Why don't you all try to work something out on that?'" The band reworked the melody completely and came up with a tune called "Philly Dog," which referenced Thomas's "dog" hits and name-checked Philadelphia because, according to Wayne Jackson, "Philadelphia was always the place where the dances came out of."[19]

"Philly Dog" was released in January 1966 and reached No. 19 on the R&B charts. Any frustration that Thomas felt over failing to make the tune work for himself was probably alleviated by the fact that he was given a writing credit on the tune.

◆ ◆ ◆

While Thomas was struggling to find the right recipe for his next hit single, his wife, Lorene Thomas, found herself with more time on her hands. Her son, Marvell, had been drafted into the army, and Carla Thomas no longer required her help as a chaperone while on tour; she was studying for her master's degree in Washington DC. In the meantime, her younger daughter, Vaneese Thomas, was now a teenager and no longer required as much of her time.

Lorene Thomas had been a member of the Memphis branch of the National Association for the Advancement of Colored People (NAACP) for several years, working closely with the legendary activist Maxine Smith, who had been promoted to executive secretary of the Memphis branch in 1962.

"My mother was really important in the civil rights story," Vaneese later recalled. "She was the recording secretary for the local branch of the NAACP, and so in the early days, she and Maxine interacted with Martin Luther King, John Lewis, and the other leaders. Whenever she sat in, picketed, all the things she was doing, she took me. I remember sitting in in the middle of a bank floor when I was eight years old. This would have been around 1960, after Dr. King had begun the bus boycotts and sit-ins. For all her life, she was committed to social justice."[20]

One of her key roles within the organization was to attract new members and encourage members of the local community to get out and vote on election day. "She would go from house to house, educating people, passing out pamphlets," said family friend Trent Cobb. "There was no such thing as early voting then; you voted on the day. There were long lines! She would go and pick people up who had no transportation, or if it was too far to walk, and take them to the polls and wait on them. She was a true advocate to improve racial injustice. She was like a Dr. Martin Luther King in the neighborhood!"[21]

Lorene Thomas was also happy playing a more active role, marching and picketing. Indeed, one famous photograph by the renowned Memphis photographer Ernest Withers, best known for his civil rights photographs, shows Lorene picketing a local store on Main Street in Memphis.

Thomas used to joke that Lorene was always busy and that they had to make do with too many TV dinners around that time, but he had a deep respect for the work she was doing and even helped out with the occasional election campaign when his schedule permitted.

In 1997, Lorene Thomas was honored by the local branch of the NAACP for forty years of membership, and when she passed away three years later, Maxine Smith spoke at her funeral. "Anything, everywhere, Lorene was there," Smith said, remembering her work with the NAACP.

"She was as close to sainthood as anybody I know. She gave so much of herself to so many people without ever expecting any kind of return. She gave it because of her greatest asset—her love for people."[22]

♦ ♦ ♦

Early 1966 saw Stax Records continuing where it had left off the previous year. Once again, Otis Redding was riding high on the charts with his version of "Satisfaction." He was joined by singer Johnnie Taylor, who had recently signed to the label and made his breakthrough with a song called "I Had a Dream," another composition by the Porter-Hayes songwriting team.

Porter and Hayes struck gold again in the spring of 1966 with a song called "Let Me Be Good to You." The song was written in conjunction with Carl Wells, who seems to have contributed the song's title and some of the lyrics. "He was one of those guys who would hang around the studio," Porter explained to author Rob Bowman. "I just liked him. I tried to do something with one of his ideas."[23]

Isaac Hayes added a superb, piano-driven, Motown-style arrangement, and they invited Carla Thomas to sing the song. It was the perfect combination, and Carla took the song to No. 11 on the R&B charts, her biggest hit since "I'll Bring It Home to You" in late 1962.

Sam and Dave's next big hit was also written by Porter and Hayes and was apparently inspired by Porter taking a bathroom break. On several occasions, Hayes told the story that he was frustrated by the lack of progress being made on a song they were working on and yelled at Porter to get back to work. "I finally struck a groove," said Hayes, "and it's taking David forever!" Porter responded by shouting back, "Hold on, I'm coming!"[24]

Porter was convinced that worked as the song's new title, and Isaac Hayes added a horn riff that he had been working on that was intended for a different song, and suddenly everything fell into place. Even now, there's something thrilling about listening to the way Sam and Dave delivered each line, but that took hard work. "When it came to laying down the vocals," Porter told the Smithsonian Institution, "I'm on one side of the mike, Sam and Dave on the other, and I'd direct them, like a choir."

The hard work paid off, and with Al Bell now coordinating the marketing, the record raced up the charts, reaching No. 1 on the R&B charts and scoring high on the pop charts too. Soon after, Hayes and Porter celebrated by both buying a new car—something they also did together.

Not everyone was impressed. Rufus Thomas was particularly vocal about his feelings. "People like David Porter had one helluva ego," said

Isaac Hayes and David Porter publicity photograph, 1971. *Memphis Press-Scimitar*, Special Collections Department, University of Memphis Libraries.

Rufus. "I said, 'You around here bragging all the time. Every time I turn around, I hear you bragging about what a helluva songwriter you are'. . . . Until you write a hit song for Rufus Thomas, you ain't shit. And he never did."[25]

In hindsight, Thomas's comments about David Porter seem unfair. For one thing, Porter had worked incredibly hard for his success. He had been working two day jobs for a number of years in order to support both his family and his ambitions as a songwriter, and his hard work was finally beginning to pay off. In addition, he tried on several occasions to write songs for Thomas, both as a solo artist and performing with his older daughter Carla. "Willy Nilly" may not have cut it, but "When You Move You Lose" was a good tune, as were later efforts like "Sister's Got a Boyfriend" and "Sophisticated Cissy."

Part of the problem was that now that Hayes and Porter had established a degree of success, they were expected to write in multiple styles, from the horn-driven R&B that seemed to work for Sam and Dave to the pop songs that suited Carla to the more rhythm-oriented tunes favored by Thomas.

David Porter thought the issue was very specific. "There was no one, in my opinion, who could do a better job of writing or producing for Rufus than Rufus himself," he explained. "Isaac and I tried on a couple of occasions to write songs—and record songs—with Rufus. They were okay but they did not strike the strand that gave Rufus the kind of energy that Rufus liked to have to sell a song. And so we missed the mark! And he was the only one we couldn't do justice on a song for . . . . But any time you would hear him doing a song that he was closely associated with, it always ended up being amazing."[26]

Porter's point is a valid one; looking back over the years, most of Thomas's biggest hits were self-penned as he latched on to a particular dance craze or a rhythm that had caught his ear.

While there may have been a personality clash with Porter himself, it seems likely that there were other factors also concerning Thomas at this time. One was that the hits appeared to have dried up—at least temporarily—and if the in-house songwriters couldn't deliver them for him, he would have to write more himself.

Looking back, singer William Bell wondered if Thomas's relentless touring also dented his creativity at this time. "When Rufus got a couple of hits under his belt, he was a hard-working man—he toured constantly," he recalled. "And the logistics of touring added pressure too, because you have all the road stuff, the promoters, and the agents to deal with—it cuts into your creativity. You have to grow as an artist, learn to pace yourself. That was a learning process for all of us, including Rufus."[27]

◆ ◆ ◆

In the summer of 1966, the Stax artists got a further glimpse of Al Bell's power as a promoter when he promoted a standalone Stax Revue at the Apollo Theater in New York without the need for the support of Atlantic Records. The week-long show featured an impressive lineup: Otis Redding, Sam and Dave, Rufus Thomas, Carla Thomas, the Mad Lads, and newcomer Johnnie Taylor. The label was reluctant to let the house band away from the studio for a whole week, so backing was provided by the theater's band, the Reuben Phillips Orchestra. The show was billed as Rocky G's Boogaloo Spectacular and was cohosted by local DJs Rocky G and Frankie Crocker. The show was well-received, and Bell was convinced that it helped to expand the label's presence in New York.

Back in Memphis, Isaac Hayes and David Porter presented Carla Thomas with a song they had written called "B-A-B-Y." "They had written something for Sam and Dave, and that's how it sounded," she remembered. "It sounded to me like 'You Don't Know Like I Know.' And I said, 'I'm not going to sing that! I don't like it.'"[28]

They persuaded her to try, but she still felt it wasn't the right song for her. "You see, when you write for an artist, you write for that artist," she later explained. "You don't just throw me a song because you've got it left over from another session, especially your top female artist at that time. You just don't do that. That was the first time I'd ever said, 'Uh-uh. I'm through. Bye!' I don't think I'd ever done that before, but sometimes you just have to!"[29]

Porter and Hayes did not want to fall out with Carla Thomas and visited her at home the next day, trying to persuade her to return to the studio. Her father, Rufus, encouraged her to stand firm, and she insisted it wasn't the right song for her.

At this point, Booker T. Jones stepped in and started working on a new arrangement of the song to try and make it more suitable for Carla's pop-oriented style. "It was one of the more stressful situations. It took a long time—around eight days," he remembered. "It wasn't working, and I finally came up with a new arrangement, and she was so happy with me."

"Booker changed the whole song," said Carla. "They [Porter and Hayes] don't like for me to say that, but Booker was on the organ, and they had come up with this little introduction on the bass line. I said, 'Now I can sing it!'" It wasn't just the organ, either—the Motown-style arrangement, the seductive way Carla sang "baby," the lush backing vocals, and Al Jackson's perfectly placed drumbeats all helped to make the song utterly irresistible.

The backing singers also featured Carla's younger sister, Vaneese, who made her first appearance on record here at the age of thirteen. "They knew me since I was a baby," she said. "When my mother would allow it, Daddy would bring me down to the studio. David knew that I could sing. I've been singing since I've been in the world. He asked if I wanted to sing on 'B-A-B-Y,' and the three of us sang background, David, Carla and me."[30]

The single was released in July 1966 and became Carla's biggest R&B hit to date, reaching No. 3 on the R&B charts and narrowly missing the Top 10 on the pop charts.

At the suggestion of Al Bell, guitarist Steve Cropper had forged a strong songwriting relationship with Eddie Floyd. They had cowritten two songs for Carla Thomas's sophomore album, *Comfort Me*, including the title track. That July, they went over to the nearby Lorraine Motel to work on some more songs.

The Lorraine Motel was popular with Stax staff for a number of reasons. "The Lorraine was the only hotel for Blacks in town," explained Booker T. Jones. "Stax staff meetings were held there over lunch at midday, then an afternoon swim before heading back to McLemore Avenue."[31]

One particular evening there was a big thunderstorm, and Floyd started to tell Cropper about the big storms he witnessed growing up in Alabama. "In Alabama, man, there's like thunder and lightning," he told Cropper. "We'd hide under the bed because we'd be frightened." Cropper liked this phrase and suggested the lyric "it's like thunder, lightning, the way you love me is frightening."

"We were trying to write a song about superstitions, and after we'd exhausted about every superstition known to man at that time, from cats to umbrellas, you name it, we said, what do people do for good luck?" Steve Cropper recalled to *Mojo* magazine. "And Ed tapped on the chair and said, 'Knock on wood, there it is.' So basically the whole theme of the song changed, and we started to sing about, I'd better knock on wood for good luck, that I can keep this girl that I got, because she's the greatest—and that's what it was about."

The song was almost there, but the arrangement still needed fleshing out. Isaac Hayes helped out with the horn line, but the key to the song's success, according to Eddie Floyd, was drummer Al Jackson Jr. "He said, "Let me put something in there," Floyd laughed. "And he put in a break where everyone stops, and he hits the drum, like knocking on the door . . . if he hadn't did that [sic], I'm convinced it wouldn't have been a hit."[32]

Floyd suggested it might make a good song for Otis Redding but was overruled by Jim Stewart, who suggested he cut it himself. "Knock On Wood" was released as a single on July 25, 1966, and rose to the top of the R&B charts. It was also a big crossover hit, reaching No. 28 on the *Billboard* Hot 100 and No. 19 on the UK singles chart. The song proved to be very popular over the years and was later covered by both David Bowie and disco singer Amii Stewart, who returned the song to the top of the charts in 1979.

In the late summer of 1966, Jim Stewart urged Carla Thomas to return to the studio to record a new album to consolidate her recent success in the singles market with "Let Me Be Good to You" and "B-A-B-Y."

Despite the inclusion of the two hit singles, her third album, simply titled *Carla*, suffers slightly in comparison with her previous album. First, *Comfort Me* was only released early in 1966; for a record label that was primarily focused on singles rather than albums—at that time, at least—to release two albums by the same artist in one year was perhaps over-ambitious. Secondly, the album was too varied stylistically and lacked any real focus. Carla sang two of the country songs that she loved when she was a teenager and also two blues tunes—Howlin' Wolf's "Little Red Rooster" and Jimmy Reed's "Baby What You Want Me to Do?"

Of the two country songs, Hank Williams's "I'm So Lonely I Could Cry" works really well. The Stax team gave the song a country-soul flavor, complete with a horn section, which is effective, and Carla's delivery is perfect. Patsy Cline's "I Fall to Pieces" is less successful and would perhaps have been a better fit on her debut album. There's nothing wrong with Carla's delivery, but it simply sounds out of place here.

The two blues tunes are okay but not great. Carla is clearly a much better singer than her father, Rufus Thomas, but he was a better blues singer, and it's hard to escape the feeling that her delivery lacks authenticity. Willie Dixon's classic "Red Rooster" lacks the necessary strut while she struggles to sound as down and dirty as Cropper's guitar on "Baby What You Want Me to Do?"

None of this makes *Carla* a bad album. Carla Thomas's own composition, "I Got You, Boy," is much better, hitting the pop-soul groove, complete with a bold horn arrangement and call-and-response backing vocals. "What Have You Got to Offer Me," a ballad composed by Carla, also works well and shows her maturing as a songwriter. There's also a gorgeous version of Dusty Springfield's smash hit, "You Don't Have to Say You Love Me," with Carla putting her own stamp on the song. This song, in particular, hints at the sophisticated pop sound that Carla would target a couple of years down the line.

If *Comfort Me* was the sound of a young lady maturing as both a person and an artist, the follow-up sounded like she had reached a crossroads and was unsure which direction she should be heading in.

Deanie Parker, who had joined Stax as a female singer-songwriter herself in 1963, had a slightly different take. "Carla was versatile, and I'm not sure she excelled at any one style enough that you knew it was Carla, like you knew it was Aretha the moment the needle hit the groove, you know?" she explained. "She could have been a number of different artists, all good, but not great."

The album certainly demonstrates Carla's versatility, but to my mind, she fails to convince as either a blues singer or a "pure" country singer; if the charts were anything to go by, pop-soul seemed to be her forte, and she probably needed someone at Stax—most likely Jim Stewart—to steer her in the right direction.

Carla was released in September 1966. The album fared similarly to *Comfort Me*, reaching No. 130 on Top LP charts and No. 8 on R&B charts.

Carla had one last crack at the singles chart that year, resurrecting "All I Want for Christmas Is You," the B-side to 1963's "Gee Whiz, It's Christmas," to celebrate the 1966 holidays. The B-side was a new Isaac Hayes original, "Winter Snow," which Carla apparently wanted as the A-side. In truth, the string-drenched tune was pretty but probably too downbeat for the Christmas market. It made little difference, as the single failed to chart, but the "Moohah" Williams's song remains a lovely Christmas tune that deserves to be better known.

Otis Redding returned to the studio again in August 1966, as so often the case, with the sketch of a song in his head. "I traveled with Otis for about a year and a half. We were writing while we were going along the highway in the car—he never wrote the whole verse down," recalled fellow singer William Bell. "He wrote the first line of a verse and had the rest in his head. That's what made his singing so great, he could ad lib around the story line that he had in his head. You'd never see him with the whole song written down. The same with the horn arrangements!"[33]

And it was those horn arrangements in his head that gave their name to his next single, "Fa-Fa-Fa-Fa-Fa (Sad Song)." And if you think that humming a horn line sounds simple, then think again. "Otis always had the hardest head arrangements," explained baritone saxophonist Floyd Newman. "James Brown did the same thing, but Otis's horn lines were entirely different from what James was doing. They were more difficult, rhythmically and harmonically. Otis always did things in keys like E, A and F sharp, the keys that nobody was playing in. The sharp keys are brilliant keys but people just don't mess around with them much. It gave his songs a lot of punch and drive and made you want to pop your fingers. He would always say, 'Floyd, if you listen to the song and your shoulders don't move, there's no groove to it.'"[34]

This helps to explain why there was always a palpable excitement in the Stax recording studio when Otis Redding was in town. The single was released in September and continued Redding's run of hits, reaching No. 12 on the R&B charts and No. 29 on the pop charts, demonstrating that he was becoming a genuine crossover artist with both national and international appeal.

But arguably, the best was yet to come. Redding's manager, Phil Walden, had suggested he cut an old standard by the name of "Try a Little Tenderness," a song which was originally recorded back in 1933 and had been covered by the likes of Bing Crosby and Frank Sinatra.

Redding had heard the song on Sam Cooke's classic *Sam Cooke at the Copa* album, where he includes the song as part of a medley, but this is an abbreviated version, which is probably why Redding only knew the first two verses.

"Otis Redding in the studio and Otis Redding on stage were quite different," recalled Booker T. Jones, who played piano on the session. "In the studio, he was very inventive, and there were many possibilities with him."[35]

On this particular occasion, Isaac Hayes had written most of the arrangement, including the horn section. But the magic started when drummer Al Jackson Jr. started picking out rim shots in the second verse. "I looked at him like he was crazy at first but soon realized those taps were in rhythm and possibly the precursor of something more exciting to come," recalled the pianist. "Sure enough, he played a big fill leading into the first turn, and I hit a B in the left hand, an inversion leading into the E7 turn, and instantly we had a turn, a build that was about to explode into something."[36]

Redding instantly recognized what was taking place, marching across the studio, improvising as he did so. "You've got ta! Squeeze her! Don't tease her! Never leave her!" At that point, Redding leaped in front of the drummer, who had kicked off the whole idea, and Jackson responded by playing a fill, and the band broke, creating a momentary silence. "Na, na, na, na! Try a little . . . tenderness!" roared the singer, prompting an explosion from the band. Amazingly, the improvised section takes up a full minute—the last one-third of the song.

Jim Stewart did not smile easily but burst into a grin as the song climaxed. "If there's one song, one performance that really sort of sums up Otis and what he's about, it's 'Try a Little Tenderness,'" he later revealed. "That one performance is so special and so unique that it expresses who he is."[37]

The single was released on November 14, 1966, and reached No. 4 on the R&B charts, again charting nationally on the pop charts and in the UK, too.

The year 1966 had been a phenomenal one for Stax Records. Otis Redding was now a major star, and Sam and Dave had delivered on their early promise, forging a strong partnership with songwriters Isaac Hayes and David Porter. Carla Thomas was the label's most successful female artist and had enjoyed a successful year with two big hit singles, while newcomers Eddie Floyd, Johnnie Taylor, and blues singer Albert King were coming through the ranks. The Memphis-based label had cemented its place nationally; now, it was time to do the same thing in Europe.

Chapter Eight

King and Queen

Stax in Europe, 1967

Stax Records continued its hot streak in the early months of 1967. The first single to be released that year was "Something Good (Is Going to Happen to You)," which paired the newly christened "Memphis Queen," Carla Thomas, and the hit songwriting duo of Hayes and Porter.

Given that Carla Thomas had released her third album, *Carla*, just four months earlier, it might have made more sense to release one more single from that album in an attempt to boost sales. The decision to record a brand-new single was no doubt because Carla was back from Washington for the Christmas holidays.

The recording session did not go particularly smoothly. The relationship between Carla Thomas and David Porter, in particular, was still somewhat frosty after the difficulties recording "B-A-B-Y" the previous summer, and Porter remembers trying out the song several times with Carla before she agreed to record it. From Carla's perspective, "that's when I started getting away from something that was basic to me."[1]

Listening now, it's hard to understand why Carla was upset over the recording. She may have thought that the song was not written specifically with her in mind, and with its upbeat tempo, was clearly not one of the "sweet little ballads" that she thought were her specialty. But it was still poppier and less gritty than many of the Hayes-Porter compositions. The horn arrangement has more of a Motown feel than many of the Stax recordings from this time. The song also features fantastic female backing vocals, which add to the pop feel, and a great piano line from Isaac Hayes on the bridge. In short, it was Carla's best single since "B-A-B-Y" and deserved to be a bigger hit than it was. Even so, the single reached a respectable No. 29 on the R&B charts and maintained Carla's chart presence.

Later that month, Hayes and Porter struck gold again with the magnificent "When Something Is Wrong with My Baby," a No. 2 hit on the R&B charts for Sam and Dave. As romantic as the song sounded, it was inspired by Porter's loveless marriage at that time; he was married to a woman he had made pregnant in high school and, by this stage, was feeling trapped and unhappy. "In the early part of my career I would fantasize about a lot of things that I would come up with for my lyrics," he revealed to Stax historian Rob Bowman. "I was fantasizing about what it would really be like to be in love."[2]

Other hits at that time included Eddie Floyd's follow-up to "Knock on Wood," "Raise Your Hand," which also reached the Top 20, "Hip Hug-Her" by Booker T. & the M.G.'s, and "Everybody Loves a Winner" by William Bell who, like Rufus Thomas, had been suffering from a lean streak in terms of hit singles.

The first new album released by Stax in 1967 paired the label's biggest male and female stars, Otis Redding and Carla Thomas. "It was my idea to put them together for *King and Queen*," revealed the label's founder, Jim Stewart. "It turned out pretty good!"[3]

Stewart was keeping an eye on Detroit's Motown record label and was aware that Marvin Gaye and Kim Weston had recorded a hit single, "It Takes Two," which had been released in early December 1966. "I thought it would be helpful to both artists' careers," Stewart explained. "Carla was always sort of special to me because she was my first artist and I felt she needed a boost. I thought the combination of his rawness and her sophistication would work. I wanted to try it."[4]

Carla Thomas and Otis Redding had been close friends since he signed for the label back in 1962. She used to tease him about how he sounded like Little Richard when he first came to Memphis. "The more he stayed here, his style became more like the bluesy things that you start hearing later like 'Dock of the Bay' and that kind of song," she told NPR Radio. For his part, Otis actually named his third child Karla after Carla Thomas, which cemented their close bond.

Both singers were apparently unsure whether the project would work. Carla was particularly apprehensive. "I didn't want to do it," she later admitted. "Not because I didn't like Otis. I loved Otis. But it was like, 'Are y'all kidding me, singing with Otis Redding?' So he came in, I think it was close to Christmas, and we just started throwing out songs. And I said, 'Whatever you sing, I'll come in there and try to sing with you.'"[5]

The first song that Redding suggested was a cover of the Lowell Fulson song "Tramp," which had been a big R&B hit earlier that year. "They wanted to make something of the fact that Otis was a country boy and Carla was a city girl," recalled pianist Booker T. Jones, who had now finished his degree in Indiana and was available in the studio on a more regular basis.[6]

Redding suggested they play up their differences, given that she was from Memphis and he was from Georgia. "He said, 'You're from the South. You know how to bless people out!'" she recalled. "I said, 'Not really. I never had nobody I had to bless out!' He said, 'Well, let's just write—whatever you feel like you come up with, we'll put the piece of paper right here.' So that's what I did. I just stood right there. I put the music stand up, and when I came up with something, I just wrote it. 'You're just a tramp! You ain't got no money!' It was just so real. He was laughing half the time, and I was laughing. It was just wonderful."

The song features a hard-hitting horn section, which was clearly Redding's idea. "Otis loved the hard brass," recalled Carla.

"Knock on Wood" was another one of the album's highlights. Cowriter Eddie Floyd had Otis Redding in mind when he wrote the song, although he ended up recording the song first. Redding tackles it the same way he did "Satisfaction" by the Rolling Stones—like a freight train! There is real chemistry between the two singers as they take turns singing below the other's lead, imbuing the song with an amazing energy.

"Tell It Like It Is" by Aaron Neville was a contemporary hit, having been released as a single in November 1966. Carla was a huge fan of Neville's and suggested they cut the song together. As a slow ballad, this was well within Carla's comfort zone, but Redding holds his own, injecting more of a deep soul feeling than the original.

"Lovey Dovey," another cover, was originally a doo-wop hit for the Clovers in 1954. Otis and the Stax house band turn it into a fast-paced foot-stomper, the vocal harmonies replaced by a steamy call-and-response duet. "Ooh Carla, Ooh Otis," was composed especially for the session by Otis Redding and Al Bell. It's not as smoochy as it sounds; it's another up-tempo tune, built on a bass riff by "Duck" Dunn that sounds like it was lifted from Henry Mancini's *Peter Gunn* theme, coupled with another monster horn riff. You can hear that Otis and Carla were having great fun recording it with the chemistry shining through.

Once these initial songs had been recorded, Redding had to leave Memphis to go away on tour and laid down his own vocal tracks for a few more songs. These were generally less successful. The main exception is the delightful "New Year's Resolution," which was written in-house by Deanie Parker, Randall Catron, and Mary Frierson (who had recorded three singles for Stax as Wendy Rene in 1964 and 1965). The two singers exchange lines about how they can improve their relationship, with Redding suggesting:

> Let's turn over a new leaf,
> And baby let's make promises that we can keep.

It's near enough impossible to tell that the vocals were recorded on different days. The only giveaway is when they simultaneously sing the line "let's make promises that we can keep," Carla sings "that we can" while Redding wails "we *both* can." Still, it's a soulful performance by the King and Queen, and one of the highlights of the album.

They also record the Hayes-Porter tune that Sam and Dave had recently cut, "When Something Is Wrong with My Baby." It's good, but not as good as the original, and the vocals do not sound quite as "together" as they might have been if they had been recorded live. The same can be said of Marvin Gaye and Kim Weston's "It Takes Two," which sounds a little under-rehearsed, the chemistry lacking.

Still, *King and Queen* was a good album, with Otis Redding sounding like he was relaxed and having fun and Carla Thomas stepping out of her comfort zone to deliver grittier-sounding soul, Stax-style. It might have sounded an unlikely pairing on paper, but Jim Stewart was right, it worked well. The album was released in mid-March 1967 and reached No. 5 on the R&B charts. It also reached No 36 on the *Billboard* pop charts and an impressive No. 18 in the UK, and in that respect, the album did boost Carla Thomas's profile, as Stewart had hoped.

"Tramp" was released as a single in mid-April, reached No. 2 on the R&B chart, and also made the Top 20 on the UK charts. Lowell Fulson was reportedly unhappy about the recording by Otis and Carla and felt that it made fun of his song, but in truth, the only thing they made fun of was themselves. "Knock on Wood" was released as a single later that year and also charted, reaching No. 8 on the R&B charts.

♦ ♦ ♦

Since the early days at the Flamingo Club in London's Soho, British interest in US R&B music had exploded. The Beatles covered Motown songs like "You Really Got a Hold on Me" and "Money" on their second British album, *With the Beatles*, in 1963, while the Rolling Stones covered both Motown ("Can I Get a Witness") and Stax ("Walking the Dog") on their debut album in 1964.

Rufus Thomas and Atlantic artists Solomon Burke and Ben E. King all toured the UK for the first time in 1964, and Motown famously sent their Motown Revue in 1965. Stax artists Otis Redding and the Mad Lads had both toured in 1966, and Solomon Burke returned for a second tour.

Stax singles now regularly appeared in the UK singles chart, with Otis Redding enjoying five Top 40 hits in 1965 and 1966. Fan magazines had also started to pop up, including the likes of *Soul Music Monthly* and *Soul Beat*. The Beatles had even raised the possibility of recording at Stax Records in Memphis in 1966, an event which never took place, much to Estelle Axton's disappointment.

In early 1967, British booking agent Arthur Howes and Polydor executive Frank Fenter approached Redding's manager, Phil Walden, about arranging a second tour, this time on a larger scale. Phil Walden approached Jim Stewart, who naturally brought Al Bell into the discussion.

Bell suggested that if they were to send a revue of Stax artists, Booker T. & the M.G.'s, together with the Memphis Horns, could serve as the house band as well as appear in their own right. Sam and Dave were obviously a big draw at that time, having enjoyed a string of recent hits. Eddie Floyd, Carla Thomas, and William Bell were also invited. William Bell had already arranged a number of US dates and was unable to attend, while Carla also had a prior commitment and was only able to attend the first part of the tour.

The other name added to the tour was a Georgia-based singer named Arthur Conley, who had just enjoyed a big crossover hit with "Sweet Soul Music." He was added at the insistence of Otis Redding, who had recently signed him to a record label he had established.

Of note, Rufus Thomas was not invited on the tour, much to his disappointment. Polydor Records was responsible for the distribution of Stax Records in the UK, and as a result, Frank Fenter is likely to have had some input into the final lineup. Rufus Thomas had not enjoyed any chart success since "Jump Back" in late 1964, and this ultimately counted against him. The fact that Arthur Conley made the tour, when he was not even a Stax artist, made Thomas particularly angry.

The billing of the tour was also the source of some controversy. The tour was officially billed as the Stax-Volt Revue, as Otis Redding was officially signed to Volt, the Stax subsidiary. It was also subtitled "Hit the Road, Stax." But some of the initial ads in the UK press referred to the tour as the "Otis Redding Show" with support from the other artists. This was probably how the idea was originally pitched to Phil Walden, before the idea of a Stax-Volt Revue finally took shape. In addition, some of the tour posters showed Arthur Conley given second billing as a "special guest star" ahead of Sam and Dave; in reality, that position belonged to Sam and Dave, and deservedly so.

For the main artists, a full European tour, taking in several dates in the UK, Paris, Copenhagen, Stockholm, and Oslo, was the opportunity of a lifetime. For the Memphis Horns—who, unlike the M.G.'s, were not salaried staff at Stax Records—the decision was more difficult. Trumpet player Wayne Jackson had a regular gig at Hernando's Hideaway and was told that if he traveled to Europe, he'd be out of a job. He made the decision to join the tour and never looked back. "That door closed and other doors opened," he later recalled, "and we walked right on through, kept on going."[7]

The musicians were accompanied by a sizeable entourage of record label executives. Phil Walden was there as Otis Redding's manager and promoter. Jim Stewart and Al Bell joined from Stax Records, with Bell scheduled to appear as MC at some of the shows. Bell also wanted to take the opportunity to meet with Frank Fenter and discuss how to better promote Stax artists in Europe going forward. Atlantic's Jerry Wexler and Tom Dowd also joined. Dowd was there to record the main shows in London and Paris with a view to releasing a live album on Atlantic Records.

The tour was scheduled to begin at London's Finsbury Park Astoria, a former movie theater with a capacity of 3,000 people, on Friday, March 17. Otis Redding had flown in the previous Saturday, and most of the other artists arrived at London's Heathrow Airport on the Monday before the show, with two days set aside for rehearsals. While Booker T. & the M.G.'s had played on many of the Stax singles, they had not played them in a live setting. Likewise, many of the horn parts were devised in the studio rather than played from charts.

Steve Cropper remembers being blown away by the number of people who met them at the airport. "That was something I don't think any musician will ever forget—period," he recalled. "We were treated like royalty, much more than we expected. We expected to land in London and no one would know who we were. Well, the Beatles sent a Rolls for us and put out a red carpet, came down to our soundcheck, and hung out! Oh, man!"[8]

Jim Stewart was also surprised at how well-known Stax Records was in England. While the musicians rehearsed, he popped out to buy some new clothes. "I decided I wanted to get a shirt," he remembered. "I paid with my credit card. The sales person said, 'Just a minute' and brought my card back to the manager. She came back and said, 'The manager would like to speak to you.' I thought there must a problem and went back to his office. He shook my hand and said, 'I just wanted to meet someone from Stax Records!' It was so English!"[9]

The various Stax artists also engaged in various promotional events before the tour started. Otis Redding was the biggest center of attention and attended a press conference held at the Speakeasy, a London nightclub. "Do you think rhythm and blues is drifting more towards rock 'n' roll, so to say?" asked a BBC reporter. "I think rock 'n' roll is drifting more towards the blues," Redding replied. "People don't want to admit it, but a lot of the pop songs today are nothing but blues songs. Rhythm and blues has been here for a hundred years."

Ahead of the opening concert, Carla Thomas had been booked to play a private show, by invite only, at a small London club called the Bag O' Nails, backed by Booker T. & the M.G.'s. The Beatles had just finished recording the album *Sgt. Pepper's Lonely Hearts Club Band* at Abbey Road a few days previously, and unbeknown to Booker T. Jones, attended the gig. "I knew their music but didn't know who to look for, exactly," he recalled. "I think the whole band was there."[10]

Carla Thomas got the chance to sing a new song she had rehearsed for the tour, "Yesterday," in front of the song's composer, Paul McCartney. "It was to get the practice and it was a real intimate little place," she later recalled. "Of course, that just made us feel really good that he came to see us. We all sat at the table and talked to him and he stayed the whole night, just about until the club closed. He was wonderful. It was just an exchange of mutual admiration."[11]

The next night, the tour kicked off in earnest with two sold-out shows—at 6.40 p.m. and 9:10 p.m.—at the Finsbury Park Astoria. There was an air of anticipation ahead of the show, with heavy traffic in the area and crowds queuing to get in despite the cold weather. "It was news to me that we were so popular in the UK," said Booker T. Jones. "I didn't have a clue until I saw the size of the audience at the first gig. It was probably the largest audience I'd played for up to that time. People we met were telling us how difficult it was to get our music, and that music was being played by ships offshore ['pirate radio']; how they'd have to walk long distances to find a store that stocked our stuff. But they came in large numbers to the shows!"[12]

The London shows were hosted by Emperor Rosko, a disc jockey on a popular pirate radio station, Radio Caroline. He took to the stage, yelling into the microphone, "Gimme an S, Gimme a T, Gimme an A, Gimme an X!" before introducing Booker T. & the M.G.'s. They took to the stage wearing fetching lime green suits courtesy of Lansky Brothers in Memphis, tailor to the stars, including Elvis Presley. They played a brief set of three instrumentals, incorporating their biggest hit, "Green Onions."

They were then joined by the Memphis Horns, who wore matching royal blue suits for the occasion. The lineup for the European tour was made up of Wayne Jackson, Andrew Love, and Joe Arnold rather than Floyd Newman. Together they were billed as the Mar-Keys, even if "Packy" Axton was no longer a part of the band. They resurrected "Last Night," which was the band's biggest hit single, and also played "Philly Dog," the single that had emerged from a Rufus Thomas recording session.

Carla Thomas was next, taking the stage in an elegant, sparkly gold dress. She charmed the audience with "Gee Whiz," her first hit single, and her version of "Yesterday," which she mistakenly introduced as "a number recorded by a London group." She closed her set with "B-A-B-Y," which had many in the audience dancing in the aisles. Arthur Conley closed the first half of the show with a rousing "Sweet Soul Music;" he may have been the "new boy" on the tour, but he knew he had to put on a show and thrilled the audience with a James Brown-style exit.

After a brief interval, Eddie Floyd opened the second half of the show. European audiences were familiar with "Knock on Wood" but less familiar with his more recent material, although "Raise Your Hand" did enter the UK charts around this time.

Emperor Rosko then returned to the stage to introduce the "dynamic duo" that was Sam and Dave. They lived up to that billing with a thrilling set that culminated in a version of "Hold On, I'm Coming" that would last for several minutes. By this stage, their jackets had been removed, and they tried to out-sing and out-dance one another, imploring the audience to "stand on up" before they leaped into the crowd. They made Otis Redding's job near impossible, bidding the crowd goodnight before returning to the stage once more, leaving themselves—and the stage—drenched in sweat.

Redding watched from the side of the stage and, on one occasion, was heard to say, "I never want to have to follow those motherfuckers again!"

On previous tours, Redding had been quite static on stage, but following Sam and Dave, he transformed his live set. "He was just like a thoroughbred racehorse waiting for the bell," recalled Al Bell. When Sam and Dave finished, Otis Redding broke from behind that stage and he started going from one end of the stage to the other. I couldn't believe what was going on—the energy that I had never seen before!"[13]

As the headliner, Redding got to play a forty-five-minute set which included "Day Tripper," "Shake," "Satisfaction," "Fa-Fa-Fa-Fa-Fa (Sad Song)," "Respect," "My Girl," and the set closer, "Try a Little Tenderness." If you listen to recordings of the shows or watch some of the video clips from later in the tour, the energy level he brought is undeniable. The only complaint that some critics made was that by increasing the tempo of most of the songs, the performance was less soulful than it might have been. "Try a Little Tenderness" particularly suffered in this regard, with the subtlety of the changes in the studio version lost as drummer Al Jackson Jr. picked up the pace at Redding's request. "We're not going to let those songs just lie there onstage," he told the band.

This caused some friction with Jim Stewart, who felt that Redding was playing them too fast. After the opening night, he spoke to drummer Al Jackson, suggesting he slow the tempos down. Redding was furious and exchanged words with Jackson before the shows in Paris.

At the Olympia, Stewart entered Redding's dressing room after the first show to complain to him directly about the tempos. "We're trying to make a recording here," he explained. Redding was livid and reportedly picked Jim up by his collar. "These people are fans of mine," he explained, "And I'm going to entertain them."

Most of the reviews were extremely positive. "Just in case you hadn't heard—the Stax Show must be one of the raviest, grooviest, slickest tour packages that Britain has ever seen," wrote Nick Jones in the influential *Melody Maker*. "And if you haven't seen it already—pull your finger out!"

The following night, the Stax stars performed a show at the Upper Cut in Forest Gate in East London, a nightclub owned by boxer-turned-playboy Billy Walker. It seems an unlikely venue, and it may have originally been intended as a warm-up gig for the musicians before the Astoria shows were confirmed.

The next stop was Paris, where most of the musicians played a slightly longer set with the intention of producing a live album. Carla Thomas added an unusually up-tempo "Got My Mojo Working," which she delivered in some style, while Otis Redding added "I Can't Turn You Loose" and "I've Been Loving You Too Long."

Tempo tantrums aside, the recording process went smoothly, with Tom Dowd happier with the sound quality than he had been in London. The only problem they experienced was when Otis Redding received an unexpected reaction from the crowd. "We were recording with Tom Dowd of Atlantic," Jim Stewart recalled. "Tom and I were in the back when we heard a noise, and they were booing Otis Redding. The reason they booed him was that he tried to do a couple of lines in French! Otis was kind of shocked."[14]

Carla Thomas was only on the London and Paris legs of the tour and was determined to make the most of her time in Europe. "I remember one time, we had a four-hour layover at the airport," she later recalled. "Everybody was just sitting there in Paris. And I said, 'I don't know about you guys, but I'm getting ready to go to the Eiffel Tower.' Just like that. And then all of us, we got all these taxis together . . . oh, it was great!"[15]

After Paris, the other musicians returned to the UK, zig-zagging their way across the country by bus. For the most part, the musicians were impressed by the manner in which they were received by hotels in Europe. Their base in London was the Mayfair Hotel, and they were pleased to see there was no segregation in place (in contrast to Memphis) and that they could all stay in the same hotel.

There were some exceptions. Booker T. Jones recalled being rudely awakened by the hotel night clerk in Sheffield, who was concerned that he was sharing the room with his white girlfriend. They were asked to leave without a word of explanation. "We walked until we found a fish-and-chips restaurant where we could at least sit inside and wait out the rest of the dark morning," he recalled in his autobiography.[16]

The Revue played several dates in Europe before returning to London, where they played one last show at the Hammersmith Odeon. The tour was a resounding success, playing to full capacity every night. "The crowds, needless to say, were awesome," remembered guitarist Steve Cropper. "When we played the big theaters, they were completely sold out. I found out later that people from the Rolling Stones were there but they couldn't get backstage. They told me later, 'We saw your show!' I said, 'You did?'" [Laughs].

♦ ♦ ♦

Back in Memphis, Carla Thomas was adding the finishing touches to her fourth solo studio album. Her album of duets with Otis Redding, *King and Queen*, had only just been released a few weeks previously, but Jim Stewart was confident that it would be a big hit. He conceived of Carla's new album as a way to take advantage of the additional publicity she would receive and named the album *The Queen Alone*.

The recording process, which had started in December 1966, had been fraught with difficulties. First of all, Jim Stewart suggested that she work more closely with David Porter and Isaac Hayes, the most successful of the various songwriting teams that were now working at Stax Records.

Stewart had always enjoyed a close relationship with Carla and desperately wanted her to be successful, and thought he was doing the right thing by pairing her with his best writers.

The problem was that her relationship with David Porter, in particular, had not really recovered from their fallout of the recording of "B-A-B-Y" the previous year. In addition, Carla still felt she was treated as being less important than Sam and Dave, and tended to be offered songs that had been rejected by them. This view was vehemently denied by David Porter, who noted that he and Hayes prided themselves on being "stylists for other artists," trying to write songs that were tailored to their particular style.[17]

Secondly, Carla made no pretense about the fact that she preferred to work with Booker T. Jones as an arranger rather than Isaac Hayes. She had a close relationship with Jones and felt that he was more responsive to her requirements. Even though Jones had finished college and was now back in Memphis, she found it difficult to get much studio time with him. The European tour had taken him away from Memphis for the best part of a month, and even when he returned, he was always in demand as a studio musician.

A third issue was that Jim Stewart discouraged her from including her own songs on the new album. This was the source of considerable disappointment as she felt that she had progressed as a songwriter. Again, Jim Stewart was trying to look after her best interests and maximize her chances of recording a hit single and probably never appreciated how much this decision had upset her.

Finally, Carla had started to see herself as more of a cabaret singer rather than a pop-soul singer. She increasingly looked to singers like Dionne Warwick as an inspiration and admired the sophisticated songs of Bacharach and David, which had quite a different feel from the more Motown-like arrangements that Porter and Hayes were suggesting.

For all of the difficulties in the recording process, *The Queen Alone* is an artistic triumph. It is more consistent in tone than her previous studio album, *Carla*, and probably the best of the studio albums she recorded for Stax Records.

Ironically, the album opens with Burt Bacharach and Bob Hilliard's "Any Day Now," a 1962 hit for Chuck Jackson, which was exactly the sort of song she had been pushing for.

"Stop Thief" was a more muscular Hayes-Porter composition written with Joe Shamwell. The song had more of a Motown flavor, complete with seductive backing vocals, but still boasted a Stax-style horn arrangement.

"I Take It to My Baby" has a distinctly Latin groove, quite unlike most Stax tunes from this era. Carla handles the vocal with aplomb and sounds like she's having fun, too.

"I Want to Be Your Baby" is a delightful ballad that clearly supports Porter's view that they were trying their best to write to Carla's strengths. After the first single, "Something Good," "When Tomorrow Comes," a fantastic, Supremes-style piece of pop-soul, brings Side 1 to a triumphant close.

"I'll Always Have Faith in You," a gospel-style ballad, was composed by one of Carla's favorite writers, Eddie Floyd, writing with Al Bell. "All I See Is You" had been a hit for Dusty Springfield and was presumably the sort of sophisticated pop that Carla was looking for. "Unchanging Love" was another super Hayes-Porter ballad with some delicious, tasteful guitar courtesy of Steve Cropper. Two more contributions from other in-house songwriting teams round out Side Two. "Give Me Enough (To Keep Me Going)" was contributed by Deanie Parker, while the excellent "Lie to Keep Me from Crying" was composed by Homer Banks and Allen Jones.

Overall, *The Queen Alone* does a good job of balancing the cabaret-style ballads that Carla was hoping to move toward and the pop-soul that had arguably made her name. The album was released in April 1967 and was probably overshadowed by *King and Queen*, peaking at No. 16 on the R&B charts. As an album, it may have lacked the killer "hit single" like "B-A-B-Y," but songs like "When Tomorrow Comes" were every bit as good. For all of Carla's reservations, it is probably the album that holds up best; interestingly, it was this album that secured her one Grammy nomination in 1968 for Best Female R&B Vocal Performance.

Vaneese Thomas, Carla's younger sister, felt that Stax Records should have been more supportive in encouraging her to move away from R&B and toward pop. "Carla's expertise lay in the 'Gee Whiz'- type material, in my opinion," she explained. "That should have been Stax's cue as to where to take her. But they didn't, and they wouldn't."[18]

She felt that only a handful of people in the company were equipped to help her achieve this, and for the most part, they were too busy on other projects. "No one at Stax had that kind of background or expertise," she said. "Jim Stewart didn't have it, Al Bell didn't have it. Isaac [Hayes] and David [Porter] could have taken her in that direction, but they were busy writing material like 'Hold On, I'm Coming' and they weren't thinking of material like 'Gee Whiz.' They kept her away from Booker, who was a master at that kind of thing, writing charts for strings and horns."

To their credit, Isaac and David had tried to adapt their writing style to suit Carla Thomas. The songs they contributed to *The Queen*

Alone were much more pop-oriented than the material they typically wrote for Sam and Dave, but Carla clearly felt that the material was too Motown-oriented, and that was not what she was looking for.

Ironically, she seemed to be turning her back on R&B at a time when Stax Records had started to invest more in marketing. She was being marketed as the "Queen of Memphis Soul" to Otis Redding's "King." The album title *King and Queen* was part of that branding, and *The Queen Alone* was designed to strengthen that image in the mind of the public.

"The other thing you can't overlook is that Stax Records' specialty was not a label that delivered pop," Deanie Parker added. "But Al Bell was the consummate promotions person for rhythm and blues—that was our genre."

In his excellent book, *Ladies of Soul*, author David Freeland's chapter on Carla Thomas is titled "Memphis's Reluctant Soul Queen," which is the perfect title; just as she was being crowned, Carla Thomas was looking to abdicate.

Carla would appear to have fallen out with David Porter and Isaac Hayes over the recording of the album. In an extensive interview with Bill Dahl for *Ponderosa Stomp* in which she discusses most of her singles and albums, *The Queen Alone* barely get a mention. Likewise, in the detailed liner notes to the *Complete Stax/Volt Singles: 1959–1968*, she dismisses the singles from that album as "getting away from something basic to me." Porter and Hayes only contributed one song to Carla's follow-up album, *Memphis Queen*, leaving Carla to look for help from people outside of the company to help her achieve her goal.[19]

♦ ♦ ♦

The following month, in May 1967, Carla was back at Howard University in Washington. One evening, she dropped into the Bohemian Caverns, a jazz club located close to her apartment, to watch a gig by the jazz pianist Ramsey Lewis. "I'm sitting there and I see the drummer come out, and I'm going, 'Wait a minute! That's Maurice [White]!' This is long before he got with Earth, Wind & Fire. He was traveling with Ramsey. He said, 'Oh, my God! That's Carla Thomas!' So, he introduced me to the owner, and that's how I got that job at the Bohemian Caverns."

Carla landed a week-long booking at the prestigious club and asked her close friend, pianist and singer Donny Hathaway, to book the band and work on arrangements with her. He assembled a top-notch band, including jazz saxophonist Herschel McGinnis, to accompany her.

Stax Records seemed to be entirely supportive of the project and flew in key people from the company to watch her perform on the second

Carla Thomas performing at Washington's Bohemian Caverns, May 1967. Photography courtesy of the Stax Museum of American Soul Music.

night. The company's founders, Jim Stewart and Estelle Axton, were there, along with Al Bell, who introduced Carla Thomas that evening, and her close friend Otis Redding and his manager, Phil Walden. Carla's father, Rufus Thomas, also flew in for the show, as did her brother, Marvell Thomas, who had just finished his service in the army. It was clearly designed to be a high-profile, prestigious event.

Carla performed an eclectic mix of jazz standards, including "You're Gonna Hear from Me" (written by Andre and Dory Previn and performed by Frank Sinatra and Andy Williams) and a medley which included Johnny Mercer's "Zip-A-Dee-Doo-Dah" and Doris Day's "It's a Lovely Day Today," pop songs ("Yesterday"), pop-soul, including "B-A-B-Y," and some well-chosen covers, including Leroy Hutson's "Never Be True." She even attempts Jorge Ben's "Mas Que Nada" in Portuguese, a tune which had recently been covered by Sergio Mendes.

Carla was in fine form throughout, performing music that was close to her heart. There's also no doubt that Donny Hathaway's arrangements were sympathetic; less horn-driven than Stax Records, with just a solitary saxophone, allowing more space for the vocals.

That evening's performance was recorded by Stax Records and even given a catalog number, so it was clearly intended for release. But for reasons lost in the mists of time, the live recording was not released that year. It's easy to understand why Stax Records would wait to release it; after all, *King and Queen* was only released in March 1967 and *The Queen Alone* in April. It would have made more sense to release the album later in the year, perhaps closer to Christmas. But Christmas came and went, and by then, Stax was engaged in a fight for survival and desperately trying to record as many albums as it could in a single year.

Could it be that Al Bell, who was nominally promotions director, simply blocked the release because he felt it did not fit with Carla's new image as the "Memphis Queen"? There's no evidence to suggest this was the case, although there's little doubt, given his marketing know-how, that he would have had some reservations. In all likelihood, the album got put on the back burner because of concerns over the timing of the launch, and by the end of the year, the record company had much bigger things to worry about.

Carla was bitterly disappointed. She considered this recording her most important performance in the United States. "When I was doing Johnny Carson, Mike Douglas, I was doing everything East Coast, that's when they should have put it out," Carla said. "Because you had those type songs on it."[20]

The album was finally released in 2007—a full forty years after the event—as *Live at the Bohemian Caverns*. Even then, it was a somewhat substandard product. The CD was only one hour long, leaving space to include more music. The CD also omitted a number of songs from her set that night, including "Yesterday," while including a few songs that her father performed as a short set at the end of the show, which seemed like a wasted opportunity. The release received generally favorable reviews, with most mentioning that it showed a different side of Carla Thomas than was less visible in her studio recordings, which generally had a more soulful feel.

Listening to the recording now, it makes it easier to appreciate that Carla Thomas felt constrained by the machinery of Stax Records; most of the writers and arrangers were geared toward R&B, and even if the likes of Isaac Hayes and David Porter tried to tailor their compositions toward her style, it tended to end up as pop-soul. This album suggests she was aiming for more sophisticated pop akin to the songs produced by Bacharach and David or even pop-jazz. In fact, the closest equivalent to her set that night was probably an album like *Pop Artistry* by jazz singer Sarah Vaughan, which came out in 1966, and also featured songs by Lennon-McCartney and Bacharach-David. In the same vein, Nancy Wilson had also recorded *A Touch of Today* that year, which also featured "Yesterday" and "You're Gonna Hear from Me."

Both Sarah Vaughan and Nancy Wilson were primarily jazz singers, and while they were quite capable of singing pop, it didn't play to their strengths, and their pop-oriented albums are not among their most highly regarded recordings. Likewise, Ella Fitzgerald's more pop-oriented album from the same era, *Sunshine of Your Love*, met with predominantly lukewarm reviews. So, while it's interesting to hear Carla Thomas produce a more pop-jazz oriented set for the cabaret crowd, it could be questioned whether it suited her style as much as the pop-soul she had recorded on *The Queen Alone*.

"Carla was a happy-go-lucky type of person who kept reaching for something no one [at Stax] could define," suggests Deanie Parker, one of the few other female singers on the label. "She had the beautiful voice; she was a gifted songstress. I really think it was timing. Everything in our industry is about timing. The stars have to align. If you are pursuing a career to become the greatest rhythm and blues performer, and you get discouraged halfway through and want to go a bit more pop, you really need to understand what is happening in the marketplace. Is this the time to incorporate pop? It's not a science."[21]

The key people at Stax Records, as Deanie Parker suggests, were struggling to find the right formula for Carla as an artist, but it can happen, despite the best of intentions. Aretha Franklin was signed to Columbia Records for five years before she signed with Atlantic Records, and in that time, they tried her with R&B, jazz, pop and easy listening, but again, failed to "define" her. Label executive John Hammond later said he felt Columbia did not understand Franklin's early gospel background and failed to bring that aspect out further during her time there. In hindsight, it would have been a good time for Carla to leave the label and try working with someone who better understood her needs as an artist. But her roots were in Memphis, her family was in Memphis, and she stayed with Stax until the bitter end.

♦ ♦ ♦

Back in Memphis, another talented African American band was emerging from the local high school system. The Impalas formed at Booker T. Washington High School in 1966, named after the car they used to drive themselves to gigs. They eventually landed a regular nightclub gig in West

Memphis. Around this time, white keyboard player Ronnie Caldwell joined the band, making them an "integrated" band, "which was still unusual at that time," according to bass player James Alexander.[22]

Soon after this, the band changed its name to the Bar-Kays. The name change was inspired by a local billboard ad for Bacardi Rum, which had some letters missing, but it was also a reference to the Stax band, the Mar-Keys. The band used to hang around the Stax studio at every opportunity, and trumpet player Ben Cauley had played on a couple of singles by Carla and Rufus Thomas, including "B-A-B-Y."

"The Thomas family, especially Rufus, played a very instrumental part in the Bar-Kays' career," explained James Alexander. "We went out several times backing Rufus Thomas. Rufus and the Bar-Kays were booked by the same booking agency, and with Rufus being a solo artist and the Bar-Kays being a band, it was the perfect fit. We got a lot of gigs because of him. The promoter would say, 'Well, we've got a band up here that can play.' But the booking agent would say, 'There's a band down here that already knows his material, already knows his stuff, they could back him.' So, they wouldn't pay the local band, would pay Rufus a little extra, and every time he got a show, we had a show. This would have been around 1966."[23]

The band auditioned for Steve Cropper at Stax on a couple of occasions without success. As they were leaving the studio after the second audition, they ran into Jim Stewart, who suggested they come back that Sunday and audition for him. At the back of Jim's mind was a feeling that Booker T. & the M.G.'s was being overworked as a house band now that Stax had expanded and that a second house band could be a useful addition.

When the Bar-Kays returned that weekend, they played an original tune called "Don't Do That," which had been well-received in local nightclubs. Jim was impressed but had to step out of the studio, and when he did, the band started to work on a groove they had discovered while playing at the Hippodrome. Jim came back in, loved what he heard, and suggested they cut it right away. The next day, David Porter suggested they add some party effects to the tune, including local schoolchildren shouting "Soul Finger," and the band's debut single was born.

"Soul Finger" was released as a single on April 14, 1967, and by May had reached No. 3 on the R&B charts and No. 17 on the *Billboard* Hot 100. All of a sudden, Stax Records had brand-new stars and a second house band.

After that, the Bar-Kays were stars. "Phalon [Jones, saxophonist] would walk into assembly late," recalls Alexander. "Girls would be screaming like it was the Beatles. We were teenagers in tailor-made suits with a thousand dollars in our pockets."[24]

Rufus in the sound booth at WDIA radio station, March 29, 1967. Photograph courtesy of the *Memphis Press-Scimitar*, Special Collections Department, University of Memphis Libraries.

That summer, the hits kept coming for Stax Records. They released two live recordings from the Stax-Volt Revue concert in London, Otis Redding's recording of "Shake," which reached No. 16 on the R&B charts, and Sam and Dave's "Soothe Me," which also reached No. 16. Carla Thomas also returned to the charts with "I'll Always Have Faith in You," the gospel-oriented tune from *The Queen Alone* album.

In late May, Rufus Thomas returned to the recording studio for the first time in more than six months. He had remained a popular draw on the live circuit but struggled to produce a hit single. His return to the charts was prompted by another popular dance, the Sissy. The tune was cowritten by

Detroit singer Mack Rice, a friend and former bandmate of Eddie Floyd, in conjunction with Isaac Hayes, David Porter, and Joe Shamwell.

Rufus Thomas and David Porter had had their differences, but "Sophisticated Sissy" was tailor-made for Rufus, with an infectious groove, an exciting horn line, and superb backing vocals courtesy of Jeanne and the Darlings. "For me, Rufus was hard to work with," admitted Porter. "Rufus knew what he wanted, knew how he wanted it, and if you wrote a song for him—you wrote the song, so you knew how you wanted it. And so it was a little bit of a challenge to get things the way you wanted them to be, certainly for Isaac and [me]. We were stylists for artists, and Rufus was the epitome of a stylist for himself."[25]

On this occasion, at least, the combination worked well. "Sophisticated Sissy" was Rufus Thomas's best single for three years and his first chart entry since "Jump Back" in 1964. It only reached No. 43 on the R&B charts, but it sent a strong signal, nonetheless—Rufus Thomas was back!

◆ ◆ ◆

Back in Memphis after his triumphant tour of Europe, Otis Redding was on the lookout for a new backing band to support him. He was advised to check out the latest Stax signing, the Bar-Kays, and went to watch them play at the Hippodrome. "He was so amazed when he sat in with us that he asked us if we would be his touring band right then," recalled bass player James Alexander. "But we were underage and we had to ask our parents. We were all still in high school so our parents really didn't want us to go on the road. All the parents unanimously said no."[26]

Otis Redding persisted. He had a prestigious gig coming up at the Monterey International Pop Festival in mid-June and needed to recruit and rehearse a band at the earliest opportunity. He even offered to hire the band a tutor, so they could join him, but the parents insisted it would have to wait until they had graduated at the end of June.

The Monterey Pop Festival was a three-day event held from June 16–18, 1967. In what became known as the "summer of love," the lineup featured a number of prominent rocks bands including the Jimi Hendrix Experience, one of the first major appearances of Big Brother and the Holding Company (featuring Janis Joplin), Canned Heat, the Who, Grateful Dead, and Jefferson Airplane. There was only a handful of African American acts appearing; singer Lou Rawls appeared on the Friday evening, Otis Redding on the Saturday night, and Jimi Hendrix on the Sunday.

In any event, Otis Redding was backed by Booker T. & the M.G.'s, who played a brief set of their own, and the Memphis Horns. The M.G.'s had the difficult task of taking the stage after the emerging psychedelic rock band, Jefferson Airplane, who used a big amplification system and light show. "And [here] came Booker T. & the M.G.'s, four pieces with their little small amps, and they did an instrumental set—their sound was so small by contrast," remembered Atlantic's Jerry Wexler in an interview with *Blues & Soul* magazine. Even "Green Onions" failed to provoke much of a reaction.

Things got a little better when they were joined by Wayne Jackson and Andrew Love—the Memphis Horns—who were again billed as the Mar-Keys. But it was Otis Redding that really shook things up, opening his set with storming versions of "Shake" and "Respect." He then won the crowd over with an impromptu speech. "This is the love crowd, right?" he asked. "We all love each other, right? Am I right?" The love crowd roared its approval, and Otis said, "Let me hear you say 'Yeah' then." As the crowd yelled, "Yeah!" Otis took his cue to slow things down a notch and went into a sublime version of "I've Been Loving You Too Long." A crowd-pleasing version of "Satisfaction" followed, picking up the tempo once more, before a lengthy version of "Try a Little Tenderness," which closed the set. "I got to go, y'all," he told the crowd. "I don't wanna go!"

Jon Landau, a rock critic before he went on to manage Bruce Springsteen, marveled at the performance. "Otis Redding's performances constituted, as a whole, the highest level of expression rock 'n' roll has yet attained," he wrote. "Otis Redding *is* rock 'n' roll."

After Monterey, Redding's schedule was full for several weeks. Once the Bar-Kays had graduated, they flew directly to New York for a series of gigs at the Apollo. There was no time to even rehearse, and the band was told which songs to rehearse ahead of the shows. Otis Redding was supported by Carla Thomas to commemorate the album they had recorded together. "We did that whole summer tour," she later recalled. "I was just amazed that we were on the show together. I said, 'Are you sure you want to do "Tramp" on this show?' He said, 'Yeah! Let's do "Tramp!"' These people are calling for "Tramp!"' I said, 'You gotta be kidding!' And 'Tramp' got to be the song!"

With a busy touring schedule, Otis Redding had bought a small private plane earlier that summer rather than having to rely on a tour bus. It was only big enough to fit Redding and his immediate entourage and not the whole band, but it made life easier for the singer. In the weeks that followed, they toured all over North America, including a show at the Expo 67 World's Fair in Montreal, Canada, on July 4.

On August 10, Al Bell had booked Otis Redding and Carla Thomas to perform at the National Association of Radio Announcers (NATRA)

Convention in Atlanta, an event that would also feature Atlantic's newest stars, Aretha Franklin and Don Covay.

The day before the NATRA Convention, Otis Redding threw a huge barbecue at his ranch. In 1966, he had bought a large plot of land in Round Oak, Georgia, and by the summer of 1967, the Big O Ranch was complete—except for the swimming pool, which had yet to be filled. He set up a stage where Sam and Dave, the Bar-Kays, and Arthur Conley performed, but Otis himself was too tired, and happy to play the gracious host. The event was attended by many fellow musicians from Stax and Atlantic, and record industry executives too. A total of eight hogs, four cows, and fifty cases of whiskey were consumed that day, but according to Redding's wife, Zelma, "[He] was so tired . . . he spoke to everybody but he just couldn't move."

After two days at the convention, the tour resumed, taking in Charlotte, Chicago, Nashville, and St. Louis. In Chicago, Otis Redding and Carla Thomas were guests of honor at the *Bud Billiken Parade and Picnic*, one of the largest annual African American gatherings in the country, with over 70,000 attendees. The King and Queen enjoyed breakfast with Mayor Richard Daley and the Governor of Illinois before riding in the parade, then performing at the picnic itself.

Otis finally returned home to his family for a few days of rest before heading out to the West Coast, where he played for one week at San Francisco's Basin Street West, again backed by the Bar-Kays. While he was there, he stayed on a houseboat at Waldo Point, Sausalito, owned by rock music impresario Bill Graham, rather than a hotel. His close friend, Earl "Speedo" Sims, recalled he spent his spare time listening to the new Beatles album *Sgt. Pepper* and working on a new song, inspired by the view from the boat.

> Sittin' in the mornin' sun,
> I'll be sittin' when the evenin' comes,
> Watching the ships roll in,
> And then I watch 'em roll away again.

Neither Otis nor his wife, Zelma, was particularly impressed with the new song at first. "I really couldn't get into it," Zelma remembered. "I said, 'Oh God, you're changing.'"[27]

His manager, Phil Walden, had much the same reaction. "Most people had doubts about it," he said. "It was a drastic change . . . it sounded like it might have been a little too pop."[28]

The constant touring had taken its toll on Redding's voice, and in early October, he had an operation to remove polyps from his throat. Otis was worried that this might put an end to his career as a singer, but a throat specialist in New York convinced him that if he stayed quiet for six weeks, he would make a full recovery. He spent those six weeks at home on his ranch, spending time with his wife and children and composing new songs for his next album.

◆ ◆ ◆

David Porter and Isaac Hayes may have struggled to find the right style to suit Carla Thomas, but with Sam and Dave, they were on a roll. Earlier that summer, Isaac Hayes had watched television footage of the 12th Street Riot in Detroit, Michigan, and noted with interest that African American-owned businesses had not been targeted by the rioters. "It was said that if you put 'soul' on the door of your business establishment, they wouldn't burn it," Hayes explained to NPR Radio. "Then the word 'soul,' it was a galvanizing kind of thing for African Americans and it had an effect of unity; it was said with a lot of pride." Porter wrote the lyrics to "Soul Man" around this theme while Hayes devised the funky arrangement. The famous Cropper guitar line in the song also came from Hayes, who suggested he play an Elmore James-style line in the chorus. The guitarist didn't have a slide with him but improvised with a cigarette lighter, prompting an excited Sam Moore to yell out, "Play it, Steve!"

"Soul Man" was the most successful Stax Records single to date. The song was released in late August and reached No. 1 on the R&B charts and an impressive No. 2 on the *Billboard* Hot 100, too. It was a bigger hit than Otis Redding had yet achieved, a fact that was on his mind as he was writing for his album.

After six weeks of keeping his voice to a whisper, Redding was delighted to find his voice had made a full recovery. Rather than rush back into touring and risk damaging his throat, he planned to ease his way back into performing. He would fly to Memphis first, to record his new album in late November, before returning to the road in December.

With a new tour approaching, Redding decided it made sense to upgrade his Cessna private plane. It was too small and not particularly comfortable for longer flights. He opted for a twin-engine Beechcraft Model 18, which was a popular corporate aircraft and within his budget. He bought a relatively new model, built in 1962, which was designed to hold seven passengers but with room to add another one or two seats. It still wasn't big enough to carry the whole entourage, but it meant that most of them could fit on the plane, with the remainder flying commercial. The plane was scheduled for delivery in late October, allowing time for it to be repainted with Redding's logo of his Otis Redding Enterprises.

Redding was in the Stax recording studio for the best part of two weeks, putting the finishing touches to his new songs. There was no evidence of the throat problems he had experienced over the preceding two months. "His voice was so clear, we couldn't get over it," recalled Cropper. "We just couldn't record enough. And when the band would leave at night, we'd break and go and have a little dinner somewhere and come back to the studio and start recording."[29]

The sessions were highly productive, yielding a string of classic songs, including "Hard to Handle," "You Made a Man out of Me," "The Happy Song," and "I'm A Changed Man." Most were fairly up-tempo, but as the sessions came to an end, Redding wanted to finalize the ballad he had started writing back in Sausalito.

Like "Speedo" Sims and Zelma Redding, not everyone in the studio was convinced by the new song. "Otis came in and he had Steve working on a song," recalled Jim Stewart. "They did 'Dock of the Bay.' It didn't knock me out when I listened to it because it was so different."

Despite the initial reservations of some of the Stax team, pianist Booker T. Jones remembered the whole studio being astonished by the final playback. "The most unlikely music you could expect from Stax's most unlikely artist, an anomaly for sure. An uncompromising tone poem of the simplest chordal structure created the setting for Otis's most heartfelt plea for love and understanding. The song took us on a journey together right there in the control room and washed us clean. For a minute, we were one."[30]

The next day, on Friday, December 8, Otis Redding and the Bar-Kays were getting ready to leave Memphis to perform the first of three gigs that weekend. "We were standing in the lobby that day, killing time, and they were getting ready to go," remembered Jim Stewart. "There was thunder and lightning, and I said, 'It's going to be pretty rough up there!' He turned to me and said, 'I'd rather be up there when it's rough, there's no else around me.'"[31]

The Friday evening gig finished early, and the band flew to Cleveland that same evening. That allowed the band to head to Leo's Casino, the club they were playing the next night, and catch the end of the show by the O'Jays and the Temptations.

The next day, the band appeared on the *Upbeat* TV show in the afternoon. The band created quite a stir by playing live on the show when most other bands would lip-sync their performance. Later, they played their gig at Leo's Casino, which bass player James Alexander recalled as "unbelievable," before spending the night in Cleveland.

Early the next morning, Redding called his wife, Zelma, who was at home on the ranch with their children. "He was depressed about something. I remember that very well," she told author Peter Guralnick. "And he talked to little Otis, who was just three. He said he would call me when he got to Madison."[32]

The band was scheduled to fly to Madison, Wisconsin, just after at lunch. "The plane that we traveled on could only carry a certain amount of people," explained James Alexander. "Two people always had to fly commercial because there wasn't enough room on the plane. It could be any two people. This particular day, it happened to be me and another gentleman. We were the two people that took the commercial flight. That's the only reason that I wasn't on the plane." With no direct flights to Madison, James Alexander and roadie Carl Sims made arrangements to fly to Milwaukee, where Redding's pilot would collect them late afternoon, ahead of an early evening gig at the Factory nightclub near the University of Wisconsin.[33]

It was a cold, foggy day, and as the plane was preparing to take off, drummer Carl Cunningham asked the flight attendant if it was possible to start the engine to warm up the cabin. The attendant explained that it was better to wait for the pilot as the battery was kind of low. The plane took off without a hitch and was given clearance to land at 3:25 p.m. The visibility was poor that afternoon, with low cloud cover and rain. Trumpet player Ben Cauley remembered waking up with the engines making a loud sound, realizing there was a problem, then unbuckling his seatbelt. Seconds later, the plane crashed into the icy waters of Lake Monona, just outside Madison.

Cauley could not swim but managed to cling to one of the aircraft seats for more than fifteen minutes before he was pulled from the water. He was the only survivor of the crash.

Otis Redding lost his life at the age of just twenty-six; his body was not recovered until the next day. The pilot, Richard Fraser, was the same age. Four of the six members of the Bar-Kays, the next generation of Memphis R&B music, also died that day—drummer Carl Cunningham, guitarist Jimmy King, saxophonist Phalon Jones, and organist Ronnie Caldwell, all aged between seventeen and nineteen. Redding's young valet, Matthew Kelly, also lost his life.

James Alexander was sitting at the airport in Milwaukee, waiting to be collected, when he heard the news. The police rushed him to the hospital in Madison, where he found Cauley in an understandable state of shock.

Jim Stewart received a call from promotions man Joe Galkin that evening, who told him to turn on the television. "It was horrible," he recalled, "I remember like it happened yesterday. Otis was almost there [as an international star], and would have been, had he lived."[34]

Carla Thomas had just gotten back from the wedding of a close family friend when she heard the news that her close friend had died. "We had gotten home and we were jiving and joking about the wedding," she recalled. "And we just happened to turn on the TV, and we were in this elated mood. And then they said 'Bulletin.' Just, 'boom.' And I knew that the kids were with him. They were traveling together. I just put my hands in my ear. I didn't even hear the rest of it. Mother and I were in there together, so after the bulletin went off, I looked at her. She looked at me. And I said, 'What did they say?' I wanted to get it second-hand. And then she told me."[35]

Redding's funeral was postponed from December 15 to December 18 so more people could attend. The funeral took place at the Macon City Auditorium, where an estimated 4,500 mourners crammed into the 3,000-capacity hall. Most of the US's R&B community was in attendance, including Rufus and Carla Thomas.

Singers Johnnie Taylor and Joe Simon were among the pallbearers. During the ceremony, Johnnie Taylor sang "I'll Stand By," accompanied by Booker T. Jones on organ, before Joe Simon sang a heartfelt version of the gospel song, "Jesus Keep Me Near the Cross." The latter proved too much for Zelma Redding, who broke down and was attended by nurses who were present.

The eulogy was delivered by Jerry Wexler of Atlantic Records. "Respect was something Otis achieved for himself in a way few people do," he said. "Otis sang, 'All I'm asking for is a little respect when I come home,' and Otis has come home."

Redding's first major song, "These Arms of Mine," was played as his glass-enclosed casket was carried out of the church. He was later laid to rest on the Big O Ranch near Round Oak, the place he thought of as home.

Christmas was a devastating period for the Stax family, who was in a state of shock. A wreath of white carnations hung from the entrance, and when Ben Cauley returned to the Stax studios, just one week after his bandmates had been buried, Estelle Axton came over and hugged him.

Atlantic Records, all business, even at a time like this, put in a call to Jim Stewart and suggested they release a single at the earliest opportunity. "I told Jim Stewart I didn't know if I could do it," Steve Cropper says. "He said 'you have to.'" Cropper put the finishing touches to "(Sittin' On) The Dock of the Bay," the sound of seagulls and waves, and overdubbing some guitar. "That was one of the first times we'd done that," recalled Jim Stewart, "because most of his tracks were live."[36]

The song was eventually released on January 8, 1968, and became the crossover hit that Redding had been looking for, reaching No. 1 on both the R&B and pop charts.

A few days after the funeral, Jim Stewart had called a meeting of the Stax staff and, with his voice breaking, told everyone that they had to keep going.

But in the months ahead, two more devastating events would occur that cast a shadow over both Stax Records and the city of Memphis. The first of those was the sale of Atlantic Records to Warner Brothers, which saw Stax lose both its distribution network and its entire back catalog. The second was the shooting of the civil rights leader, Martin Luther King, which took place just blocks from the label's recording studio on McLemore Avenue. Those events will be examined in the next chapter.

Chapter Nine

Memphis Queen

The Soul Explosion, 1968–1970

Earlier it was suggested that in 1965, nothing changed at Stax, but everything changed. But in 1968, everything changed, after which nothing was ever the same: the ownership of the company changed, the distribution changed, the stars changed, the focus changed, the internal politics changed, and the external politics, too. And although Stax Records survived—and for a few years, thrived—it was no longer the same company that Jim Stewart and Estelle Axton had founded.

The problems started in October 1967, when Atlantic Records first announced that it had reached an "agreement in principle" with Warner Bros.-Seven Arts to be purchased by the larger entity for approximately $20 million in cash and stock. The deal saw Ahmet Ertegun and Jerry Wexler staying with Atlantic Records and continuing to run the company, and was finalized on November 24, 1967.

At first, Jim Stewart did not give the deal much thought. The arrangement with Atlantic, he assumed, was primarily a distribution arrangement and was clearly favorable to both companies; after all, Stax Records had produced some of Atlantic's biggest hits in 1967, including those by Sam and Dave and Otis Redding.

Jim Stewart assumed that Atlantic Records would want to take Stax Records with them as part of the agreement, and so there was clearly a deal to be done. Failing that, Jim Stewart had insisted on a key man clause being inserted in the 1965 contract, which gave him the right to terminate the agreement if ownership of Atlantic Records were to change. As a result, Stewart was in no hurry to finalize the new arrangement. With the tragic death of Otis Redding and the Bar-Kays in December 1967, he felt he had more important things to worry about. He was wrong.

Going into January 1968, Stewart's initial inclination was to try and negotiate a deal with Atlantic Records to include Stax as part of the sale.

He was wary of going independent again and losing the nationwide distribution deal that he had. Jim Stewart, Estelle Axton, and Al Bell flew to New York hoping to negotiate terms. However, Atlantic was only willing to pay a paltry $2 million for the Memphis label. "Atlantic wanted to buy the company, so I went to New York and had a meeting," Stewart recalled. "Wexler came up with some ridiculous figure. At least, I thought it was ridiculous. Basically, I got up and walked out of the room."[1]

Stewart later admitted that he felt personally insulted by Wexler's low offer, given the amount of business they had generated for Atlantic Records over the years. "You realize how many millions of dollars we've run through that company since 1960," he complained to author Rob Bowman. "Seven years, and their total outlay of money from 1960 through '67, their cost to get that deal, was five thousand dollars. From there on, they have had not one penny invested. They were using our money all during that period of time."[2]

Stewart then approached Warner Bros.-Seven Arts directly, but their offer was similarly unacceptable to Stax.

When that failed, Stewart attempted to negotiate more favorable distribution terms with Atlantic figuring they might be able to secure a better deal. But Atlantic refused to budge, leaving Stax with a difficult decision to make.

The negotiations were going nowhere, and time was ticking away; Stax Records had a six-month window in which they could invoke the key man clause, so a decision had to be made. Stewart and Axton discussed the options with Al Bell, who was still nominally in charge of promotion; despite the promise of a stake in the company, no arrangement had yet been finalized.

Bell had an ambitious plan named after *Star Trek*, his favorite TV show, called Enterprise Records. He wanted the label to move beyond R&B and showcase different kinds of music. Taking the analogy further, he wanted to present "a whole new galaxy of stars" and become "universal" rather than just national.

With this in mind, Bell suggested bringing the company's other key employees into the discussion and calling a company meeting. Bell later recalled that drummer Al Jackson was particularly vociferous about the benefits of leaving Atlantic and going it alone. With the backing of their employees, Stax made their decision known to Atlantic Records, and both parties agreed to terminate the agreement on May 6, 1968.

It was then that Stewart was informed by Wexler that Atlantic's lawyers had included a clause in the 1965 distribution contract that gave Atlantic all rights, including any rights of reproduction, to all Stax's

Atlantic-distributed recordings between 1960 and 1967. In effect, only its unreleased recordings remained the property of Stax; all of the masters delivered to Atlantic between 1960 and 1967 became the property of Atlantic's new parent company, Warner Music Group.

The clause itself stated that Stewart agreed to "sell, assign, and transfer ... the entire right, title and interest in and to each of such masters and to each of the performances embodied thereon," and was halfway through a thirteen-page contract filled with similar legal jargon.

"I trusted Wexler and didn't even bother to read the contract," revealed Stewart, who admitted that he had been naive. "We'd been operating without a contract without a problem. I learned a lesson the hard way."[3]

Wexler always denied that he had any knowledge of the clause concerning the masters. "I didn't know that until the end," he explained to Peter Guralnick, author of Sweet Soul Music. "It was a loaded deal, and I tried to give them back their catalog, but I couldn't, because the lawyers had put it over. What are you getting at, that we were slick?"[4]

Wexler was smart, with a degree in journalism, and it seems highly unlikely that he had either failed to read the contract or had his lawyers talk him through the key clauses. "Slick" was too generous a term for his behavior. It also helps to explain why he made such a paltry offer to Jim Stewart to buy the company in January 1967; there was no point paying too much because they owned the masters already.

Did Otis Redding's untimely death play a part in this? Ultimately, it probably did. Redding was the key asset that Stax "owned" from Atlantic's point of view, and he was tied into a long-term contract. Wexler had been openly courting Redding for months with a view to prizing him away from Stax Records, assisting with his promotion both home and abroad. Without Redding, the future recordings of Stax artists were worth far less to Atlantic Records.

Jim Stewart tried to negotiate with Atlantic Records over the terms, both by telephone and in person, but without success. To rub salt into the wound, Wexler insisted that if the contract was coming to an end, the "loan" deal for Sam and Dave, who were still signed to Atlantic Records, would also be terminated.

All the Stax artists felt betrayed by Wexler's behavior. "Jerry Wexler pulled a fast one on Jim Stewart," said Booker T. Jones. "Jim was a nice guy, but he wasn't fast enough for a New York attorney, and he lost all of his valuable masters."[5]

Sam and Dave were also unhappy with this development. "Sam and Dave at Stax was a family thing," admitted Sam Moore. "That chemistry works. And when you separate that nucleus between those four

people—Sam and Dave, Hayes and Porter—something happens." There
was enough material for the duo to release another album, *I Thank You*,
in 1968, but it appeared on Atlantic Records, not Stax, even though it had
been recorded in Memphis. Atlantic issued *The Best of Sam and Dave* in
early 1969, which sold well, and consolidated their success, but in reality,
these were all Stax recordings. Jerry Wexler tried bringing them down
to Muscle Shoals in Alabama to record later that year, but they found it
hard to replicate their earlier success and never had another hit record.
The duo split in June 1970, and although they reunited periodically, the
game was up.[6]

In the space of just six months, Stax Records had lost its two biggest
artists, Otis Redding and Sam and Dave; one of its most promising acts,
the Bar-Kays, who were also considered a second house band; and their
distribution deal with Atlantic Records.

Jim Stewart felt the loss of Otis Redding, in particular, having watched
him develop as an artist over the preceding five years. "It was really a
tragic time for all of us," he recalled. "Otis was not only an artist but a
dear friend."

"(Sittin' On) The Dock of the Bay" reached the top of the charts in
March and stayed there for four weeks. Shortly after, it was certified as
a gold record, and Redding's widow, Zelma Redding, flew into Memphis
to receive the gold record from Jim Stewart himself.

"I'm not sure that any of us—for quite a while—were in touch with
our feelings," said Deanie Parker, who was working as the publicist for
Stax Records. "We never got over Otis because he'd made too much
of an impact. And we never got over the Bar-Kays because we would
constantly reference the fact that we had these kids in training. This was
our future. They were the product of the teachers teaching the children,
helping us to prepare them for the profession they wanted to embrace."[7]

♦ ♦ ♦

The tumultuous events at Stax Records in late 1967 and early 1968 were
taking place against a backdrop of massive political and social change
within the city of Memphis itself.

Taking inspiration from the broader civil rights movement, the Memphis branch of the NAACP, led by the indefatigable Maxine Smith, had
waged a series of campaigns against bastions of discrimination within the
city, starting with the segregated schooling system and then turning their
attention to other city-run institutions such as the public libraries, parks,
and art galleries. By the early 1960s, Smith—strongly supported by Rufus

Thomas's wife, Lorene Thomas—turned her attention to privately owned businesses, arranging sit-ins at segregated banks and department stores.

By 1967, the NAACP was taking a more active interest in employment rights, which Smith saw as a natural extension of her prior efforts, fighting against employment discrimination within both the government and private institutions. It was only natural, then, that the NAACP became involved in the Memphis sanitation strike that started on February 12, 1968, in response to the deaths of two sanitation workers earlier that month.

The riots that took place in Memphis on March 28—a few days prior to King's death—ripped through the city's more poverty-stricken districts like a wildfire, looters ransacking small businesses and setting buildings on fire. The neighborhood around Stax Records on East McLemore was hit hard, but miraculously, the studio and record shop were left unscathed, most likely in recognition of all the company had done to help the local community.

When King was killed by a sniper's bullet just a few days later, the city braced itself for another night of unrest. But while riots raged in numerous other American cities, most notably Washington, DC, Chicago, and Baltimore, Memphis remained relatively subdued, with the union leaders joining forces to arrange a silent march on April 8 through the streets of the city, an event which attracted over 40,000 participants. The sanitation strike finally ended on April 16, and a settlement was reached; it was widely regarded as a turning point in both Black activism and union activity in Memphis.

Both the rioting that took place and the subsequent assassination of Dr. King had a profound impact on the atmosphere within the confines of Stax Records.

These days, guitarist Steve Cropper chooses his words extremely carefully when discussing the events that took place in the spring of 1968. At the time, however, he was less mindful of white privilege and the impact his words might have on the fragile tension within the local community.

"You know, Memphis was a refuge for Black people, it really was," he told one interviewer. "Blacks were Blacks and whites were whites, and everybody was cool. We all loved each other. The Black people were perfectly happy with what was going on. I don't think anywhere in the universe was as racially cool as Memphis was until Martin Luther King showed up."

The insensitivity of Cropper's comments was not lost on his bandmate Booker. T. Jones. "It hit me hard," he revealed in his autobiography, *Time Is Tight*. "This was the guitar player in my band speaking! How could I knowingly collaborate with anyone who supported the mindset that made Dr. King's murder possible?"[8]

The East McLemore neighborhood around the recording studio was badly scarred by the riots. Many of the local businesses had been looted, and some—especially those that were white-owned—had been burned to the ground. "I found out when we got back that the only building that wasn't torched in that block where Stax was, was Stax itself," Steve Cropper recalled. "I was told that one of Isaac's friends stood out front and said, 'You ain't torching this place!' They got the bakery, they got everything!"[9]

The atmosphere around the neighborhood also changed quite dramatically. "With the looting and everything [that followed King's death], there were a lot of things happening outside of the confines of Stax that we were confronted with when we came out of Stax," recalled singer William Bell. "The Blacks had to stand up for the whites, and the police were very hostile if you were driving one of your coworkers home and he was white. They would stop and harass you, and all that sort of stuff. It put a strain on our relationship. We were still respectful and working together, but it was difficult."[10]

One example of these changes was that a local gang started to operate in the car park opposite the recording studio. Steve Cropper and Donald "Duck" Dunn were regularly threatened, in return for money, while the gang even threatened Booker T. Jones's family with his kidnapping.

As a result of these changes, a number of the Stax musicians started to carry handguns. "It got pretty intense around there," Dunn remembered. "Al [Jackson] sent me to West Memphis, Arkansas. I bought five .38 pistols. He said, 'Anybody gives you shit, pull the trigger.'"[11]

Given the increased security threat, Al Bell brought in an acquaintance of his driver to act as the nominal head of security. Jim Stewart described Johnny Baylor as a "New York street hustler," but "gangster" would probably have been closer to the mark.

Alabama-born Baylor had served as a Special Ops ranger before moving to Harlem, New York, where he briefly worked as a boxer, even working in the ring for the great Sugar Ray Robinson.

Baylor saw himself as far more than just an enforcer, however. He had a peripheral interest in the music industry, having founded a small label, Koko Records, in 1964. The sole artist signed to the label was a singer by the name of Luther Ingram, who went on to have a big hit in 1972 called "(If Loving You Is Wrong) I Don't Want to Be Right." The song would also later be covered by both Millie Jackson (1974) and Rod Stewart (1977).

Baylor's lofty ambitions were also apparent from his self-penned Stax publicity release. It described him as a "serendipitous thinker" and a "free spirit, [who] feels that experience is the absolute basis for learning and feeling." His sense of style reflected that worldview, with most photographs showing him wearing a sharp tailor-made suit. It was primarily the sunglasses, even worn indoors, and the handgun tucked into his suit, which suggested he was more than just a business executive at Stax Records.

Baylor's gangster-like behavior would see him pull a gun on many of the musicians at Stax in the months that followed, including Marvell Thomas, Rufus Thomas's son. But it was his sense of ambition that would eventually cause bigger problems for the record label and ultimately play a part in its downfall.

In Baylor's initial role as head of security, his right-hand man was Memphis-born Dino Woodard. Woodard had also worked as a boxer in New York and sparred with Sugar Ray Robinson, which is where he met Baylor. Woodard was more monosyllabic than "serendipitous thinker" and was nicknamed after his favorite catchphrase, which was "boom." Accompanied by an appropriate hand-gesture, it could be used to refer to impending violence, disagreement, approval, or even love, so it was important to gauge his mood.

Shortly after he had been hired by Stax Records, Baylor dispatched Woodard to have a quiet word with the gang that was operating in the car park. Woodard explained that they were disrupting the musicians' creative juices, and "boom," they were gone, never to return.

With so many changes taking place—the death of Otis Redding and most members of the Bar-Kays, the ending of ties with Atlantic Records, the loss of Sam and Dave, the assassination of Dr. King, and the changes that had been brought about to the neighborhood—the key players at Stax Records had to pull together and remember what was most important to them.

"We had worked like hell to start up a company," recalled Deanie Parker, the label's publicist. "We were doing well, we were succeeding, were doing everything to the best of our ability, and then Atlantic snatches the world from under our feet and Otis dies. We didn't have the time to get used to the idea of not having Otis or not having the Bar-Kays and determining what our Plan B was gonna be. We had to get in touch with our souls again, throw away the tissues we'd used to dry the tears, and get up and kick ass!"[12]

◆ ◆ ◆

Inevitably, it was music, of course, that allowed the musicians at Stax to get in touch with their souls again.

In February 1968, William Bell wrote a tribute to Otis Redding titled "A Tribute to a King." "It was like therapy for me," he later recalled. "It was like cleansing, I needed closure on this idea that he's dead. I saw him on the Friday before he left [Stax's studio] and Sunday he'd gone. I wrote it to give [Redding's wife] Zelma and the family. I didn't have any idea to release it."

Jim Stewart loved Bell's demo and suggested they record it. Booker T. Jones worked on an elegant arrangement, adding strings, and they sent the recording to Zelma. She wanted the song released as a single, as did Jim Stewart and Estelle Axton. In the end, Bell compromised and agreed to put it out as a B-side, as he didn't want to be seen as capitalizing on Redding's death. "But when the jocks [disk jockeys] got the record they all went on the B-side," Bell said.

The song eventually reached No. 16 on the R&B charts and helped to provide both a fitting tribute to Redding and an element of closure over his untimely death.

Rufus Thomas released his first single of 1968 in March, a stomping number called "The Memphis Train." The song had been cowritten by occasional Stax songwriter Mack Rice and Willie Sparks, a harmonica-playing friend from Detroit. Thomas added some lyrics of his own in the studio and was also given a cowriting credit.

The song was produced by Steve Cropper, who also plays guitar on the song. Because of this, it is widely assumed that the M.G.'s are also on the recording, but it was actually the original version of the Bar-Kays. Listen carefully, and you can hear Rufus yell, "Come on, Carl" before one of the drum breaks, referring to Carl Cunningham, the band's original drummer. As a result, the song must have been recorded in late 1967, before the Bar-Kays went on tour with Otis Redding.

It was a fantastic single, paving the way for some of Thomas's more funk-oriented singles that were to follow, but failed to break into the nationwide charts. "We had a little bit of success with that song locally, and then Buddy Miles cut it," recalled Cropper. "They flew me up to New York and I played on the Buddy Miles session of 'The Memphis Train' for Mercury Records. It came out as a single and did pretty good. Buddy Miles was a great guy. I met him at Monterey Pop and we became friends later. He's not listed, but he's on my *With a Little Help from My Friends* album [1969]. Nobody knows that 'cos it's not [listed] on there."[13]

The B-side to "The Memphis Train" is also worth a mention. "Rufus was a comedy man at heart," explained William Bell. "What he excelled at were songs about comedic things. Being a comedian on stage and a dancer, he could put those songs across. He could do blues and stuff like that, but if you put a soul ballad on him, he was not that kind of singer." Bell wrote a song called "I Think I Made a Boo Boo" with Thomas in mind, and it was recorded as the flip side. "He loved it—he loved those kind of songs, that's what his personality was—comedy and up-tempo dance stuff."[14]

Music also helped the surviving Bar-Kays, bass player James Alexander and trumpeter Ben Cauley, get back in touch with their souls. In April 1968, they put together a new version of the band featuring Harvey Henderson on saxophone, Michael Toles on guitar, Ronnie Gorden on organ, and Willie Hall on drums. As a consequence, Stax once again had a second house band to help out with studio recordings.

The following month, music also helped to ease the tensions within the main house band, Booker T. & the M.G.'s. One morning, just before the band were about to start work, drummer Al Jackson pulled Booker T. Jones into the record store to listen to some calypso music that was playing. "The music was different from anything I'd ever heard," Jones later recalled. "Immediately I connected to it emotionally."

Al Jackson tried to reproduce that same beat in the studio, and over the next few days, Jones came up with an organ riff and bass line that worked with the tune. "Duck" Dunn played the organ bass line, and Steve Cropper added a calypso rhythm, and the basis of a new tune was in place. Al Bell liked what he heard but thought it needed a little more work.

Cropper took the tapes over to engineer Terry Manning at nearby Ardent Studios. He had been doing "overflow" studio work for Stax for some time and suggested they add more percussion. The two of them tried using spoons on glasses, and when that didn't produce the desired effect, hit upon the idea of using marimba to add steel drum-type sounds, which worked well. All that remained was for Isaac Hayes to add some additional cowbell percussion and a touch of piano, and "Soul Limbo" was born.

The song was a big crossover hit, reaching No. 7 on the R&B charts and No. 17 on the pop charts. The song also reached the Top 30 in the UK, where it later became synonymous with the sport of cricket when it was adopted by the BBC as the main theme to their cricket coverage for many years.

It had taken a few months, but with a steady stream of hit singles, Stax had started to find its groove once again, and with that, a sense of belief.

◆ ◆ ◆

Having taken the decision to walk away from a cut-price deal with Atlantic Records, Jim Stewart and Estelle Axton faced a tough decision:

whether to operate alone, as an independent label, or find a new buyer. They opted for the latter; cash flow was a potential issue as a pure independent, but in addition, Jim Stewart felt it was the right time to finally take some money out of the company, having previously reinvested any gains. "I might as well get something out of it," he recalled. "We were looking for capital gains, basically."[15]

Over the course of the spring of 1968, they had engaged in discussions with several potential suitors but struggled to find a buyer. In the end, an acquaintance of Al Bell—a music executive named Clarence Avant, nicknamed "the Black godfather"—agreed to help. He knew Charlie Bluhdorn, the owner of the conglomerate Gulf & Western, which owned a variety of businesses ranging from businesses that sold automobile parts to companies like New Jersey Zinc and Consolidated Cigars. In 1967, they had purchased Paramount Pictures, which in turn owned Dot Records, a pop music label. Bluhdorn was keen to expand in the music business, so it felt like a good fit.

In May 1968, *Billboard* magazine revealed that Paramount would buy the Stax Records complex. "Jim Stewart . . . will continue to helm the Stax/Volt companies reporting directly to Arnold D. Burk, Paramount Pictures' vice president in charge of music operations . . . Burk added that Stax would continue to be handled mostly by independent distributors." "We were still responsible for recording and promotion, but they were supposed to help with promotion," revealed Jim Stewart. "We thought they were big in Hollywood, and we could profit from that."[16]

Gulf & Western agreed to a price of $4.3 million to buy East/West, Stax's publishing company. Less than one quarter was paid in cash; the remainder was paid in stock and convertible debentures which were issued to Stax and valued on their net revenues. What this meant, in essence, was that Jim Stewart and Estelle Axton would get paid over time, provided Stax Records was profitable.

Jim Stewart also wanted to honor the verbal agreement he had made with Al Bell when he joined the company back in 1965. He proposed to Estelle Axton that they each give 10 percent of the publishing company to Al Bell so that he owned 20 percent. Estelle Axton refused and wanted to give 10 percent of the company to Steve Cropper instead, as he had been there since the very beginning. Jim agreed to this, but the deal had the effect of turning Al Bell against Estelle Axton.

From a distribution perspective, nothing much changed. "I just picked up the phone and said to the distributor, 'You won't be paying Atlantic next month, you'll be paying us,'" Jim Stewart explained. The difference was that Stax Records now kept most of the gains rather than paying the majority share to Atlantic.

The first single released under the new arrangement was "Soul Limbo," which was given the catalog number STA-0001. The second single, also released in late May, was "I've Never Found a Girl (To Love Me Like You Do)" by Eddie Floyd. The song was another big hit, reaching No. 2 on the R&B charts.

The new deal with Gulf & Western had gotten off to the strongest possible start.

◆ ◆ ◆

With the new agreement in place, the full extent of Al Bell's ambition became clear. He had waited three years to obtain the stake in the company that Jim Stewart had promised and was named executive vice president of the company. The initial changes he proposed seemed innocuous enough, but over time, they started to threaten the family atmosphere that had developed over the years, which caused significant unrest among key members of staff.

One of the first changes he proposed was a new logo for Stax Records to give the company a more modern image. Al Bell worked with Paramount's creative team on this project and out went the "stack" of records, which had represented an old-fashioned jukebox, and in came the "snapping fingers" logo, because "Stax was finger-snappin' music," as Bell saw it.

The second change was to revamp Stax's distribution network, giving the label a more formidable nationwide and international presence. As a former disc jockey, he knew the domestic market well, and signed up companies like Weis Records in Chicago and Arch Records in St. Louis. He also signed new distribution deals in Canada, England, and France around this time.

The third change was more controversial and brought him into direct conflict with Estelle Axton. Bell invoked a clause in the Gulf & Western deal which said that none of the three key Stax principals, Jim Stewart, Estelle Axton, or Al Bell, could have any affiliation with another music-oriented business and used this to insist that the Satellite Record Shop be closed.

The record shop had been there since the beginning; it had been used to gauge the market, check out new artists, and influence the staff songwriters; as a meeting place, a resting place, and a neighborhood hangout. In more recent years, *Billboard* had used the shop's sales figures when pulling together their regional and nationwide charts.

Estelle was offered a nominal role in the publicity department, one that had already been filled by Deanie Parker, and given a small office next to her brother. She was paid a small base salary, just one-third of what Jim and Al were being paid by the parent company. From that point on, Al Bell made a point of excluding her from key staff meetings, effectively squeezing her out. "I could see the writing on the wall," she later admitted. "I said, 'If I can't have a hand in the decision-making, I don't want no part of it.'"[17]

Jim Stewart chose to side with Al Bell, given his apparent corporate expertise and vision for the company, rather than his sister, who had been so supportive when the company started out. When Al Bell threatened to leave the company, Jim suggested his sister step down.

Both sides engaged lawyers, and eventually, on July 17, 1969, an agreement was reached whereby Estelle Axton was paid a total of $490,000 in an earn-out agreement over the next five years. She would continue to draw her base salary over that period but was subject to a non-compete clause. After the non-compete agreement expired, Axton went on to form Fretone Records, which enjoyed some success with the novelty disco song "Disco Duck" in 1976.

Al Bell had now established a platform to take the label beyond "southern soul"—or what some disc jockeys referred to as 'Bama (short for Alabama) music—and showcase different kinds of Black music. "When I was a DJ on the radio, I played Stax and I played Motown," he explained. "So why shouldn't we have a company here that reflects the sum total of Black music?"[18]

With that vision in mind, Bell set about recruiting a number of new names to the record label in the months that followed the Gulf & Western deal.

The most important of these was a gospel-oriented group called the Staple Singers, who were comprised of father Roebuck "Pop" Staples, a guitarist; son Pervis Staples; and daughters Cleotha and Mavis. The family had their roots in Mississippi but had been based in Chicago for many years.

The Soul Children were another new signing around this time. The songwriting duo of Hayes and Porter were on the lookout for new artists to effectively replace Sam and Dave and formed a male-female vocal quartet around a singer called John Colbert, who performed under the name J. Blackfoot. He was joined by Norman West, a former member of the Del-Rios, Anita Louis, a former Teen Town singer and Shelbra Bennett.

One new signing that slipped through the cracks was an Arkansas-born singer by the name of Al Green. "Al Bell told me that we missed getting Al Green by ten minutes!" explained Steve Cropper, laughing. "He told me that had we not have had a meeting, we would have signed him. He called Al Green and said, 'We just had a meeting, and we definitely want to sign you.' He said, "I wished you called me ten minutes ago—I just made a deal with Joe Cuoghi [founder of Hi Records]. I'm sort of thankful we didn't sign him, because it would have been a very competitive situation."[19]

These new arrivals unsettled many of the existing stars at Stax Records, who faced the prospect of more competition for the attention of the in-house songwriters and more competition for studio time, too. "Let's put it this way," said Carla Thomas. "Well, we see Carla and Rufus all the time, but oooh, the Beatles just showed up down here! See what I'm saying? It's okay to get excited, but don't forget the people that actually brought you there, that even brought the Beatles there, and Elvis, and all these people . . . ."[20]

Finally, in order to help him implement his vision, Al Bell brought in producer Don Davis with a view to bringing a more polished, Detroit feel to the label's sound. Davis had been a guitarist with Motown in the early years before spinning out on his own and establishing his own recording studio and record label. Al Bell had first brought him to Memphis in late 1967 to produce Carla Thomas and, in the summer of 1968, made the decision to hire him as a full-time producer.

The hiring of another apparent "outsider" further ruffled the feathers of the more established members of the Stax family. First up, credit as the producer had historically been given to members of the in-house "production pool," also referred to as the Big Six—Booker T. & the M.G.'s, Isaac Hayes and David Porter; being given producer royalties had been a way in which these key members of staff were provided with additional compensation for the work they did on behalf of the label.

"After Stax left Atlantic's distributionship, they brought in a lot of outside people to hold down positions that—quite honestly—Booker, Steve, Duck and Al—thought they would be elevated up to, as they'd played on 99% of the hits," explained singer William Bell. "The new executives took over the production, and that put some discord into the operation."[21]

In addition, some of the singers—most notably Carla Thomas—disliked his production methods. Davis tended to prerecord the back music and have singers add a vocal later rather than interact with musicians live in the studio.

Deanie Parker, as head of publicity, downplayed the effect of most of these changes. "I don't think things changed at Stax that much—the heart of Stax, the architecture of Stax—as much as the furniture was rearranged."[22]

But not everybody shared her view. Steve Cropper went to Al Bell and explained the problems the changes had created. "He did not want to hear that," Cropper told Peter Guralnick, author of *Sweet Soul Music*. "All of a sudden, after being such a longtime friend, I became Al Bell's enemy."

Rufus Thomas broadly shared Cropper's view and felt that the old "family" feel at Stax was starting to erode. "It was like family for a long while, until it got to be a corporation," he later explained to the Smithsonian Institution. "And I had sense enough to know that when it gets to be a corporation, it's different. Where I used to go into the office when I wanted to, I had to get an appointment. It got big; they really got big. But then it wasn't family anymore."[23]

♦ ♦ ♦

Thomas returned to the recording studio for the first time since the Gulf & Western deal was finalized in the summer of 1968 to record a song titled "Funky Mississippi" written by Eddie Floyd while on a fishing trip to Byhalia, Mississippi. "It was written for a little town called Byhalia," Thomas later recalled. "The mayor heard the song and called the company not knowing what 'funky' meant. You know how them white boys down in Mississippi are—'funky, that's bad.' He didn't know nothing. 'What you mean say Byhalia, Mississippi, is funky?' He never did get it correct."[24]

The song was the first of a number of more blatantly funk-oriented tunes that he would record in the late 1960s, and although the single failed to chart, it probably deserved a better fate.

Around this time, Carla made the decision to take a break from her master's degree in English and relocate from Washington, DC, to New York. She had struggled to juggle her studies with her music career and embarked on a course at drama school at the American Academy of Dramatic Arts.

The course had been proposed by her new manager, Sandy Newman, who thought that she might consider a potential career in television or movies, considering Stax Records' close ties to Paramount Pictures. In an interview with *Stax Fax*, the label's new in-house magazine, Carla admitted that she would also consider theater. "I feel that theater experience would be good for me," she revealed, "because if you can make it on stage, you can make it anywhere."[25]

At that stage, however, she expressed her desire to eventually return to her master's degree. "I think I'm going to try to finish up this year," she suggested. In the end, she never completed her master's and eventually relocated to Los Angeles to try and forge a career in television.

While she was in New York, she conducted her next recording session, which was supervised by Al Bell and his new hire, Don Davis. The plan was to record a song called "Where Do I Go" from the popular counterculture theater production *Hair*. Rather than fly the in-house band to New York, Davis opted to use a local band which was comprised of guitarist Carl Lynch, bassist Chuck Rainey, and drummer Bernard "Pretty" Purdie on drums.

Carla also recorded her own composition, "I've Fallen in Love," which featured the Sweet Inspirations on backing vocals, a group which was founded by Cissy Houston, mother of the late Whitney Houston. The new song was very well-received by the session musicians. "I hadn't even started singing yet," she remembered. "Bernard, he stopped, he hit the bass drum with his foot, threw his sticks up in his air. He said, 'This is a hit record!'"[26]

Al Bell was adamant that "Where Do I Go" should be the A-side, and Carla's song was relegated to the B-side, despite her protestations. The single just about broke the Top 40 that fall. Carla did not give up on her new composition, and it remained an integral part of her live set at that time. Local disc jockeys started to play the song, and it was later released as a single in its own right in 1969, also scraping into the lower reaches of the chart.

One of Don Davis's next sessions for Stax became his big breakthrough. The songwriting team of Homer Banks, Bettye Crutcher, and guitarist Raymond Jackson had penned a raunchy new tune, "Who's Making Love," which was one of the first overtly sexual songs written for the label. They had presented the song to the "production pool," but the song had been rejected.

Don Davis had been looking for a new song to record with a veteran singer named Johnnie Taylor, who had signed to the label back in 1966 but failed to achieve any real commercial breakthrough. Al Bell had high hopes for Taylor, who had replaced Sam Cooke in the gospel group, the Soul Stirrers, back in 1957.

Davis heard the demo that had been recorded by Homer Banks and thought it would be perfect for Taylor. His decision to override the decision of the production pool went down badly with the older members of the Stax family and reinforced his position as an "outsider" in the organization. But Davis saw the song's potential as "an anthem for women" and pushed ahead with the recording, which was released as a single in September 1968.

The single was a massive crossover success, reaching No. 1 on the R&B charts and an impressive No. 5 on the pop charts, too. It became the biggest-selling song in the label's history, outstripping earlier hits by Sam and Dave and Otis Redding, and eventually hitting two million in sales.

Al Bell saw the success of "Who's Making Love" as vindicating the hiring of an outside producer to shake things up, as the song had a more modern feel than the traditional Stax recordings. However, it also reinforced the divide between the original Stax "insiders" and the newer "outsiders."

"We didn't have a real outlet for our material until Don Davis came," noted Bettye Crutcher. "As a result, we got a lot of songs on Johnnie Taylor because, as far as Don Davis was concerned, there was no other place to turn."[27]

Johnnie Taylor's follow-up single, "Take Care of Your Homework," was also well-received. It was another Banks/Crutcher/Jackson composition, produced by Don Davis, and again hit No. 2 on the R&B charts. A new star had emerged.

♦ ♦ ♦

As Christmas approached, Al Bell was busy putting together the final arrangements for the second annual Stax/Volt Records Christmas party, an event known as the "Yuletide Thing." The event was scheduled to take place at the Mid-South Coliseum on December 20. The concept was loosely based Motown's annual "homecoming" shows in Detroit and was designed to showcase some of the label's biggest stars; scheduled to appear that year were, among others, Isaac Hayes, Rufus and Carla Thomas, Johnny Taylor, Booker T. & the M.G.'s, Eddie Floyd, and the new-look Bar-Kays.

Al Bell, ambitious as always, wanted to broaden the appeal of Stax's music and made the decision to invite the counterculture rock star, Janis Joplin, to appear at the event. The idea wasn't quite as crazy as it sounded. The singer had recently disbanded her blues-rock oriented outfit, Big Brother and the Holding Company, and assembled a new band, the Kozmic Blues Band, which aimed to be more soulful and even featured a horn section. Moreover, according to Stuart Cosgrove, author of the excellent book, *Memphis 68: The Tragedy of Southern Soul*, the singer had been listening to Carla Thomas non-stop, wearing out the stylus as she tried to absorb every nuance of her style.

Sadly, a number of unfortunate events marred Joplin's performance. First of all, the band was newly formed and had not had much time to work on their repertoire. "Janis wanted to emulate Aretha and Otis," recalled guitarist Sam Andrew, the only bandmember retained from Big Brother. "But before we had the repertoire down, we were going to play in front of one of the most demanding audiences in the country, our heroes from Stax."

In addition, the schedule for the event was extremely busy, and the visitors did not have much time to rehearse. "It was truly one of the most awkward situations I'd ever been in," said Bill King, the band's original pianist. "First, the studio floor was on a slope due to its previous incarnation as a public cinema. Secondly, the number of certified superstars walking about not only excited but also added a level of intimidation. I mean these were my big heroes."²⁸

The soundcheck at the Mid-South Coliseum was also a disaster. The band was used to using far more amplification than the local R&B performers, leaving them feeling concerned as to how they would sound. Joplin also spotted a poster of the event with her name in much larger letters than the other participants; this had been arranged by her manager, but left her feeling embarrassed and apologetic in front of her hosts.

Bill King remembers the Bar-Kays as stealing the show that night. "Booker T. did the M.G. thing in a cool almost self-effacing manner," he recalled. "The Bar-Kays stole the night with an upbeat rhythm set dressed in zebra-striped flannel jumpsuits."²⁹

By contrast, the under-rehearsed newcomers bombed. The sound was poor, with the organ cutting out and Janis Joplin's mike distorting. To make matters worse, the audience offered minimal support. "It was intimidating, playing the blues for Black people," Sam Andrew later admitted. "We just blew it."³⁰

Still, there seemed to be no hard feelings after the show, with the Stax entourage inviting Joplin and members of her band over to Jim Stewart's new home where he and his wife were hosting a Christmas party.

Having made the decision to cash in on his investment in Stax Records, Jim had spent almost a quarter of a million dollars on a sprawling new ranch-style home on the outskirts of the city. The house boasted fifty acres of land, four swimming pools, and a tennis court. "He had this house I could not believe," recalled saxophonist Don Nix, who had been in the original Mar-Keys with Steve Cropper. "They had a trout stream running through the living room!"³¹

One can only imagine what Jim Stewart's new neighbors made of his flamboyant guests that evening. Rufus Thomas had dressed appropriately, wearing a dark suit and tie, but Isaac Hayes was wearing a leopard print suit and the Bar-Kays sported matching fur jackets and polyester pants, while Janis Joplin looked every inch the hippie, with long beads and ostrich feathers on each wrist.

Jim and his wife had put on a lavish spread, but guests remember
a largely somber and reflective evening. "Stewart had rigged various
rooms with monstrous-sized Voice of the Theater [*sic*] speakers," Bill
King remembered. "Through the night he played unreleased tapes of Otis
Redding, who had perished in a plane crash along with four of the original Bar-Kays on December 10, 1967. There were many tears. As much
as it was an occasion to celebrate it was nearing Christmas Eve, one in
which all knew the great singer would be unable to attend."[32]

Somber it may have been, but sober it wasn't. As the evening wore
on, Janis Joplin started to stub out her cigarettes on the living room's
brand-new white carpet. Jim's wife was furious and asked her to leave.
Joplin never returned to Memphis after that ill-fated trip. She died of a
heroin overdose less than two years later, in Hollywood, California. She
was just twenty-seven years old.

♦ ♦ ♦

In late 1968, Al Bell launched an ambitious new project to rebuild Stax's
back catalog, which had effectively been snatched away from them by
Atlantic Records earlier that year. Aware that long-playing records,
or LPs, were becoming increasingly popular, he planned to record
twenty-eight new albums over an eight-month period, with a view to
presenting them to the music industry at a sales conference in May 1969.
Singles still served a purpose, of course, and hit singles could help to promote an album, so he also planned to release thirty singles. "Hit records
are the number one thing on our list," he explained in the first edition of
Stax Fax, the newly launched in-house magazine.[33]

The idea was to showcase the various Stax artists, old and new, and
prove to the industry that Stax Records had a broad back catalog that had
both national and international appeal. The project is regularly referred
to as the *Soul Explosion*, which takes its name from a Stax compilation
album released at the time.

The scale of this endeavor should not be underestimated. Each album
typically contained around ten songs, so this would mean completing
more than one song a day for several months. In order to achieve this,
Al Bell instructed Paramount Pictures, Stax's parent company, to issue a
memo to the studio musicians; going forward they would have to work
in shifts: 3 p.m.–11 p.m., 11 p.m.–7 a.m., or 7 a.m.–3 p.m. "Under Al
Bell's direction, the directive was activated, and I was forced on to the
3 p.m.–11 p.m. shift," noted Booker T. Jones. "The old recording studio
became a 45-record/song-production conveyor belt, quite different
from the little studio of years before where I carried my baritone sax

and haphazardly played an intro to a twelve-bar blues by Rufus and Carla Thomas."[34]

The plan also relied on the fact that Stax essentially had two house bands, Booker T. & the M.G's and the Bar-Kays. Other in-house musicians and staff found themselves essentially multitasking. "I joined Stax in late 1967," recalled Bobby Manuel, who had played guitar with Rufus Thomas when he was still in high school. "The first six months I was an engineer, and then I started playing guitar, doing some sessions— Bar-Kays' stuff, Mad Lads, groups like that. Then I started writing with Bettye Crutcher and other people, with some Bar-Kays songs. Then I just eased into production . . . I became a bit of a utility guy. There was no telling what I'd be doing on a particular day."[35]

In addition, the hiring of an outside producer, who used session musicians in Detroit or Muscle Shoals rather than Memphis, also made this task possible.

Two of the twenty-eight albums planned for May 1969 involved Carla Thomas. The first of these was a new solo album, *Memphis Queen*.

She had already recorded two songs for the album—"Where Do I Go" and the self-penned "I've Fallen in Love"—and returned to the studio in January 1969 to record a new single, "I Like What You're Doing to Me." The song had been composed by the songwriting trio of Bettye Crutcher, Homer Banks, and Raymond Jackson, who were still riding high after two consecutive hit singles with Johnnie Taylor.

It had been a long time since Carla's last solo hit single. "B-A-B-Y" had been a big hit back in 1966, and although she had enjoyed chart success in 1967, they were primarily duets with Otis Redding, such as "Tramp" and "Knock on Wood." Jim Stewart tried to apply pressure on the main songwriters to come up with a hit. Songwriter Bettye Crutcher was in the studio with Jim when he said, "Bettye, we need some songs for Carla."

Crutcher rose to the challenge. She remembered Carla's fantastic performance of the song "B-A-B-Y" clearly. "The very first word in it, it has always amazed me how Carla can say 'baby.' Anything that Carla did that had the word 'baby' in it with any emphasis sold!"[36]

The recording of the song was problematic, however. Producer Don Davis turned up at the recording studio with the backing track already completed. "The whole song was finished [but] I didn't know it," Carla recalled. "He just had the rhythm tracks up and I was cutting. After he started turning the horns on I turned blue. I said 'This is awful, the horns are awful.' I said, 'This is not Stax!'"[37]

While the song was a big hit on the R&B charts, reaching No.9, Carla was convinced it could have been a crossover hit with a more sympathetic arrangement. "If he had let [saxophonist] Andrew [Love] and [trumpeter] Wayne [Jackson] just cut it. But you see, it was his thing, and Memphis musicians were not good enough."[38]

The same thing happened with the album's follow-up single, "Some Other Man (Is Beating Your Time)," and the flip side, "Guide Me Well," which had been composed by Hayes and Porter; the rhythm tracks were cut in Detroit and featured Rudy Robinson on keyboards, Ray Monette on guitar, and Melvin Davis on drums.

Carla Thomas found the whole recording process of the album extremely difficult and found herself longing for the earlier days at Stax, when she had more interaction with the in-house musicians. "[Davis] was very, very gifted," she later recalled, "but I missed the interaction between me and Booker. And that's what started happening. All these people were coming in, and they were doing productions, and they were taking the masters somewhere else to put on the strings and the horns. I mean, we had everything right there [Memphis] you could have ever needed."[39]

Carla was also involved in an ambitious double album of duets, *Boy Meets Girl*—the first double album that Stax had issued. After the success of "Private Number" by Judy Clay and William Bell, they planned a number of duets featuring some of the label's finest singers. The plan was clearly to try and replicate Motown's success with the pairing of Marvin Gaye and Tammi Terrell. Carla Thomas featured on eleven of the album's twenty-two songs, including a group song, "Soul-A-Lujah," and a series of duets featuring William Bell, Johnnie Taylor, Eddie Floyd, and Pervis Staples.

The recording took place in Memphis and was apparently a more rewarding experience than her solo album. "Carla and I were always talking about doing a duet, even after she did the duet with Otis," recalled William Bell. "We finally got the chance to do that with *Boy Meets Girl*. It worked out fine. Carla and I loved working and singing together!"[40]

Carla's only regret over *Boy Meets Girl* was that her father was not invited to sing a duet with her on the album. "I feel so bad because Daddy wasn't on that album, and he felt bad about it, too," she later explained. "I didn't bother to ask him. See a lot of it had to do with because I was away. And, I would come home and do my little part, then I was gone. I always just assumed he was doing it, until maybe the album came out or something."[41]

A total of six singles were released from the album, including the opening track, "Soul-A-Lujah," two of Carla's duets with William Bell, "I Need You Woman" and the Everly Brothers classic "All I Have to Do Is Dream," and "Just Keep on Loving Me," which she sang with Johnnie

Taylor. It's notable that none of these singles charted. Part of the problem may have been that Stax was releasing too much material at that time, with eleven singles in June 1969 alone. But it's hard to escape the feeling that the songwriting teams at Stax were being stretched a little thin by the Soul Explosion.

Of the six singles, only "All I Have to Do Is Dream" really stood out, helped by an extended improvised ending to the song where the chemistry between the two singers really came through. The album, *Boy Meets Girl*, was also somewhat hit-and-miss; like most double albums, it would probably have been better to eliminate the filler and release it as a single LP.

Incidentally, around this time, Carla filled in for an ailing Tammi Terrell and performed a number of shows with Marvin Gaye in New York. Terrell had collapsed on stage while performing with Marvin Gaye in October 1967 and was diagnosed with a brain tumor the following year and had a series of operations. She retired from live performances in 1969 but did get the chance to see Carla sing with Marvin Gaye and was highly complimentary about her performance. After an eighth and final operation in early 1970, she passed away; she was still one month shy of her twenty-fifth birthday.

If Carla was disillusioned by the recent developments at Stax Records—the treatment of her close friend, Booker T. Jones, and the hiring of outside producers and musicians—her father, Rufus Thomas, felt disrespected, most notably by Al Bell.

He also returned to the studio in early 1969 to record a cover of Calvin Arnold's 1968 hit, "Funky Way." He was pleased with the results, describing it as "funkier than nineteen yards of chitlins with onions and sardines on the side. Now is that funky, or is that funky?" The answer was a resounding yes, but as with his earlier funk single, "Funky Mississippi," it failed to make the charts.[42]

His only gripe over the recording session was that Steve Cropper was again credited as producer. Thomas usually claimed that he "produced" his own recording sessions—which included directing the arrangements, giving parts to individual musicians, and even encouraging the musicians to get down to work—rather than mess around. "I been doing that since way back, I mean since I was quite young, putting this together. But I never got credit for it." By contrast, Cropper was often listed as the producer and paid for it. "Some of the songs that Steve Cropper's name appeared on as producer and all that . . . had no business at all on there," he explained to author Charles Hughes.[43]

A Rufus Thomas album was planned as part of the Soul Explosion titled *May I Have Your Ticket, Please?* The production notebook for the sales conference suggests that Stax Records was not quite sure how to pitch the album: "We are experimenting with this album . . . . The album should be a hot underground item; also, if it comes through, it will open the door to establishing Rufus as a comedian."

Thomas had already recorded two funk-oriented singles for the album, "Funky Way" and "Funky Mississippi," but the references to comedy suggest that more comedic songs like "I Think I Made a Boo Boo" may also have been planned for the album. The Stax Archives suggest that a number of other, still unreleased, songs had been completed. "'Get A Groove' rings with exuberance, 'Soul Food' gives an unusual view of this tasty menu; and 'I Would If I Could' is a hilarious up-tempo tune that finds Rufus 'letting all his funky spirit hang out.'"[44]

In addition to the above, guitarist Bobby Manuel recalls doing some slower tunes. "I know we did a lot of ballads on that album—'I Love You for Sentimental Reasons,' songs like that."[45]

"I Love You for Sentimental Reasons" might sound like an unlikely tune for Rufus to be singing, given the funk-oriented songs he seemed to be gravitating toward at this time, but it is worth noting that it was a regular part of his live set. But Manuel's comments perhaps help to explain why the Stax publicity team was struggling to pitch the album; part funk, part comedy, part ballad—only Rufus Thomas could conceive of carrying that off.

In any event, *May I Have Your Ticket, Please?* was the only one of the twenty-eight albums that was never completed. This was clearly not intentional; notes had been prepared for the sales conference, the cover art had been shot, and a catalog number was given to the album. The problem was almost certainly down to securing studio time in Memphis, which was clearly at a premium, given the tight deadline.

Rufus Thomas took this as a personal insult, however, and Bobby Manuel remembers a very tense atmosphere between Thomas and Al Bell around this time. From his perspective, his family was part of the foundation of Stax Records, and without their early successes, the company would never have taken off the way it did. For him to be overlooked in this way, while newcomers recorded their debut albums, was unforgivable.

◆ ◆ ◆

As promised, the Soul Explosion delivered a wide variety of new music. There were new albums by Stax stalwarts such as Carla Thomas, William Bell, and Eddie Floyd. Booker T. & the M.G.'s tipped their hats to the pop scene with The Booker T. Set, which included covers of "Lady Madonna" and "Michelle" by the Beatles, and "Light My Fire" by the Doors. There were new blues recordings by Albert King and John Lee Hooker, and debut albums by the Soul Children and Mavis Staples, who recorded her first solo record.

But the pick of the bunch was the second solo recording by one of the label's in-house songwriters, Isaac Hayes. His debut album, *Presenting Isaac Hayes*, had been a jazz-oriented album, a far cry from the perfect miniatures he composed with his songwriting partner David Porter. The album sold poorly, so expectations for his new album were low.

The new album was built around two extended versions of pop classics, Bacharach and David's "Walk On By" and "By the Time I Get to Phoenix" by Jimmy Webb. "Back in the old days, [we] were the only two people at Stax who had musical taste that was almost identical," revealed pianist Marvell Thomas, who played piano on the new album and helped with the arrangements. "We wanted to do things that the company people weren't ready to deal with. We wanted to get into more pop stuff—Burt Bacharach and Jimmy Webb stuff, but Stax was not interested."[46]

His backing band on the new album was the Bar-Kays. Hayes had sat in with the newly reformed band at the Tiki Club in Memphis, where the band had a weekend residency. Over the course of several weeks, Hayes found a way for his organ to work with the band's piano, bass player James Alexander and drummer Willie Hall learned to improvise beneath Hayes's vocal and instrumental improvisation, and guitarist Michael Toles built up a strong rapport with Hayes, playing a supporting role at times but delivering wild, passionate solos when required.

"By the Time I Get to Phoenix," which brought the album to a close, had its origins at the club. Over the opening organ and bass, Willie Hall would play the ride cymbal while Hayes talked to the crowd, moaning and groaning to attract their attention. "I'm talking about the power of love," he would explain. Hayes would then provide an improvised backstory, missing from Jimmy Webb's word-perfect original, which would draw the noisy club audience in and have them hanging on every word. By the time the song had built to its climax, Hayes had made the song his own, transforming from a song of regret to a song of redemption as the singer looked to a brighter future. It was a truly astonishing performance.

Hayes had asked Al Bell for artistic freedom when recording the new album and got just that, in part because the album was recorded at nearby Ardent Studios rather than Stax Records. "The Isaac project . . . was almost an afterthought," explained Marvell Thomas. "Stax was throwing 60 records together at once, and this album wasn't part of the plan. We went into Ardent and did *Hot Buttered Soul*, breaking all kinds of rules. Seventeen-minute songs had never been done before. The

Marvell Thomas in the recording studio at Stax Records. Photography courtesy of the Stax Museum of American Soul Music.

company didn't think it was gonna do anything; otherwise, they would've been stricter about what was done."[47]

The arrangements on *Hot Buttered Soul* were also groundbreaking and a far cry from the small string section occasionally used at Stax Records. "Part of the whole symphonic texture of that album came again from my and Isaac's interest in that sort of stuff," said Marvell. "Standard Stax orchestration at that time was just a couple of horns and a rhythm section. We wanted to go past that. This project gave us the opportunity to do that. We got an arranger out of Detroit, Johnny Allen, who did strings

THE SOUL EXPLOSION, 1968-1970

and all the orchestral stuff. I'd designed the tracks to accommodate an orchestral top end, and it worked out fine."[48]

The album's cover also told listeners to expect something new, featuring Isaac's shaved head looking down. He was wearing sunglasses and a thick gold chain, suggesting both Black masculinity and sexuality. The album's lush, orchestral sound paved the way for the likes of Barry White in the early 1970s, the records made on Philedelphia International Records (known as "The Sound of Philadelphia)," and the bold arrangements that tended to dominate the so-called "blaxploitation" movie soundtracks of that era. Hayes's spoken monologues were also influential, laying the foundations for Barry White, Millie Jackson, and Teddy Pendergrass.

"Isaac's success caught us all by surprise," admitted Jim Stewart. "We knew Isaac was a good artist. He started as a studio musician. Later he said he kept pestering me to record him, but I don't remember that!"[49]

Before the sales conference took place, Stax Records recorded a one-hour TV Special titled *Getting It All Together* for WNEW in New York. The recording took place on March 20, 1969, and featured Carla Thomas, Booker T. & the M.G.'s, and Sam and Dave. The inclusion of Sam and Dave might seem curious, given that they had left Stax Records for Atlantic Records by that time. Their inclusion probably reflects the fact that they had been nominated for a Grammy Award in 1968 for "Thank You," their final recording for Stax Records. The awards ceremony took place on March 12, 1969, just one week before the TV special. "The New York broadcast in April will also give our major album release in May a terrific boost," Al Bell suggested in *Stax Fax*. Sadly, no recording of the broadcast seems to have survived.

The sales conference itself took place over two weekends in mid to late May. The main purpose of the event was to impress the label's new owners, Gulf & Western, and show the record distributors that Stax had an impressive pipeline even if they had lost their back catalog to Atlantic.

The event was hosted at the high-end Rivermont Hotel overlooking the Mississippi River. The first weekend, May 16–18, was dedicated to distributors and wholesalers from around the country. The following weekend was devoted to the press and key influencers from within the music industry; this included *Rolling Stone* and *Billboard*, *Vanity Fair*, *Jet*, *Time* magazine, and even members of the key European publications. Al Bell was not afraid to aim high, and also invited advertising agencies and movie production companies to the event.

Guests were treated to a slideshow set to accompanying music, speeches and presentations, a tour of the studios, and live performances from some of the key artists on the label, including established artists such as Booker T. & the M.G.'s, Carla Thomas, William Bell, and newer signings such as the Staple Singers and Albert King.

The event was judged to be a resounding success. While it had cost an estimated quarter of a million dollars to stage, the wholesalers loved what they heard and preordered $2 million worth of new product, according to *Billboard* magazine; moreover, this figure multiplied once the success of *Hot Buttered Soul* was taken into account. The album went on to sell over one million copies, topping the R&B and even the jazz charts, and reached No. 8 on the *Billboard* Top 200 pop charts, too. In Isaac Hayes, Stax Records now had a major new solo star.

"With those twenty-eight albums at one time, folk began to forget we didn't have a catalog," Al Bell later explained. "Out of that meeting was born Mavis [Staples] as an individual artist, Isaac Hayes as a giant, and on and on. We came back from the dead not with the vintage Stax sound of Otis Redding and Sam and Dave. We came now as a diversified new company."[50]

While there is no doubting that the Soul Explosion was a financial success, it did come at a price. A number of the original members of the Stax family felt that quality had been sacrificed for quantity. "It's like a great shirt company farming out to some other country to make their shirts and they wear out after three weeks," suggested Steve Cropper. "They're not the same shirt anymore."[51]

Steve Cropper makes a good point. Stax Records became far more prolific in the post-Atlantic era as the Complete Stax/Volt Singles box sets made clear; two of three boxed sets document the post-Atlantic era. While the label continued to produce some superb singles and albums in the late 1960s and early 1970s, the output was arguably less consistent.

The company's cash flow improved significantly post the Soul Explosion. Al Bell had taken the company from a small family-run enterprise to a multi-million-dollar corporation, complete with a sprawling new suite of offices. But increased cash flow also resulted in increased greed and opportunities for corruption, too, all of which would play a part in the label's eventual downfall.

Finally, Al Bell's single-handed ambition alienated many of the original members of the Stax family. Estelle Axton had been forced out, and some of the key musicians were not far behind. In late 1969, Booker T. Jones paid a visit to Al Bell with a personal, heartfelt new song he had written and performed called "Ole Man Trouble." Bell did not feel it was the right song for Stax Records to be releasing at that time. In his biography *Time Is Tight*, Jones described his feelings at the time as "surprised, disappointed, and heartbroken." He drove back to the Stax recording studios for one last time, erased the tape, and made the decision to relocate to California. The original lineup of Booker T. & the M.G.'s stayed together for one more album, *Melting Pot*, and while it was a fine record, it was recorded in New York, not Memphis.

Saxophonist Andrew Love and trumpet player Wayne Jackson, better known as the Memphis Horns, also asked Jim Stewart if they could leave around this time. As session musicians, they could charge far more, and with their immense reputation in the industry, they found themselves in high demand, appearing on the likes of Neil Diamond's "Sweet Caroline," Al Green's "Let's Stay Together," and Elvis Presley's "Suspicious Minds," to name but a few.

Guitarist Steve Cropper stuck around for another year but eventually left to set up his own studio, TMI Studios, in conjunction with Jerry Williams and former Mar-Key, Ronnie Stoots, where he would record the likes of John Prine, Jeff Beck, Rod Stewart, and even Ringo Starr.

But one of the founding members of the Stax family, Rufus Thomas, decided to stick around; while the old "family" feel of the label had disappeared, he figured it was still the family he knew best.

Chapter Ten

Funkiest Man Alive

The Funk Years, 1970-1975

As 1970 approached, Rufus Thomas felt like the forgotten man at Stax Records. He had not scored a chart hit since "Sophisticated Sissy" three years earlier, and even then, it had only troubled the lower reaches of the charts. He hadn't achieved a Top Thirty hit since "The Dog" and "Walking the Dog" back in 1963.

When Al Bell launched his Soul Explosion in 1969, he had been overlooked in favor of new signings such as the Soul Children, the Staple Singers, and the Emotions. Not only was his album *May I Have Your Ticket, Please?* left unfinished, but in addition, the label did not even release any of the songs recorded for that album as a single. In fact, it had been almost exactly one year since his last single, "Funky Way," was released in December 1968.

Looking back on the late 1960s in later years, Rufus would occasionally try to pin the blame on the label's house band, the M.G.'s. "The Stax sound was a hollow sound," he explained to Stax historian Rob Bowman. "If you listened to it, it sounded hollow, there was space. But not with mine. Something happened that I filled it up."[1]

In truth, Thomas's observation seems a little unfair. While it is true that he enjoyed bigger hits in the 1970s with what was essentially the Bar-Kays' rhythm section supplemented by a horn section, it probably had more to do with the growing popularity of funk as a genre than the musicians themselves.

Part of Thomas's grudge may have stemmed from the fact that he simply found it hard to get studio time with the M.G.'s during the Soul Explosion; even with the musicians working in shifts, the label was struggling to meet its ambitious album launch plan.

But there was another element to the singer's complaints about the late 1960s that is worthy of further examination. On several occasions, he singled out guitarist Steve Cropper for particular criticism. Part of this stemmed from the fact that the guitarist was occasionally given production credits which Thomas felt were unwarranted, as previously discussed. But on other occasions, Thomas went further, suggesting there was a racial element to Cropper's behavior, too. The disputes seem to have centered around who was responsible for controlling the recording session. "Steve Cropper had that *white* thing that said because you're Black, you're supposed to do exactly what this white man says," Thomas later suggested.[2]

In another interview, Thomas suggested that Cropper's control in the studio acted as a constraint on his ability to arrange the records as he wanted. "After Steve Cropper eventually left," he explained, "I started doing the records without Steve and the records came along very well without him."[3]

Charles Hughes, author of the excellent essay "You Pay One Hell of a Price to Be Black" which is part of the book *An Unseen Light: Black Struggles for Freedom in Memphis, Tennessee*, suggests that this provides evidence that Stax Records was not perhaps as "colorblind" as authors such as Peter Guralnick, author of *Sweet Soul Music*, have suggested.

Certainly, Rufus Thomas and Steve Cropper were no longer as close as they had been in the early 1960s when they recorded hits like "The Dog" and "Walking the Dog" together, and Rufus would invite the young guitarist to dinner at the family home.

Part of this stemmed from the fact that Cropper was far busier than he had been and was in demand as a songwriter, a guitarist, and an engineer, which Rufus seemed to resent, particularly when he felt overlooked. But there was also a degree to which Thomas himself could be difficult and demanding to work with in the studio, and insisted on doing things his way. "He had a very strong personality, very much in charge," admitted Booker T. Jones. "To be honest with you, not always pleasant—it would be at whatever cost. But none of us are perfect. But now that I'm 75, I know you have to have a passion in life, you have to have an aim. He was very purposeful."[4]

Was there also a racial element to Cropper's behavior that exacerbated the friction in the studio? As Jones himself has admitted, the guitarist's behavior could be racially insensitive, as demonstrated by the comments made in the light of the assassination of Martin Luther King, and there would appear to have been some similar interactions with Thomas in the recording studio that left an unpleasant taste in the singer's mouth.

At the end of the day, the two musicians were no longer as close as they had once been, and this was the result of several factors—and more to do with business; in this case, the making of hit records—than race itself.

Perhaps the situation is best summarized by Deannie Parker, the label's publicist, who was asked about this issue. "I used to cringe when I heard in Memphis about things that were prejudiced, as opposed to things that were racist, because there is a distinct difference, and I'm not sure that people do a good job of distinguishing the two," she explained. "Racism concerns behavior and policies that are woven into the fabric, by design, to ensure that certain things do and do not happen to certain groups of people. At Stax I saw Jim Stewart and Al Bell exercise all kinds of opportunities, putting into place all kinds of mechanisms, to ensure that there was racial equality, gender equality, writer equality, producer equality—they were conscious of that at all times. And so, while we were a family, and we really were a family—all families have conflict, play games with each other, love on each other, misunderstand each other, take each other for granted. But when it came to racial equality, I think we achieved it. Now racial harmony? I think that's determined by your prejudices. I don't recall a situation at Stax, an interaction with anybody that I would say was racist."[5]

◆ ◆ ◆

Despite Thomas's problems in the recording studio, he remained a popular live attraction, and he toured constantly. James Alexander of the Bar-Kays remembers that the band still occasionally backed Thomas at this time, despite their own commitments. "In 1969, we did a show in Washington, DC," Alexander recalled. "The headliner of the show was Al Green, and on that show was Rufus Thomas. Rufus was the type of artist who would play anywhere; a nightclub one night, or like the shows in Washington DC, we played for five days at the Warner Theater."[6]

And it was one of his live performances that provided the inspiration for his next single. He was playing a gig at a club called the Crestview in Covington, Tennessee, backed by Willie Mitchell's band. A couple of his earlier hit singles had been based on dance crazes that were popular in the nightclubs, including "the Dog" and "the Sissy," so Thomas was always on the lookout for the latest trends. He had heard about a new dance that had started in Chicago known as "the Chicken." "The dance was so hot I said, 'I got to have me a song,' and I don't know how it came about but we had a groove going," Thomas later explained.[7]

With the band playing a funky beat behind him, Thomas started to improvise. "I did it in the middle of doing another song . . . and the words just started to come," he explained to Stax historian Rob Bowman. "I don't know how, they just came out of the blue. I just separated it. 'You raise your left arm up, and your right arm too.'"[8]

The biggest problem, Thomas later admitted, was finding a word that rhymed with "chicken."

The middle section of the song is based on some of the riffs and one-liners he had used over the years, both working as a host on Amateur Night with "Bones" Crouch and as a radio announcer at WDIA.

> Oh, I'm feeling it now, I feel so unnecessary,
> This is the kind, this is the kind of stuff,
> To make you feel like you want to do something nasty,
> Like waste some chicken gravy on your white shirt,
> Right down front, here we go y'all.

The song was recorded in December 1969 with his son Marvell Thomas on keyboards and the Bar-Kays' rhythm section. The Bar-Kays' horn section was not used, with the Memphis Horns, Andrew Love, and Wayne Jackson brought back in, supplemented by Fred Ford on baritone saxophone and Ed Logan on tenor saxophone.

"The recording session was quick," Alexander recalled. "Rufus would always come to the studio with an idea, how he wanted it to go. Rufus was very particular—he knew exactly what he wanted, how he wanted it to be, you know. He was very patient with us, and would wait until he got what he wanted—we were so young at that time."[9]

"Do the Funky Chicken" opens with Thomas's goofy chicken impression, and then guitarist Michael Toles joins the fun, creating a chicken lick of his own. The fuller sounding horn section also contributes to the song's success. But it's Thomas's tune, and there are few other singers that could carry a novelty song like that and make it sound convincing.

Of note, it was the first song produced by another newcomer at Stax Records, Tom Nixon, who had recently been appointed as director of production control, yet another new role created by Al Bell. Nixon had previously worked as an engineer with Motown on the West Coast and had helped to build a studio there for Venture Records. He had been introduced to Bell by Mickey Stevenson, the former Motown producer, who had been impressed by his abilities.

Bell was impressed by the fact that Nixon used a stopwatch to analyze songs on the charts, effectively monitoring the popularity of certain songs by measuring beats per minute, or BPM, long before that became more popular through disco. "Tom Nixon seemed to me a very important addition to our creative team," said Bell.[10]

Harold "Scotty" Scott, one of the singers with the Temprees, recalled that Nixon knew how to keep things simple in the studio. "Tom Nixon was a wonderful guy to work with, he was very smart, very savvy. He did not want to overproduce any of our records," he explained. "Some producers add strings, tom-toms, chimes, and stuff like that, and when you're on stage, it doesn't sound like that. Tom liked to keep it simple and focus on the singing. If you notice, he recorded Rufus the same way with very simple tracks, with just the rhythm section and horns. He wanted everyone to sound like they did on the record. We added handclaps to three or four Rufus tracks. If you listened to the songs with and without the handclaps, it could really make a difference, providing a backbeat. Tom Nixon was a very smart man."[11]

Nixon developed a good relationship with Rufus Thomas while he was at Stax Records, however, and worked closely with him for the next six or seven years.

"Do the Funky Chicken" was released as a single in December 1969 and became his biggest hit since "Walking the Dog," reaching No. 5 on the R&B charts but also achieving some crossover success and scraping in to the Top 30 on the *Billboard* pop charts, too. The single also reached No. 18 in the UK, his only European chart hit.

Goofy it may have been, but the "Funky Chicken" had staying power. Welsh singer Tom Jones performed the song, complete with white chicken tassels, on his TV show *This Is Tom Jones* in 1970. The song remained a core part of Thomas's live repertoire for the rest of his life; the song would often last for fifteen to twenty minutes, with Thomas inviting women onto the stage and teaching them how to do the dance, making sure that they "followed his instructions." He even performed the song on a late-night music TV show *Sunday Night* in 1989 at the age of seventy, teaching saxophonist David Sanborn and the house band the moves. The song was also sampled by a number of rap artists. Eazy-E sampled a section of the song on his 1988 track "Still Talkin," while Missy Elliott sampled Thomas's chicken sounds for "Don't Be Comin' (In My Face)" in 1997.

Emboldened by the success of "Funky Chicken," Thomas returned to the recording studio to cut a cover of "Sixty Minute Man," which had been a gospel-influenced R&B hit in 1951 for Billy Ward and the Dominoes. The Dominoes were a Black vocal group led by pianist and main songwriter Billy Ward. He was joined by Bill Brown, Charlie White, Joe Lamont, and Clyde McPhatter, who later left the group to form the Drifters. "Sixty Minute Man" was the band's third single and featured Bill Brown's bass voice, rather than McPhatter's tenor, as the lead.

Rufus Thomas demonstrates the "Funky Chicken" at the Mid-South Coliseum for the annual Starlite Revue charity show sponsored by WDIA, July 6, 1970. Photograph courtesy of the *Memphis Press-Scimitar*, Special Collections Department, University of Memphis Libraries.

Gospel-influenced the song may have been, but the contents of the song would probably make the preacher blush.

> There'll be fifteen minutes of kissin',
> Then you'll holler 'Please don't stop' (Don't stop!)
> There'll be fifteen minutes of teasin',
> Fifteen minutes of squeezin',
> And fifteen minutes of blowin' my top.

Thomas returned to the studio with the same band that had recorded "Funky Chicken." The song opens with a looping bass line, courtesy of James Alexander, before Willie Hall joins on bass drum and hi-hat followed by some tambourine percussion and Michael Toles on guitar.

When Thomas joins, he turns the song inside out. He begins by repeating the line, "I feel my body." "It was Africa where I got that from," the singer later admitted. "That came from a Tarzan or Harry Carey movie. It sounded to me like [they] said 'I found my bonnie,' but it was a chant, an African chant. Just a whole tribe when they decided they were gonna kill some of the white folks, put them on the stake—this is the way they were sounding. I just took it from there."[12]

Thomas also delivers a tribal chant, his unique take on an African-style Cab Calloway. The full song lasts for over seven minutes, and an edited version was released as a single. Overall, it's a quite remarkable performance, unlike anything he had ever recorded previously, and effectively previews Thomas's growing interest in African culture prior to his visits to Liberia and South Africa.

The B-side, also recorded at that time, was an old song called "The Preacher and the Bear." It tells the story of a church pastor who appeals to God after being caught in a tree by a bear while out hunting on the Sabbath. Ragtime singer Arthur Collins had recorded the song back in 1905, and Thomas recalled hearing the song as a young child growing up in Memphis. Thomas had recorded the song for a local television broadcast in the late 1950s, prompting some complaints that the song was sacrilegious. Thomas later explained to Rob Bowman that hearing Jack Benny's bandleader perform the song convinced him that by the late 1960s, it was safe to record the song. Thomas puts a Chuck Berry, early rock and roll spin on the song, which also features the Stax vocal group Ollie & the Nightingales on gospel-style backing vocals.

The single was released in May 1970, and while it did not perform as well as "Funky Chicken," it still reached a creditable No. 42 on the *Billboard* R&B charts, giving Thomas his first back-to-back hit singles since 1964.

Around this time, Thomas started recording his second full-length album, *Do the Funky Chicken*, which was released in the summer of 1970. In addition to the singles released from the album, "Do the Funky Chicken" itself and "Sixty Minute Man," he dusted off a couple of old classics—a Louis Jordan cover and one of his older hits.

"Let the Good Times Roll" was a 1946 jump blues song cocomposed by Sam Theard, a New Orleans songwriter, and cocredited to Fleecie Moore, Jordan's wife, presumably in an attempt to circumvent Jordan's publishing contract. It's given an up-tempo read here with some funky guitar licks courtesy of Michael Toles and soulful backing vocals. In the middle of the guitar solo, Thomas announces to listeners, "You know, everything I'm gonna do from now on is gonna be funky—yeah!"

Thomas also applied a layer of funk to a remake of his controversial 1953 hit "Bear Cat," but this time took care to credit the song to the original composers, Leiber and Stoller, to avoid any potential lawsuits.

One of the album's other highlights is "Soul Food," a song that had been recorded for the *May I Have Your Ticket, Please?* sessions. The song was written by Nashville songwriter Dallas Frazier and sees Thomas singing his way through the menu, adding touches of his trademark humor along the way.

The album's only misstep is his two-part read of the old children's nursery rhyme "Old McDonald Had a Farm." Thomas had made a children's rhyme work on "Walking the Dog," of course, but "Old McDonald" stretches the joke a little thin. Part 1 sees him give the tune a gospel makeover, which may have been fun to witness in concert but doesn't stand up to repeated listening. Part 2 sees the band return to full funk mode, and while it works better than you might think, it still feels like filler.

As ever, Thomas was quite the perfectionist in the studio, and on one occasion, it quite literally bit him on the backside. "I remember one time, myself, Lester Snell and Michael Toles—I forget who was on bass—it could have been James Alexander," recalled Bar-Kays drummer Willie Hall. "We were locked in the studio with Rufus working on a song which shouldn't have taken more than three hours, and ended up taking around five hours. I don't know what kind of day Rufus was having, but at that point, he was kind of upset. He'd say, 'No, that's not it, play it again!' A lot of times in the recording studio it takes time to capture the right feel.

"Everyone was tired and frustrated. We felt that we were close, and thought that we had captured it in a couple of previous takes. This went on for a while. Everyone was getting a bit agitated, and wanted to go home, because as the studio band, we didn't get to spend much time with our families. In the studio there was an aluminum ladder, just three or four foot tall. Rufus went to sit down on the ladder but it was not completely closed, so when he sat down, it pinched him on the butt—and it got a good piece of him, too! Rufus jumped straight up the air, grabbed his butt cheek with one hand, and he had that look on his face—and he had some looks! Everybody fell on the floor laughing, rolling on the floor. It was just what we needed. And right after that, we collected ourselves, and nailed it in two takes!"[13]

The album was released in June 1970 and is rightly regarded as being one of his finest full-length albums. The CD rerelease is even better than the original album, adding some of Thomas's underrated late 1960s funk recordings, such as "Funky Mississippi" and "Funky Way," and non-album singles such as "Itch and Scratch" from 1972.

After the difficulties he had experienced in the late 1960s, struggling to even get studio time at Stax Records, Rufus Thomas was now on a roll. He returned to the studio in the fall on 1970 to record another funk-oriented dance number, "Do the Push and Pull."

Rufus returns home from his European tour, 1971. Photograph courtesy of the Stax Museum of American Soul Music.

Again, Thomas was joined by the Bar-Kays rhythm section, but after the success of "Funky Chicken," he persuaded the Stax executives to let him use an even bigger seven-piece horn section, underpinned by the Memphis Horns. After an intro by the Bar-Kays, Thomas storms in with a loud whoop, just as he did on Memphis Train two years earlier.

> Hey everybody, Mr. Rufus in town,
> Came here to take care of business, ain't messing around . . .

And with that fuller band sound, he certainly wasn't messing around. The band works up an irresistible beat, and the horn section engages in some fine call-and-response with Thomas on the chorus. The lyrics are loosely based around a "brand-new dance" that Thomas claims to have found and even name-check James Brown in the final verse, but the song is all about the groove, and Thomas knows that, drilling the band to perfection in the studio.

The single was released in October 1970, and Thomas was incensed to discover that Tom Nixon's right-hand man, keyboard player Carl Hampton, had been given credit as the arranger; as usual, he had come up with the arrangement himself in the studio, including the distinctive horn arrangement, and he felt like he was being ripped off yet again by the management team at the label.

The single gradually climbed the charts, and by February 1971, got to No. 1 on the *Billboard* R&B charts, his biggest ever hit. It was also a sizeable crossover hit, reaching an impressive No. 25 on the *Billboard* Hot 100 pop charts. It capped the most unlikely of turnaround stories; in the space of just eighteen months, Rufus Thomas had gone from being the label's "yesterday man," overlooked in Al Bell's Soul Explosion, to their best-selling singles artist of 1970. What made this all the more remarkable was that by late 1970, Thomas was almost fifty-four years of age.

In the year that followed, Thomas took full advantage of what was, in effect, his third wave of chart success—from "Bear Cat" in the early 1950s to "The Dog" and "Walking the Dog" in the early 1960s, through to full-fledged funk star in the early 1970s.

Three consecutive hit singles meant that he remained a hot ticket as a live performer. He was the big star at WDIA's annual Starlite Revue in July 1970, where he got on stage at the Mid-South Coliseum to teach the packed crowd how to dance the "Funky Chicken."

On January 15, 1971, Thomas embarked on his second European tour, a month-long trip that took in England, France and Germany. "Fans will get the chance to see him doing the 'Funky Chicken,' 'The Dog,' and the 'Push-and-Pull,'" noted Stax Records in their press release.

And on his return, Thomas recorded his first (and best) live album, *Doing the Push and Pull at P.J.'s*, which was recorded at P.J.'s club in Hollywood, California. The album featured his most recent hit, several songs from "Do the Funky Chicken," including an eight-minute version of the title track and "Old McDonald," and a couple of older favorites like "Ooh Poo Pah Doo" and "Walking the Dog." The album captures Thomas at the peak of his powers, working the audience, who was clearly in the palm of his hand.

The album was rushed out weeks later, in March 1971, and featured a cover photograph by Thomas's former WDIA colleague and photographer, Mark Stansbury, and liner notes by his mentor Nat D. Williams, who clearly regarded his success with a sense of pride. "[Thomas] makes no pretensions to a great voice," he noted, "but has a natural sensitivity to entertainment, song and dance," a talent that he had nurtured from the days when he hosted the BTW (Booker T. Washington) Ballets in the early 1930s.

◆ ◆ ◆

Rufus Thomas's higher chart positions also raised his profile from a polit-ical perspective. On May 18, 1971, he left for a ten-day trip to Monrovia, the capital of Liberia, where he was the guest of the country's president, William Tubman.

His trip pre-dated the famous Zaire '74 concert that took place in Kinshasa ahead of the famous "Rumble in the Jungle" fight between Muhammed Ali and George Foreman in September 1974—an event that featured US performers such as James Brown, Bill Withers, and B.B. King, as well as African artists such as Miriam Makeba and TPOK Jazz.

"I had a distorted impression of what Africa was really like," Thomas noted on his return. "I was certainly relieved that Africa wasn't like what most of us are used to seeing on television and movies."[14]

Later that year, he was called upon by Mayor Loeb in Memphis—for the second time—to quell a sense of unrest in the local African American community.

On October 15, 1971, Black teenager Elton Hayes was apprehended by police after a high-speed chase and was subsequently beaten to death while in police custody. Five days of rioting followed, and Thomas was one of several Stax representatives invited to appeal for an end to the rioting; they also persuaded the mayor to lift the curfew he had imposed on sections of the city.

As a result of their work to help the mayor, both Rufus Thomas and Isaac Hayes were recognized by the Memphis City Council in March 1972 for their "outstanding contributions to the city" and received the key to the city from Mayor Loeb.[15]

♦ ♦ ♦

Back in the recording studio, Rufus Thomas's hot streak continued. An early advocate of recycling, in April 1971, he recorded a funk version of his 1965 recording "The World Is Round," which in turn had been based on his 1956 Meteor B-side, "The Easy Livin' Plan." On the flip side, Thomas rerecorded his version of "I Love You for Sentimental Reasons," another leftover from the 1969 *Ticket* sessions.[16]

On this occasion, the single was coproduced by Rufus Thomas him-self and his son, Marvell Thomas. The makeover achieved modest chart success, reaching No. 34 on the R&B charts, but failed to make any impression on the broader pop charts.

Three months later, Thomas returned with another dance-oriented tune, "The Breakdown (Part 1)." Mack Rice had started to compose the song in Detroit, apparently with the Bar-Kays in mind, and when he returned to Memphis, teamed up with Eddie Floyd to finish the song.

Al Bell suggested that as it was dance-based tune, it might be a better fit for Rufus Thomas.

The Bar-Kays rhythm section was unavailable on this occasion, so Thomas was paired with what was effectively Isaac Hayes's backing band; the band featured Harold Beane and Charles "Skip" Pitts on guitar, Lester Snell and Marvell Thomas on keyboards, Ronald Hudson on bass, and drummer Willie Hall.

As usual, Thomas amended the arrangement in the studio and was given a cowriting credit as a consequence. "Skip" Pitts contributed a distinctive slide guitar sound throughout, which producer Tom Nixon wanted to edit from the final take. "I said, 'No, Tom, can't do that,'" Thomas explained to Rob Bowman. "That's an important part in there 'cause it's different from anything we have done. Leave that in there."[17]

Thomas clearly had a good ear, because the single again soared up the charts, reaching No. 2 on the R&B charts while narrowly missing the Top 30 on the *Billboard* pop charts.

Later that year, Thomas tried repeating the trick with "Do the Funky Penguin (Part 1);" it uses the same band, the same guitar effect, and even some of the same words, with Thomas opening with:

Hey everybody, Mr. Rufus is back,
I've got another dance, I know you're gonna like . . .

If it was starting to sound a little repetitive, no one seemed to care, either on the dance floor or among the record-buying public. "Funky Penguin" didn't do quite as well as "The Breakdown," but it was close, reaching No. 11 on the R&B charts—and providing Thomas with his fourth Top 20 hit in just two years.

Thomas's only gripe, once again, was over the writing credits, with Mack Rice, producer Tom Nixon, and Jo Bridges all being cocredited for writing the song. "Mack Rice and none of them have anything to do with 'Funky Penguin,'" he explained to Rob Bowman. "I get my bass lines first and then I put my words in there. Doing it in the United States, way over in England. That was my past experiences . . . they didn't put nothing in there. I just got screwed royally 'cause I didn't know. When you think about it, it burns your butt. I was interested, like most Blacks, in making a record."[18]

Looking back, it's perhaps interesting to ask why Rufus Thomas enjoyed a surge in popularity in the early 1970s after his late 1960s singles had flopped. Fellow singer and label mate William Bell felt that James Brown's transition from soul to funk, starting around the time of

"Cold Sweat" in 1967, helped to pave the way for Thomas's funkier sound. "They were rhythmic from day one," he noted. "James was a drummer originally, and Rufus was a comedian and dancer, and rhythm was really important for both of them."[19]

Deanie Parker, Stax Records' publicist, broadly agreed but felt that the trend toward gimmick-oriented dance crazes also played a part. "It was good timing for Rufus," she said. "It was rhythm, it was dance, it was gimmick. I think Rufus had his finger on the pulse because he created dance songs. He was a gimmick artist. If you got him to sing a blues song and tried to sell a million copies, you would have failed. He was a phenomenal entertainer, a natural entertainer. He could work a crowd. He had the look, the gestures, and he had the songs we could all remember. 'Do the Funky Chicken'! Really?"

◆ ◆ ◆

While Rufus Thomas was flying high on the charts, his older daughter, Carla Thomas, was still struggling to find her niche. Since the split with Atlantic Records in May 1968, she had recorded three solo singles; according to Stax historian Rob Bowman, they had been recorded in three different cities with three different rhythm sections and two different producers.

In April 1970, the label released "Guide Me Well," a Hayes and Porter composition from *Memphis Queen*. The song had previously been released as the B-side of "Some Other Man (Is Beating Your Time)" in November 1969. The song opens with a spoken monologue, or "rap" as it was known at the time, and features a Detroit-based band that included Rudy Robinson on keyboards, Ray Monette on guitar, and Melvin Davis on drums and was again produced by Don Davis. The single crept into the lower reaches of the R&B charts, peaking at No. 41.

The following month, Carla reunited with her older college friend and former musical director, Donny Hathaway. Hathaway had just finished recording his debut album, *Everything Is Everything*, which was released later that summer. Thomas heard a tune that he had written back in college titled "Never Be True" and suggested that they record it. Once again, there is an opening monologue from Carla, which was something of a trend at this time. It has a more organic feel to it compared with the songs she had recorded with Don Davis, and featured some superb background vocals that had been arranged by Hathaway himself.

For the B-side, Carla recorded "The Time for Love Is Anytime," which had been composed by industry heavyweights Quincy Jones and Cynthia

Promotional photograph of Carla Thomas, December 1970. Photograph courtesy of the *Memphis Press-Scimitar*, courtesy of the Special Collections Department, University of Memphis Libraries.

Weil for the soundtrack to the 1969 movie *Cactus Flower* and sung by Sarah Vaughan, who was much admired by Carla Thomas.

Despite being a superb single, "Never Be True" failed to chart. It's hard to escape the feeling that when a song was recorded without the Stax production machine behind it, which included the approval of Al Bell, the marketing team did not push the song so hard.

Carla's final single in 1970 was a ballad titled "I Loved You Like I Love My Very Life." The song had been penned by Toni Wine, the wife of former Stax producer Chips Moman, who had written the song in conjunction with Irvin Levine and Phil Spector. By this time, Moman's American Sound Studio was highly successful, after producing a string of hits for the likes of Elvis Presley, such as "In the Ghetto" and "Suspicious Minds," "Son of a Preacher Man" by Dusty Springfield, and "Sweet Caroline" by Neil Diamond.

Carla Thomas recorded the song with Moman's house band—yet another new rhythm section—and strings were later overdubbed.

"That's one of my favorite songs," Carla later recalled. "Just working with Toni was like, 'Ah!' But Jim [Stewart] said, 'I don't know if we can push that.' I'm going, 'Now I see why Chips left!'"[20]

If Jim Stewart and presumably, Al Bell, failed to get behind her latest single, Carla's manager, Sandy Newman, tried her best. She secured her a place on musician John Hartford's short-lived variety show, *Something Else*, for which she recorded her first music video, lip-syncing as she walked along the beach. Despite Newman's best efforts, the song failed to make the charts. In truth, it's a pretty song, but the arrangement—in particular the heavy-handed strings that were added—overpowers the melody.

Carla only released one single in 1971, and it was her final single to reach the charts with Stax Records. "You've Got a Cushion to Fall On" was composed by Homer Banks and Raymond Jackson and saw her return to a more R&B sound, complete with the Emotions on backing vocals. Like "Guide Me Well" the previous year, it edged its way into the lower reaches of the R&B charts but probably deserved a better fate.

♦ ♦ ♦

While Rufus Thomas was one of the most consistent singles artists for Stax Records in 1970 and 1971, he was not the only one, as the label continued to produce a stream of hits.

Johnnie Taylor continued his hot streak working with producer Don Davis, with "Steal Away" reaching No. 3 on the R&B charts in mid-1970 and "I Am Somebody" landing one place lower as the year came to a close. In early 1971, Taylor scored his second No. 1 with "Jody's Got Your Girl and Gone," cementing his place as one of the label's biggest post-Atlantic stars.

Two of the new artists that emerged as part of the Soul Explosion also met with chart success. Mavis Staples enjoyed her first solo hit single in 1970 with "I Have Learned to Do Without You," while her family's group, the Staple Singers, enjoyed a string of hits in 1971, culminating in "Respect Yourself," which achieved crossover success later that year, reaching No. 2 on the R&B charts and No. 12 on the *Billboard* Hot 100.

The surprise star of the Soul Explosion, Isaac Hayes, also proved that *Hot Buttered Soul* was no fluke. He released two studio albums in 1970—*The Isaac Hayes Movement* and . . . *To Be Continued*—both of which topped the R&B charts while doing well in the broader pop charts, too, reaching No. 8 and No.11, respectively. Both albums essentially followed the same formula as *Hot Buttered Soul*, with just two songs per side, which allowed plenty of space to demonstrate his smooth-talking skills and lush arrangements.

The following year, Hayes cemented his superstar status. The MGM movie studio was looking to make a movie aimed at the African American market and asked if Hayes would consider composing the soundtrack.

He agreed to do so, on the condition that he could also audition for the movie itself. He was disappointed to learn that Richard Roundtree, a model, had already been offered the lead role as a private detective named Shaft, but settled for a cameo role in the movie.

Director Gordon Parks sent Hayes raw footage from the movie, and he composed three pieces, including the opening scene sequence. Parks was pleased with the results, and Hayes worked on the remainder of the score between his heavy touring schedule. To the astonishment of the movie studio, the soundtrack was recorded in just three days; one day with the Bar-Kays, who provided the rhythm section, one day for the orchestral tracks, and one day to add vocals to a couple of the pieces.

When *Shaft* was released in June 1971, the album shot to the top of both the R&B and *Billboard* 200 charts. The album also made history as the first double album to ever be released by an R&B artist. In September, "Theme from *Shaft*" was released as a single, its lyrics describing the protagonist as the "Black private dick who's a sex machine to all the chicks." Despite the racy lyrics, the single repeated the feat, also topping the charts. The following year, Hayes won three awards at the Grammys, two of which were for "Theme from *Shaft*" and also an Oscar for Best Original Song.

With the Soul Explosion, Al Bell had set out to make a "product that was appealing to and accepted by the masses in America." With success at both the Grammy Awards and the Oscars in 1972, Bell could certainly claim to have achieved that. Stax was looking more secure financially, too; in 1971, gross income had risen to an impressive $17 million. The problem was they kept finding new ways to spend this money.

◆ ◆ ◆

While the company appeared to be prospering, there were numerous problems lurking beneath the surface.

The first of these was that the label had expanded too quickly. Around the time of the Soul Explosion, Al Bell had changed the name of the company from Stax Records to the more corporate-sounding Stax Organization. The company had taken over stores adjoining the studio to create office space and eventually rented additional offices closer to the center of the city to house Jim Stewart, Al Bell, and most of the administrative staff. The expansion got out of hand, and by the end of 1971, there were around two hundred staff—a far cry from the small business Jim and Estelle had established. Administrative costs were rising and, just as important, Jim Stewart and Al Bell no longer had such close control of day-to-day developments.

The second issue is that elements of corruption were creeping in. For a record label with independent distribution to get airplay, DJs and distributors had to plug the new releases. They might be given various forms of "encouragement," from lunch to extra "promotional" copies of an album—that could then be sold—to cash incentives or even drugs. To be clear, this was an industry-wide phenomenon and certainly not limited to the Stax Organization.

But things took a darker turn in 1972 when Johnny Baylor, the former head of security, was promoted by Al Bell to work in the Promotions department. Baylor, together with his sidekick, Dino "Boom Boom" Woodard, had spent the preceding two years working as part of Isaac Hayes's ever-growing entourage but had fallen out in a violent dispute over money. So in that respect, Al Bell knew exactly what he was doing.

"Dino was an ex-boxer and he promoted records," explained Stax attorney Seymour Rosenberg. "He would open up a briefcase and inside it was mounted a revolver. He would say, 'Boom!' and close it back up and, miraculously, his records got played."[21]

Things came to a head on November 30, 1972, when Baylor was stopped by airport security at Memphis International Airport boarding a flight to Birmingham, Alabama. His briefcase was found to contain $129,000 in cash, and he carried a check for half a million dollars, written by the Stax Organization.

In later years, both Bell and Stewart rejected any suggestion of corruption, claiming that these were legitimate payments. Baylor's client, Luther Ingram, had just recorded his biggest hit single, "(If Loving You Is Wrong) I Don't Want to Be Right," and Baylor had reputedly signed a favorable deal on royalties. But when a record label reports a turnover of around $17 million and pays out $0.5 million for just one single, something doesn't smell right. The IRS agreed and launched an investigation. Soon after, noted Rob Bowman, the noted Stax historian, the $0.5 million entry in the company's accounts was changed from "loan" to "royalty payment" and later to "promotional fee." While it would take a forensic accountant to unravel the full details, it was clear that something didn't add up.

There were also lingering issues over the ownership of the company. Stax Records had effectively been owned by Paramount Pictures, part of the Gulf & Western conglomerate, since mid-1968, but the relationship had not worked out as planned. "We thought they were big in Hollywood, and we could profit from that," explained Jim Stewart. "But it didn't work; we were in constant disagreement. They wanted to move the company to California, and we said no. It resulted in us buying back the company from Paramount and we started being an independent label."[22]

Deutsche Grammophon, the German label specializing in classical music, had expressed an interest in crossing over into pop music. Gulf & Western demanded $4.5 million from Stax to buy back their stake.

A deal was finalized in July 1970. Deutsche Grammophon paid an estimated $3.5 million for a minority stake in Stax Records and international distribution rights. The remaining $1 million was borrowed from Union Planters National Bank and amortized over two years. The success of the Soul Explosion, and the label's growing album sales, particularly by Isaac Hayes, saw the company repay the loan in just five months. Union Planters National Bank was shocked at how much money Stax Records was making and figured it had found a new client.

One year later, the relationship with Deutsche Grammophon also turned sour. In the interim, the European label had purchased James Brown's recording contract, distributing him through their own label, Polydor. But when they proposed a tighter relationship with Stax Records, Al Bell felt uncomfortable. He again proposed that Stax buy out their minority stake, with the European company demanding $4.8 million—a healthy return on a one-year investment. Stax Records had half of that in cash in the bank and borrowed the other half from Union Planters National Bank; again, the bank loan was paid back quickly. The fact that Stax Records had to pay a premium to buy back a minority stake does suggest, however, that Al Bell and Jim Stewart had not been well-advised.

There was one other ownership issue that had not been resolved, one that would ultimately help to bring about the company's downfall. Jim Stewart wanted out. Over the preceding few years, he had taken a back seat in the running of the company, allowing Al Bell to execute his ambitious plans for expansion. He felt the time was ripe to finally cash in and asked Al Bell to look out for a potential deal that would allow him to do so. But that was further down the line, after what would be one of the label's finest moments: Wattstax.

◆ ◆ ◆

For Stax Records, 1972 began as 1971 had ended, with regular chart success in the singles market and cash flow remaining strong.

Isaac Hayes was back on the charts with "Do Your Thing," his second single from the soundtrack album *Shaft*. The song was edited down from the near twenty-minute version that appeared on the album to a more radio-friendly sub-four minutes and hit No. 3 on the R&B charts, achieving some pop success, too. Johnnie Taylor, nicknamed "the Soul Philosopher," kept up his strong track record with producer Don Davis, with "Doing My Own Thing (Part 1)" reaching No. 16 on the R&B charts.

Stax promotional photograph of Rufus around the time of *Did You Heard Me?*, 1972. Photograph courtesy of the Stax Museum of American Soul Music.

The Soul Explosion continued to pay off for the label, too, with the Soul Children enjoying their biggest success to date with "Hearsay" and the Staple Singers reaching the top of both the R&B and pop charts with their smash hit, "I'll Take You There."

And there were big hits for some of the label's new signings. The Dramatics, a Detroit vocal group, brought to the label by Don Davis, enjoyed crossover success with "In the Rain," while newcomer Frederick Knight reached No. 8 on the R&B charts with his distinctive falsetto on "I've Been Lonely for So Long."

Luther Ingram's "(If Loving You Is Wrong) I Don't Want to Be Right" was another big hit for Stax that year. The song had been written by the Stax songwriting team of Homer Banks, Raymond Jackson, and Carl Hampton and provided Ingram with his breakthrough single, which was a big hit on both the R&B and pop charts, reaching No. 1 and No. 3, respectively. The single was released on Koko Records, which was owned by Ingram's manager, Johnny Baylor, but was distributed by Stax Records, who also owned the publishing rights. When Baylor discovered that Stax's publishing company owned the copyrights, he paid a visit to Tim Whitsett, executive vice president of the publishing companies, and asked for 50 percent of the rights. He reminded Whitsett that he knew where he lived, and suggested he call Al Bell to get the contracts changed.

In the meantime, veteran singer Rufus Thomas looked to cash in on his long run of hit singles by releasing his third album in three years. *Did You Heard Me?* was released in March 1972 and included "Do the Push and Pull (Part 1 & 2)," "The World Is Round," "The Breakdown (Part 1 & 2)," and "Do the Funky Penguin (Part 1 & 2)," as well as the B-side to "The World Is Round," "(I Love You) for Sentimental Reasons."

Some of the singles were divided into two parts, Part 1 and Part 2, because Rufus Thomas liked to improvise in the studio, ad-libbing to the funky beat, usually for comic effect. James Brown worked in a similar way, albeit with less comedy. Part 2 was often released as the B-Side to the single, effectively anticipating the trend toward 12" singles, featuring extended versions of a song, which was seen later in the decade.

One more single, "6-3-8," was released from the album in April 1972. The song, an ode to gambling at the dog track, had been composed by Stax producer and songwriter Randy Stewart with additional lyrics (and a dog whistle) provided by Rufus himself. Despite some fine piano from his son, Marvell Thomas, and a great horn riff, the single failed to chart, perhaps reflecting the fact that it was not geared toward a particular dance trend. For all that, it was a great slice of funk and deserved to chart.

◆ ◆ ◆

Encouraged by the company's success, Al Bell sought to expand way beyond the company's R&B base. He signed a deal with Ardent Studios, where Stax sent some of their overflow work, and agreed to distribute their own label, Ardent Records, which included the power pop band Big Star. "We were ginning money at that time," Al Bell told Stax historian Robert Gordon. "We had hit records—like great apples falling off a tree."[23]

A simple distribution deal felt like an obvious expansion for the Stax Organization, but elsewhere it felt like the company was moving away from its core strengths into markets they knew little about. The Black country singer, O. B. McClinton, was launched on the Enterprise label, designed for "all kinds of music," while new labels were established for gospel (Gospel Truth) and even comedy (Partee), which released the third album by up-and-coming comedian Richard Pryor in May 1974, titled *That Nigger's Crazy.*

There was also an ill-considered foray into theater, with Stax backing two Broadway productions in 1972. "I was troubled by it, these layers and layers," admitted Deannie Parker. "I always wanted to say, 'Why can't we be what we are?'"[24]

Movies were also under consideration, and Al Bell established a new subsidiary, Stax West, in Los Angeles. The company was headed by concert promoter Forrest Hamilton, who was the son of the esteemed jazz drummer Chico Hamilton. Hamilton suggested the company get more involved in the local community to raise its profile and floated the idea of the label helping to support the Watts Summer Festival, which had become an annual event.

The Watts Summer Festival had been established to commemorate the 1965 Watts Rebellion, the riots that had been witnessed by a number of Stax recording artists in the days that followed their appearance at the 5/4 Ballroom. Al Bell supported the idea and originally proposed sending two artists, but other Stax stars liked the idea and offered to appear for free. When Isaac Hayes also agreed to take part, Al Bell got involved in the arrangements, knowing that a big venue would be required.

The LAPD was concerned about the scale of the event, and tentatively suggested the LA Coliseum, home to the LA Rams, as a potential venue. "They didn't want to see that many Black people in Watts 'uncorralled,'" explained, Tommy Jacquette, a local resident, participant in the original riots, and organizer of the festival. "It was a win/win for all of us. Their motives were different, but it was still a win/win."[25]

A date was set for Sunday, August 20, 1972, the last day of the festival. Ticket prices were set at just $1 so that most people could afford to attend. The event was sponsored by Schlitz beer, which allowed most of the event's proceeds to go to charities and local organizations, including the Martin Luther King Hospital in Watts, the Sickle Cell Anemia Foundation, the Reverend Jesse Jackson's Operation PUSH (People United to Save Humanity), the Watts Labor Community and Action Committee, and the festival itself.

Al Bell's promotional experience went into overdrive. The former radio station of local disc jockey Magnificent Montague agreed to broadcast the event live. Hollywood producer David Wolper was brought in to film the event, and he in turn hired Mel Stuart—who had just made *Willy Wonka and the Chocolate Factory*—to direct. Al Bell later claimed he wanted to hire the finest producers, Black or white, and having hired two white moviemakers, set about hiring an all-Black camera crew. "What was important was to get the very best, it wasn't about color," explained Bell. "There was enough color in putting the event on."[26]

The event was christened Wattstax, and Mayor Yorty declared the final day of the festival "Wattstax Day."

As the day unfolded, an air of excitement began to build. Local radio stations held competitions, giving away tickets to the event. Stax recording artist Carla Thomas, who was now based in Los Angeles, appeared on a radio show to promote the event. "They were asking me about the riot and different things," Carla later recalled. "And, I told them how Booker and all of us had been there right before, and how we were so happy to be back and be a part of the rebuilding, instead of tearing something down."[27]

Just after lunch, the crowds started to gather outside the gates of the stadium, a mass of vibrant colors, some wearing multicolored wide-brimmed hats which had been designed for the occasion. When the gates finally opened, a crowd estimated at 112,000 took to their preallocated seats around the stadium; no seating was permitted on the pitch itself, as the Rams were due to play the next day.

The event opened with the "Salvation Symphony," which had been composed by Dale Warren and was performed by the Wattstax '72 Orchestra. Soul singer Kim Weston, best known for her duet with Marvin Gaye, "It Takes Two"—but then signed to Volt, a subsidiary of Stax—then took the stage to sing the national anthem, "Star-Spangled Banner." Her rendition was well received, but the majority of the crowd remained seated.

Soon after, Jesse Jackson, sporting a multicolored dashiki, addressed the crowd. "We've gone from 'burn, baby, burn' to 'learn, baby, learn,'" he claimed, urging the crowd to chant, "I Am Somebody!" With that, Weston was invited back to sing the unofficial Black national anthem, "Lift Every Voice and Sing." And with that, the crowd rose as one, punching the air. Wattstax had begun.

Melvin Van Peebles, director of the cult African American movie *Sweet Sweetback's Baadasssss Song*, introduced the first main act, the Staple Singers, who had enjoyed a string of recent hits. They opened with "Heavy Makes You Happy," followed by the Black pride anthems "I Like the Things about Me" and "Respect Yourself." Of the former, Mavis said, "We felt it was a good song to sing at that event. With Pops saying, 'There was a time I wished my hair was fine.' Well, no. Not anymore. We want our hair the way we came here with it—nappy. That's what was happening. Black people were showing they were proud to be Black. We were singing songs to lift the people."[28]

The day was too short for every artist to play a full set, and even established acts like William Bell and Eddie Floyd were limited to just one song each, while timing issues meant that more recent stars like Johnnie Taylor and the Emotions did not appear that day, despite being present and ready to perform.

Somewhat surprisingly, given the time constraints, Carla Thomas was allocated a twenty-minute set. It had been three years since her last Top 10 hit and her final album for Stax, *Love Means*—much of which had been recorded and produced by her brother, Marvell Thomas, in Memphis, and had struggled to just No. 42 on the R&B charts—her lowest charting album to date.

Carla looked resplendent that day, taking the stage in a long multicolored dress, her hair grown out naturally into a large Afro. Her set was a mix of old and new. She opened with "I Like What You're Doing (to Me)," her most recent hit, before going back to two of her earliest hits, "Gee Whiz" and "B-A-B-Y," holding the crowd's attention with her strong, pitch-perfect performance. She closed her set with a brand-new song. "Throughout my success," she explained in the intro, "I say I owe it mostly to God, and I can't forget him, so I wrote this song about myself and my God." The song, "I Have a God Who Loves," was a strong reminder that Stax Records had failed in the marketing of one of their biggest home-grown talents; it was both a powerful composition and performance that showed she could still hold her own in any company.

Earlier that day, the Bar-Kays had demonstrated that they were one of the label's rising stars with a dynamic set that included their latest hit single, "Son of Shaft." The band's saxophonist, sporting an outsized white Afro wig, introduced the song claiming "freedom is a road seldom traveled by the multitude"—a line later sampled by Public Enemy on their classic debut album, *It Takes a Nation of Millions to Hold Us Back.*

Powerful messages were delivered throughout the day, both from the artists themselves and the celebrities who introduced each act. But beneath this, there was a party atmosphere, too; it was a hot sunny day in Los Angeles, with six hours of soul and funk to enjoy.

Nobody captured that side of Wattstax better than Rufus Thomas, who took to the stage just before dusk sporting a custom-made pink cape and stack-heeled, knee-high white boots. "Hey!" he greeted the crowd, beaming. "Can I ask you something? I said, can I ask you something? Ain't I'm [sic] clean?" dusting off his old catchphrase from the nights at the Palace Theater.

And with that, he parted his cape, revealing a matching pink jacket with a large medallion beneath and pink Bermuda shorts, to rapturous applause from the audience. And with that he introduced the tight funk of his big hit, "The Breakdown," removing the cape as he did so. The cameramen panned around the vast stadium, capturing the joy that he brought that afternoon, from hand-clapping to spontaneous dancing.

As he introduced the second song, "Do the Funky Chicken," he announced, "I don't want anyone on the field . . . not yet," referring to the playing field which was supposed to be kept clear. "Now, when I tell you to get on the field, then you get on the field—then I just might get on the field with you!" And with the crowd's laughter still ringing around the stadium, he launched into the crazy chicken sounds that open the song.

As the groove started, Thomas urged the crowd to "come on right down the front, I've got something I wanna show you," prompting a few thousand people to jump the security fences and make their way across the pitch to the stage. Al Bell panicked, worrying about the company's insurance policy, and sent Randy Stewart and Larry Shaw to have a quiet word with Thomas. As the song came to a close, Thomas reminded the crowd that they needed to return to the stands. "Power to the people," he said, adopting the tone of the day. "Now let's go back to the stands." It was a masterclass in how to get the audience eating out of the palm of your hand and showed that even at the age of fifty-five, with receding hair and white sideburns, Rufus Thomas still had what it took.

Remarkably, there were some people within the Stax organization, including Al Bell himself, who felt that Rufus Thomas had misjudged the occasion. Bell felt that frivolous songs like "Do the Funky Penguin" did not fit with the message being delivered by the likes of the Reverend Jesse Jackson and the Staple Singers and that his outfit looked back to the days of minstrel rather than looking forward to a new era of Black power. But over 100,000 people thought otherwise, and many of those felt he had stolen the show.

Headliner Isaac Hayes was not easily outdone, however. Rufus Thomas had removed his cape to reveal pink Bermuda shorts, but when Hayes removed his own psychedelic-print cape to the opening bars of "Theme from *Shaft*," he revealed a thick gold chain vest over his glistening, ripped torso. "Who's the Black private dick who's a sex machine to all the chicks?" he asked the crowd. Hayes knew the answer and delivered a spectacular one-hour set that also included an extraordinary version of "Ain't No Sunshine" by Bill Withers.

Looking back, even after the events that followed, Al Bell still felt that Wattstax reflected the Black Power ideologies. "Here was a little Black company that was able to go to LA, where you had all the giant corporations, and get the musicians out there, hire Mel Stuart, take a stadium and finance the production, then get Columbia to distribute it, and not ask any of them for any money," he explained. "Now, from an economic standpoint, that was the ultimate in Black Power!"[29]

Stax released a double album, *Wattstax: The Living Word*, on January 18, 1973. The album featured live recordings from the event as well as a handful of studio recordings, including "Oh La De Da" by the Staple Singers, overdubbed with audience reactions. A follow-up, *The Living Word: Wattstax 2*, was released later that year, and even included sketches by comedian Richard Pryor, who had not appeared at the event.

The movie premiered on February 4, 1973 at the Los Angeles Music Center, but before it could be released nationwide, Metro-Goldwyn-Mayer (MGM), the producers of *Shaft*, insisted that the clip of Isaac Hayes performing "Theme from *Shaft*" be removed from the final cut. This was eventually replaced with a video of Hayes performing his next single, "Rolling Down a Mountainside," which had not been performed at the event. Despite this last-minute change, the movie was successful and went on to make a sizeable profit at the box office.

◆ ◆ ◆

In many respects, Wattstax was the pinnacle of Stax Records' success; just two years later, the hit singles dried up, and within three years, the company was on the verge of bankruptcy.

The story of the label's fall from grace is long and complex, and readers are advised to check out *Soulsville U.S.A.: The Story of Stax Records* by Rob Bowman or *Respect Yourself: Stax Records and the Soul Explosion* by Robert Gordon to appreciate the finer details.

The root of the problems stemmed from Jim Stewart's desire to cash out of the business and Al Bell's attempts to strike a deal that would allow him to buy out Stewart's stake.

Earlier that year, Al Bell had met with Clive Davis, the President of Columbia Records (hereafter referred to as CBS), at an industry convention. Bell admitted to Davis that Stax Records was still struggling to penetrate the white market, and while CBS had a strong nationwide marketing team, it was struggling to reach the Black market. CBS had signed a distribution deal with Philadelphia International Records, the new label formed by Kenny Gamble and Leon Huff, but made no secret of the fact that he wanted to compete with Motown Records. On paper, at least, it felt like a good fit.

Bell originally proposed that CBS buy 50 percent of the company, but Davis discussed it with the company's attorneys, who saw potential anti-trust problems, so a nationwide distribution deal was worked out instead.

A deal was finalized on October 24, 1972, whereby CBS would loan Stax Records $6 million for distribution rights. Al Bell would pay $2.5 million of this to Jim Stewart up front and use the remainder as working capital. To ensure a degree of continuity, Jim Stewart would stay on as the nominal president of Stax Records but would relinquish day-to-day responsibilities, something he was happy to do. In return, Stewart would be paid a salary of $62,500 per month for the next five years until January 1978, and then a final lump sum payment of $1.5 million.

Despite his past experiences with Atlantic Records, Jim Stewart claims he never read the contract. This time, however, it looked like a good deal for him. If things worked out, he would be paid a total of $7.5 million for his stake over a five-year period.

For the next few months, it seemed to be business as usual. In January 1973, the Soul Children reached No. 11 on the R&B charts with "It Ain't Always What You Do (It's Who You Let See You Do It)," while the following month, the Staple Singers reached No. 4 with "Oh La De Da." Sales of *Wattstax: The Living Word*, the soundtrack album, were also strong, while the movie itself was well received at the Cannes Film Festival in May 1973. However, just below the surface, things were starting to unravel.

In February 1973, the Stax Organization was informed that it was being investigated by both the Internal Revenue Service and the US Attorney's Office, which was a double blow. The announcement came just three months after Johnny Baylor had been caught with a briefcase full of cash and a suspiciously large check at Memphis International Airport.

Two months later, in April 1973, Union Planters Bank in Memphis issued a $3 million line of credit to the Stax Organization. There was nothing unusual in this per se. Stax had become an increasingly important customer to the bank. The record label had paid back the $2.5 million they had borrowed to buy back Deutsche Grammophon's stake and had repaid a further $1.75 million they had borrowed subsequently. The company was seen as being a good credit risk.

On this occasion, however, the Stax Organization's publishing company, East/Memphis, took half of that line of credit on April 10, 1973, and promptly wrote a check to Johnny Baylor for $1 million—all of this despite the fact that both Baylor and the Stax Organization were under investigation by the Internal Revenue Service. Al Bell claimed the payment was legitimate and related to royalties, but again, the numbers simply don't add up. Even Bell himself was only drawing an annual salary of $90,000.

Worse was to follow. On May 29, 1973, Clive Davis was fired by CBS for using company money to fund his personal expenses, including the redecoration of his Manhattan apartment and his son's bar mitzvah. For his own part, Davis claimed the dispute was down to a personality conflict. Either way, Davis was out, and without him, CBS seemed less interested in the Stax Organization.

Davis's successors at CBS failed to make sense of the deal that Davis had signed with the Stax Organization; essentially, albums retailed for just under $6. Of this total, Stax received $2.26, while CBS, as the distributor, received around $0.50. The dispute went beyond just the split. CBS did not see why they would spend additional money on promoting records made by the Stax Organization, given that they received such a small portion of the profit. In short, there was a big gap between the two sides.

As a result of these factors, the CBS marketing machine failed to promote the latest singles and albums produced by Stax, instead focusing on their own records by the likes of Earth, Wind & Fire and the Isley Brothers. By the fall of 1973, reports were coming back to Stax that retailers in major cities such as Chicago and Detroit were struggling to get hold of the latest releases. The hits, and more importantly the cash flow, were starting to dry up. To finance the shortfall, the Stax Organization turned to the Union Planters Bank. It had burned through the $3 million line of credit offered in April 1973, and by the turn of the year, Stax owed them almost $10 million.

To make matters even worse, Union Planters Bank was now facing problems of its own. Oil prices and interest rates were going through the roof, the country was slipping into recession, and like the Stax Organization, the bank had overextended itself. Against that backdrop, they sought more collateral from their biggest creditors, including Stax.

The company had limited collateral that it could offer, but its cofounder Jim Stewart was sitting on a fifty-six-acre estate, having just pocketed a cool $2.5 million from the deal with CBS. At this point, he should have just walked away; the hits were drying up, and he clearly disapproved of many of Al Bell's ambitious plans, which he saw as a drain on cash flow. Even if he had forfeited his agreed salary and the final $1.5 million payout, he could still have retired a very wealthy man.

But Stewart had always been ruled by his heart, not his head, and in February 1974, he pledged his personal assets to Union Planters Bank in a bid to keep the company going. "It was an emotional [decision], not a prudent, sensible one," he later admitted to Rob Bowman. In addition to that, he put a further $0.5 million into the company to help with operating cash flow, which was now negative.

In March 1974, CBS further squeezed the Stax Organization. They claimed that records were starting to be returned and announced that in order to cover their own costs, they would automatically withhold 40 percent of the monies owed to the Stax Organization. It's not clear what was causing this to happen. Rob Bowman, in his liner notes of *The Complete Stax/Volt Singles, 1972–1975*, argues that "the quality of records that Stax [was] releasing through the summer and early fall of 1973 was pretty inconsistent." The gradual rise of dance-oriented disco music was also a factor. Ironically, some of the early disco records that hit the charts were recorded on Philadelphia International Records and distributed by CBS itself; this included songs like "Love Train" by the O'Jays and "The Love I Lost" by Harold Melvin & the Blue Notes. However you looked at it, the unilateral decision to change the contract by CBS was disastrous for cash flow at Stax and another nail in the coffin; the end was in sight.

◆ ◆ ◆

Against this rapidly deteriorating backdrop, Rufus Thomas's own fortunes also took a turn for the worse. From 1969 through 1972, he had scored a steady stream of hits, from "Do the Funky Chicken" through "Do the Funky Penguin (Part 1)." But his final single of 1972, "Itch and Scratch (Part 1)," failed to chart, despite being launched to coincide with his appearance at Wattstax. The song had all the right ingredients: Thomas had again teamed up with producer Tom Nixon, who had been at the helm for three years, guitarist Charles "Skip" Pitts, who again produced his "scratching" guitar sound, and the big horn section. The only unusual element was that the song was recorded at Malaco Studios in Jackson, Mississippi, rather than Memphis, Tennessee, for reasons now lost in the mists of time. As usual, it was great fun, but maybe the public was beginning to grow tired of his somewhat formulaic dance-oriented tunes; while he described the "Itch and Scratch" as a brand-new thing, it didn't sound quite as new the third or fourth time around.

A similar fate awaited his February 1973 release "Funky Robot," which again tried to tap into the latest dance craze. As Rob Bowman later noted, this track was unusual in that it employed New York session musicians rather than members of the Bar-Kays or Isaac Hayes's band. Thomas had tried to record the track on two other occasions but failed to achieve the results he was looking for. It wasn't one of his more inspired lyrics, and the formula was starting to wear a little thin.

Thomas seemed to be aware that this was a potential issue and changed direction with his September 1973 release, "I Know You Don't Want Me No More." The song was a cover of Barbara George's 1961 hit, and as was often the case, Thomas added his own touches: some additional lyrics and a clarinet line, which gave the song a slight Dixieland feel. It was great fun and worked fine as an album track, but was arguably the wrong choice as a single.

Rufus Thomas released his final album for Stax Records, *Crown Prince of Dance*, in October 1973. While it is not as strong as his two previous studio albums, *Do the Funky Chicken* (1970) and *Did You Heard Me?* (1972), it still has its moments.

The highlight is undoubtedly the song "Funkiest Man Alive," a barnstorming tune that never outstays its welcome, despite clocking in at almost eight minutes. The song was cowritten with Memphis concert promoter Don Dortch and demonstrates clearly that Thomas could compete with anyone on funk terms, with or without a dance craze to hang it on. The horn section sounds enormous on this tune, helped by a fantastic baritone sax line from James Mitchell.

Another highlight was the soulful, gospel-tinged "Bring It On Home," which was written by Sam Cooke's manager, J. W. Alexander. Thomas was never the most refined singer on the label but delivers one of his finest vocals here, supported by his daughter Carla, who contributes to the gospel feel.

The self-composed "Git On Up and Do It" may not break any new ground but still packs a funky groove, while elsewhere Thomas reinvents Little Richard's "Tutti Frutti," adding a funk groove, handclaps, and party effects, which make for an irresistible combination.

There were a handful of final singles. In December 1973, Rufus had one final crack at the Christmas market, recording a song titled "I'll Be Your Santa Baby." The song was apparently cowritten by the curiously monikered Oriell Roberts, sometimes spelled as "Robberts." According to Rob Bowman, this was a pseudonym for an exotic dancer known to Rufus Thomas. Whether she really was a budding songwriter or Thomas was looking to help her or perhaps reduce the tax payments on his songwriting royalties, we'll probably never know; either way, her name crops up on a few Rufus Thomas compositions around this time, and indeed songs written by fellow Memphis-based singer, Bobby "Blue" Bland.

It's not one of his finer efforts—the band sounds a little thin after *Crown Prince of Dance* and apparently included a number of younger session musicians rather than the more experienced band that he was used to working with.

Rufus performing live, July 17, 1973. Photograph courtesy of the *Memphis Press-Scimitar*, Special Collections Department, University of Memphis Libraries.

Thomas always kept his finger on the pulse of what was happening on the dance floor and cut a few more disco-oriented singles in the months that followed. Released in July 1974, "Boogie Ain't Nuttin' (But Gettin' Down) (Part 1)" was little more than a groove, but managed to name-check both Temptations singer Eddie Kendricks, who had just topped the charts with his solo single "Boogie Down," and Kool and the Gang. "Do the Double Bump (Part 1)" followed in early 1975, but by then, Stax was struggling to get too much in the way of distribution and promotion. Both singles struggled into the lower echelons of the R&B charts, peaking at No. 63 and No. 74, respectively.

Stax released one final Rufus Thomas single in October 1975. "Jump Back '75" was, as the name suggests, a funk remake of his 1964 single. The sleeve notes to *The Funkiest Man: The Stax Funk Sessions 1967–1975*, written by Dean Rudland, suggest there was some doubt as to whether the single was actually released. Rob Bowman spoke to Thomas about this issue when he wrote the sleeve notes of *The Complete Stax/Volt Singles, 1972–1975*, and Thomas was fairly certain that a few copies of the single were pressed. This is borne out by online record retailers, which reveal that some US and UK pressings can still be found.

But by then, the game was effectively over. In September 1974, Isaac Hayes took Stax to court, filing a $5.3 million civil suit. The lawsuit had been brought about by the fact that a July 26 check for $270,000 had bounced, leaving him facing financial problems: a burgeoning team of hangers-on to support and a sizeable tax bill of his own. He eventually reached a settlement that allowed him to sign a new contract with ABC Records, and with that, Stax's biggest revenue generator was gone.

More lawsuits followed. CBS filed a lawsuit against Stax, Stax responded by countersuing, and then Union Planters Bank got into the act, suing both of them. By mid-1975, many employees were no longer being paid and, in September 1975, the telephone lines were disconnected. Stax Records was forced into Chapter 11 bankruptcy on December 19, 1975, and closed by order of a bankruptcy judge on January 12, 1976.

Chapter Eleven

I Ain't Getting Older

The Post-Stax Years, 1976–1988

On January 13, 1976, Jim Stewart drove to work as usual, reported the *Memphis Commercial Appeal.* "But according to guards posted at the business, he sat in his car at the parking lot behind the old Capitol Theater, barred from entering the business he had founded. After about thirty minutes, he drove away . . . ."

The aftershocks from the closure of Stax Records were still being felt several years later.

Al Bell was arrested and charged with "conspiring to obtain more than $18 million in fraudulent bank loans" from Union Planters Bank, reported the Memphis Press-Scimitar. Also charged was bank officer Joseph Harwell, who later confessed to forging Bell's signature on various loan guarantees. In August 1976, after a three-week trial, Bell was acquitted of those charges, while Harwell was found guilty of making false entries on a bank record and other charges.

Still only thirty-six years of age, Bell remained in the music industry. He went on to become president of Motown Records in the late 1980s, working with Berry Gordy, and worked with Prince and former Stax colleague Mavis Staples in the 1990s.

In the 2014 documentary, *Take Me to the River,* Bell claimed that the city's white power structure conspired to take down a successful Black-owned business. This is a view shared by many of the musicians interviewed for this book.

"How can you say it grew too fast when you start at zero in terms of master tape value in 1968, and by 1974, the company is valued at $67 million?" he asked Stax historian Robert Gordon. But the company's cash flow could not support such a lofty valuation, and by 1974, had clearly started to deteriorate. This reflected a variety of factors, including the nonsensical publishing deals signed with the likes of Johnny Baylor, a dubious distribution system, over-expansion away from the company's core competence, changing musical tastes away from soul to disco, and a distribution deal with CBS that turned sour. No one factor was to blame, but together they brought the company to its knees.

The impact on the company's founder, Jim Stewart, was even more profound. He had stepped up to help, rather than ride off into the sunset, and had to sit and watch as the bank put his house and its contents up for sale in the fall of 1981. "The only excuse I can give is that I love the company," he explained to author Peter Guralnick. "I thought it was worth saving."

Around the same time, Union Planters Bank sold the record label's former headquarters on McLemore Avenue to the Southside Church of God in Christ for just ten dollars. The church originally intended to build a community center at that location, but in 1989, the building was torn down, leaving just an empty lot. It was not for a number of years that the city began to appreciate its rich musical heritage, and the site was finally redeveloped.

Among the numerous musicians signed to Stax Records, none was hit harder than poor Isaac Hayes, who had sued the company for monies owed back in September 1974. He filed another lawsuit in January 1976, claiming the company was supposed to have returned his copyrights and master tapes, but by this stage, he was one of many making claims. By mid-1976, Hayes was being pursued by the Internal Revenue Service, Union Planters Bank, and his ex-wife, who claimed he had missed alimony and child support payments. On November 11, 1976, he filed for personal bankruptcy.

◆ ◆ ◆

In many respect, Rufus Thomas was in a fortunate position. He had enjoyed a resurgence in his recording career in the late 1960s and early 1970s, when—for a couple of years—he was one of the label's best-selling stars. While he occasionally had cause to complain about writing and production credits, the company's cash flow was still strong at this time, and he had benefited enormously. By the time the company was getting into trouble, sales of his records had started to slow; as a result, the amount owed to him by the company for royalties and radio play was modest compared with some of the other artists on the label.

In addition, Rufus Thomas and his wife Lorene had invested wisely over the years, rather than fritter the money away on a gold-plated Cadillac with a fur-lined interior, as Isaac Hayes had done in 1972. After the

Marvell Thomas and his wife, Jimmie, Vaneese Thomas, Carla Thomas, Lorene and Rufus Thomas. Photograph courtesy of the Stax Museum of American Soul Music.

success of "Do the Funky Chicken" in late 1969, the family had moved to a new house on Joanne Street in the Cherokee neighborhood. They had also invested in their children's education, with both Carla and her younger sister Vaneese going on to college.

While Rufus had only released a handful of singles after his album *Crown Prince of Dance* in late 1973, he remained active in the studio, working on new material with some of the new musicians in the house band. When the label folded, both Union Planters Bank and CBS tried to claim ownership; however, the court ruled that they should be sold for the benefit of numerous creditors, and they were made available for auction. In early 1977, they were sold for the paltry sum of just $1.3 million to NMC Company, a Los Angeles-based bankruptcy specialist. Later that year, the tapes were sold—at a substantial profit—to Fantasy Records of Berkeley, California.

A number of these unreleased Rufus Thomas tracks started to appear on various compilations released by Fantasy over the years. The song

"Funky Hot Grits," which some sources suggest dates back to 1973, appeared on a compilation titled *Stax of Funk—The Funky Truth*, in 2000. As was often the case, Thomas injects this serious slice of funk with less than serious lyrics, to great effect. So much so that it was even released as a single in 2002, with another superb unreleased song, "Give Me the Green Light," on the flip side.

Two more unreleased songs were included on the fantastic 2002 compilation, *The Funkiest Man—The Stax Funk Sessions*, 1967–1975, which includes many of his finest recordings. They included an updated version of the criminally overlooked "Memphis Train" titled "Memphis Train '75" and another Thomas classic, "I'm Getting Better." In the sleeve notes, Dean Rudland suggests that these sides were recorded without producer Tom Nixon, but this seems unlikely, as Thomas continued to work with him even after Stax had folded. He also hints that there were other unreleased tracks from this period, claiming "we have taken three of the best of the tracks." To date, these other tracks have not been released, but hopefully that will eventually change.

In 1977, when it became apparent that the Stax master tapes had been sold, Rufus Thomas reunited with Tom Nixon to rerecord some of the unreleased Stax material, some new songs, and a handful of covers. The resulting album, *If There Were No Music*, was released on AVI Records, an independent Los Angeles-based label that was starting to make its name in disco-oriented recordings. Nixon tried to update Rufus Thomas's trademark funk sound on this album, with more prominent backing vocals and the occasional use of synthesizer, but it was still unmistakably Thomas.

The excellent title track was released as a single and scraped into the lower reaches of the R&B charts, peaking at No. 92—the last occasion on which he would enjoy a hit single. The follow-up, a cover of "Who's Makin' Love to Your Old Lady," a hit in 1968 for Johnnie Taylor, failed to chart.

The album also included "Hot Grits," which had been recorded—but not yet released—for Stax Records as *Funky Hot Grits*. While it was the same song, this version was credited to Rufus Thomas and Oriel Robberts, his mystery friend who worked as an exotic dancer. By contrast, the Stax recording is credited to Rufus Thomas alone, which again suggests that the cocredit was just a ruse to reduce tax expenses. In fact, Ms. Robberts is cocredited on three tracks on the album. The song's title, incidentally, may be a sly reference to Al Green, whose girlfriend had poured boiling hot grits over his body in October 1974 before taking her own life.

Little else is known about the recording of this album, with no credits given as to where the album was recorded or which musicians appeared on the album. The main Stax musicians who played on *Did You Heard*

Rufus with Clementine Byers, September 18, 1976, at a charity event in Memphis for diabetes. Photograph courtesy of the *Memphis Press-Scimitar*, Special Collections Department, University of Memphis Libraries.

Me? and *Crown Prince of Dance* deny playing on this album, but it may well have featured Marvell Thomas on keyboards and some of the younger Stax session musicians who were around in the label's final years. The original album claims to have been produced by "Tom Dixon" rather than Tom Nixon, but it sounds like a Nixon production, and other online resources suggest that he was indeed the producer. Either way, the album itself failed to chart and was never released on CD—despite the inclusion of some fine material.

A follow-up album, *I Ain't Gettin' Older, I'm Gettin' Better*, was released in 1978, again on AVI Records. The highlight of this album was the title track, a thirteen-minute version of the song "I'm Getting Better" that Thomas had recorded for Stax Records. It's one of the best—but least-known—of his funk-oriented recordings. Despite being released as a two-part single in late 1977, it failed to chart. Disco ruled supreme at that time; Funkadelic ("One Nation Under a Groove"), Chaka Khan ("I'm Every Woman"), and Chic ("Le Freak") all topped the US R&B charts in 1978, while the Bee Gees ruled the *Billboard* Hot 100 with "Night Fever" and "Stayin' Alive," both taken from the soundtrack to *Saturday Night Fever*. With the help of Tom Nixon, Rufus had adapted his sound—but at sixty-one years of age and still sporting his trademark cape, he was no longer the hottest thing on the dance floor.

Rufus Thomas's deal with AVI Records seems to have come to an end in 1978, and he made the decision to team up with his old friend, Willie Mitchell, over at Hi Records. Mitchell had enjoyed an incredible run of hit records with singer Al Green with soulful albums like *Let's Stay Together* (1972), *Call Me* (1973), *Explores Your Mind* (1974), and *Al Green Is Love* (1975) all topping the *Billboard* R&B album charts and reaching the Top 30 on the pop charts, too. But even Al Green was not immune to the changes taking place in R&B, and his last two secular albums, *The Belle Album* and *Truth N' Time*, struggled in the face of the trend toward disco.

Thomas had composed another novelty dance-oriented song, "Fried Chicken," and proposed to Mitchell that he record it over at Hi Records. Like anything Thomas recorded at that time, it was enormous fun, but not really in keeping with the changing times; had it been released in the early 1970s, it might well have charted. The single was released in 1978, and having failed to chart, no album followed.

With royalty payments from Stax Records effectively drying up, Thomas tried a change of tack, and in the summer of 1979, he rere-corded many of his biggest Stax hits, hoping that he could achieve greater payments on any subsequent sales and airplay. The album, simply titled *Rufus Thomas*, was released on Nashville-based Gusto Records. By this stage, Rufus was no longer working with Tom Nixon, and his back catalog was rearranged by John Komrada Jr., an experienced studio musician who also worked as a musical director for Rosemary Clooney.

Songs like "Do the Funky Chicken," "Walking the Dog," and "The Breakdown" were effectively rerecorded with session musicians with a couple of covers, including "In the Midnight Hour" and "Mustang Sally," thrown in for good measure. "It was explained to us that Mr. Thomas had already recorded most of these songs previously, and even had some hits with them, but did not own the rights," explained saxophonist Ron

Rudkin, "so he had to rerecord them in order to rerelease them. So the arranger tried to recreate all the horn and rhythm parts as closely to the original recordings as possible."[1]

Unfortunately, the session musicians found it hard to recreate the magic of the originals, and the session sounded very flat in comparison with the original Stax recordings. The album was released on vinyl in 1980 and was later reissued on CD in Japan only, but is now hard to find.

Thomas had one final attempt to break into the disco market, releasing "Everybody Cried (the Day Disco Died)" in 1981 and an ill-fated attempt at rap, "Rappin' Rufus," in 1984, before resigning himself to the fact that his days of chart success were probably behind him.

With his hit singles drying up and disco taking over from funk, Rufus Thomas became less of a draw on the US concert circuit, too. He would still play regularly in and around Memphis but was no longer a regular on the college circuit that had been his mainstay in the 1960s.

He was offered a second opportunity to travel to Africa in 1977, when he was invited to play in South Africa. His decision to accept the invitation was met with anger from students at Memphis State University who were concerned about the government's anti-apartheid policies. To his credit, Thomas agreed to meet with the local students to address their concerns. "I had a Snack and Rap session at Memphis State and the students told me I shouldn't go," he later explained. "I said, "If I lived through the era which I had to come up through this point and I made it through that, then I can make it through South Africa or any other part of the country. So I went. I had a beautiful time!"[2]

"He debated whether to go," recalls his younger daughter Vaneese. "You know, I think people don't equate apartheid in South Africa with apartheid in the United States, but it's the same thing, just called something different. And he lived through some of the worst of it."[3]

By all accounts, Thomas found it difficult to adjust to these changes. He had lost his job at WDIA back in 1974 and felt that he was less connected to the local community than he had been. For a man who thrived on being an entertainer, whether it was on the radio or as a live performer, it was hard for him to accept.

◆ ◆ ◆

Soon after Stax had closed, Carla Thomas relocated from Los Angeles back to Memphis and moved back in with her parents on Joanne Street. Her move to Los Angeles, which had been encouraged by her manager, Sandy Newman, had been a mixed success. She had appeared on television locally on a number of occasions, including *Soul Train* (October

Carla, Lorene, and Rufus at home, August 8, 1978. Photograph courtesy of the *Memphis Press-Scimitar*, Special Collections Department, University of Memphis Libraries.

1971) and the *Merv Griffin Show* (June 1973), but plans to launch her as an actress after attending the American Academy of Dramatic Arts in New York failed to materialize.

Unlike her father, Carla seemed to accept that she was no longer in the spotlight. After her final album for Stax Records, *Love Means*, she released just two further singles: "I May Not Be All You Want" and "Love Among the People," in 1973 and 1974, respectively.

She seemed happy to be back in her hometown, immersing herself in the local community. She still performed locally, sometimes appearing as a solo performer, sometimes with her father; more often than not, her brother Marvell played for her at these shows.

A close friend of the family, keyboard player James Nelson, recalled that Carla also started to play more gospel shows around this time. He had first encountered the Thomas family back in 1961, when he had been hit by a car. Rufus Thomas's wife, Lorene, was working as a nurse at this time and effectively saved his life, rushing to find a doctor when he suffered from internal bleeding. He was in the hospital for several weeks while he recovered from his injuries. "While I was in the hospital, she sent me a card every day," he later recalled. "I had more cards than anybody. She kept up with me after my release and in November she called my great-aunt, who raised me, and asked if I could come to their house for Thanksgiving dinner."[4]

Thereafter, the Thomas family took Nelson under their wing. As a member of the Teen Town singers in the early 1960s, he was nicknamed "Big Man"—a nickname he kept for life—but Thomas would always joke with him, nicknaming him "Big Mule."

Nelson regularly accompanied Carla at her gospel shows around this time. "We used to do a Mother's Day concert up at Jackson, Tennessee, at this church every year for about six years," he remembered. "One year we did it [1977], a lady from Memphis was Miss Black America. Because of Carla, I ended up playing for her, too! The young lady's name was Claire Ford. Claire's mother came to me and said, 'Carla said you would play for her!' They were like a second family to me. I got more opportunities than I ever would have by being a part of that Thomas family."[5]

In the late 1970s, Carla Thomas started working on a local community project known as *Artists in the Schools*, established by the Tennessee Arts Commission. "The artists go in with pictures of the era and say, 'Look, this is what we did,'" she explained to David Freeland. "And then [the students] send you letters . . . it's all so rewarding. They're those little things that really keep you going in this business."

Carla worked on this program for around ten years, even taking on the role of rehearsing the children in both singing and dancing prior to a local community performance. She also encouraged her father to take part in the *Artists in the Schools* program, with the *Commercial Appeal* reporting that his appearances always made the children howl with laughter.

The Thomas family would help the local community in other respects, too. Lorene Thomas was less active in the NAACP than she had been in the 1960s but remained very active with the church. "Mother—they all called her Mother," explained James Nelson, "was a member of a very famous church here in Memphis, the New Salem Baptist Church. Every Sunday morning, she would get up early and pick up the four mothers that were on the board at New Salem. She would pick them up, take them to church, take them home again—after having fed them. She was like that."[6]

A few years later, James Nelson found himself in financial trouble. In the intervening years, he had finished college and later found work with Al Green, playing organ and singing backing vocals on a number of his gospel albums.

He left Al Green's band in 1983 to get married to his second wife, but a few days after the wedding, his wife's father suffered a massive stroke.

Carla and Rufus at the Opera Ball, Memphis, April 13, 1979. Photograph courtesy of the *Memphis Press-Scimitar*, Special Collections Department, University of Memphis Libraries.

"My wife is from Charleston, South Carolina, and we were in the middle of packing a trailer to drive back to Memphis," he explained. "I had to cancel all of that. I stayed with her father in the hospital that first night. I had to stay in Charleston, and didn't know how long we were gonna be. My wife had quit her job, and I was running low on money. I started calling people to ask if I could borrow money. I called Rufus's house but Carla answered, and I told her what had happened. The next day, Carla called me back, and said, 'James, go to Western Union.' I said, 'How much am I going to owe you?' She said, 'You're not going to owe me anything. Daddy pitched in some money as well when I told him what had happened.' When I got there, I was completely flabbergasted at the amount of money they had sent me. It was almost $3,000. Who does that, right?

I had only asked for four hundred dollars. I was moved to tears. They would not let me pay them back."[7]

On another occasion, a Christmas Eve in the late 1980s, Rufus Thomas was parking his car in front of the old Wall Street Deli at East St. and Union Avenue in Memphis, right across from where the Baptist Memorial Hospital then stood. He heard some loud snoring and discovered a young homeless man named Lee Brown. Thomas roused the young man and said, "Watch my car for the next hour while I visit my friend in the hospital and I'll take care of you when I get back."

True to his word, Thomas returned an hour later and invited Brown to his home to spend the Christmas holidays. Brown accepted his invitation and found himself surrounded by the warmth of the Thomas family and their friends. "Rufus told me he'd been down and out himself once upon a time and he understood what I was going through," Brown revealed to WMC Action News many years later.[8]

♦ ♦ ♦

Although Carla Thomas seemed content to be out of the spotlight after the closure of Stax Records, her younger sister, Vaneese—ten years her junior—was taking her first tentative steps toward a career in music.

While she had sung backing vocals for her sister as early as 1964—singing on "A Boy Named Tom," the B-side of the hit "I've Got No Time to Lose"—Vaneese had never performed in public. In part, this reflected an innate fear of the music business, having seen it close up while she was growing up. But looking back, she felt it also took a number of years for her to fully appreciate her family's legacy.

In 1970, she started at Swarthmore College, located just outside Philadelphia. "My mother had no desire for me to be in the record business at all—she wanted me to be a lawyer," Vaneese recalled. "But I was not going to be a lawyer in my head! I was studying to be an interpreter. I studied French in school and went to France to live for a while, on three different occasions. So that was where I was headed."[9]

At college, Vaneese sang in the school gospel choir, and by the time she graduated, she was ready to try her luck in music. "My girlfriend Carolyn [Mitchell] and I met a keyboard player and a percussionist—we didn't have a real drummer at that time. Carolyn was playing bass. We decided to form a band called Drift Silver and started playing in the suburban Philadelphia area. And that was the end of my interpreter dreams!"[10]

In addition to playing, Vaneese and Carolyn sang backing vocals at both the Alpha and Sigma recording studios in Philadelphia, both of which were associated with the so-called "sound of Philadelphia" that was popular in the disco era. "We wound up sort of as the B-team for the Sweethearts of Sigma, who sang on all of those records that came out of Sigma Sound," Vaneese remembers. "We got some of that work. We were singing backup for Gamble and Huff and at Alpha Studios. We wound up singing for the John Davis and the Monster Orchestra. They were fabulous. John was a great arranger. That's sort of where we got our feet wet in the studio. As a result of that, the two of us got several record deals."[11]

John Davis helped to get them a record deal with Polydor, which was releasing a lot of dance records at that time. He arranged their first single, "Let Me In," which was released in 1977 under the name of Vaneese & Carolyn. A second single, "Goodbye Song," was released the following year and featured Vaneese's own composition, "Just a Little Smile," on the flipside. Neither song charted, but the duo found regular work, playing club gigs in New York and elsewhere.

A third and final single emerged on the Midsong International label in 1979. The duo, identified as Siren presumably in an attempt to circumvent their previous deal, performed a song called "Morning Music," which was again produced and arranged by John Davis. This single was marginally more successful, spending five weeks on *Billboard*'s Hot Soul Singles chart and peaking at No. 79.

For the next few years, Vaneese remained out of the limelight. She got married, moved back to Memphis with her husband, and found work as a schoolteacher. "I was singing locally, but not much—my then husband was not very supportive," she explained.[12]

In the early 1980s, Vaneese got a call from a singer named Debra Henry, who later sang with Bruce Hornsby, to let her know about a recording project in New York that was looking for a female singer. Vaneese auditioned and landed the gig, but the record was never released because of problems with the production company. Nevertheless, it alerted her to the opportunities that existed in New York, and Vaneese decided to get a divorce and stay on in the city.

She started singing with a jazz fusion band, Nite Sprite, which featured a young Dave Weckl—who was still at college—on drums. For the next five years, Vaneese worked in the commercial jingle business in New York. "That's the reason I wasn't recording," she explained. "They used to call it the velvet glove, because it held you tight—you were making so much money you didn't want to record and tour, because you didn't have to!"

Around this time, Vaneese also worked at Minot Sound Studios in White Plains, New York, where she met her future husband and song-writing partner, Wayne Warnecke, who worked as an engineer. They teamed up with Ernie Poccia to form their own production company. "We called it Predawn Productions because we'd go in at midnight, work all night, and come out as the sun would just be rising," Vaneese later explained. "We did a lot of our demos that way."[13]

Fellow songwriter Rob Aries played one of those demos to Charles Huggins of Hush Productions, then husband of singer Melba Moore, and the very next week, Vaneese was signing a record deal. "The production company had a brand-new deal with Geffen; they were not known for doing R&B at that time—they were doing Whitesnake, Elton John, stuff like that, but they wanted to venture into R&B and I was their experiment!"

The album's first single, "Let's Talk It Over," which was cowritten by Vaneese Thomas and Ernie Poccia, reached No. 10 on the *Billboard* R&B charts in 1987, and the follow-up, "(I Wanna Get) Close to You," was almost as successful, reaching No. 12. Suddenly there was a new star in the Thomas family.

"Warner Bros. was promoting Geffen at the time," said Vaneese. "They were such a big help. My record was No. 1 on the Quiet Storm chart for weeks, and I attribute that to Warner Bros. They did such a great job of promoting my record."[14]

Unfortunately for Vaneese, her self-titled debut album never came out on CD. "They never made a digital copy of it," she explained. "It was backwards-thinking, because in the next two years, CDs were the predominant format."[15]

After the album's release, Vaneese experienced problems with Hush Productions, the production company, which lost its deal with Geffen, which effectively gave up getting into the R&B market after that. As a result, Vaneese Thomas never released a follow-up album on Geffen, despite scoring two hit singles.

Vaneese Thomas remained active in music in the years that followed, however, writing a song called "One Shining Moment" for Diana Ross, which was a Top 10 hit in the UK in 1991, and doing a considerable amount of television and commercial work.

◆ ◆ ◆

The 1980s had been a difficult period for Rufus Thomas from a commercial perspective. The self-styled "world's oldest teenager" was now approaching seventy years of age, and while he still played occasional gigs, there was less demand for him to bring out his trademark cape and Bermuda shorts. Of note, he had not released a hit single since 1973 and had not recorded an album of original material since 1978.

Rufus leaves an impression, Memphis, October 1979. Photograph courtesy of the *Memphis Press-Scimitar*, Special Collections Department, University of Memphis Libraries.

He still kept himself busy, landing a job to host the W. C. Handy Awards, known as the Handy's, which were presented by the Blues Foundation to promote the heritage of blues. "I remember he hosted together with Ruth Brown, and it was hilarious," recalled Bruce Iglauer, owner of the Chicago-based blues record label Alligator Records. "They were both very smart people, with quick wit and an instant sense of humor. They really loved each other, and it made for a very warm atmosphere. In those days, the W. C. Handy Awards were still quite amateurishly done—there would be long pauses while musicians set up behind a curtain, or nobody knew who was coming on next, and Rufus was good at filling up that space, telling stories or improvising. He was a very charming man, and full of energy."[16]

Rufus also served on the Memphis and Shelby County Music Commission in the early 1980s. He also emceed and performed at numerous events associated with the regeneration of Beale Street, sometimes working with his old friend from WDIA, Reverend "Gatemouth" Moore.

Nevertheless, Rufus Thomas was both a hard-working man and a natural performer, and he yearned for the days when he spent more time in the public eye, not just around Memphis but nationally and internationally, too.

In the late 1980s, two events occurred in quick succession, which helped to remind the public of his unique skill set, both as an entertainer and as a singer, and paved the way for one of the more unlikely musical comebacks in history.

The first of these occurred in 1986 when he was unexpectedly invited to return to WDIA, the radio station he had worked for between 1950 and 1974.

The fortunes of the radio station had dwindled since its heyday in the 1950s, of course. Radio no longer played such a pivotal role, either in the home or the community, and many of the incredible personalities that had made WDIA so unique had long since gone. In addition, WDIA still broadcast on AM at a time when most pop music radio stations had moved to FM. Amid declining ratings, a new, younger broadcaster, Bobby O'Jay, was invited to join the station in 1983 in an attempt to shake things up.

"I was born down in Panola County, Mississippi, about fifty miles south of Memphis, and as a child I grew up listening to Rufus on the radio, and listening to and dancing to his music," O'Jay explained. "In 1983, when I came to WDIA, I was looking to take the radio station to a higher level. I created a blues show in 1986, on Saturday morning, and thought it would be a good idea to make Rufus a part of that. So I called him, and asked him if he would be part of the All Blues Saturday morning show with another host, Jaye Michael Davis. Rufus agreed and continued to cohost the show until about a year before he passed."[17]

Rufus had met Jaye Michael Davis before, in the early 1970s, but they had never worked together. Davis quickly figured out he was working with a consummate professional who possessed a sharp wit and naturally settled into the role as the straight man. "When they teamed up, there was an instant connection, like magic," recalled O'Jay. "They loved each other, and they did great work on the air—it was the perfect union. Rufus was a very lovable, likeable [sic] guy. When he was at work he was on—he was funny, he was witty, he was a very easy guy to work with—he was so professional."[18]

The All Blues Saturday morning show lasted from 6 a.m. until 10 a.m., and the two hosts would intersperse classic blues and old R&B recordings with Rufus's stories and anecdotes. On one memorable occasion, Rufus Thomas read a poem he had written, titled "The Golden Years," which reduced Davis to tears of laughter:

> I cannot see
> I cannot pee
> I cannot chew
> I cannot screw
> My body shrinks
> My memory stinks
> The golden years
> Have come at last
> The golden years
> Can kiss my ass.

The impact on WDIA's rating was immediate. "The listeners loved it," O'Jay recalled. "They were number one on Saturday mornings in Memphis, Tennessee, for as long as they were on air together. After they had been on air for a year, the ratings were so good, we decided to dump the R&B program for the rest of the day, and make it all blues! That was around 1987, and we still do the all blues day now, from 6 a.m. until midnight on a Saturday at WDIA because it's that popular—but it all started with Rufus and Jaye!"[19]

Rufus was thrilled to be back at WDIA, entertaining the public, and even used to swing by the station between shows, just as he had done in the 1950s. "He would even come to the radio station in the week, just to chop it up with everybody at the station—hang out for a while, see what was going on," said O'Jay, laughing at the memory.

Rufus remained incredibly grateful for his support, and when O'Jay's father passed away in 1996, Rufus offered to sing at the funeral—even though they had never actually met. "Rufus got into his automobile, drove sixty miles down to Mississippi, and he sang at this small church down in Batesville, Mississippi," said O'Jay. "It was incredible, I couldn't believe it. He sang a gospel song and he did it acapella. As he was singing, I was laughing to myself and thinking, 'my Daddy would be floored—he would never stop talking about that in his life—having someone as famous as Rufus Thomas!'"[20]

Promotion photograph of Rufus Thomas, mid-1980s. Photograph courtesy of the Vaneese Thomas family collection.

The second event that boosted Rufus Thomas's profile once more took place a year or so later, most likely because of a chance encounter at the W. C. Handy Awards in Memphis. Thomas was introduced to a record producer by the name of Bob Greenlee, who owned King Snake Studios down in Sanford, Florida. Greenlee had recorded a number of modern blues artists such as Kenny Neal and Root Boy Slim, as well as older musicians like Noble "Thin Man" Watts and former B.B. King drummer Tony Coleman. Greenlee suggested that Thomas return to his musical roots and record a straight-ahead blues album.

Thomas jumped at the opportunity. As he noted in the album's liner notes, he had been grounded in the blues from a very young age. "The blues you heard in the Beale Street theaters was a more polite, uptown kind of blues," he explained. "To hear the real, down-in-the-alley blues, you'd have to go out to the rougher joints, in neighborhoods like Orange Mound. The Beale Street crowd would talk about going to those places like it was slumming, but we'd go! Because those were the places where you go to know the blues."

Greenlee put together a superb band for the occasion, including guitarists Bryan Bassett and Ernie Lancaster, Lucky Peterson on keyboards, renowned R&B saxophonist Noble "Thin Man" Watts, and Kenny Neal, who guested on harmonica.

The King Snake Studios were built above a large garage next to a rambling old house that Greenlee had inherited from his uncle. "It was very makeshift," recalled Bruce Iglauer, who worked with Bob on a number of recordings. "Recording studios are supposed to have high ceilings, so the sound doesn't bounce around, they're supposed to have a lot of isolation spaces so you can record without getting into other people's microphones, and they're supposed to have equipment that works well—and Bob had none of these things! Bob would often put the guitar amp in the bathtub in the bathroom so that we could isolate it, and get a little bounce off the porcelain. The drums were under a very low ceiling. The early records that I got from Bob, I had to do a lot of difficult and time-consuming replacement of drums because the drum sound was so bad!"[21]

Thomas dusted off some old songs that had been in his repertoire for some time, such as "All Night Worker" and "Big Fine Hunk of Woman," and some newer tracks like "That Woman Is Poison!" and "Blues in The Basement," which had first appeared on *If There Were No Music* in 1977. He also covered two old Jimmy McCracklin R&B songs, "The Walk" and "Just Got to Know," the band giving them a more contemporary blues flavor.

Bruce Iglauer, who ran Alligator Records, insisted on remixing the album at Streeterville Studios in Chicago, where the label was based, to improve the sound for release. He was joined by Bob Greenlee, who had made the original recording, and Jay Shilliday, an engineer. "Rufus was there too, with a half-gallon of vanilla ice cream and a spoon, sitting on the couch, and when I arrived, he was consuming the entire half-gallon, explaining how much he enjoyed ice cream on every possible occasion!"[22]

The resulting album was called *That Woman Is Poison!* and the cover featured Rufus, in a bright yellow cape, holding a glass bottle marked "poison, be careful" containing a young lady in a pink dress. "We shot that cover in Chicago," Iglauer recalled. "The girl was Bob Greenlee's daughter, from his first marriage, I think. She was a model, and she happened to be in Chicago. Rufus is in his 'world's oldest teenager' costume, so he must have had it shipped up from Memphis. I think we shot it outside the building that Alligator is in, and then it was retouched, putting the woman in the bottle. Peter Amft was a very talented photographer but was also a convicted felon for drug dealing and a habitual thief!"

The album met with the most positive reviews that Thomas had enjoyed for a number of years. In the *Chicago Reader*, for example, David Whiteis concluded that "Thomas has chosen on this album to walk a fine line between sophistication and blues grit. He fuses blues tradition with deep-soul variations on timeless themes, and the result is a masterful expression of exuberance, musicality, and joy."[23]

Rufus Thomas hosted a launch party for the album—his first in more than eight years—in his hometown of Memphis. "I remember we had a record release party at the Rum Boogie in Memphis, and somewhere there's a photo of me attempting to do the funky chicken, which is particularly hilarious!" said Bruce Iglauer, laughing at the memory.[24]

The "world's oldest teenager" was back in the spotlight, complete with his cape, shorts, and boots, and loving every second of it.

Chapter Twelve

Age Ain't Nothin' but a Number

Final Years, 1988-2001

By the time *That Woman Is Poison!* was released in 1988, Rufus Thomas was seventy-one years old and had been making records for almost forty years.

In the meantime, over in Italy, advertising executive and soul music aficionado Graziano Uliani was on the verge of taking his first tentative steps into the music industry. The seeds were sown in December 1986, when he traveled to Zurich to see R&B legend Solomon Burke perform at the Congress Palace. "I saw this big man, 240 kilos, arriving in a limousine. My English was very bad, because I studied French in school, but I told him, 'Mr. Solomon, I'm your Italian fan and I've founded the Solomon Burke fan club.' I had invented that colossal lie to catch his attention and be able to have a picture with him. Solomon was very nice to me. During the concert he saw me in the crowd and he called me on stage."

Inspired by this chance encounter and a copy of Peter Guralnick's R&B bible, *Sweet Soul Music*, Uliani decided to establish The Sweet Soul Music cultural association to promote soul music in Italy. "In the spring of 1987, I introduced the Italian singer Zucchero to the Memphis Horns for his first R&B album in Italian," Uliani revealed. "We called them to do a session in Bologna in 1987."[1]

Six months later, in November 1987, a new music show launched on Italian television that featured rock music but also blues and soul. "I convinced their anchorman, Renzo Arbore—a true soul fan—to call Solomon [Burke]," Uliani later recalled. "And Solomon came! I organized a concert with Solomon and a band on November 7, just after the TV gig, in the Castanea Hotel in my town of Porretta Terme. The concert lasted three hours and people went crazy!"

One month later, the idea of hosting an R&B festival in Italy started to take shape. "I was a guest at Wayne Jackson's home in Nashville and

Promotional poster for the inaugural Sweet Soul Music Festival in Porretta, Italy, 1988. Photograph courtesy of Graziano Uliani, Porretta Soul Festival.

made a trip to Muscle Shoals, Macon, and Memphis," he remembered. "I visited Macon, Georgia, for the twentieth anniversary of Otis Redding's death, and I promised his widow to do something to keep Otis's memory alive. Wayne Jackson then went with me to Memphis and introduced me to Rufus Thomas, Willie Mitchell, and the Stax people."

Uliani hit it off with Rufus Thomas and invited him to Italy in June 1987 to film an Italian TV special with the Memphis Horns. After that, the musicians traveled to Uliani's hometown of Porretta Terme for the inaugural Sweet Soul Music festival, which was billed as a Tribute to Otis Redding, as promised. "I decided to do the first show as a one-time show," Uliani explained. "The other bands were Italian R&B bands. But it was a big success, mostly because of Rufus!"

The Italian singer, Zucchero—now regarded as the "father of Italian blues"—was a special guest at the festival and was introduced to Rufus Thomas by Uliani. "I convinced Zucchero to record his next album at Ardent Studios in Memphis," he remembered. "It was a very popular album, *Oro, Incenso & Birra* [*Gold, Frankincense & Beer*], selling 1.5 million copies. Rufus helped us with the session, putting together a gospel choir with many Stax musicians including Jay Blackfoot, Ruby Wilson, Homer Banks, and William Brown. We thought Zucchero would call the album *Zio Rufus* [*Uncle Rufus*] as a tribute to him, but in the end, an Italian beer company paid him money to change the title of the album." Zucchero ended up forming a close bond with Rufus over the years, even naming one of his later songs "Funky Gallo" (meaning "Funky Chicken"), the song name-checking "Uncle Rufus."[2]

The success of the first festival convinced Uliani that he could make it an annual event, albeit with the help of the regional government and corporate sponsors. Rufus Thomas returned to the festival on numerous occasions in his later years, usually accompanied by his son Marvell, who was his bandleader and arranger. Thomas was also instrumental in introducing Uliani to other Memphis-based artists, who soon found themselves with a brand-new fan base in Italy. "In 1991, Rufus brought Jay Blackfoot and Ruby Wilson," Uliani recalled. "We also had another fabulous artist that [*sic*] had only performed one time previously in Europe, Eddie Hinton. Now he is a cult figure. He lives near Muscle Shoals, and has worked with Percy Sledge and many others."[3]

Whenever Rufus appeared, he was the star of the show, both on and off stage. "He started each concert with the introduction, 'Hellooooo, Porretta!'" Uliani remembered, laughing. "And the audience responded with 'Hello, Rufus!' It was funny!"

Musically, there were numerous highlights. In 1994, Thomas headlined an amazing lineup that also featured two of his Stax Records contemporaries, William Bell and Mavis Staples. Toward the end of his set, Rufus—wearing his now trademark custom-made Bermuda shorts—encouraged Mavis Staples to join him on stage and dance the "Funky Chicken" to the obvious delight of the capacity crowd.

The following year, Thomas returned but found himself playing second on the bill to the former Atlantic Records recording artist Wilson Pickett. Never one to be upstaged, Thomas invited dozens of girls on stage to

Promotional poster for the Sweet Soul Music Festival in Porretta, Italy, 1993. Photograph courtesy of Graziano Uliani, Porretta Soul Festival.

dance an extended version of "Funky Chicken," taking him beyond his allotted set time. Pickett was furious and threatened to walk out, but Thomas rallied the crowd, which was going crazy. "This is my park," he exclaimed, "and you are my people!" Pickett eventually made it on stage that evening, but not until 1:30 a.m.

In 1997, his sixth and final appearance at Porretta, Thomas tried to entice his friend Zucchero on stage with him. "I want to know," he asked, "who is the real Funky Chicken . . .?" Marvell Thomas had arranged a version of Zucchero's "Funky Gallo" especially for the occasion, but even as a big star, the Italian knew there was no way he could upstage Thomas. "When they called Zucchero onstage, he panicked and left to eat a pizza," Uliani laughed. "He chickened out!"[4]

The only downside to Thomas's success in Italy was that it damaged his relationship with his son, Marvell, who was effectively the bandleader, responsible for both the arrangements and hiring the musicians. "Marvell was difficult to get along with, in a lot of ways," explained saxophonist Jim Spake, who regularly backed Rufus in his later years. "Everyone knew that Marvell would get what he could first, and we'd get what was left over. Rufus felt that he was taking over his career. 'He thinks he should be making as much as I make,' he once told me. Towards the end, it kind of broke Rufus's heart, a little bit."

Marvell was Rufus's bandleader for his first three appearances at Porretta; thereafter, he was replaced by the legendary Stax Records guitarist Michael Toles.

Thomas also endeared himself to the local people of Porretta, even if they were occasionally confused by his dietary habits. While staying at the distinctly old-school Hotel Salus, Thomas used to request an omelet rather than the traditional "continental" style breakfast. The hotel staff explained that omelets were not on the menu, and if other guests saw him eating eggs for breakfast, others might start to request it. "I am the King of Soul," Thomas explained to the official interpreter, "and I am the only one who can claim an omelet in the morning!" The hotel soon realized the error of their ways, and the King of Soul got the breakfast he wanted.

Uliani recalled that Thomas would sometimes eat a raw onion with a glass of milk as a snack before the show. "He once had heartburn and the doctor on call told him that he probably had to change his diet," he explained. "The doctor did not give him a prescription but invited him to his house for a dinner of crescentine [Italian flatbread] and local products. The cure worked and a few nights later Rufus repeated the experience at the home of the local cheese shop owner, with dinner of tagliatelle with meat sauce. His spirit was that of a boy, and not for nothing Rufus was known as "the World's Oldest Teenager!"[5]

Thanks to the vision of Graziano Uliani, the town of Porretta in Italy will always be associated with R&B and with Rufus Thomas, too. The local park that hosts the annual festival was renamed Rufus Thomas Park in 1994. "We have a park dedicated to Rufus, a big mural with the image of Rufus, and a restaurant called Rufus Rhythm and Burger—it's very popular," Uliani explained. "The connection between Rufus and Porretta is very well known. We also have a Soul Museum in Porretta now. The museum has many memorabilia that the artists left in Porretta. Rufus gave us the green shorts and jacket he wore from the first edition of the festival. We also have a bridge dedicated to Solomon Burke, and a street dedicated to Otis Redding—where I lived for many years."

♦ ♦ ♦

The resurgence in Thomas's popularity in Italy brought him to the attention of other promoters, too, including the legendary Freddy Cousaert, a Belgian club owner and concert promoter, perhaps best known for taking care of R&B singer Marvin Gaye while he lived in the Belgian seaside town of Ostend.

Cousaert arranged a few European tours for Rufus, including a doubleheader in 1993, which paired Thomas with Motown saxophone legend Junior Walker. "We put the two of them together; it was called 'Motown Meets Stax,'" he later recalled. "It was fantastic—two old troupers."

Cousaert's favorite memory of that first tour was traveling between gigs by car. "Junior was very much in love with France, and I had a six-cylinder Mercedes. He drove it, with Rufus sitting next to him," he said. "I was sitting in the back, with these two warriors driving between Holland and France. I said, 'Hey, Junior, you're going over 125 miles an hour.' He said, "You're jiving, but I'm driving. I'm the road runner, you have to adapt to me.' Months later, I received a speeding ticket!"[6]

♦ ♦ ♦

And it wasn't just Europe; the self-styled "world's oldest teenager" saw a resurgence in demand back home, too. Granted, he was no longer playing fraternity houses as he did in the 1960s or conducting nationwide tours, but he would play regular gigs in and around Memphis, Tennessee, and neighboring states. "There were local gigs that would go on, community events, street festivals—and he was always the headliner at those," recalled saxophonist Jim Spake, who started working with him around this time. "Generations of people, mostly people of color, had grown up seeing Rufus—in a tent, or at the Cotton Carnival, or the Cotton Makers' Jubilee. He was like everybody's grandfather. He would get the women up on stage to do the funky chicken. He would do his facial stuff with the crowd—that stuff doesn't exist anymore!"[7]

Shortly after he had joined the band, Spake was invited to attend an informal recording session over at Sun Studios. "Around 1990, Sun Studio relaunched," he explained. "They'd been running tours through the old studio, but then they started to allow people to come in after museum hours. By this time, I'd played with Rufus a few times and he wanted me in the band with him. We cut things live on the floor with monitors—there weren't even earphones or anything—and some of that came out eventually."[8]

The songs recorded that day were left untouched until 1998, when Thomas remembered that he had them and brought them over to his old friend, the former Stax guitarist and engineer Bobby Manuel. "He brought all those tapes to me, maybe thirty or forty cuts, and said, 'You can have them, Bobby!' You can imagine how I felt."[9]

Most of the songs had been recorded at Sun Studios, but they were not in the best of shape, according to Manuel, because of the "leakage" in the sound. But the big surprise was there was also a handful of cuts from a previous recording session that had taken place with Willie Mitchell over at Hi Records. While the precise date is not known, it most likely stems from the recording session for the single "Fried Chicken," which took place back in 1977 or 1978. Further evidence that these are the dates of the Hi sessions can be heard in the song "Age Ain't Nothin' But a Number," on which Thomas sings the line "sixty years of age, and I'm still here on the scene."

As far as Manuel remembers, Thomas told him that he had got into a fight with Willie Mitchell during the course of that recording session. "They were doing some blues—I think it was 'Just Because I Leave'—and Willie Mitchell told him how to phrase blues. Rufus said, 'Man, you can't tell me anything about singing blues. I got gold records on my wall!' And Willie Mitchell said, 'I got gold records too!' That was it, man. Two bulls in a china shop. Rufus went and took his tapes!"[10]

"I don't think I would have done that!" said Manuel, laughing. "You pretty much let Rufus do what he wanted to do. If it was something you'd written, you might teach him some melody, but for the most part, he did what heard and felt."[11]

Bobby Manuel cleaned up the recordings as best he could. "I had to overdub a guitar solo on 'Just Because I Leave, That Don't Mean I'm Gone,' which I felt was a great blues song, because there was so much leakage in the studio. And I think I put a rhythm guitar on a couple of other things, mainly that he had done at Willie's." He also added background vocal overdubs on certain tracks using Carla Thomas, Vaneese Thomas, and their family friend, James Nelson.[12]

The resulting album, *Swing Out*, was released in May 1999 and was the final studio album to be released in Thomas's lifetime. The album deserves to be better known, as it is probably the best of his later recordings. Half of the songs on the album were recorded over at Hi Records in the late 1970s, when his voice was still in good shape, while the later recordings, from Sun Records, capture him in 1990 and are a good example of how he sounded with the band he was playing with on a regular basis.

Two years after the Sun sessions, Thomas teamed up with his European promoter Freddy Cousaert to record an album called *Timeless Funk* which was recorded at Peak Top Studios in Dusseldorf, Germany. Despite the presence of Stax veteran Michael Toles on guitar, it's primarily a poor rehash of Thomas's Stax recordings, including "Walking the Dog," "Funky Chicken," and "Jump Back," all of which were vastly superior the first time around.

In 1995, Rufus made a guest appearance on an album titled *Bluesiana—Hurricane*. It was the fourth album in the "Bluesiana" series, which paired musicians from a jazz, blues, R&B, and even rock background to record New Orleans-style music. The album was interesting, pairing Thomas with the likes of Lester Bowie, the renowned avant-garde jazz trumpet player and jazz saxophonist Bobby Watson, who had spent a few years working as the musical director for Art Blakey's Jazz Messengers. Thomas recorded brand-new funky versions of "Big Fine Hunk of Woman," "The World Is Round," and "Walking the Dog." Thomas clearly enjoyed the session and was in fine form, entertaining the other musicians with stories about people he had encountered over the years, including Wilson Pickett, whom he described as a "complete fool."

Thomas even appeared on *Late Night with Conan O'Brien* to promote *Bluesiana—Hurricane*. It had been an ambition of his to be on the show, apparently, because he liked the house band, the Max Weinberg 7, led by Max Weinberg, the drummer of Bruce Springsteen's E Street Band.

During the taping, Thomas got into an argument with Max Weinberg about the arrangement of "Walking the Dog." Weinberg and his band had arranged a version especially for the show, but Thomas wanted to use the new arrangement written for the album. Charlie Dahan, A&R Director of Shanachie Entertainment—which conceived the *Bluesiana— Hurricane* project—had to explain to Thomas who Max Weinberg was. "I don't care about Bruce Springstone [*sic*]," he replied. "I am Rufus Thomas; we'll do it my way." In any event, Rufus got his way and put in a great performance for the show.

The final studio album recorded by Thomas was another Freddy Cousaert project titled *Blues Thang!* It appears to have been recorded in late 1995 and early 1996, again at the Peak Top Studios, but also at the Power House studio back in Memphis. The band included, among others, Michael Toles on guitar, Marvell Thomas on electric piano, and a horn section comprised of Dirk de Schoenmaker on saxophone, Pete Lamont on trombone, and Eddie Thornton on trumpet.

The album was effectively an unofficial follow-up to *That Woman Is Poison!* and as the title suggests, focused on more blues-oriented tunes. In fact, the album went right back to the beginning of his career and even featured a song he had picked up during his time with the Rabbit Foot Minstrel show called "The Last Clean Shirt." The album was also note-worthy for including three new Rufus Thomas compositions—"Walking in The Rain," "I Came Home This Morning," and "Miss Bunny"—as well as well-chosen covers, including "What Do You Want Me to Do" (Mighty Sam McClain) and "Don't Put No Headstone on My Grave" (Charlie Rich).

The album generally received favorable reviews. "The Memphis music legend possesses a richer-than-molasses low voice that's now frayed around the edges," *DownBeat's* Frank-John Hadley wrote, adding that Thomas "taps a bottomless well of accumulated wisdom and endearing playfulness." And while it's true that his voice sounds well worn, it's worth remembering he had just turned seventy-nine years old at the time of the album's release.

Thomas supported the new album with a UK tour that spring and made it clear to journalists that he was not about to give up performing. "I'll carry on doing this if I have to sit down to do it," he informed the *Times*. "To me it is just a part of living and music will be a part of me until I die."

♦ ♦ ♦

Thomas's late-career revival also included numerous TV and movie appearances. He appeared on *Sunday Night*, a late-night music TV show in 1989, performing "Walking the Dog" with the house band, which was led by jazz saxophonist David Sanborn. And later, as the credits rolled, Rufus changed into his trademark cape and boots and taught the band how to do the "Funky Chicken." Incidentally, the same episode also fea-tured his older daughter, Carla Thomas, who performed "Gee Whiz."

Also in 1989, he had a small role in Jim Jarmusch's acclaimed inde-pendent movie *Mystery Train*, which was set in Memphis. The movie featured a triptych of separate but connecting stories, each featuring tourists or outsiders. As so often with Jarmusch's films, it featured a mix of established actors and non-professionals; in this case, the movie featured cameos from singer Joe Strummer (The Clash) and R&B singer Screamin' Jay Hawkins, among others. Remarkably, the director had never previously visited Memphis before filming and was attracted to the city because of its rich musical history as well as its decline, in the way that Elvis only lived on through Graceland, his former home.

The first story featured two Japanese tourists who come to pay homage to their heroes; for one of them, because of Elvis Presley, and for the other, Carl Perkins. When they arrive at the train station, they are met by an African American man who asks for a light for his cigarette; neither of them realizes that it is the real king of Memphis, Rufus Thomas. The movie also features his son Marvell, who can be seen playing pool in the bar.

Later that same year, Thomas made a cameo appearance in *Great Balls of Fire!* which starred Dennis Quaid as Jerry Lee Lewis. Thomas played a dancer at Haney's Big House, the bar in which Lewis reputedly absorbed blues and R&B music played by African American musicians in his formative years.

Thomas made further movie appearances in the years that followed, playing Theo Johnson in Robert Altman's 1999 comedy *Cookie's Fortune* and himself in *Only the Strong Survive*, a 2002 D. A. Pennebaker documentary about R&B musicians. "You knew he was an old person, but he acted like a sixteen-year-old," Pennebaker revealed. "He was always full of funny takes on things and he always gave the impression he was a goofball. But when he talked about the music, you realized he knew a lot."

♦ ♦ ♦

In the summer of 1996, Rufus Thomas headlined at the Southern Crossroads Festival, a show put on at the Centennial Olympic Park as part of the Summer Olympics in Atlanta. The Friday night event was attended by an estimated 60,000 people—the biggest audience Thomas had played to since Wattstax back in 1972.

The event was a showcase for Memphis music and also featured singer Ann Peebles, a former Hi Records artist, and William Bell, who performed a number of Otis Redding hits as well as his own. Still, the star of the show was Rufus Thomas, who closed the show in his trademark style, inviting a group of girls onto the stage to dance the Funky Chicken. Marvell Thomas was the bandleader for the occasion and remembered it as being one of his favorite performances with his father. "Everyone was on their feet," he later recalled, "and we were all in top form."

The concert was recorded and later released as *Rufus Live!* on Ecco Records. Thomas was particularly proud of his performance that day, according to his daughter Vaneese, and was glad to see it released on CD.

On March 26, 1997, Rufus Thomas turned eighty years old. The mayor of the city of Memphis took this opportunity to rename a section of Hernando Street—where it intersected with Beale Street—as Rufus Thomas

Boulevard. The location seemed appropriate, as this was where the Palace Theater had once stood, one of the key venues in which Thomas had cut his teeth as an entertainer. In addition, the city also gave him an honorary reserved downtown parking space which he used on a regular basis.

A birthday celebration was held in one of the city's downtown theaters that evening, with Thomas as the guest of honor. He divided his time between the stage, where he sang like a man possessed, and the theater floor, where he caught up with old friends. At the end of the evening, most of the guests were weary, but Thomas still found the energy to thank everyone for attending.

In an interview around that time, however, he did admit that the years were finally catching up with him. "I have a stretch of a few months where, man, I'm way up there," he said. "But then, I'll have to take a few days to come back down. You may say I'm like a rubber band. I always snap back. On that, you can count on [sic]."[13]

Later that year, he also appeared at the Smithsonian Folklife Festival in Washington, DC. Vaneese Thomas recalls traveling down to the event and that her father used a carved wooden cane to walk as he approached the stage. "He didn't use it that often, as he didn't want people to think he was incapacitated," she explained. "It wasn't really age so much as a congenital back problem that he'd had all his life." He took to the stage in his trademark pink Bermuda shorts and matching jacket and bellowed, "Hello DC! Say, 'Hello Rufus!'"

When the show was over, Vaneese climbed the steps to the stage and tried to hand the cane back to her father, but he refused to accept it. "He was a proud man," she explained, laughing.

In early 1998, Thomas was again the guest of honor—this time at a gig by the R&B artist Prince, who played a "secret" concert at the New Daisy Theater in Memphis. Prince played a number of his biggest hits and a selection of cool covers, including James Brown, Parliament and Funkadelic. "The highlight of the show, however, was when Prince—always the biggest star in the room—introduced his special guest: eighty-year-old Stax royalty, Rufus Thomas, who made his supremely groovy appearance in shorts and knee socks," recalled local journalist Chris Davis, who had been lucky enough to land tickets for the event. "Then the unflappable Purple One proceeded to nerd the hell out, saying he didn't want his time on stage with Rufus to end."

The performance culminated in some nursery rhyme-style freestyle rapping and a funky version of "Walking the Dog." "I wish I could tell you what was said and sung, but the details have slipped (or were possibly sipped) away," Davis wrote several years later. "All that remains is the memory of a grin so big it threatened to crack my face. And a similar memory of so many other people wearing the same dopey expression."[14]

Thomas finally cut back on his touring schedule in his final years but remained a colorful figure in and around the city of Memphis, whether he was presenting his Saturday morning radio show on WDIA with Jaye Michael Davis, acting as an unofficial ambassador for the city, hosting the annual New Year's Eve party on Beale Street, or simply espousing his homespun philosophies on life.

Thomas Hackett, who wrote an article titled "Rufus Thomas, Man of the House of Happiness," remembers meeting him at WDIA in 1999. "Rufus, you are one handsome devil!" Thomas exclaimed within minutes of dropping by WDIA'S scruffy, shag-carpeted studios. "Well-dressed all the time!" Thomas went on. "Even on your off days! You can hear them saying it as soon as they pass you on the street: 'Damn, that Rufus is sharp! Uh-huh!' And for a man your age, who is still able to go out on the street and look sharp, it's remarkable . . . you just don't have it in your brain to be looking shabby!"[15]

Thomas took his role as an ambassador for the city very seriously. On one occasion, in typically forthright fashion, he told journalist Richard Knight that "Memphis has made more of a contribution to music than any other one city in the whole world, and that includes New York."

Likewise, when a group of Chicago musicians and promoters claimed that their city was the birthplace of the blues—at a press conference in Memphis, no less—Thomas leaped in to set them straight on this matter and gave them his version of the history of the blues.

One interviewer asked Thomas if his sense of fun was the secret to long life and happiness. "Hell, yeah!" he replied. "You gotta have fun in life. Music to me is fun. You see me, and you'll see how much fun I have with it. More, I'll bet, than anybody else you ever have!"[16]

On other occasions, he would reflect how far he'd come from the segregated minstrel shows back in the late 1930s and how hard he had to fight to get to where he was now, sixty years later. "You pay one hell of a price to be Black," he explained to Pete Daniel in an interview with the Smithsonian Institution. "But I am not going to die from it. I'm going to survive, and I'm going to live. And I'm going to do something recognizable, so when I pass off this land of the living, I will be remembered for what I have done—what I have done for the community, what I have done for my people, what I have done for the whole universe. Because I am liked from Mississippi to Japan and from Africa to Alabama, I've been no place yet that I was not liked. And I appreciate that."[17]

◆ ◆ ◆

In 1998, at the age of eighty-one, Thomas had triple bypass heart surgery and was fitted with a pacemaker. It didn't keep him down for long. "Wayne and I went in to visit him after his operation, and he had contracts all over the bed," said Vaneese, laughing. "He was ready to get back on stage!"

"When he went back in for tests before Christmas, he was so full of energy that hospitalizing him was like putting a rabbit in a box," noted his publicist at High Stacks Records. "The other patients have the benefit of his great smile and his constant jokes."

While Thomas's energy returned, his singing voice—which was gravelly at the best of times—was beginning to fade. In late 1998, he recorded one song for an album compiled by guitarist Bobby Manuel, which reunited many of his old friends from Stax Records, titled *926 East McLemore*. "The last cut I did with Rufus he could barely do it," Manuel later recalled. "It was a song called 'Hey Rufus,' and we only got a couple of lines out of him. It was kind of a New Orleans groove thing. His voice was fading at that point, of course, and I had to duplicate and manipulate a lot of things to get what I did get. But it was still fun, and it's got a good groove on it."[18]

Around this time, the health of his wife, Lorene, also started to fail. "She had diabetes, and was having a series of mini[-]strokes, so little by little, her memory was getting bad—just for everyday stuff," recalled her younger daughter Vaneese. "She was still fully lucid when it came to family and friends, stuff like that."[19]

Lorene died of heart failure on February 7, 2000, after suffering complications from another stroke. "She really died too early, she was only eighty—and had she have kept up with her diabetic medicine and her diet the way she should have, she could have lived much longer," Vaneese noted. "But she wasn't always dutiful about that."[20]

Her long-standing friend Maxine Smith, the former executive secretary of the Memphis Branch of the NAACP, spoke at her funeral. "So many know the family . . . better because they're in the limelight. I know Lorene as the driving force behind all their success," she recalled. "She was such a strong and supportive mother and wife. She made many sacrifices to make sure that all of those who were in the limelight in her family looked good."[21]

Retired Criminal Court Judge H. T. Lockard, who was president of the Memphis Branch of the NAACP in the late 1950s, also remembered her as a tireless worker. "She was just on top of everything," he said. "She was such an advocate of what the branch stood for . . . and of course everybody listened when she got up to speak."[22]

Lorene's passing had a huge impact on Carla Thomas, who still lived with her parents at this time. "Our nuclear family was really, really important to all of us," explained Vaneese. "Daddy had a million friends, and each of us had a million friends, but nothing was as important as the five of us. The fact that any one of us were lost was a big blow to us."

♦ ♦ ♦

After Lorene's passing, Thomas started to spend more time with a local seamstress by the name of Katie Woods, who was his companion in his final years. She would accompany him to dinner, and they would occasionally drop in to the clubs on Beale Street together.

Shortly after this, Vaneese recalls hearing that Katie would also drive Thomas to his hospital appointments. "I didn't know until much later that Daddy had been diagnosed with colon cancer and was seeing a doctor at the West Clinic," she revealed. "It was only when I heard it was the West Clinic that it occurred to me, because it was a cancer clinic."[23]

Thomas's illness meant that he had to finally give up his Saturday morning radio show with WDIA, much to his disappointment. "He used to come over to the studio almost every day; we'd just have lunch and talk," Bobby Manuel remembered. "He just needed a place to come. He was taking these injections that cost a fortune just to get his blood straight— serious money—and it was very tough to see him go through that."[24]

Thomas's eyesight was also starting to fail around this time, and his family would try to dissuade him from driving and use a local driver, Will "Bardahl" McDaniel, who had been a friend of Elvis Presley in the late 1950s. Rufus would occasionally ignore this advice and sneak out, and eventually, Marvell had to confiscate his driving license to avoid a potential accident.

Many of his old friends would swing by the house or telephone him to keep him company. "I would call him up and we'd tell each other jokes on the telephone," said singer William Bell, who had known Thomas for over forty years. "He was not supposed to laugh because he was ill, but we would just be telling jokes and laughing. Sometimes Marvell or somebody would come by and say, 'You guys have got to stop telling them jokes, he's not supposed to be laughing!'"[25]

Thomas's condition deteriorated, and he was taken to the St. Francis Hospital on November 22, 2001. "My aunt—my mother's sister—was in the hospital at the same time," Vaneese remembered. "She died first, and then he died. So it was a very difficult period, from Thanksgiving until the Christmas holiday."[26]

Rufus Thomas passed away on December 15, 2001; he was eighty-four. "He was not in the hospital for very long, which was good," said Vaneese. "Daddy would not have been able to stand being incapacitated for any length of time. I think his quick demise was a blessing."[27]

In the days that followed, newspapers and magazines around the world mourned his passing. The *New York Times* described him as "the jovial patriarch of Memphis soul," while on the West Coast, the *LA Times* ran with the headline, "Singer boosted Sun Records before Elvis," touching upon his importance in the early history of R&B.

In the UK, *The Guardian* described Thomas as an "irreverent champion of American Black music" and singled out his contribution to Black radio as being particularly significant. And in Porretta, Italy, Graziano Uliani arranged a remembrance service which was attended by the many friends he had made there, which was held at Caffe Italia, just in front of Rufus Thomas Park. As Thomas himself had suggested several years earlier, there was not a place in the world he was not liked.

Another element of Thomas's legacy was touched upon by Pat Kerr Tigrett, a local fashion designer, philanthropist, and socialite, who highlighted his sense of fashion at the pre-funeral visitation. "He was the original icon of styling," she said, singling out his trademark cape and shorts, "before Elvis, before any of them."[28]

But the more personal tributes came from those who attended his funeral service, which took place at the Mississippi Boulevard Christian Church on Thursday, December 20. An estimated 2,500 people attended to pay their respects, including the two founders of Stax Records, Jim Stewart and Estelle Axton; many of the musicians he worked with at the label, such as Steve Cropper and Isaac Hayes; colleagues from WDIA, where he had worked for so many years; and countless numbers of the close-knit Memphis music community, including Sam Phillips, Little Milton, Calvin Newborn, and Cordell Jackson, to name but a few. Blues legend B.B. King, an early "discovery" at Rufus's talent shows and later a colleague at WDIA, was also in attendance and acted as an honorary pallbearer.

The ceremony, which lasted for more than two hours, was broadcast live on WDIA and featured music by gospel singer O'Landa Draper and the Associates, Kirk Whalum, the Reverend Dwight "Gatemouth" Moore, and Isaac Hayes. Hayes performed one of his trademark "raps," noting that Thomas "had so many titles, so many titles,"—referring to nicknames such as "crown prince of dance" and "the world's oldest teenager." He ended with a version of "Have Yourself a Merry Little Christmas," a song choice that had been approved by his family, and with the funeral taking place just five days before Christmas, many were reduced to tears.

"He did it all; he saw it all," said Rob Bowman, who spoke at the funeral at the request of the family. "Rufus was born a couple of months before the first jazz record was ever recorded. He was born three years before the first blues record, seven years before the first country record and light years before rock, rhythm and blues, soul and funk were even thought of. He was part of it all."[29]

B.B. King also stepped up to pay his respects. "He was a mentor to me, one of the great, great people in our business, and to be honest with you, one of the greatest entertainers I ever met," he said.

State and city leaders also celebrated aspects of his long and colorful life. Tennessee Governor Don Sundquist spoke about Thomas as an ambassador of unity. "He taught us not to see the world in Black or white," he said, "but in shades of blues."

Shelby County Mayor Jim Rout spoke of the time he ran into Thomas, who complained, "Somebody is parking in my space!" Mayor Rout apologized and said he would call the city mayor to have it towed away.

City of Memphis Mayor Willie Herenton himself was up next. He explained that he used to have lunch with Thomas at a local café and said, "You know that Rufus had an ego and he came to me and said you know you the mayor," to which he replied, "Yes, I know." And Rufus said, "I need a parking space," and then he mentioned that he needed a street named after him. Mayor Herenton then said that if Rufus had been around much longer, he was sure he would be trying to get the city of Memphis to change its name. He also sent a warning: "Rufus, don't be trying to change any names up there!" which brought much laughter.

Others who paid tribute that day included WDIA disc jockeys Robert "Honeyboy" Thomas and Jaye Michael Davis, and the head of the National Academy of Recording Arts and Sciences, Michael Greene.

Paul Shaffer, the musical director for the *Late Show with David Letterman*, also sent a powerful video testimonial. "His music will live forever," he said. "His melodies, his riffs, his grooves are really like Beethoven. They're simple, they're direct, they hit hard, and they'll never be forgotten."

♦ ♦ ♦

After the ceremony, a motorcade took Thomas through downtown Memphis one last time. WDIA requested that everyone in the funeral parade and the countless cars lining the street tune in to the station so all the cars could be playing Thomas's music as he embarked on his final journey. Once again, Beale Street reverberated to the sound of Rufus Thomas and *The Breakdown*. He was buried at the New Park Cemetery, next to his wife of almost sixty years, Lorene Thomas.

"This is the end of an era, and the world will miss him dearly," noted his son, Marvell. It was an era that had begun with the birth of the blues, encompassed the age of minstrel shows, the beginnings of R&B, the development of soul and funk, and even disco. Rufus Thomas had seen it all and played an important role throughout. And whether you regarded him as the world's oldest teenager, the crown prince of dance, or the funkiest man alive, he was always one of the world's greatest entertainers, which was all he ever aspired to be.

Postscript

Marvell Thomas had always been a staunch advocate of his father's and family's legacy and was encouraged to see Rufus and Carla inducted into the Memphis Music Hall of Fame.

In 2011, his own achievements were formally recognized, and he was inducted to the Beale Street Walk of Fame. He was humbled by the honor, telling the Commercial Appeal, "I was very flattered, because the general public doesn't know about people like me. They know singers, but they don't know the producers and songwriters and session guys. So, it's good to be recognized." Stax artists from around the country flew in for the occasion, and Stax historian Rob Bowman flew in from Canada to speak at the event.[1]

Sadly, Marvell passed away on January 23, 2017, after suffering a stroke on the operating table, and was unable to take part in the events planned to celebrate the 100th anniversary of his father's birth. "Marvell Thomas was one of those rare behind-the-scenes musicians," said Stax spokesman Tim Sampson. "He contributed so much to the 'Memphis Sound' but never quite got the mass recognition he merited, although he always seemed to accept that role. The keyboards, arrangements and production talents he lent to everyone from his sister Carla Thomas to Isaac Hayes were absolutely essential to the success of Stax Records."[2]

♦ ♦ ♦

Carla Thomas has maintained a relatively low profile since her father's death but continues to live in Memphis, where she occasionally performs.

A live album, *Carla Thomas and Friends, Live in Memphis*, was recorded in early 2001 and released the following year. In 2004, she performed live on *Late Night with Conan O' Brien*, duetting with Sam Moore to promote the D. A. Pennebaker documentary, *Only the Strong Survive*, in which she appeared with her father.

In addition, Carla has continued to work with the Tennessee Arts Commission, getting involved in education-related projects, a cause that is close to her heart.

Carla appeared with her sister, Vaneese, at the 2017 Porretta Soul Festival at Rufus Thomas Park in Porretta Terme, continuing the rich family heritage, and in 2021 she made a guest appearance on "Call Me a Fool," a new song by Memphis singer-songwriter Valerie June, contributing a spoken-word introduction and backing vocals. The song was later nominated for Song of the Year at the Americana Awards and a Grammy for best American roots song, and effectively introduced Carla Thomas to a new audience.

On September 22, 2021, Carla Thomas was presented with a Lifetime Achievement Award at the 20th annual Americana Awards show at the Ryman Auditorium in Nashville, bringing her back to her country roots. She also performed on stage that evening with both Valerie June and her sister, Vaneese.

Speaking to the Memphis Commercial Appeal, she explained that receiving "lifetime" recognition from the Americana Music Association has caused her to contemplate her own legacy and even the possibility of future recordings. "Now my name is getting out there again, and I think, 'Uh-oh, I better try to do something.'"[3]

♦ ♦ ♦

Vaneese has been the most active of Rufus's children from a musical perspective in recent years. She recorded a gospel album, *When My Back's Against the Wall*, in 1999, which was described by *Billboard* as "a small label masterpiece that begs for attention from savvy majors."

"Talk Me Down," a UK release, followed in 2001, followed by *A Woman's Love* (2003) and *Soul Sister, Vol. 1: A Tribute to the Women of Soul* (2009), both of which were released on her own label, Segue Records.

In 2013, Vaneese released an album called *Blues for My Father*, which included an amazing "duet" with her father on "Can't Ever Let You Go," which was originally recorded back in 1962, and a duet with her sister on "Wrong Turn." "That was my first foray into the blues," she later explained. "So I did that really in honor of Daddy, obviously. And because people don't know that he sang blues all through his career, from the beginning to the end. So I wanted to dab my toe in that, and I've grown to love it. And I want to sing more earthy stuff."

Outside of her recording career, Vaneese has also worked in film and television, voicing Clio the Muse in the Disney movie, *Hercules*, singing on numerous movie soundtracks, including *Anastasia*, and appearing regularly on the *Late Show with David Letterman*. She has also sung backing vocals for countless artists, including Aretha Franklin.

Like Carla, Vaneese has also been involved in teaching and education. She taught at the City College of New York for several years. She also helped to found the Swarthmore College Gospel Choir and continues to direct the Alumni Gospel Choir. Her most recent album, *Fight the Good Fight*, was released in 2022.

◆ ◆ ◆

Since his passing, Rufus Thomas's rich legacy has lived on. Stax Records released two excellent compilations of his recordings, *The Funkiest Man—The Stax Funk Sessions* (2002) and *The Very Best of Rufus Thomas* (2007). The former was a particularly noteworthy release, including some unreleased songs such as "Funky Hot Grits," which was even released as a single in Europe.

Rufus's old friend, guitarist, and producer Bobby Manuel discovered that he still had some unreleased tapes in his possession that dated back to the recording sessions made at Sun Records in 1990. After Rufus's death, he passed the tapes on to his son, Marvell. Vaneese worried that Marvell was not storing the tapes properly and offered to take them and make a digital transfer. "We wound up releasing the record on our label," she explained. "We had some internal issues with my brother, and we wound up not promoting it at all. At some point I would like to revisit the release of that record, because they were some of the last things that were recorded."[4]

The album was released as *Just Because I'm Leavin'* . . . in 2005 and featured the funky "Old Dog, New Tricks," some revisited old songs, including "Juanita" and "If There Were No Music," and even a duet with daughter Carla on "God Bless America." As with *Swing Out*, some of which stemmed from the same sessions, it is a good representation of the music he was performing with his band at that time, with his voice still in relatively good shape.

Given all that he achieved in his long and varied career, it seems astonishing that Rufus Thomas has still not been inducted into the Rock and Roll Hall of Fame twenty years after his death. His daughter Vaneese has been pushing for his recognition for several years. "The Rock and Roll Hall of Fame is a political animal—it has very little to do with talent—obviously, because they inducted Kiss!" she said with a laugh. "That's the era they're starting to induct, so they're politicizing it, monetizing it, trying to get people to come, rather than induct the people who got it off the ground. Daddy has not been inducted and that needs to be corrected." After reading this book, hopefully others will agree with that sentiment.[5]

Rufus Thomas Discography

Singles (US–Complete)

1950: "I'll Be a Good Boy" / "I'm So Worried" (Star Talent 807)

1950: "Gonna Bring My Baby Back" / "Beer Bottle Boogie" (Bullet 327)[1]

1951: "Night Workin' Blues" / "Why Did You Dee Gee" (Chess 1466)

1952: "No More Doggin' Around" / "Crazy 'Bout You, Baby" (Chess 1492)

1952: "Juanita" / "Decorate the Counter" (Chess 1517)

1953: "Bear Cat" / "Walking in the Rain" (Sun 181)

1953: "Tiger Man (King of the Jungle)" / "Save Your Money" (Sun 188)

1956: "I'm Steady Holdin' On" / "The Easy Livin' Plan" (Meteor 5039)

1960: "'Cause I Love You" / "Deep Down Inside" (Satellite 102/Atco 6177)[2]

1961: "I Didn't Believe" / "Yeah, Yea-Ah" (Atco 6199)[3]

1962: "Can't Ever Let You Go" / "It's Aw'right" (Stax 126)

1963: "The Dog" / "Did You Ever Love a Woman" (Stax 130)

1963: "Walking the Dog" / "You Said" (Stax 140)[4]

1964: "Can Your Monkey Do the Dog" / "I Wanna Get Married" (Stax 144)

1964: "Somebody Stole My Dog" / "I Want to Be Loved" (Stax 149)

1964: "That's Really Some Good" / "Night Time Is the Right Time" (Stax 151)[5]

1964: "Jump Back" / "All Night Worker" (Stax 157)

1965: "Little Sally Walker" / "Baby Walk" (Stax 167)

1965: "Willy Nilly" / "Sho' Gonna Mess Him Up" (Stax 173)

1965: "When You Move You Lose" / "We're Tight" (Stax 176)[6]

1965: "The World Is Round" / "Chicken Scratch" (Stax 178)

1966: "Birds and Bees" / "Never Let You Go" (Stax 184)[7]

1967: "Sister's Got a Boyfriend" / "Talkin' 'Bout True Love" (Stax 200)

1967: "Sophisticated Sissy" / "Greasy Spoon" (Stax 221)

1968: "Down ta My House" / "Steady Holding On" (Stax 240)

1968: "The Memphis Train" / "I Think I Made a Boo-Boo" (Stax 250)

1968: "Funky Mississippi" / "So Hard to Get Along With" (Stax 0010)

1969: "Funky Way" / "I Want to Hold You" (Stax 0022)

1969: "Do the Funky Chicken" / "Turn Your Damper Down" (Stax 0059)

1970: "Sixty Minute Man" / "The Preacher and the Bear" (Stax 0071)

1970: "(Do the) Push and Pull (Part 1)" / "(Do the) Push and Pull (Part 2)" (Stax 0079)

1971: "The World Is Round" / "I Love You for Sentimental Reasons" (Stax 0090)
1971: "The Breakdown (Part 1)" / "The Breakdown (Part 2)" (Stax 0098)
1971: "Do the Funky Penguin (Part 1)" / "Do the Funky Penguin (Part 2)" (Stax 0112)
1972: "6-3-8 (That's the Number to Play)" / "Love Trap" (Stax 0129)
1972: "Itch and Scratch (Part 1)" / "Itch and Scratch (Part 2)" (Stax 0140)
1973: "Funky Robot (Part 1)" / "Funky Robot (Part 2)" (Stax 0153)
1973: "I Know You Don't Want Me No More" / "I'm Still in Love with You" (Stax 0177)
1973: "I'll Be Your Santa Baby" / "That Makes Christmas Day" (Stax 0187)
1974: "The Funky Bird" / "Steal a Little" (Stax 0192)
1974: "Boogie Ain't Nuttin' (But Gettin' Down) (Part 1)" / "Boogie Ain't Nuttin' (But Gettin' Down) (Part 2)" (Stax 0219)
1975: "Do the Double Bump (Part 1)" / "Do the Double Bump (Part 2)" (Stax 0236)
1975: "Jump Back '75 (Part 1)" / "Jump Back '75 (Part 2)" (Stax 0254)
1976: "If There Were No Music" / "Blues in the Basement" (Artists of America 126)
1977: "Who's Making Love to Your Old Lady" / "Hot Grits" (AVI 149)
1977: "I Ain't Gittin' Older, I'm Gittin' Better (Part 1)" / "I Ain't Gittin' Older, I'm Gittin' Better (Part 2)" (AVI 178)[8]
1978: "Fried Chicken" / "I Ain't Got Time" (Hi 78520)
1979: "Funky Chicken" / "Walkin' the Dog" (Gusto 2037)
1981: "Everybody Cried (The Day Disco Died)" / "I'd Love to Love You Again" (XL 151)
1982: "Christmas Comes But Once A Year" / "I'll Be Your Santa Baby" (Stax 1073)[9]
1984: "Rappin' Rufus" / "Rappin' Rufus (Instrumental Mix)" (Ichiban 85-103)
1984: "Rappin' Rufus" / "Rappin' Rufus (Drum & Vocal Mix)" / Rappin' Rufus (Instrumental Mix) 12" Single Ichiban 12-103)
1987: "Ramesses Rap" / "Memphis Train" (PWP 7387)
1998: "Hey Rufus!" / "Body Fine" (High Stacks HS9801-7)[10]
Unknown: "Walking the Dog" / "The Dog" (Atlantic Oldies Series 13093)
Unknown: "Bear Cat" / "Tiger Man" (Collectables COL 3915)
Unknown: "Do the Funky Chicken" / "Sixty Minute Man (Part 2)" (Collectables 71042)

Albums

1963: *Walking the Dog* (Stax 704)
1969: *May I Have Your Ticket Please?* (Stax 2022—Unreleased)
1970: *Do the Funky Chicken* (Stax 2028)
1971: *Rufus Thomas Live—Doing the Push and Pull at P.J.'s* (Stax 2039)
1972: *Did You Heard Me?* (Stax 3004)
1973: *Crown Prince of Dance* (Stax 3008)
1977: *If There Were No Music* (AVI 6015)
1978: *I Ain't Gettin' Older, I'm Gettin' Better!* (AVI 6046)
1980: *Rufus Thomas* (GT 0064)
1988: *That Woman Is Poison!* (AL 4769)
1992: *Timeless Funk* (Prestige CDSGP 036)
1996: *Blues Thang!* (Sequel 1054)
1997: *Rufus Live!* (ECD 1013)
1999: *Swing Out with Rufus Thomas* (HS 9982)

2002: *Live in Porretta* (SD 44022)

2005: *Just Because I'm Leavin'* . . . (SRRT 05)

Key Compilations

1991: *Can't Get Away from This Dog* (CDSXD 038)—Twenty previously unreleased Stax recordings, with sleeve notes by Rob Bowman.

1996: *The Best of Rufus Thomas—Do the Funky Somethin'* (R2 72410)—Excellent compilation by Rhino Records, including some non-Stax recordings.

2002: *The Funkiest Man—The Stax Funk Sessions 1967–1975* (SX2 135/SCD 8611)—Not a greatest hits collection, but a round-up of Rufus's best funk-oriented tunes.

2007: *The Very Best of Rufus Thomas* (Stax STXCD-30307)—The best of the Stax years.

2008: *Tiger Man: Earliest Recordings 1950–1957* (DOCD 5683)—Well-annotated collection of Thomas's pre-Stax recordings.

Notes

Introduction

1. Rob Bowman, interview with author, August 2021.
2. Rob Bowman, interview with author, August 2021.
3. Rob Bowman, interview with author, August 2021.
4. Rob Bowman, interview with author, August 2021.
5. Robert Gordon, interview with author, May 2021.
6. Rob Bowman, interview with author, August 2021.
7. Vaneese Thomas, interview with author, July 2020.
8. Peter Guralnick, from memphismusichalloffame.com.
9. William Bell, interview with author, July 2020.

Chapter One: Memphis Blues—The Early Years, 1917-1950

1. Vaneese Thomas, interview with author, October 2020.
2. More details can be found in James Cobb's book *The Most Southern Place on Earth* (Oxford University Press, 1992).
3. Vaneese Thomas, interview with author, July 2020.
4. Vaneese Thomas, interview with author, October 2020.
5. Formally known as the World's Fair: Columbian Exposition, held to celebrate the 400th anniversary of Columbus's arrival in the New World in 1492.
6. W. C. Handy, excerpt from *Father of The Blues* (Seacoast Publishing, 2003).
7. W. C. Handy, excerpt from *Father of The Blues.*
8. Rufus Thomas, excerpt from interview by Margaret McKee and Fred Chisenhall, Everett R. Cook Oral History Collection, Memphis and Shelby County Public Library and Information Center (Cook Collection).
9. Rufus Thomas, excerpt of an interview on *Open Vault* from WGBH.
10. Carla Thomas, excerpt from an interview with Portia Maultsby, September 1984 (Portia K. Maultsby Collection, Indiana University).
11. Rufus Thomas, excerpt from *The Blues Route* by Hugh Merrill.
12. Rufus Thomas, excerpt from *The Blues Route.*
13. The song has often been attributed to Memphis Minnie, but "Kansas" Joe McCoy is now thought to have been the songwriter. Memphis Minnie plays second guitar.
14. Rufus Thomas, excerpt of interview by Ray Ann Kremer and Pat Faudree, Cook Collection.
15. Rufus Thomas, excerpt from www.706unionavene.nl.

16. Rufus Thomas, interviewed by Pete Daniel, David Less, and Charles McGovern, Memphis, 8/5/1992, *Rock 'n' Soul Video History Project Collection*, interviews, National Museum of American History, Archives Center, Smithsonian Institution, Washington, DC.

17. Rufus Thomas, interviewed by Daniel, Less, and McGovern.

18. Rufus Thomas, interviewed by Daniel, Less, and McGovern.

19. Rufus Thomas, interviewed by Daniel, Less, and McGovern.

20. Robert Morris, excerpt from *Wheelin' on Beale* by Louis Cantor (Pharos Books, 1992).

21. Rufus Thomas, interviewed by Pete Daniel, David Less, and Charles McGovern, Memphis, 8/5/1992, *Rock 'n' Soul Video History Project Collection*, interviews, National Museum of American History, Archives Center, Smithsonian Institution, Washington, DC.

22. Rufus Thomas, excerpt from *Sun Records: An Oral History* by John Floyd (Devault-Graves Agency, 2015).

23. Rufus Thomas, *Sun Records: An Oral History* by John Floyd.

24. Rufus Thomas, excerpt from www.706unionavene.nl.

25. Rufus Thomas, interviewed by Pete Daniel, David Less, and Charles McGovern, Memphis, 8/5/1992, *Rock 'n' Soul Video History Project Collection*, interviews, National Museum of American History, Archives Center, Smithsonian Institution, Washington, DC.

26. Rufus Thomas, excerpt from *Wheelin' on Beale* by Louis Cantor (Pharos Books, 1992).

27. Vaneese Thomas, interview with author, July 2020.

28. Rufus Thomas, interviewed by Pete Daniel, David Less, and Charles McGovern, Memphis, 8/5/1992, *Rock 'n' Soul Video History Project Collection*, interviews, National Museum of American History, Archives Center, Smithsonian Institution, Washington, DC.

29. Rufus Thomas, excerpt from *Sun Records: An Oral History* by John Floyd (Devault-Graves Agency, 2015).

30. Paul Oliver, excerpt from *The Story of The Blues* (Barrie & Rockliff, 1978).

31. Rufus Thomas, excerpt of an interview on Open Vault from WGBH.

32. Rufus Thomas, excerpt from *The Blues Route* by Hugh Merrill.

33. Rufus Thomas, excerpt from staxrecords.com.

34. Rufus Thomas, excerpt from staxrecords.com.

35. Rufus Thomas, excerpt from staxrecords.com.

36. Rufus Thomas, excerpt from staxrecords.com.

37. Rufus Thomas, excerpt from a Grammy Foundation Living History interview.

38. Rufus Thomas, excerpt from a Grammy Foundation Living History interview.

39. Rufus Thomas, excerpt of interview by Ray Ann Kremer and Pat Faudree, Cook Collection.

40. Rufus Thomas, excerpt from staxrecords.com.

41. Rufus Thomas, interview with Peter Guralnick, from www.706unionavene.nl.

42. Vaneese Thomas, interview with author, July 2020.

43. Vaneese Thomas, interview with author, October 2020.

44. Rufus Thomas, interviewed by Pete Daniel, David Less, and Charles McGovern, Memphis, 8/5/1992, *Rock 'n' Soul Video History Project Collection*, interviews, National Museum of American History, Archives Center, Smithsonian Institution, Washington, DC.

45. Robert Golden, from "King Vidor's 'Hallelujah'" by Greg Akers, *Memphis Magazine*, August 28, 2014.

46. Rufus Thomas, excerpt from *Sun Records: An Oral History* by John Floyd (Devault-Graves Agency, 2015).

47. Rufus Thomas, interviewed by Pete Daniel, David Less, and Charles McGovern, Memphis, 8/5/1992, *Rock 'n' Soul Video History Project Collection*, interviews, National Museum of American History, Archives Center, Smithsonian Institution, Washington, DC.

48. Rufus Thomas, excerpt from Sun Records: An Oral History by John Floyd (Devault-Graves Agency, 2015).

49. Vaneese Thomas, interview with author, July 2020.

50. Vaneese Thomas, interview with author, July 2020.

51. Gloria Wade-Gayles, excerpt from *Pushed Back to Strength: A Black Woman's Journey Home* (Avon Books, 1995).

52. Rufus Thomas, excerpt from *Wheelin' on Beale* by Louis Cantor (Pharos Books, 1992).

53. Rufus Thomas, excerpt from *Wheelin' on Beale*.

54. Vaneese Thomas, interview with author, July 2020.

55. Rufus Thomas, interviewed by Pete Daniel, David Less, and Charles McGovern, Memphis, 8/5/1992, *Rock 'n' Soul Video History Project Collection*, interviews, National Museum of American History, Archives Center, Smithsonian Institution, Washington, DC.

56. Marvell Thomas, interviewed by David Less, Memphis, November 11, 1999, *Rock 'n' Soul Video History Project Collection*, interviews, National Museum of American History, Archives Center, Smithsonian Institution, Washington, DC.

57. Marvell Thomas, excerpt from an interview with memphisdowntowner.com.

58. Carla Thomas, excerpt from blog.ponderosastomp.com.

59. Marvell Thomas, excerpt from obituary in *Memphis Commercial Appeal* by Bob Mehr.

60. Marvell Thomas, excerpt from an interview with memphisdowntowner.com.

61. Carla Thomas, excerpt from *Ladies of Soul* by David Freeland.

62. Rufus Thomas, from *New York Times* obituary by John Pareles, December 19, 2001.

63. Marvell Thomas, excerpt from an interview with memphisdowntowner.com.

64. Marvell Thomas, excerpt from an interview with memphisdowntowner.com.

65. Marvell Thomas, excerpt from *Country Soul: Making Music and Making Race in the American South* by Charles L. Hughes (University of North Carolina Press, 2016).

66. Marvell Thomas, excerpt from an interview with memphisdowntowner.com.

67. Marvell Thomas, excerpt from an interview with memphisdowntowner.com.

68. Carla Thomas, excerpt from blog.ponderosastomp.com.

69. Marvell Thomas, excerpt from an interview with memphisdowntowner.com.

70. Biographical details from "B.B. King, American Blues Musician" by Quincy Troupe, jazzandbluesmasters.com.

71. Charles Lloyd, Facebook page, December 15, 2019.

72. Rufus Thomas, excerpt from staxrecords.com.

73. Rufus Thomas, interviewed by Pete Daniel, David Less, and Charles McGovern, Memphis, 8/5/1992, *Rock 'n' Soul Video History Project Collection*, interviews, National Museum of American History, Archives Center, Smithsonian Institution, Washington, DC.

74. Rufus Thomas, excerpt from an interview with Portia Maultsby, September 1984 (Portia K. Maultsby Collection, Indiana University).

75. Rufus Thomas, excerpt from *Memphis Music Hall of Fame* by Peter Guralnick.

Chapter Two: WDIA–Rufus on the Radio, 1950-1960

1. Rufus Thomas, excerpt of an interview on Open Vault from WGBH. In fact, Robinson was not the first professional Black baseball player but the first in the Major Leagues.

2. Technically Williams (and Rufus Thomas) were announcers, rather than disc jockeys. The music itself was played by a (white) control board operator, who would open up the announcer's microphone once a record had ended. However, the announcer is usually referred to as the disc jockey, and Louis Cantor refers to the announcers as disc jockeys in his history of WDIA, *Wheelin' on Beale* (Pharos Books, 1992).

3. These radio stations did broadcast occasional live Black music, primarily gospel, but such broadcasts were a very small part of their programming. Likewise, there were occasional remote or syndicated broadcasts of jazz, blues, etc.

4. Christine Cooper Spindel, excerpt from "Let's Put Him on the Air," February 2, 2014, *Oxford American* magazine.

5. Bert Ferguson, excerpt from "How America Got Its First Black Radio Station" by Teresa Bitler, June 18, 2019.

6. Naomi Williams Moody, excerpt from *Wheelin' on Beale* by Louis Cantor (Pharos Books, 1992).

7. Christine Cooper Spindel, excerpt from "Let's Put Him on Air," February 2, 2014, *Oxford American* magazine.

8. Nat D. Williams, excerpt from *Wheelin' on Beale* by Louis Cantor (Pharos Books, 1992).

9. Reverend Dwight "Gatemouth" Moore, excerpt from *Wheelin' on Beale* by Louis Cantor (Pharos Books, 1992).

10. Reverend Dwight "Gatemouth" Moore, from "WDIA History" by Robert Gordon, Pan-African News blog.

11. Reverend Dwight "Gatemouth" Moore, excerpt from *Wheelin' on Beale* by Louis Cantor (Pharos Books, 1992).

12. Christine Cooper Spindel, excerpt from "Let's Put Him on the Air," February 2, 2014, *Oxford American* magazine.

13. B.B. King, from pagesix.com, November 18, 2008.

14. David James Mattis, excerpt from *Wheelin' on Beale* by Louis Cantor (Pharos Books, 1992).

15. Rufus Thomas, excerpt from *Wheelin' on Beale* by Louis Cantor (Pharos Books, 1992).

16. David James Mattis, excerpt from *Wheelin' on Beale* by Louis Cantor (Pharos Books, 1992).

17. David James Mattis, excerpt from *Wheelin' on Beale*.

18. Rufus Thomas, excerpt from *The Blues Route* by Hugh Merrill.

19. Rufus Thomas, excerpt from *The Blues Route*.

20. Phillips also licensed Wolf's recordings to RPM Records at this time.

21. Vaneese Thomas, interview with author, November 2020.

22. Trent Cobb, interview with author, September 2020.

23. Marvell Thomas, excerpt from an interview with memphisdowntowner.com.

24. Marvell Thomas, interviewed by David Less, Memphis, November 11, 1999, *Rock 'n' Soul Video History Project Collection*, interviews, National Museum of American History, Archives Center, Smithsonian Institution, Washington, DC.

25. Trent Cobb, interview with author, September 2020.

26. Trent Cobb, interview with author, September 2020.

27. Trent Cobb, interview with author, September 2020.

28. Trent Cobb, interview with author, September 2020.

29. Marvell Thomas, excerpt from an interview with memphisdowntowner.com.

30. Rufus Thomas, excerpt of an interview on Open Vault from WGBH. The song is thought to have been "Hootin' the Blues" by Sonny Terry, but recorded under various titles over the years.

31. Trent Cobb, interview with author, September 2020.

32. Vaneese Thomas, interview with author, July 2000.

33. Carla Thomas, excerpt from interview, memphisflyer.com, December 14, 2017.

34. Carla Thomas, excerpt from interview, memphisflyer.com, December 14, 2017.

35. Carla Thomas, excerpt from interview, memphisflyer.com, December 14, 2017.

36. Carla Thomas, excerpt from *Ladies of Soul* by David Freeland (University Press of Mississippi, 2001).

37. Carla Thomas, interview with David Less and Pete Daniel, November 10, 1999, for Rock 'n' Soul exhibit, Smithsonian Institution.

38. Thomas, interview with Less and Daniel, November 10, 1999.

39. Marvell Thomas, interviewed by David Less, Memphis, November 11, 1999, *Rock 'n' Soul Video History Project Collection*, interviews, National Museum of American History, Archives Center, Smithsonian Institution, Washington, DC.

40. Dora Todd, excerpt from *Wheelin' on Beale* by Louis Cantor (Pharos Books, 1992).

41. Toni Bell, from "How America Got Its First Black Radio Station" by Teresa Bitler, June 18, 2019, atlasobscura.com.

42. Bert Ferguson, from "How America Got Its First Black Radio Station" by Teresa Bitler, June 18, 2019, atlasobscura.com.

43. Bert Ferguson, from *Wheelin' on Beale* by Louis Cantor (Pharos Books, 1992).

44. Deanie Parker, interview with author, September 2020.

45. Mark Stansbury, interview with author, August 2020.

Chapter Three: Bear Cat—Rufus and Elvis, 1950-1956

1. Boots Bourquin, excerpt from www.706unionavenue.nl.

2. Rufus Thomas, excerpt from interview in the *Dallas Observer*, June 4, 1995.

3. Rufus Thomas, excerpt from interview in the *Dallas Observer*, June 4, 1995.

4. Donald Canestrari, from Historic-Memphis.com.

5. Rufus Thomas, excerpt from www.706unionavenue.nl.

6. Sam Phillips explained to Peter Guralnick in *Sam Phillips: The Man Who Invented Rock 'n' Roll* (Hachette UK, 2015) that the profits would be split 50/50 with Chess, provided Leonard Chess had the right of first refusal. "Rocket 88" was the first song Sam Phillips offered to Chess.

7. While "Rocket 88" was credited to Jackie Brenston on the label, Ike Turner is thought to have done most of the writing, but the song borrows heavily from a 1947 song, "Cadillac Boogie," by Jimmy Liggins.

8. The unlikely tale of Doris Genius can be found in Dave Clarke's liner notes to *Tiger Man: Earliest Recordings, 1950–1957* on Document Records.

9. Peter Guralnick, excerpt from *Sam Phillips: The Man Who Invented Rock 'n' Roll* (Hachette UK, 2015).

10. Sam Phillips, excerpt from *Sam Phillips: The Man Who Invented Rock 'n' Roll* by Peter Guralnick (Hachette UK, 2015).

11. See https://www.706unionavenue.nl/108206818.

12. The way the *Billboard* article is written suggests that Alex Bradford and the Caravans worked with WDIA, but they were in fact national gospel stars.

13. Excerpt from the liner notes of *Elvis, The King of Rock 'n' Roll—The Complete 50's Masters* by Peter Guralnick.

14. Marion Keisker, from *Flowers in the Dustbin: The Rise of Rock and Roll* by James Miller. Given that it was 1954, it is more likely that Sam Phillips would have said "a million dollars."

15. This was in fact Presley's third visit to Sun Records. He had cut a second acetate in January 1954.

16. Scotty Moore, excerpt from *Last Train to Memphis: The Rise of Elvis Presley* by Peter Guralnick.

17. Scotty Moore, excerpt from *Last Train to Memphis: The Rise of Elvis Presley*.

18. Sam Phillips, excerpt from https://www.706unionavenue.nl.

19. Johnny Cash, interview with Peter Guralnick from www.706unionavenue.nl.

20. Rufus Thomas, interview with Peter Guralnick from www.memphismusichalloffame.com.

21. Rufus Thomas, excerpt from an interview in the *Telegraph*, September 21, 1996.

22. Rufus Thomas, excerpt of an interview on *Open Vault*, WGBH.

23. Rufus Thomas, excerpt of an interview on *Open Vault*, WGBH.

24. Vaneese Thomas, interview with author, July 2000.

25. Rufus Thomas, excerpt from *Devil's Music, Holy Rollers and Hillbillies: How America Gave Birth to Rock and Roll* by James Cosby (McFarland, 2016).

26. Vaneese Thomas, interview with author, July 2000.

27. Rufus Thomas, excerpt from radio interview on *Open Vault*, WGBH.

28. George Klein, from *Wheelin' on Beale* by Louis Cantor (Pharos Books, 1992).

29. Rufus Thomas, excerpt from radio interview on *Open Vault*, WGBH.

30. Rufus Thomas, excerpt from radio interview on *Open Vault*, WGBH.

31. Robert "Honeymoon" Garner, from *Wheelin' on Beale* by Louis Cantor (Pharos Books, 1992).

32. Rufus Thomas, excerpt from *The Blues Route* by Hugh Merrill.

Chapter Four: Steady Holdin' On—Memphis Talent, 1956-1960

1. Jack Clement, excerpt from *Goin' Back to Memphis* by James L. Dickerson (Cooper Square Press, 2000).

2. Rufus Thomas, excerpt of an interview on *Open Vault*, WGBH.

3. Rufus Thomas, interviewed by Pete Daniel, David Less, and Charles McGovern, Memphis, 8/5/1992, *Rock 'n' Soul Video History Project Collection*, interviews, National Museum of American History, Archives Center, Smithsonian Institution, Washington, DC.

4. Rufus Thomas, interviewed by Daniel, Less, and McGovern.

5. Rufus Thomas, interviewed by Daniel, Less, and McGovern.

6. Rufus Thomas, excerpt from *The Blues Route* by Hugh Merrill.

7. Robert Gordon, excerpt from "Plantation Inn: Where Stars Rose in the West," *Commercial Appeal*, October 19, 2007.

8. Howard Grimes, interview with author, August 2020.

9. William Bell, excerpt from interview by Richard Scheinin, May 30, 2019, sfjazz.org.

10. William Bell, interview with author, July 2020.

11. William Bell, excerpt from an interview with soulexpress.net.

12. William Bell, interview with author, July 2020.

13. William Bell, excerpt from interview by Richard Scheinin, May 30, 2019, sfjazz.org.

14. William Bell, interview with author, July 2020.

15. William Bell, excerpt from interview by Richard Scheinin, May 30, 2019, sfjazz.org.

16. William Bell, interview with author, July 2020.

17. William Bell, excerpt from an interview with soulexpress.net.

18. David Porter, interview with author, July 2020.

19. Isaac Hayes, excerpt of an interview from *The Guardian*, August 15, 2008.

20. Don Bryant, interview with author, August 2020.

21. Don Bryant, interview with author, August 2020.

22. Don Bryant, interview with author, August 2020.

23. Don Bryant, interview with author, August 2020.

24. Howard Grimes, interview with author, August 2020.

25. Howard Grimes, interview with author, August 2020.

26. Howard Grimes, interview with author, August 2020.

27. Booker T. Jones, interview with author, September 2020.

28. Steve Cropper, interview with author, August 2020.

29. Vaneese Thomas, interview with author, July 2020.

30. Booker T. Jones, interview with author, September 2020.

31. Deanie Parker, interview with author, September 2020.

32. David Porter, interview with author, July 2020.

33. Marvell Thomas, excerpt from an interview in memphisdowntowner.com.

34. Marvell Thomas, interviewed by David Less, Memphis, November 11, 1999, *Rock 'n' Soul Video History Project Collection*, interviews, National Museum of American History, Archives Center, Smithsonian Institution, Washington, DC.

35. Marvell Thomas, excerpt from an interview in memphisdowntowner.com.

36. Marvell Thomas, interviewed by David Less, Memphis, November 11, 1999, *Rock 'n' Soul Video History Project Collection*, interviews, National Museum of American History, Archives Center, Smithsonian Institution, Washington, DC.

37. Marvell Thomas, excerpt from an interview in memphisdowntowner.com.

38. Carla Thomas, excerpt from *Ladies of Soul* by David Freeland.

39. Carla Thomas, excerpt from blog.ponderosastomp.com.

40. Carla Thomas, interview with David Less and Pete Daniel, November 10, 1999, for *Rock 'n' Soul* exhibit, Smithsonian Institution.

41. Mark Stansbury, interview with author, August 2020.

42. Carla Thomas, excerpt from blog.ponderosastomp.com.

43. Carla Thomas, excerpt from *Ladies of Soul* by David Freeland.

44. Carla Thomas, excerpt from *Ladies of Soul* by David Freeland.

45. Carla Thomas, excerpt from blog.ponderosastomp.com.

Chapter Five: Gee Whiz—The Birth of Stax, 1957-1962

1. Rufus Thomas, *The Story of Stax Records*, documentary.

2. Robert Talley, from *Respect Yourself, Stax Records and the Soul Explosion* by Robert Gordon.

3. Biographical details of Jim Stewart from *Soulsville U.S.A.: The Story of Stax Records* by Rob Bowman (Music Sales, 2006).

4. Moman plays guitar on the third Satellite release by Donna Rae and the Sunbeams, according to an interview with Jim Stewart by Rob Bowman.

5. Estelle Axton, from *Respect Yourself, Stax Records and the Soul Explosion* by Robert Gordon.

6. "Prove Your Love" by Charles Heinz (Satellite 101). Details from *Soulsville U.S.A.: The Story of Stax Records* by Rob Bowman.

7. Steve Cropper, interview with author, August 2020.

8. Steve Cropper, interview with author, August 2020.

9. Rent details from an interview with Jim Stewart, conducted by Rob Bowman.

10. Steve Cropper, interview with Barney Hoskyns, *Guardian*, May 15, 2012.

11. Carla Thomas, excerpt from blog.ponderosastomp.com.

12. Rufus Thomas, *The Story of Stax Records*, documentary.

13. Carla Thomas, excerpt from blog.ponderosastomp.com.

14. Carla Thomas, excerpt from blog.ponderosastomp.com.

15. The tip came from either Buster Williams or Norma Reuben, who worked at Plastic Products, according to interviews conducted with Jim Stewart and Jerry Wexler by Rob Bowman.

16. From interviews with Jim Stewart and Estelle Axton by Rob Bowman for *Soulsville U.S.A.: The Story of Stax Records* by Rob Bowman.

17. Jim Stewart from *Sweet Soul Music* by Peter Guralnick.

18. Jim Stewart, excerpt from *Soulsville U.S.A.: The Story of Stax Records* by Rob Bowman.

19. Incidentally, this chain of stores also gave name to the Memphis-based band, Big Star, which was formed by Alex Chilton and Chris Bell in the early 1970s.

20. William Bell, excerpt from *Respect Yourself, Stax Records and the Soul Explosion* by Robert Gordon.

21. William Bell, interview with author, July 2020.

22. William Bell, interview with author, July 2020.

23. Marvell Thomas, excerpt from *Respect Yourself, Stax Records and the Soul Explosion* by Robert Gordon.

24. David Porter, interview with author, July 2020.

25. Carla Thomas, excerpt from blog.ponderosastomp.com.

26. Carla Thomas, interview with David Less and Pete Daniel, November 10, 1999, *for Rock 'n' Soul* exhibit, Smithsonian Institution.

27. Rufus Thomas, excerpt from *Sweet Soul Music* by Peter Guralnick.

28. Carla Thomas, excerpt from *Ladies of Soul* by David Freeland.

29. Jim Stewart, interview with author, November 2020.

30. Carla Thomas, excerpt from *Ladies of Soul* by David Freeland.

31. Carla Thomas, excerpt from *Ladies of Soul* by David Freeland.

32. Vaneese Thomas, interview with author, July 2020.

33. Jim Stewart, interview with author, November 2020.

34. Rufus Thomas, excerpt from radio interview on *Open Vault*, WGBH.

35. Rufus Thomas, excerpt from *Respect Yourself, Stax Records and the Soul Explosion* by Robert Gordon.

36. Jim Stewart, interview with author, November 2020.

37. Jerry Wexler, excerpt from *Respect Yourself, Stax Records and the Soul Explosion* by Robert Gordon.

38. Vaneese Thomas, interview with author, July 2020.

39. Donald "Duck" Dunn, *The Story of Stax Records*, documentary.

40. Steve Cropper, excerpt from *Soulsville U.S.A.: The Story of Stax Records* by Rob Bowman.

41. Carla Thomas, interview with David Less and Pete Daniel, November 10, 1999, for *Rock 'n' Soul* exhibit, Smithsonian Institution.

42. Steve Cropper, interview with author, August 2020.

43. Jim Stewart, excerpt of an interview with Rob Bowman.

44. William Bell, excerpt from interview on soulexpress.net.

45. William Bell, excerpt from interview, May 30, 2019, sjjazz.org.

46. Carla Thomas, excerpt from blog.ponderosastomp.com.

47. Steve Cropper, interview with author, August 2020.

48. Steve Cropper, interview with author, August 2020.

49. Steve Cropper, interview with author, August 2020.

50. Steve Cropper, interview with author, August 2020.

Chapter Six: Walking the Dog—Rufus and the British "Mod" Scene, 1963-1964

1. Booker T. Jones, excerpt from *Time Is Tight* (Omnibus Press, 2019).

2. Booker T. Jones, interview with author, September 2020.

3. Steve Cropper, interview with author, August 2020.

4. Booker T. Jones, interview with author, September 2020.

5. Steve Cropper, interview with author, August 2020.

6. Steve Cropper, interview with author, August 2020.

7. Rufus Thomas, excerpt from interview by Richard Harrington, the *Washington Post*, May 8, 1982.

8. Rufus Thomas, liner notes to *The Complete Stax/Volt Singles, 1959–1968* by Rob Bowman.

9. Rufus Thomas, liner notes to *The Complete Stax/Volt Singles, 1959–1968* by Rob Bowman.

10. Rufus Thomas, excerpt from interview by Richard Harrington, the *Washington Post*, May 8, 1982.

11. Jim Stewart, interview with author, October 2020.

12. Jeffrey Kruger, excerpt from "Absolute Beginnings" from recordcollectormag.com.

13. Jeffrey Kruger, excerpt from "Absolute Beginnings" from recordcollectormag.com. The music played at that stage was more likely ska, as reggae did not emerge until the late 1960s.

14. Mick Eve, excerpt from *Mods: The New Religion by Paul Anderson* (Omnibus Press, 2014).

15. Mick Eve, excerpt from *Mods: The New Religion by Paul Anderson* (Omnibus Press, 2014).

16. Deanie Parker, interview with author, September 2020.

17. Deanie Parker, interview with author, September 2020.

18. Steve Cropper, interview with author, August 2020.

19. Steve Cropper, interview with author, August 2020.

20. The title of the song might also reference the 1916 hit by vaudeville singer Shelton Brooks. While this was a different song entirely, it is possible that Thomas came across the song during his minstrel years.

21. Tom Dowd, excerpt from *Respect Yourself, Stax Records and the Soul Explosion* by Robert Gordon.

22. Jerry Wexler, excerpt from *Respect Yourself, Stax Records and the Soul Explosion* by Robert Gordon.

23. Jim Stewart, interview with author, October 2020.

24. Rufus Thomas, interviewed by Pete Daniel, David Less, and Charles McGovern, Memphis, 8/5/1992, *Rock 'n' Soul Video History Project Collection*, interviews, National Museum of American History, Archives Center, Smithsonian Institution, Washington, DC.

25. Steve Cropper, interview with author, August 2020.

26. Steve Cropper, interview with author, August 2020.

27. Marvell Thomas, excerpt from an interview in memphisdowntowner.com.

28. Steve Cropper, interview with author, August 2020.

29. Steve Cropper, interview with author, August 2020.

30. Jim Stewart, excerpt from *Icons of R&B and Soul, Vol. 1* by Bob Gulla (Greenwood Press, 2007).

31. Jerry Wexler, excerpt from *Sweet Soul Music* by Peter Guralnick.

32. Carla Thomas, excerpt from blog.ponderosastomp.com.

33. Carla Thomas, excerpt from blog.ponderosastomp.com.

34. Rufus Thomas, excerpt from *Sweet Soul Music* by Peter Guralnick.

35. Bobby Manuel, interview with author, July 2020.

36. Carla Thomas, excerpt from *Ladies of Soul* by David Freeland.

37. Carla Thomas, excerpt from *Ladies of Soul* by David Freeland.

38. Steve Cropper, interview with author, August 2020.

39. Steve Cropper, interview with author, August 2020.

40. Booker T. Jones, interview with author, September 2020.

41. Carla Thomas, excerpt from blog.ponderosastomp.com.

42. David Essex, excerpt from an interview in the *Daily Mail*, January 11, 2013.

43. Vaneese Thomas, interview with author, November 2020.

Chapter Seven: B-A-B-Y—Stax in Ascendance, 1965-1966

1. Robert Gordon, excerpt from *Respect Yourself, Stax Records and the Soul Explosion* by Robert Gordon.

2. Isaac Hayes, excerpt from *Respect Yourself, Stax Records and the Soul Explosion* by Robert Gordon.

3. Marvell Thomas, excerpt from an interview in memphisdowntowner.com.

4. Steve Cropper, liner notes to *The Complete Stax/Volt Singles, 1959–1968* by Rob Bowman.

5. Sam Moore, excerpt from *Respect Yourself, Stax Records and the Soul Explosion* by Robert Gordon.

6. Eddie Floyd, excerpt from blog.ponderosastomp.com.

7. Carla Thomas, excerpt from blog.ponderosastomp.com.

8. Carla Thomas, excerpt from *Soulsville U.S.A.: The Story of Stax Records* by Rob Bowman.

9. Booker T. Jones, interview with author, September 2020.

10. William Bell, interview with author, July 2020.

11. Steve Cropper, interview with author, August 2020.

12. Al Jackson Jr., excerpt from *Aretha Franklin: The Queen of Soul* by Mark Bego (Da Capo Press, 2001).

13. Steve Cropper, excerpt from *Soulsville U.S.A.: The Story of Stax Records* by Rob Bowman.

14. Carla Thomas, excerpt from *Ladies of Soul* by David Freeland.

15. Steve Cropper, interview with author, August 2020.

16. Booker T. Jones, interview with author, September 2020.

17. David Porter, liner notes to *The Complete Stax/Volt Singles, 1959–1968* by Rob Bowman.

18. Rufus Thomas, liner notes to *The Complete Stax/Volt Singles, 1959–1968* by Rob Bowman.

19. Floyd Newman, liner notes to *The Complete Stax/Volt Singles, 1959–1968* by Rob Bowman.

20. Vaneese Thomas, interview with author, July 2020.

21. Trent Cobb, interview with author, September 2020.

22. Maxine Smith, from Lorene Thomas's obituary, *Memphis Commercial Appeal*, February 9, 2000.

23. David Porter, liner notes to *The Complete Stax/Volt Singles, 1959–1968* by Rob Bowman.

24. Isaac Hayes, excerpt from *Respect Yourself, Stax Records and the Soul Explosion* by Robert Gordon.

25. Rufus Thomas, excerpt from *Sweet Soul Music* by Peter Guralnick.

26. David Porter, interview with author, July 2020.

27. William Bell, interview with author, July 2020.

28. Carla Thomas, excerpt from blog.ponderosastomp.com.

29. Carla Thomas, excerpt from blog.ponderosastomp.com.

30. Vaneese Thomas, excerpt from "Fabulous Flip Sides," *Goldmine Magazine*, November 18, 2019.

31. Booker T. Jones, excerpt from *Time Is Tight* (Omnibus Press, 2019).

32. Eddie Floyd, excerpt from *Respect Yourself, Stax Records and the Soul Explosion* by Robert Gordon.

33. William Bell, interview with author, July 2020.

34. Floyd Newman, liner notes to *The Complete Stax/Volt Singles, 1959–1968* by Rob Bowman.

35. Booker T. Jones, interview with author, September 2020.

36. Booker T. Jones, excerpt from *Time Is Tight* (Omnibus Press, 2019).

37. Jim Stewart, excerpt from *Otis! The Otis Redding Story* by Scott Freeman (St. Martin's Press, 2001).

Chapter Eight: King and Queen–Stax in Europe, 1967

1. Carla Thomas, liner notes to *The Complete Stax/Volt Singles, 1959–1968* by Rob Bowman.

2. David Porter, liner notes to *The Complete Stax/Volt Singles, 1959–1968* by Rob Bowman.

3. Jim Stewart, interview with author, October 2020.

4. Jim Stewart, excerpt from liner notes to *The Otis Redding Story* by Rob Bowman.

5. Carla Thomas, excerpt from blog.ponderosastomp.com.

6. Booker T. Jones, interview with author, September 2020.

7. Wayne Jackson, excerpt from *Respect Yourself, Stax Records and the Soul Explosion* by Robert Gordon.

8. Steve Cropper, interview with author, August 2020.

9. Jim Stewart, interview with author, October 2020.

10. Booker T. Jones, interview with author, September 2020.

11. Carla Thomas, excerpt from *Memphis Mayhem: A Story of The Music That Shook Up the World* by David A. Less.

12. Booker T. Jones, interview with author, September 2020.

13. Al Bell, excerpt from *Respect Yourself, Stax Records and the Soul Explosion* by Robert Gordon.

14. Jim Stewart, interview with author, October 2020.

15. Carla Thomas, excerpt from *Ladies of Soul* by David Freeland.

16. Booker T. Jones, excerpt from *Time Is Tight* (Omnibus Press, 2019).

17. David Porter, interview with author, July 2020.

18. Vaneese Thomas, interview with author, July 2020.

19. Carla Thomas, liner notes to *The Complete Stax/Volt Singles, 1959–1968* by Rob Bowman.

20. Carla Thomas, excerpt from blog.ponderosastomp.com.

21. Deanie Parker, interview with author, September 2020.

22. James Alexander, interview with author, September 2020.

23. James Alexander, interview with author, September 2020.

24. James Alexander, excerpt from "Try a Little Tenderness" by George Larrimore, *Memphis Magazine*, December 12, 2017.

25. David Porter, interview with author, July 2020.

26. James Alexander, excerpt from *The Story of the Bar-Kays*, vinyldialogues.com.

27. Zelma Redding, excerpt from *Sweet Soul Music* by Peter Guralnick.

28. Phil Walden, excerpt from liner notes to *The Otis Redding Story* by Rob Bowman.

29. Steve Cropper, excerpt from *Otis Redding, An Unfinished Life* by Jonathan Gould.

30. Booker T. Jones, excerpt from *Time Is Tight* (Omnibus Press, 2019).

31. Jim Stewart, interview with author, October 2020.

32. Zelma Redding, excerpt from *Sweet Soul Music* by Peter Guralnick.

33. James Alexander, excerpt from *The Story of the Bar-Kays*, vinyldialogues.com.

34. Jim Stewart, interview with author, October 2020.

35. Carla Thomas, excerpt from *Respect Yourself, Stax Records and the Soul Explosion* by Robert Gordon.

36. Jim Stewart, interview with author, October 2020.

Chapter Nine: Memphis Queen—The Soul Explosion, 1968–1970

1. Jim Stewart, interview with author, October 2020.

2. Jim Stewart, interview with Rob Bowman from the movie *Respect Yourself: The Stax Records Story* directed by Morgan Neville and Robert Gordon.

3. Jim Stewart, interview with author, October 2020.

4. Jerry Wexler, excerpt from *Sweet Soul Music* by Peter Guralnick.

5. Booker T. Jones, interview with author, September 2020.

6. Sam Moore, excerpt from *Respect Yourself, Stax Records and the Soul Explosion* by Robert Gordon.

7. Deanie Parker, interview with author, September 2020.

8. Booker T. Jones, excerpt from *Time Is Tight* (Omnibus Press, 2019).

9. Steve Cropper, interview with author, August 2020.

10. William Bell, interview with author, July 2020.

11. Donald "Duck" Dunn, excerpt from *Respect Yourself, Stax Records and the Soul Explosion* by Robert Gordon.

12. Deanie Parker, interview with author, September 2020.

13. Steve Cropper, interview with author, August 2020.

14. William Bell, interview with author, July 2020.

15. Jim Stewart, excerpt from *Respect Yourself, Stax Records and the Soul Explosion* by Robert Gordon.

16. Jim Stewart, interview with author, October 2020.

17. Estelle Axton, excerpt from *Soulsville U.S.A.: The Story of Stax Records* by Rob Bowman.

18. Al Bell, excerpt from *Respect Yourself, Stax Records and the Soul Explosion* by Robert Gordon.

19. Steve Cropper, interview with author, August 2020.

20. Carla Thomas, excerpt from blog.ponderosastomp.com.

21. William Bell, interview with author, July 2020.

22. Deanie Parker, interview with author, September 2020.

23. Rufus Thomas, interviewed by Pete Daniel, David Less, and Charles McGovern, Memphis, 8/5/1992, *Rock 'n' Soul Video History Project Collection*, interviews, National Museum of American History, Archives Center, Smithsonian Institution, Washington, DC.

24. Rufus Thomas, excerpt from the liner notes to *The Complete Stax/Volt Singles, 1968–1971* by Rob Bowman.

25. Carla Thomas, excerpt from *Stax Fax, Issue 1*.

26. Carla Thomas, excerpt from blog.ponderosastomp.com.

27. Bettye Crutcher, excerpt from the liner notes to *The Complete Stax/Volt Singles, 1968–1971* by Rob Bowman.

28. Bill King, excerpt from billkingmusic.blogspot.com.

29. Bill King, excerpt from billkingmusic.blogspot.com.

30. Sam Andrew, excerpt from *Scars of Sweet Paradise: The Life and Times of Janis Joplin* by Alice Echols (Virago, 2000).

31. Don Nix, excerpt from *Respect Yourself, Stax Records and the Soul Explosion* by Robert Gordon.

32. Bill King, excerpt from billkingmusic.blogspot.com.

33. Al Bell, excerpt from *Stax Fax, Issue 1*.

34. Booker T. Jones, excerpt from *Time Is Tight* (Omnibus Press, 2019).

35. Bobby Manuel, interview with author, July 2020.

36. Bettye Crutcher, excerpt from the liner notes to *The Complete Stax/Volt Singles, 1968–1971* by Rob Bowman.

37. Carla Thomas, excerpt from the liner notes to *The Complete Stax/Volt Singles, 1968–1971* by Rob Bowman.

38. Carla Thomas, excerpt from the liner notes to *The Complete Stax/Volt Singles, 1968–1971* by Rob Bowman.

39. Carla Thomas, excerpt from blog.ponderosastomp.com.

40. William Bell, interview with author, July 2020.

41. Carla Thomas, interview with David Less and Pete Daniel, November 10, 1999, for *Rock 'n' Soul* exhibit, Smithsonian Institution.

42. Rufus Thomas, excerpt from the liner notes to *The Complete Stax/Volt Singles, 1968–1971* by Rob Bowman.

43. Rufus Thomas, excerpt from Charles Hughes in the essay "You Pay One Hell of a Price to Be Black" in *An Unseen Light: Black Struggles for Freedom in Memphis, Tennessee* (University Press of Kentucky, 2018).

44. http://staxarchives.com/gettin-it-all-together.

45. Bobby Manuel, interview with author, July 2020.

46. Marvell Thomas, excerpt from www.andrialisle.com/blog.

47. Marvell Thomas, excerpt from www.andrialisle.com/blog.

48. Marvell Thomas, excerpt from www.andrialisle.com/blog.

49. Jim Stewart, interview with author, October 2020.

50. Al Bell, excerpt from *Respect Yourself, Stax Records and the Soul Explosion* by Robert Gordon.

51. Steve Cropper, excerpt from *Respect Yourself, Stax Records and the Soul Explosion* by Robert Gordon.

Chapter Ten: Funkiest Man Alive—The Funk Years, 1970-1975

1. Rufus Thomas, excerpt from the liner notes to *The Complete Stax/Volt Singles, 1968–1971* by Rob Bowman.

2. Rufus Thomas, excerpt from *Country Soul: Making Music and Making Race in the American South* by Charles Hughes.

3. Rufus Thomas, excerpt from interview by David Less and Robert Palmer, *Civil Rights History Project Audio Collections*, Mississippi Valley Collections, University of Memphis.

4. Booker T. Jones, interview with author, September 2020.

5. Deanie Parker, interview with author, September 2020.

6. James Alexander, interview with author, September 2020.

7. Rufus Thomas, "Still walkin' the dog and doin' the funky chicken" interview with Geoff Brown, the *Independent*, April 18, 1996.

8. Rufus Thomas, excerpt from the liner notes to *The Complete Stax/Volt Singles, 1968–1971* by Rob Bowman.

9. James Alexander, interview with author, September 2020.

10. Al Bell, excerpt from *Soulsville U.S.A.: The Story of Stax Records* by Rob Bowman.

11. Harold Scott, interview with author, November 2020.

12. Rufus Thomas, excerpt from the liner notes to *The Complete Stax/Volt Singles, 1968–1971* by Rob Bowman.

13. Willie Hall, interview with author, October 2020.

14. Stax press release, August 1971: "King of the Canines (Rufus Thomas) Meets the King of Liberia."

15. Stax press release, April 1, 1972: "Stax's artists Rufus Thomas and Isaac Hayes Receive 'Recognition Rewards.'"

16. This version of "I Love You for Sentimental Reasons" was recorded on May 15, 1970, according to Rob Bowman's liner notes to the CD *Did You Heard Me/Crown Prince of Dance*, and seems to have been different from the version that had been recorded for "May I Have Your Ticket, Please?"

17. Rufus Thomas, excerpt from the liner notes to *The Complete Stax/Volt Singles, 1968–1971* by Rob Bowman.

18. Rufus Thomas, excerpt from the liner notes to *The Complete Stax/Volt Singles, 1968–1971* by Rob Bowman.

19. William Bell, interview with author, July 2020.

20. Carla Thomas, excerpt from blog.ponderosastomp.com.

21. Seymour Rosenberg, excerpt from *Respect Yourself, Stax Records and the Soul Explosion* by Robert Gordon.

22. Jim Stewart, interview with author, October 2020.

23. Al Bell, excerpt from *Respect Yourself, Stax Records and the Soul Explosion* by Robert Gordon.

24. Deannie Parker, excerpt from *Respect Yourself, Stax Records and the Soul Explosion* by Robert Gordon.

25. Tommy Jacquette, excerpt from "Loud and Proud" by James Maycock, *The Guardian*, July 20, 2002.

26. Al Bell, excerpt from "Loud and Proud" by James Maycock, *The Guardian*, July 20, 2002.

27. Carla Thomas, interview with David Less and Pete Daniel, November 10, 1999, for *Rock 'n' Soul* exhibit, Smithsonian Institution.

28. Mavis Staples, excerpt from "Loud and Proud" by James Maycock, *The Guardian*, July 20, 2002.

29. Al Bell, excerpt from "Loud and Proud" by James Maycock, *The Guardian*, July 20, 2002.

Chapter Eleven: I Ain't Getting Older—The Post-Stax Years, 1976-1988

1. Ron Rudkin, interview with author, February 2021.

2. Rufus Thomas, Cook Collection, 18.

3. Vaneese Thomas, interview with author, April 2021.

4. James Nelson, interview with author, August 2020.

5. James Nelson, interview with author, August 2020.

6. James Nelson, interview with author, August 2020.

7. James Nelson, interview with author, August 2020.

8. Lee Brown, excerpt from "Memphians Mourn Death of Formerly Homeless Friend to Many" by Joe Birch, WMC Action News, July 24, 2018.

9. Vaneese Thomas, interview with author, July 2020.

10. Vaneese Thomas, interview with author, April 2021.

11. Vaneese Thomas, interview with Lee Hildebrand, *Living Blues*.

12. Vaneese Thomas, interview with author, April 2021.

13. Vaneese Thomas, excerpt from the *Voice, Swarthmore College Bulletin*, Winter 2017.

14. Vaneese Thomas, interview with Lee Hildebrand, *Living Blues*.

15. Vaneese Thomas, interview with author, July 2020.

16. Bruce Iglauer, interview with author, August 2020.

17. Bobby O'Jay, interview with author, August 2020.

18. Bobby O'Jay, interview with author, August 2020.

19. Bobby O'Jay, interview with author, August 2020.

20. Bobby O'Jay, interview with author, August 2020.

21. Bruce Iglauer, interview with author, August 2020.

22. Bruce Iglauer, interview with author, August 2020.

23. David Whiteis, "That Woman Is Poison!" *Chicago Reader*, May 11, 1989.

24. Bruce Iglauer, interview with author, August 2020.

Chapter Twelve: Age Ain't Nothin' but a Number—Final Years, 1988-2001

1. Graziano Uliani, interview with author, July 2020.

2. Graziano Uliani, interview with author, July 2020.

3. Graziano Uliani, interview with author, July 2020.

4. Graziano Uliani, interview with author, July 2020.

5. Graziano Uliani, email to author, July 2020.

6. Freddy Cousaert, excerpt from "(He's a) Road Runner," adampwhite.com, January 25, 2019.

7. Jim Spake, interview with author, August 2020.

8. Jim Spake, ibid.

9. Bobby Manuel, interview with author, July 2020.

10. Bobby Manuel, interview with author, August 2020.

11. Bobby Manuel, interview with author, August 2020.

12. Bobby Manuel, interview with author, August 2020.

13. Rufus Thomas, excerpt from "Rufus Thomas Tribute," www.staxrecords.free.fr/rufus tribute.

14. Chris Davis, *Memphis Flyer*, April 22, 2016.

15. Thomas Hackett, excerpt from "Rufus Thomas, Man of the House of Happiness. Southern Cultures, Vol. 19, No. 1: *Global Music*, March 2013, University of North Carolina Press.

16. Rufus Thomas, excerpt from "Rufus Thomas Tribute," www.staxrecords.free.fr/rufus tribute.

17. Rufus Thomas, interviewed by Pete Daniel, David Less, and Charles McGovern, Memphis, 8/5/1992, *Rock 'n' Soul Video History Project Collection*, interviews, National Museum of American History, Archives Center, Smithsonian Institution, Washington, DC.

18. Bobby Manuel, interview with author, July 2020.

19. Vaneese Thomas, interview with author, June 2021.

20. Vaneese Thomas, interview with author, June 2021.

21. Maxine Smith, from Lorene Thomas's obituary, *Memphis Commercial Appeal*, February 9, 2000.

22. H.T. Lockard, from Lorene Thomas's obituary, *Memphis Commercial Appeal*, February 9, 2000.

23. Vaneese Thomas, interview with author, June 2021.

24. Bobby Manuel, interview with author, July 2020.

25. William Bell, interview with author, July 2020.

26. Vaneese Thomas, interview with author, June 2021.

27. Vaneese Thomas, interview with author, June 2021.

28. Pat Kerr Tigrett, from "Heaven's Youngest Teenager" by Bill Ellis, *Memphis Commercial Appeal*, December 21, 2001.

29. Rob Bowman, excerpt from "Heaven's Youngest Teenager" by Bill Ellis, December 21, 2001.

Postscript

1. Marvell Thomas, excerpt from his obituary, *Memphis Commercial Appeal*.

2. Tim Sampson, excerpt from Marvell Thomas's obituary, *Memphis Commercial Appeal*.

3. Carla Thomas, interview with John Beifuss, *Memphis Commercial Appeal*, September 2021.

4. Vaneese Thomas, interview with author, June 2021.

5. Vaneese Thomas, interview with author, July 2020.

Rufus Thomas Discography

1. Credited to Mr. Swing with Bobby Plater's Orchestra.

2. Credited to Carla and Rufus.

3. Credited to Rufus and Friend (Carla).

4. B-side was "Fine & Mellow" on some early copies.

5. Credited to Rufus & Carla.

6. Credited to Rufus & Carla.

7. Credited to Rufus & Carla. Note that it is a cover of Jewel Akens's 1964 recording "The Birds and the Bees" (Era 3141). Stax shortened the title.

8. Note that the single is spelled differently from the album version of the same song.

9. A-side by Albert King, B-side by Rufus Thomas.

10. B-side by the Bar-Kays.

Bibliography

This is intended to be a select bibliography, highlighting the books that were particularly useful when researching *Funkiest Man Alive*. It only refers to books that were used and not liner notes, documents, newspaper articles, and other sources.

The key books used are as follows:

Bowman, Rob. *Soulsville U.S.A.: The Story of Stax Records* (Music Sales, 2006).

Cantor, Louis. *Wheelin' on Beale: How WDIA-Memphis Became the Nation's First All-Black Radio Station and Created the Sound That Changed America* (Pharos Books, 1992).

Freeland, David. *Ladies of Soul* (University Press of Mississippi, 2001).

Gordon, Robert. *Respect Yourself: Stax Records and the Soul Explosion* (Bloomsbury USA, 2014).

Guralnick, Peter. *Sweet Soul Music: Rhythm and Blues and the Southern Dream of Freedom* (Canongate Books, 2002).

Hoppe, Sherry L., and Bruce W. Speck. *Maxine Smith's Unwilling Pupils: Lessons Learned in Memphis's Civil Rights Classroom* (University of Tennessee Press, 2007).

Hughes, Charles L. "You Pay One Hell of a Price to Be Black" in *An Unseen Light: Black Struggles for Freedom in Memphis, Tennessee*. Eds. Aram Goudsouzian and Charles W. McKinney Jr. (University Press of Kentucky, 2018).

Other books that are useful include:

Cosgrove, Stuart. *Memphis 68: The Tragedy of Southern Soul* (Polygon, 2018).

Merrill, Hugh. *The Blues Route: From the Delta to California, A Writer Searches for America's Purest Music* (William Morrow, 1990).

Dickerson, James L. *Goin' Back to Memphis: A Century of Blues, Rock 'n' Roll, and Glorious Soul* (Cooper Square Press, 2000).

Guralnick, Peter. *Last Train to Memphis: The Rise of Elvis Presley* (Abacus, 1995).

Guralnick, Peter. *Sam Phillips: The Man Who Invented Rock 'n' Roll* (Hachette UK, 2015).

Hughes, Charles L. *Country Soul: Making Music and Making Race in the American South* (University of North Carolina Press, 2016).

Jones, Booker T. *Time Is Tight: My Life, Note by Note* (Omnibus Press, 2019).

Index

About the Author

Photo by Tash Dillon

Matthew Ruddick is the cofounder and editor of the jazz website Kind of Jazz (www.kindofjazz.com) and has worked as a music critic for a variety of publications, including *Beats* magazine in Hong Kong. He is the author of *Funny Valentine: The Story of Chet Baker*, published to widespread acclaim in 2012.

CPSIA information can be obtained
at www.ICGtesting.com
Printed in the USA
LVHW031913050423
743578LV00001B/1/J